HONORIFICS EXPLAINED

Throughout the Kodansha Comics books, you will find Japanese honorifics left intact in the translations. For those not familiar with how the Japanese use honorifics and, more important, how they differ from American honorifics, we present this brief overview.

Politeness has always been a critical facet of Japanese culture. Ever since the feudal era, when Japan was a highly stratified society, use of honorifics—which can be defined as polite speech that indicates relationship or status—has played an essential role in the Japanese language. When addressing someone in Japanese, an honorific usually takes the form of a suffix attached to one's name (example: "Asuna-san"), is used as a title at the end of one's name, or appears in place of the name itself (example: "Negi-sensei," or simply "Sensei!").

Honorifics can be expressions of respect or endearment. In the context of manga and anime, honorifics give insight into the nature of the relationship between characters. Many English translations leave out these important honorifics and therefore distort the feel of the original Japanese. Because Japanese honorifics contain nuances that English honorifics lack, it is our policy at Kodansha Comics not to translate them. Here, instead, is a guide to some of the honorifics you may encounter in Kodansha Comics books.

-san: This is the most common honorific and is equivalent to Mr., Miss, Ms., or Mrs. It is the all-purpose honorific and can be used in any situation where politeness is required.

-sama: This is one level higher than "-san" and is used to confer great respect.

-dono: This comes from the word "tono," which means "lord." It is an even higher level than "-sama" and confers utmost respect.

-kun: This suffix is used at the end of boys' names to express familiarity or endearment. It is also sometimes used by men among friends, or when addressing someone younger or of a lower station.

-chan: This is used to express endearment, mostly toward girls. It is also used for little boys, pets, and even among lovers. It gives a sense of childish cuteness.

Bozu: This is an informal way to refer to a boy, similar to the English terms "kid" and "squirt."

Sempai/
Senpai: This title suggests that the addressee is one's senior in a group or organization. It is most often used in a school setting, where underclassmen refer to their upperclassmen as "sempai." It can also be used in the workplace, such as when a newer employee addresses an employee who has seniority in the company.

Kohai: This is the opposite of "sempai" and is used toward underclassmen in school or newcomers in the workplace. It connotes that the addressee is of a lower station.

Sensei: Literally meaning "one who has come before," this title is used for teachers, doctors, or masters of any profession or art.

-[blank]: This is usually forgotten in these lists, but it is perhaps the most significant difference between Japanese and English. The lack of honorific means that the speaker has permission to address the person in a very intimate way. Usually, only family, spouses, or very close friends have this kind of permission. Known as *yobisute*, it can be gratifying when someone who has earned the intimacy starts to call one by one's name without an honorific. But when that intimacy hasn't been earned, it can be very insulting.

6

Ninja Girls

Hosana Tanaka

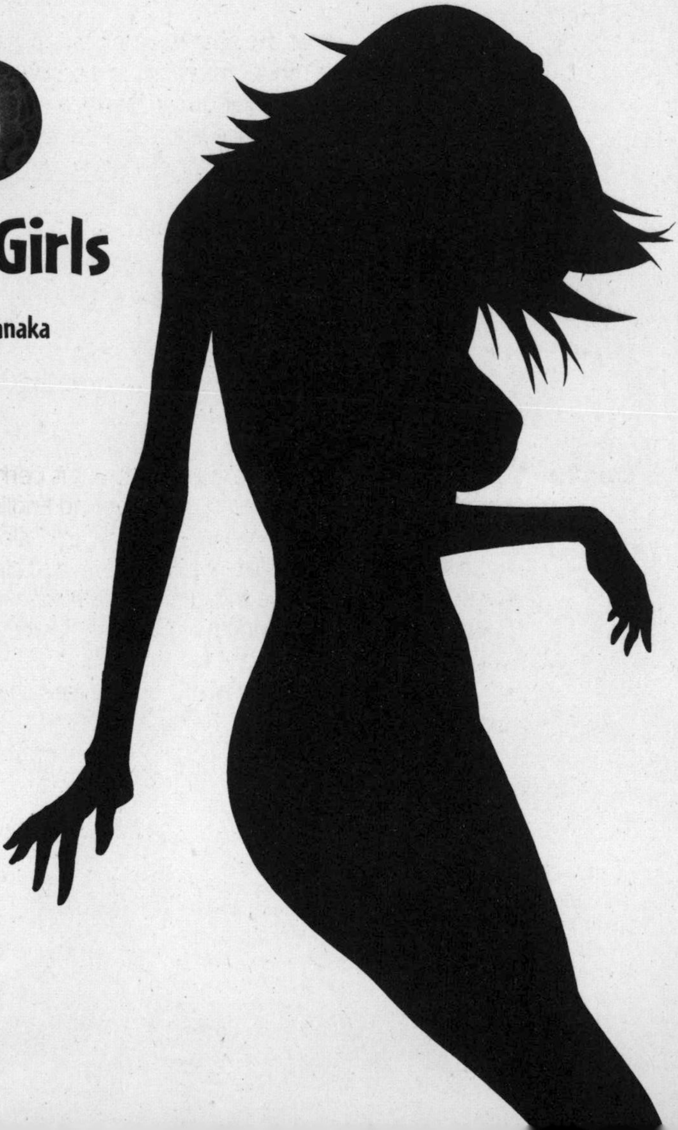

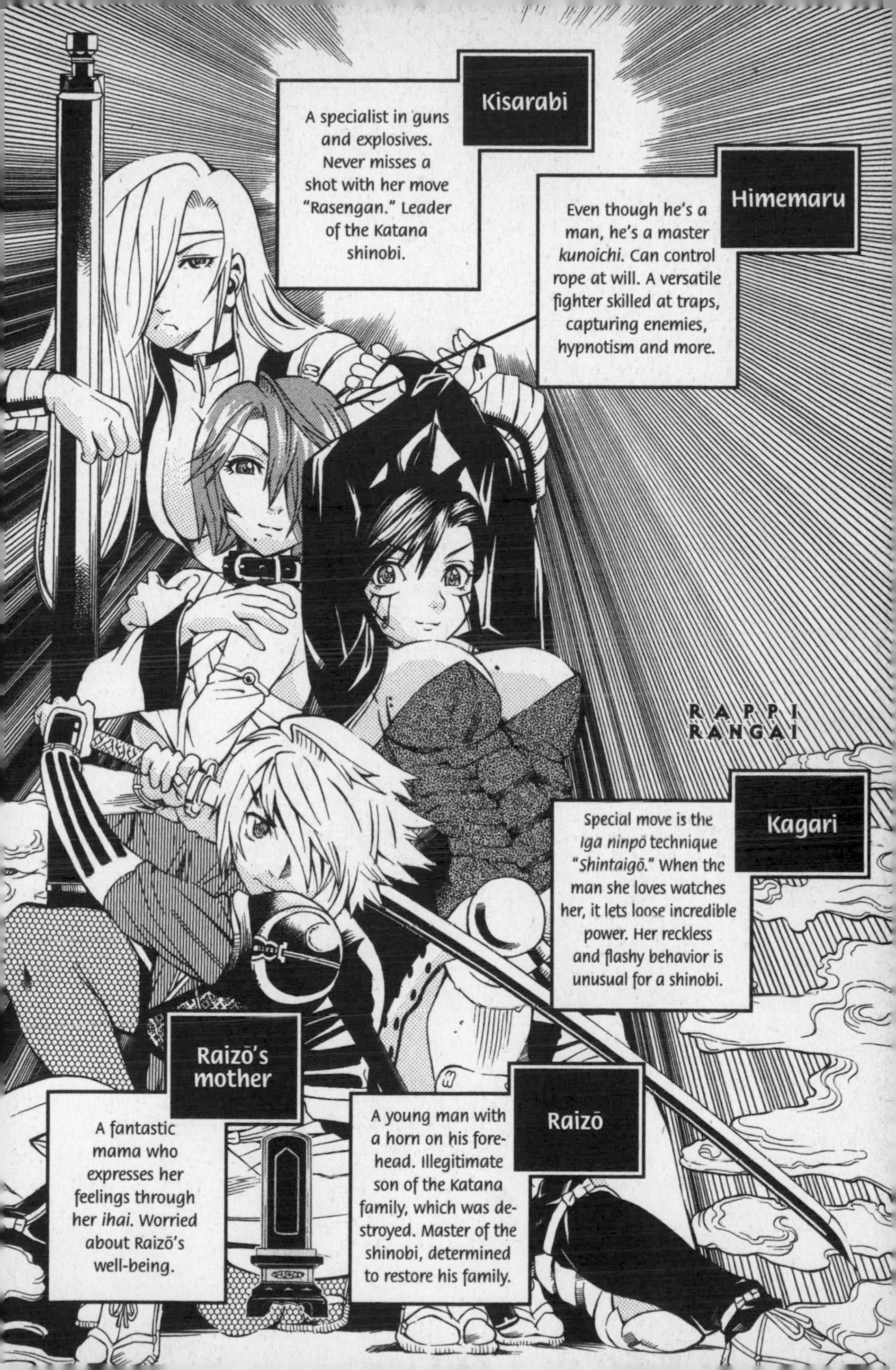

Kisarabi
A specialist in guns and explosives. Never misses a shot with her move "Rasengan." Leader of the Katana shinobi.
Himemaru
Even though he's a man, he's a master *kunoichi*. Can control rope at will. A versatile fighter skilled at traps, capturing enemies, hypnotism and more.
RAPPI RANGAI
Kagari
Special move is the *Iga ninpō* technique "*Shintaigō*." When the man she loves watches her, it lets loose incredible power. Her reckless and flashy behavior is unusual for a shinobi.
Raizō
A young man with a horn on his forehead. Illegitimate son of the Katana family, which was destroyed. Master of the shinobi, determined to restore his family.
Raizō's mother
A fantastic mama who expresses her feelings through her *ihai*. Worried about Raizō's well-being.

The Rebellion so far:

The only surviving member of the Katana family, Raizō, set off on a journey with the Katana *shinobi*: Kagari, whose special technique is *Shintaigō*; Kisarabi, a clairvoyant sniper, and Himemaru, a shape-shifting rope-master. Raizō's life is thrown into chaos by these three beautiful yet dangerous *shinobi*. Their goal is to restore the Katana family.

Last time, our heroes set sail to Shima, where they met the Princesa Pirata Tsunami, the only surviving member of the Kuki Clan. Raizō and the shinobi decided to help her in her quest for vengeance against the Portuguese pirate Shiuba. They found out Shiuba was under the influence of the Katana family's sworn enemy, Kabuki Seigan, who had changed Shiuba's blood to poison. He kidnapped Tsunami, but soon after our heroes rescued her. Now the fight against Shiuba begins...

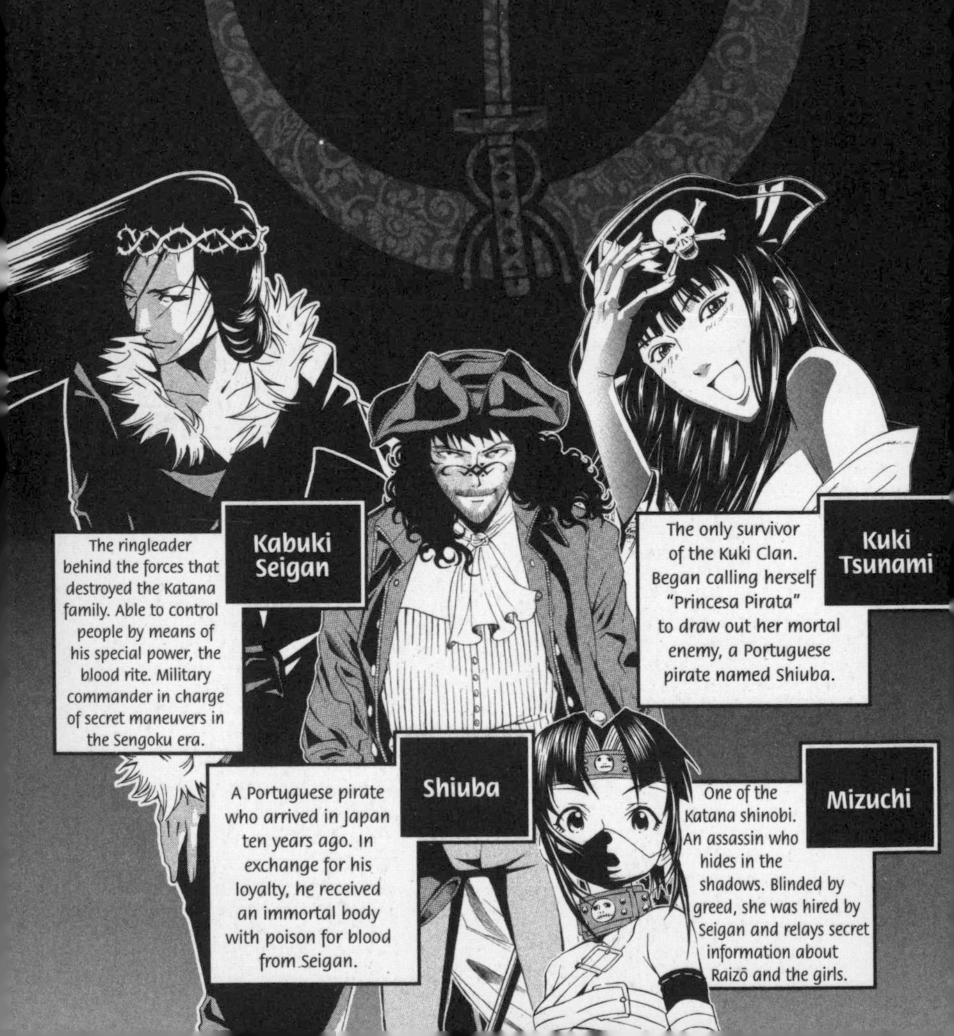

Kabuki Seigan
The ringleader behind the forces that destroyed the Katana family. Able to control people by means of his special power, the blood rite. Military commander in charge of secret maneuvers in the Sengoku era.
Kuki Tsunami
The only survivor of the Kuki Clan. Began calling herself "Princesa Pirata" to draw out her mortal enemy, a Portuguese pirate named Shiuba.
Shiuba
A Portuguese pirate who arrived in Japan ten years ago. In exchange for his loyalty, he received an immortal body with poison for blood from Seigan.
Mizuchi
One of the Katana shinobi. An assassin who hides in the shadows. Blinded by greed, she was hired by Seigan and relays secret information about Raizō and the girls.

Ninja Girls
Volume 5

Contents

30 Resolution Rebellion 5

31 Angel Rebellion 61

32 Enlightened Rebellion 86

33 Miraculous Rebellion 120

34 Fallen Angel Rebellion 151

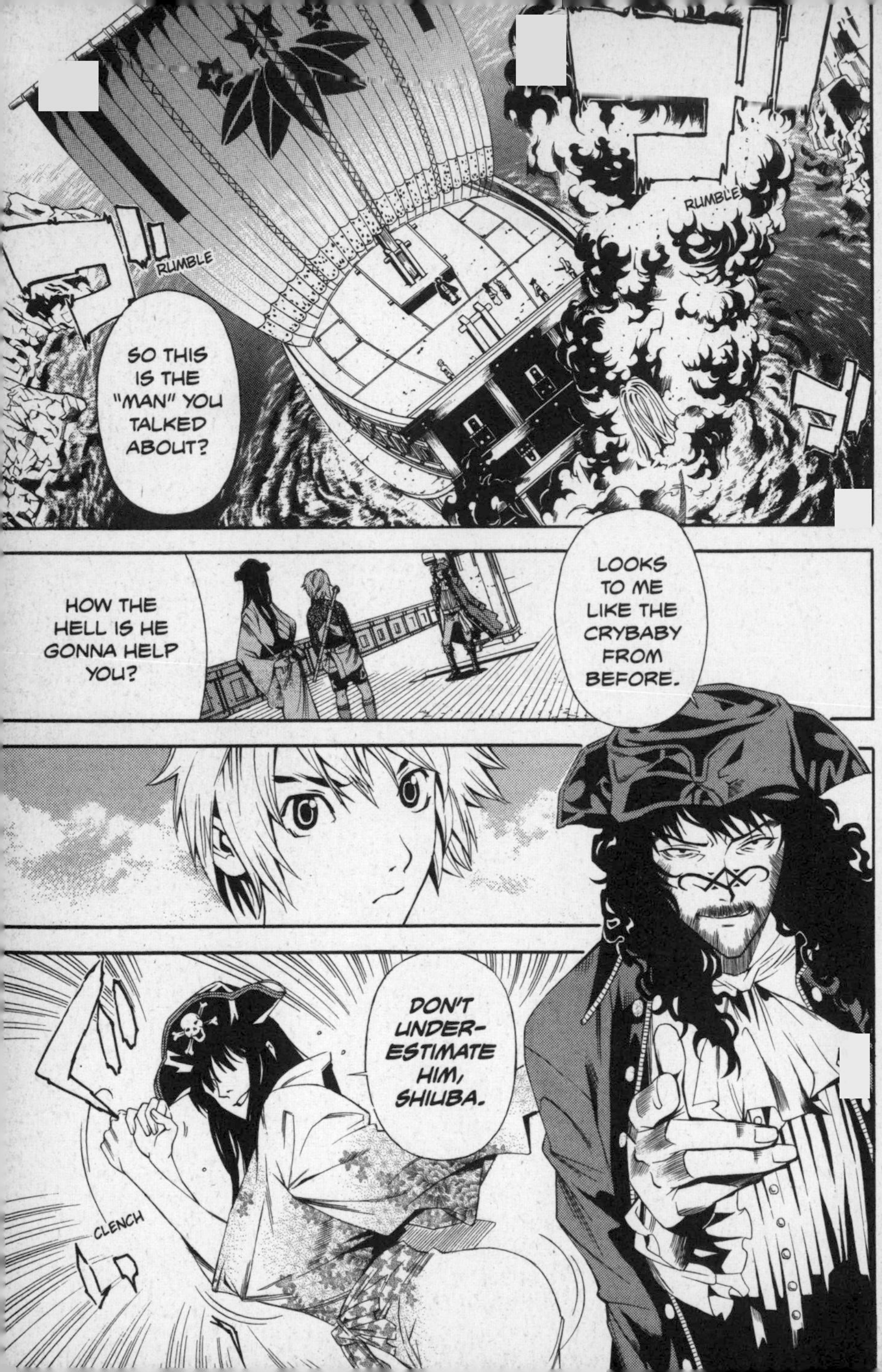
RUMBLE
RUMBLE
SO THIS IS THE "MAN" YOU TALKED ABOUT?
LOOKS TO ME LIKE THE CRYBABY FROM BEFORE.
HOW THE HELL IS HE GONNA HELP YOU?
DON'T UNDER-ESTIMATE HIM, SHIUBA.
CLENCH

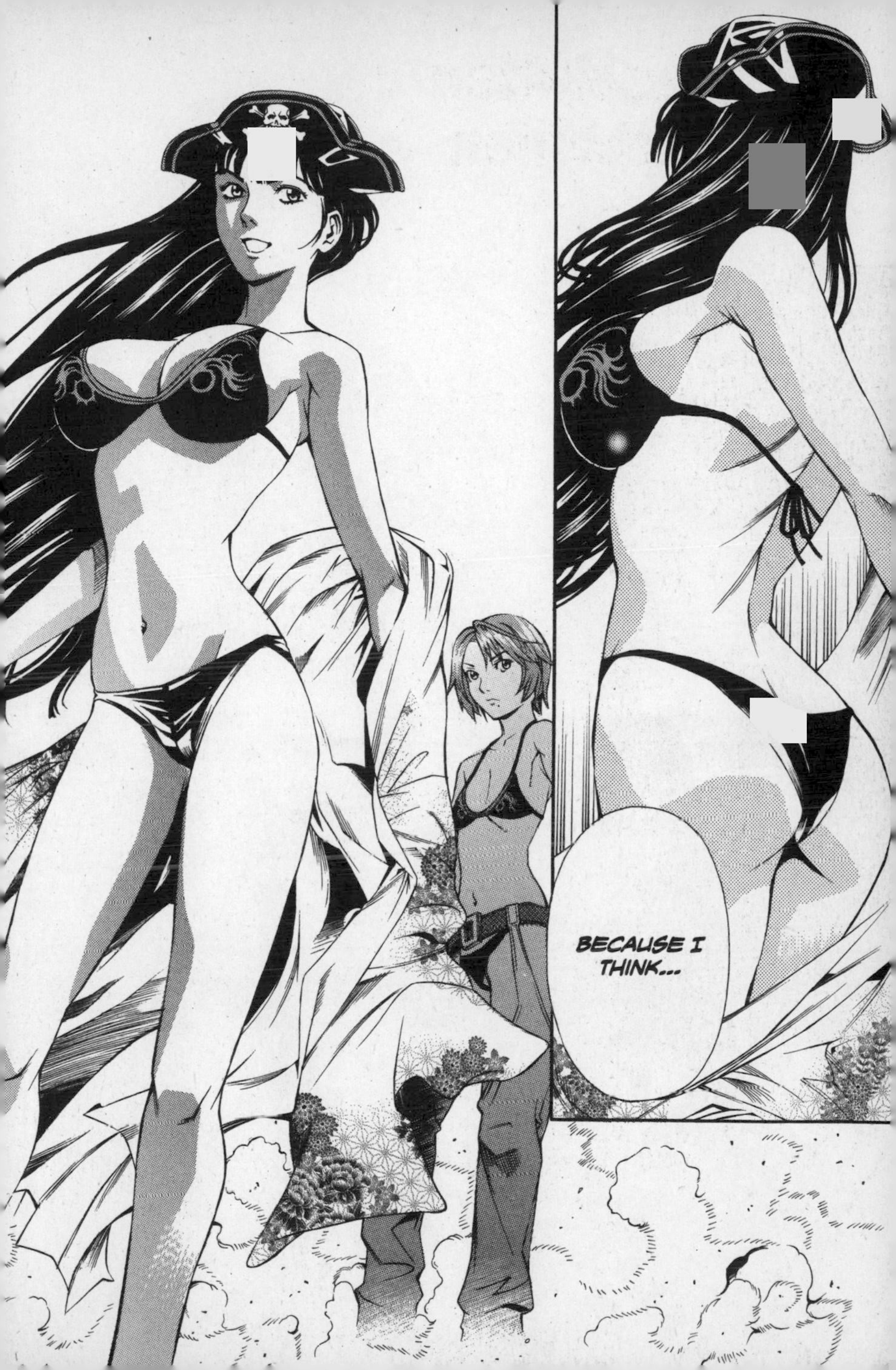
BECAUSE I THINK...

30 Resolution Rebellion

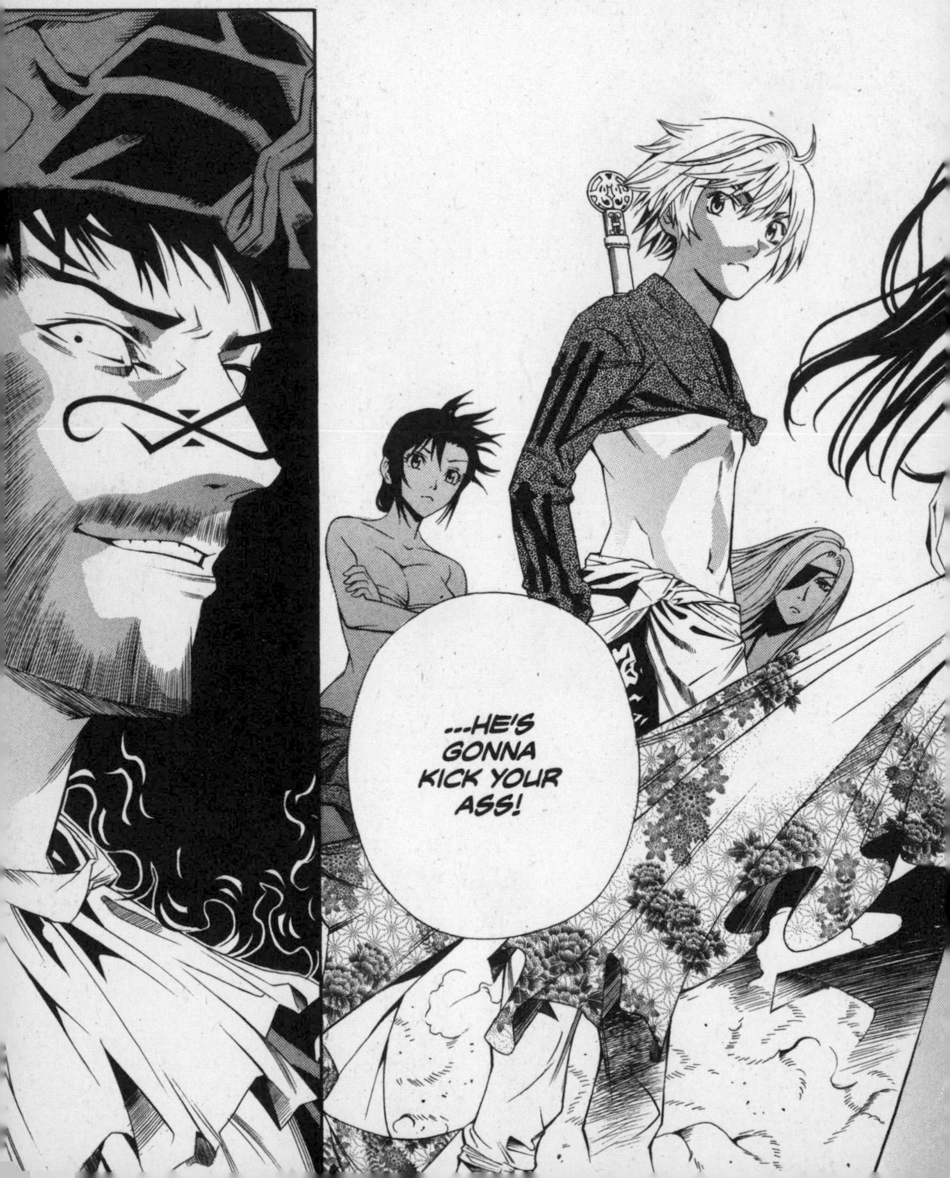
...HE'S GONNA KICK YOUR ASS!

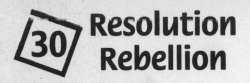

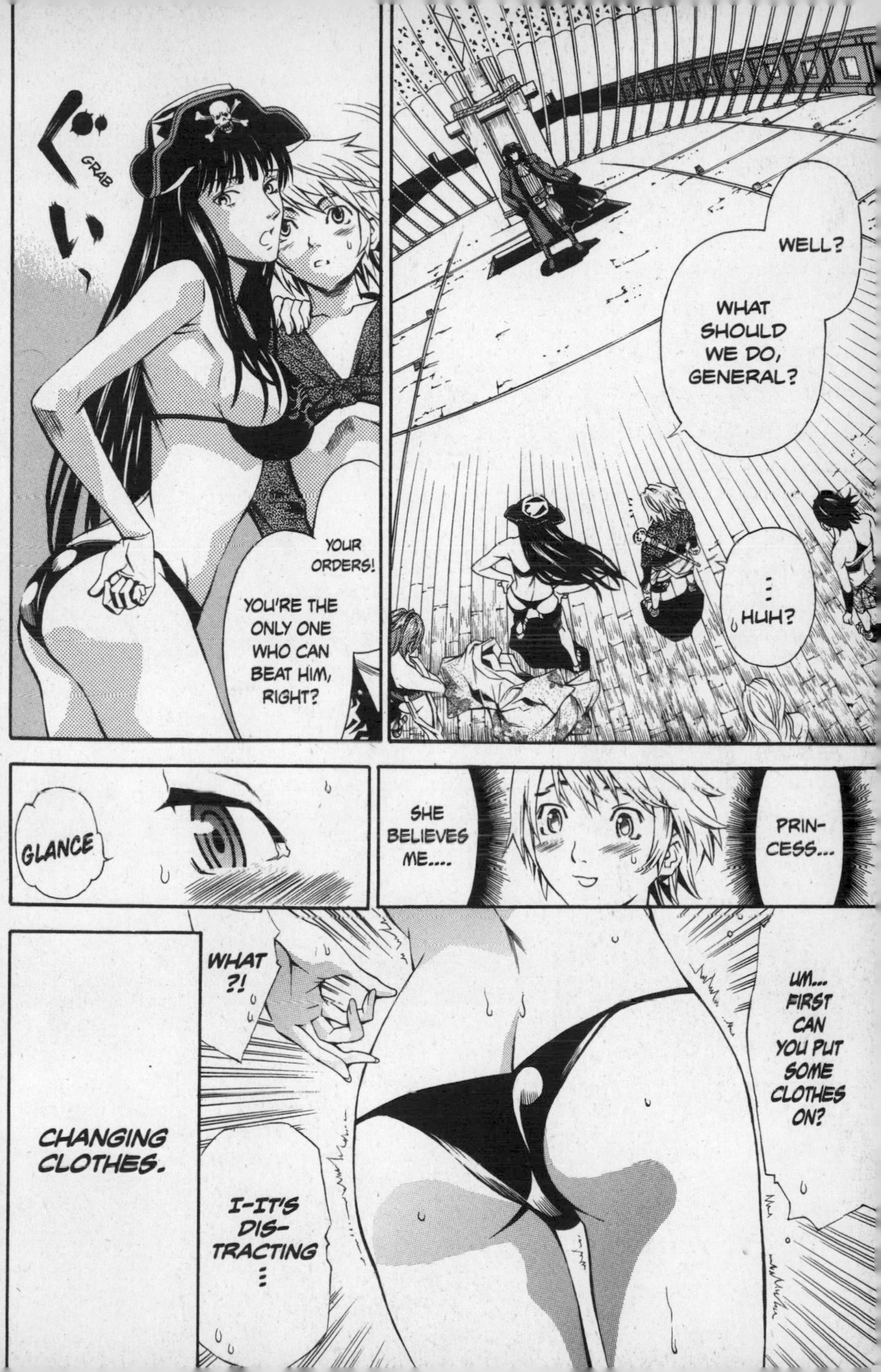
WELL?
WHAT SHOULD WE DO, GENERAL?
... HUH?
GRAB
YOUR ORDERS!
YOU'RE THE ONLY ONE WHO CAN BEAT HIM, RIGHT?
PRIN-CESS...
SHE BELIEVES ME....
GLANCE
UM... FIRST CAN YOU PUT SOME CLOTHES ON?
WHAT?!
I-IT'S DIS-TRACTING...
CHANGING CLOTHES.

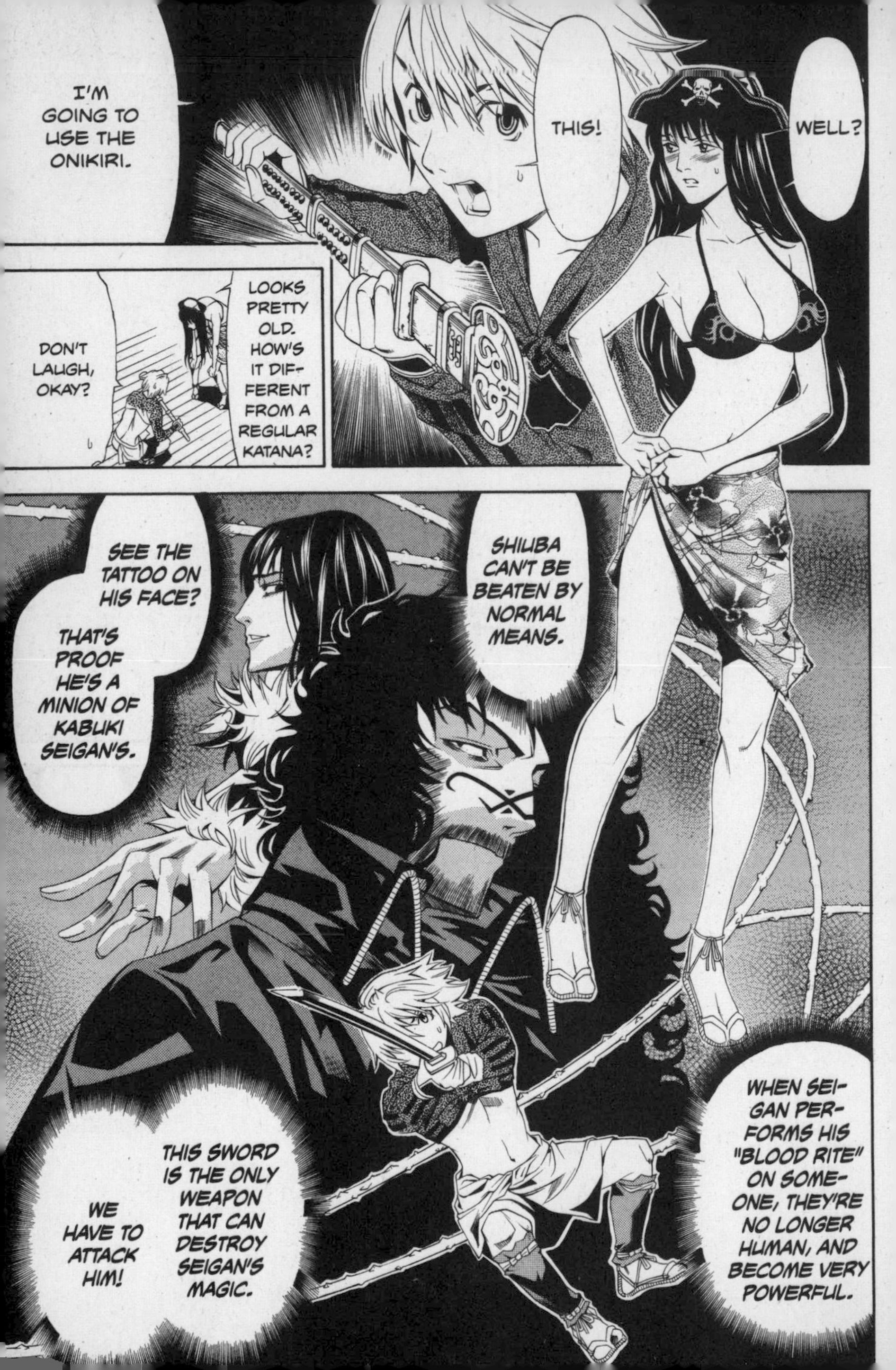
WELL?
THIS!
I'M GOING TO USE THE ONIKIRI.
LOOKS PRETTY OLD. HOW'S IT DIF-FERENT FROM A REGULAR KATANA?
DON'T LAUGH, OKAY?
SHIUBA CAN'T BE BEATEN BY NORMAL MEANS.
SEE THE TATTOO ON HIS FACE?
THAT'S PROOF HE'S A MINION OF KABUKI SEIGAN'S.
WHEN SEI-GAN PER-FORMS HIS "BLOOD RITE" ON SOME-ONE, THEY'RE NO LONGER HUMAN, AND BECOME VERY POWERFUL.
THIS SWORD IS THE ONLY WEAPON THAT CAN DESTROY SEIGAN'S MAGIC.
WE HAVE TO ATTACK HIM!

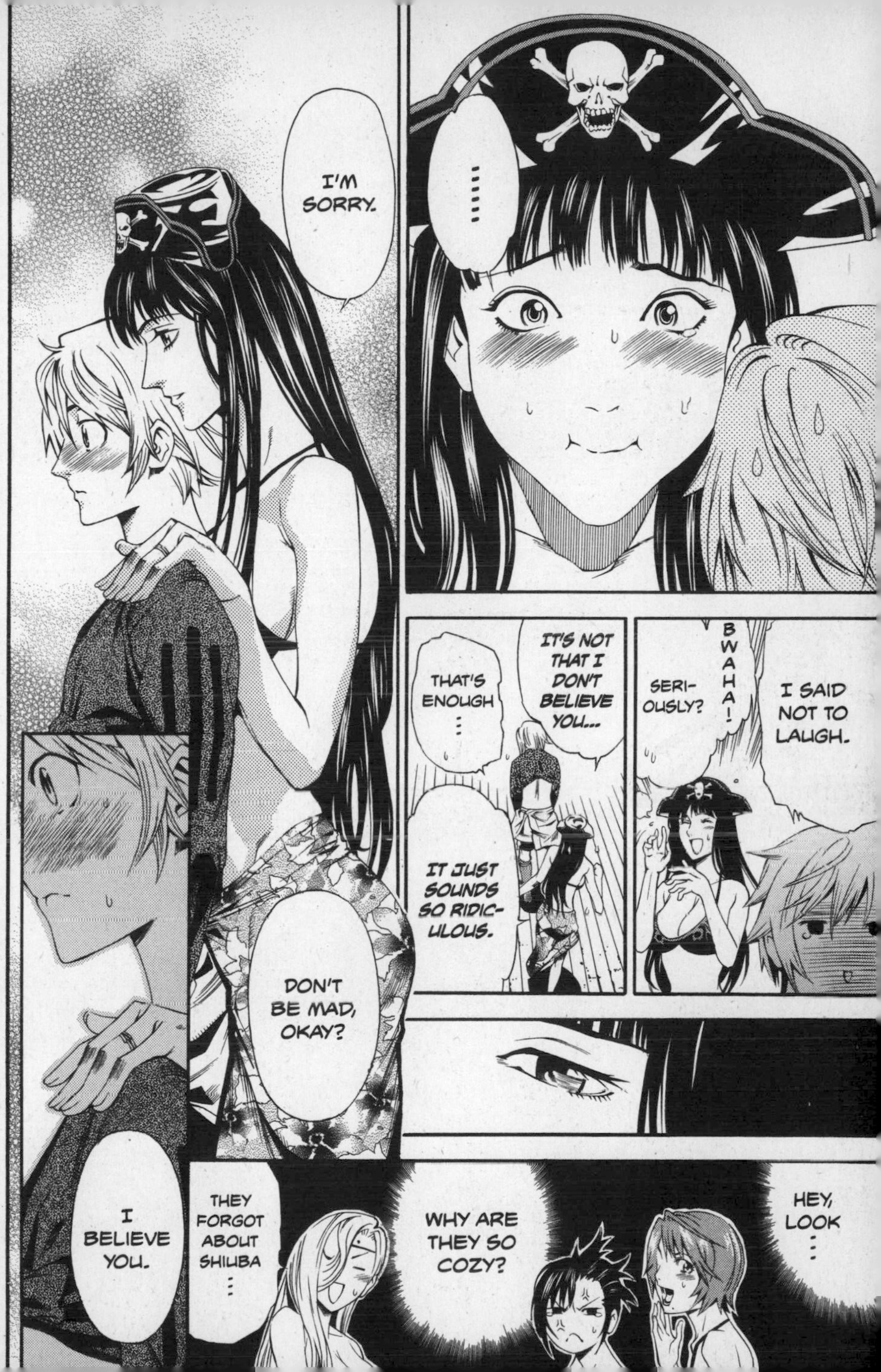
......
I SAID NOT TO LAUGH.
BWAHA!
SERI-OUSLY?
IT'S NOT THAT I DON'T BELIEVE YOU...
THAT'S ENOUGH...
IT JUST SOUNDS SO RIDIC-ULOUS.
I'M SORRY.
DON'T BE MAD, OKAY?
HEY, LOOK...
WHY ARE THEY SO COZY?
THEY FORGOT ABOUT SHIUBA...
I BELIEVE YOU.

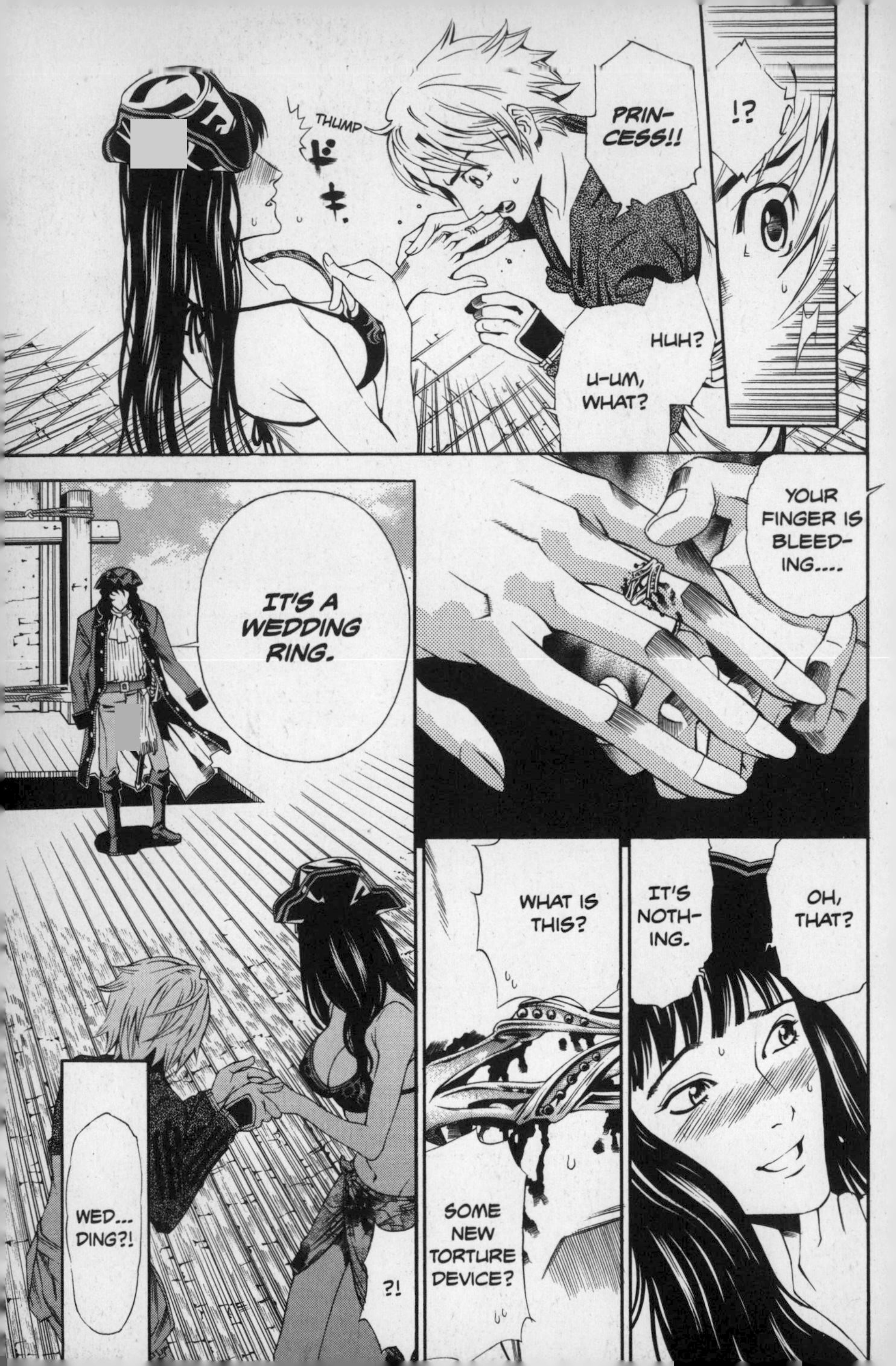
!?
PRIN-CESS!!
THUMP
ドキ
HUH?
U-UM, WHAT?
YOUR FINGER IS BLEED-ING....
OH, THAT?
IT'S NOTH-ING.
WHAT IS THIS?
SOME NEW TORTURE DEVICE?
IT'S A WEDDING RING.
?!
WED... DING?!

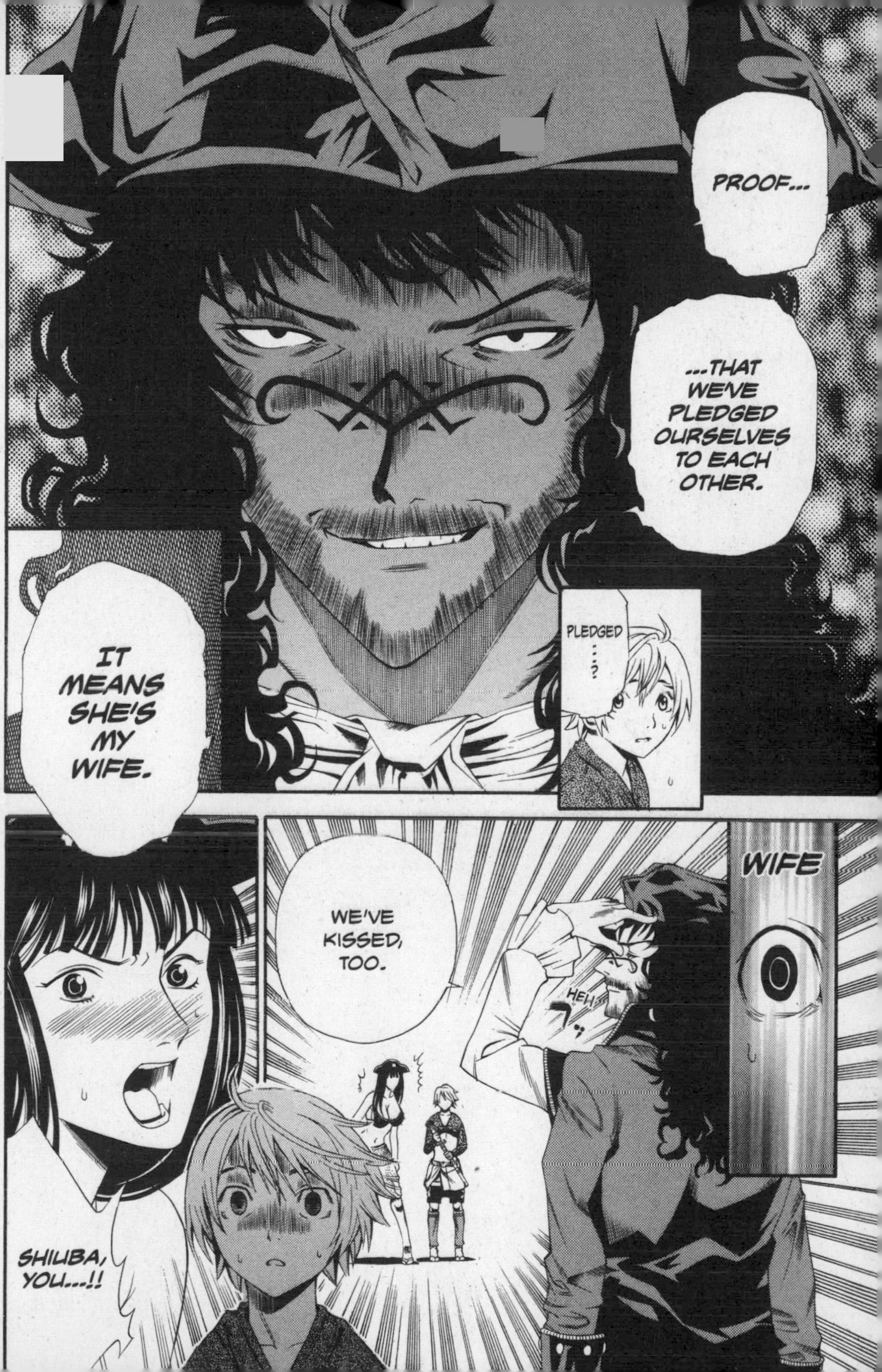
PROOF...
...THAT WE'VE PLEDGED OURSELVES TO EACH OTHER.
PLEDGED...?
IT MEANS SHE'S MY WIFE.
WIFE
HEH
WE'VE KISSED, TOO.
SHIUBA, YOU...!!

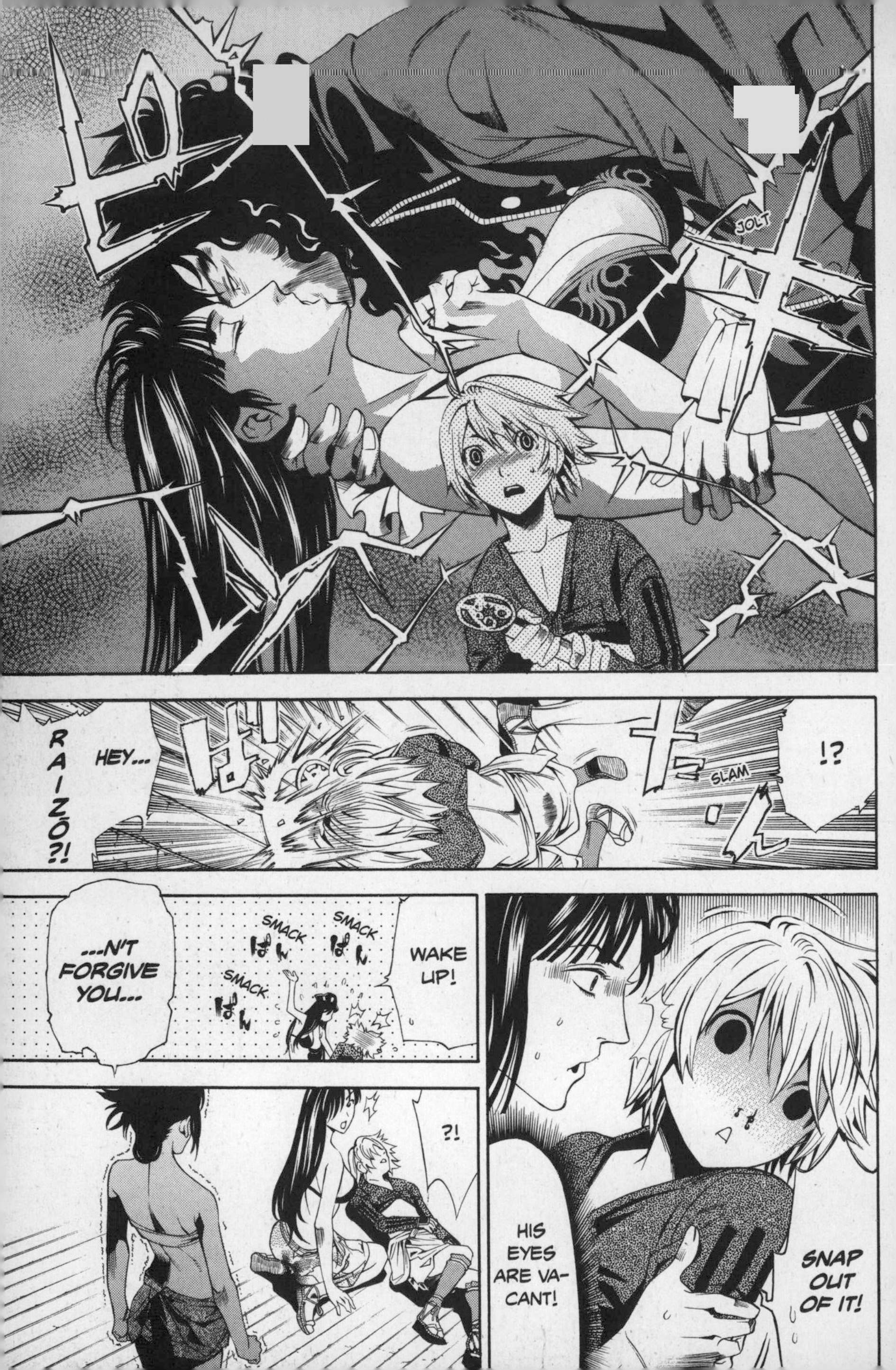
JOLT
!?
SLAM
HEY...
RAIZŌ?!
SNAP OUT OF IT!
HIS EYES ARE VA-CANT!
WAKE UP!
SMACK
SMACK
SMACK
...N'T FORGIVE YOU...
?!

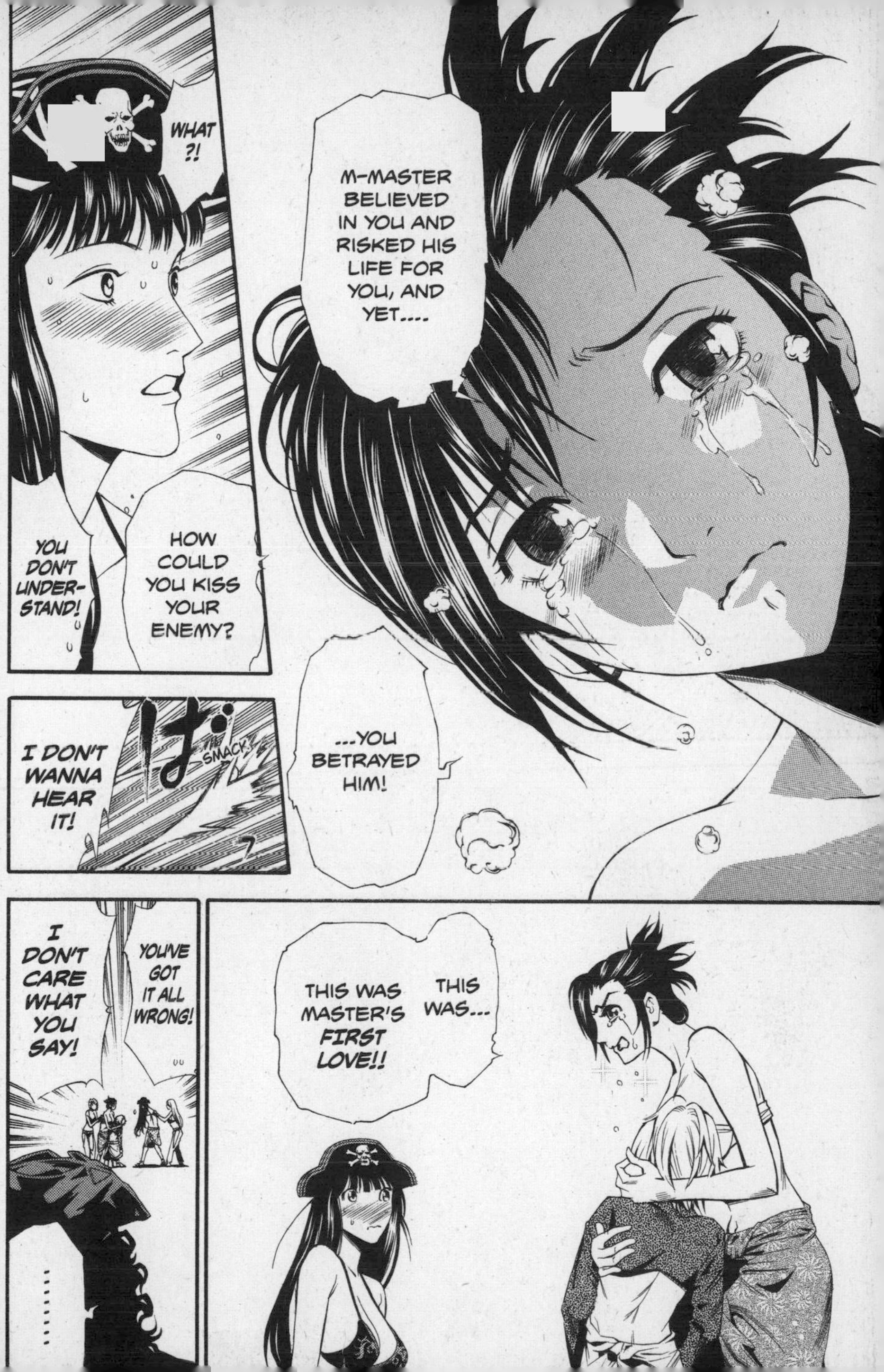
M-MASTER BELIEVED IN YOU AND RISKED HIS LIFE FOR YOU, AND YET....
...YOU BETRAYED HIM!
WHAT ?!
HOW COULD YOU KISS YOUR ENEMY?
YOU DON'T UNDER-STAND!
SMACK
I DON'T WANNA HEAR IT!
THIS WAS...
THIS WAS MASTER'S FIRST LOVE!!
YOU'VE GOT IT ALL WRONG!
I DON'T CARE WHAT YOU SAY!
....

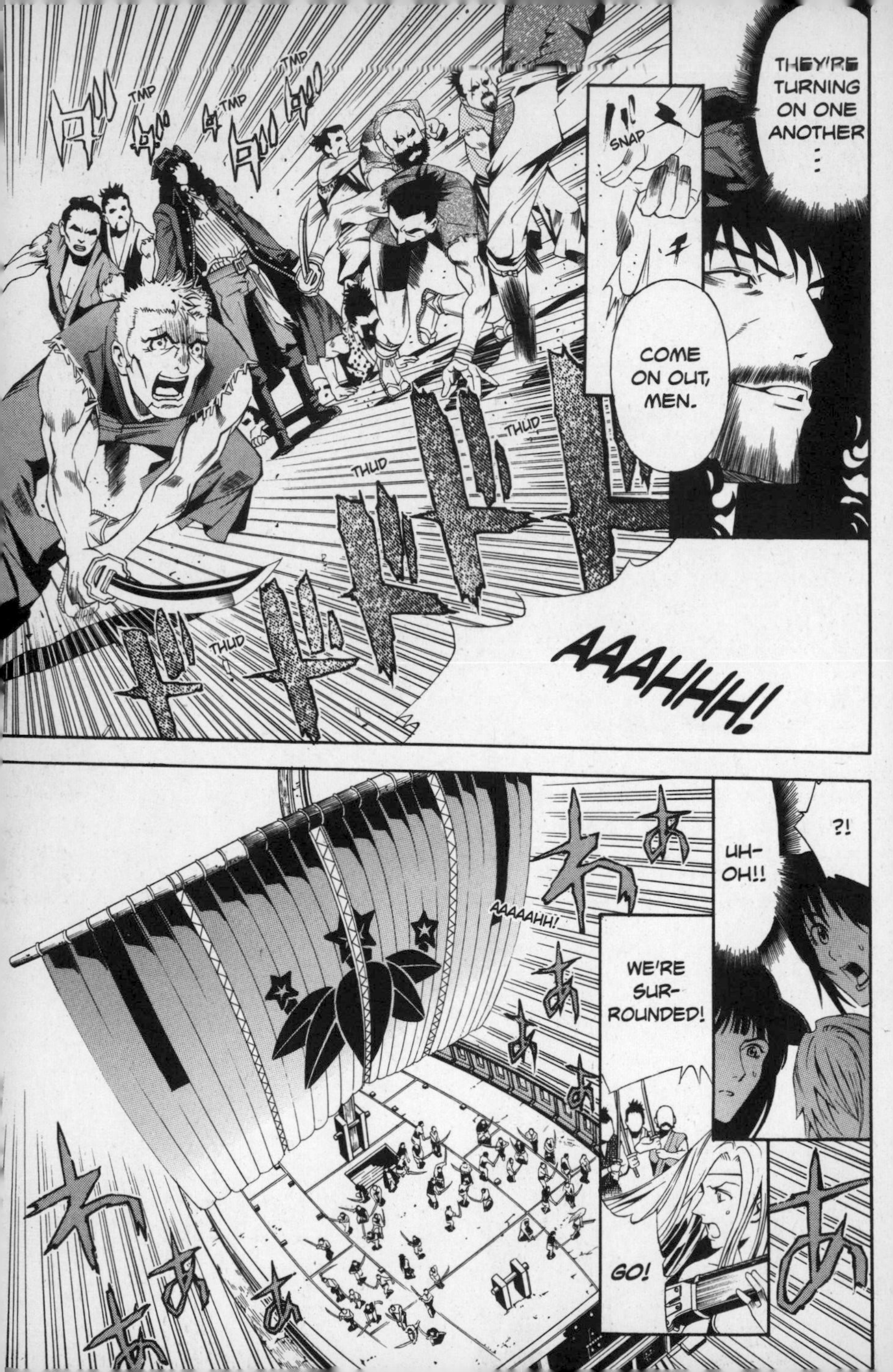

THEY'RE TURNING ON ONE ANOTHER...
SNAP
COME ON OUT, MEN.
TMP
TMP
TMP
THUD
THUD
THUD
AAAHHH!
?!
UH-OH!!
WE'RE SUR-ROUNDED!
AAAAAHH!
GO!

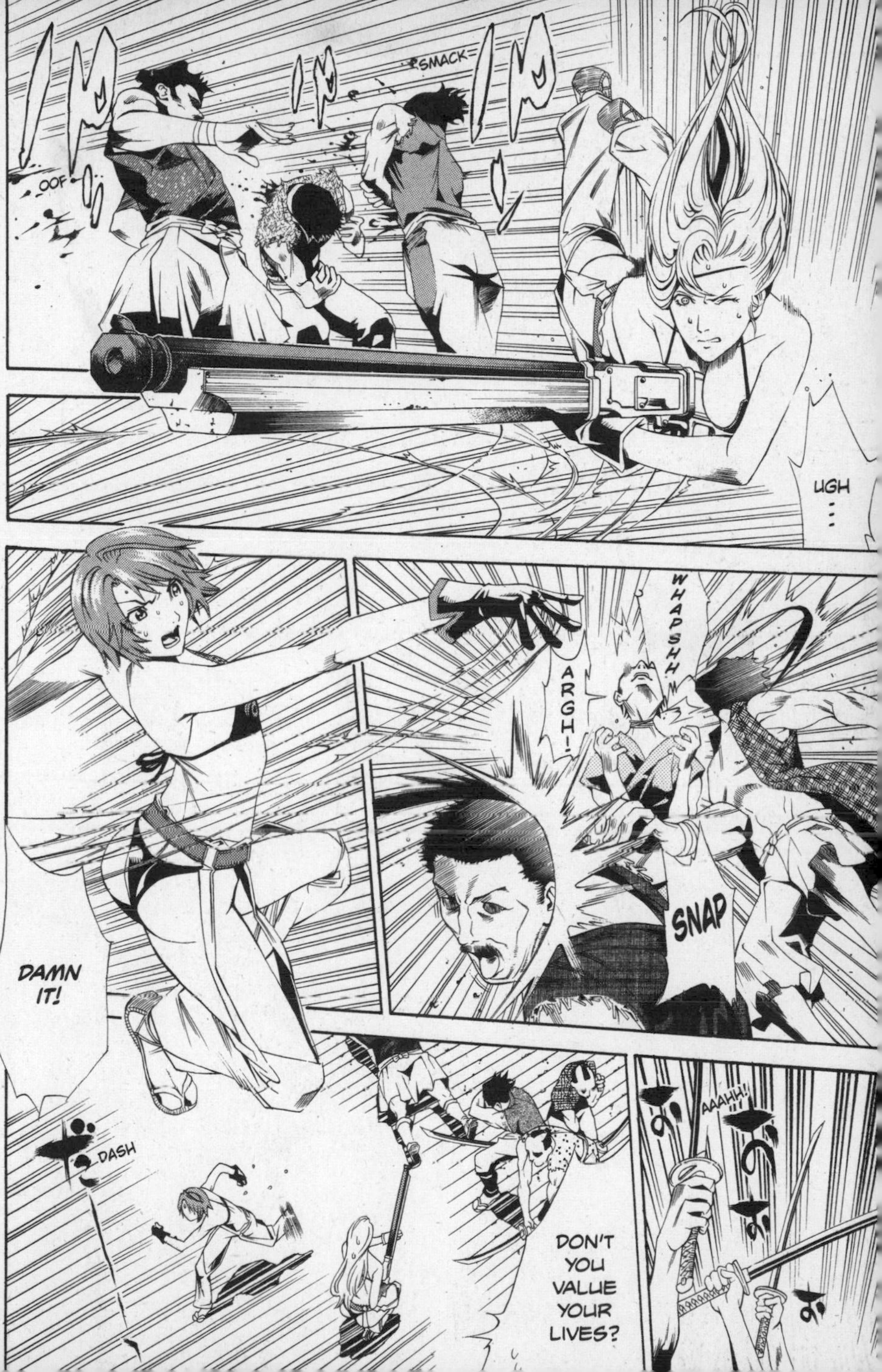
SMACK
OOF
UGH...
WHAPSHH
ARGH!
SNAP
DAMN IT!
AAAHH!
DON'T YOU VALUE YOUR LIVES?
DASH

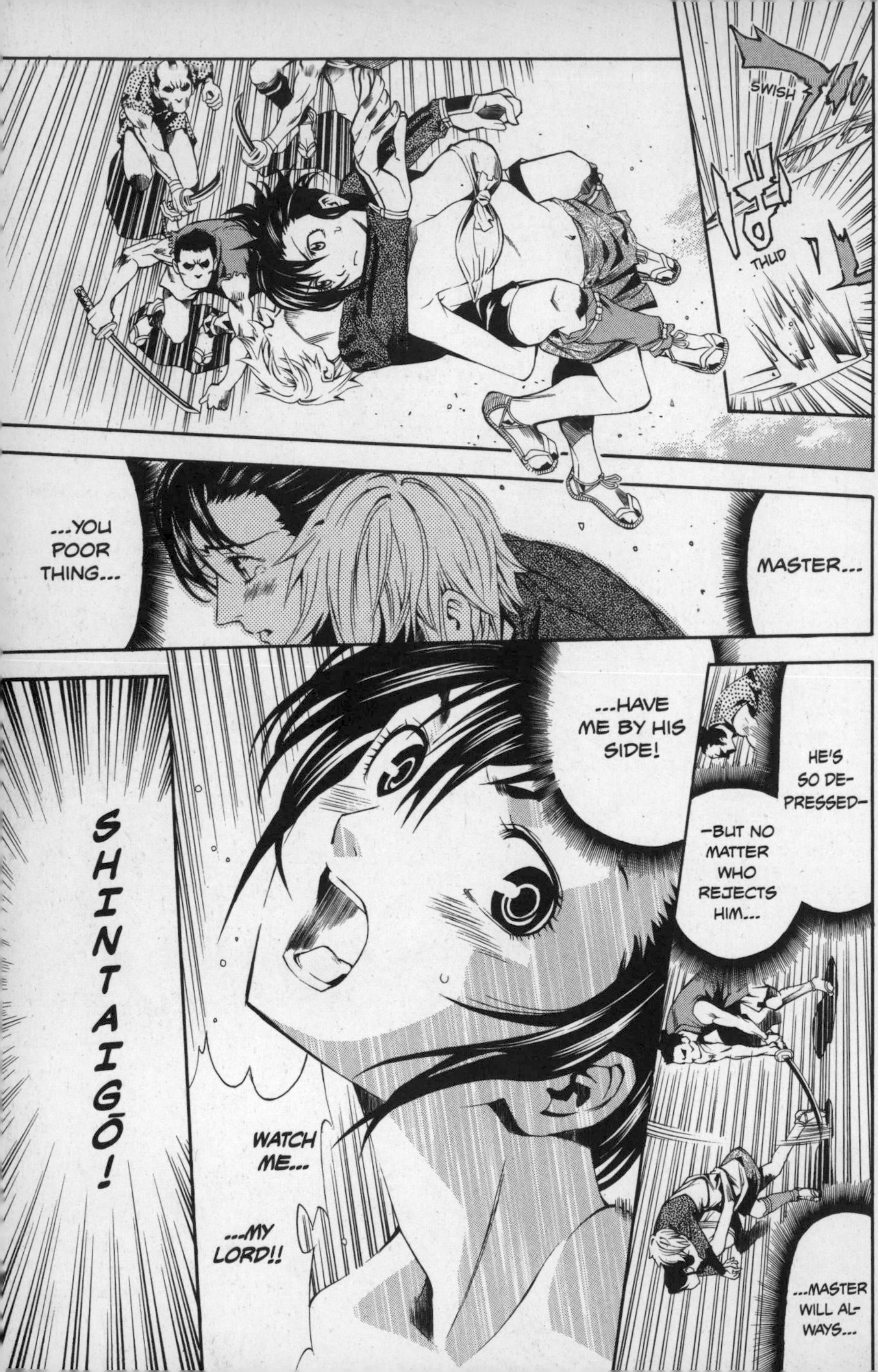
SWISH
THUD
MASTER...
...YOU POOR THING...
HE'S SO DE-PRESSED—
—BUT NO MATTER WHO REJECTS HIM...
...MASTER WILL AL-WAYS...
...HAVE ME BY HIS SIDE!
WATCH ME...
...MY LORD!!
SHINTAIGŌ!

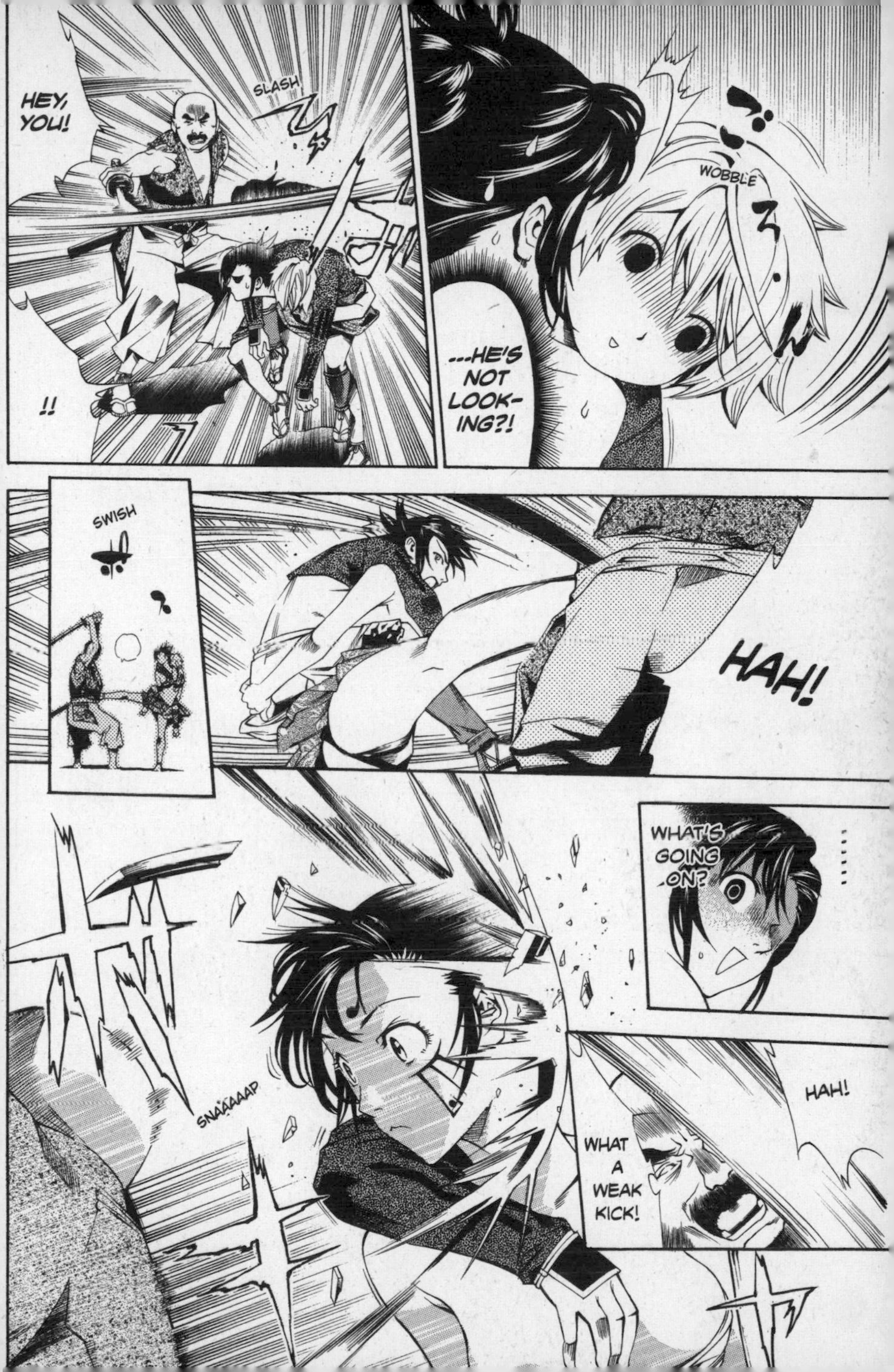
WOBBLE
---HE'S NOT LOOKING?!
SLASH
HEY, YOU!
!!
HAH!
SWISH
WHAT'S GOING ON?
HAH!
WHAT A WEAK KICK!
SNAAAAAP

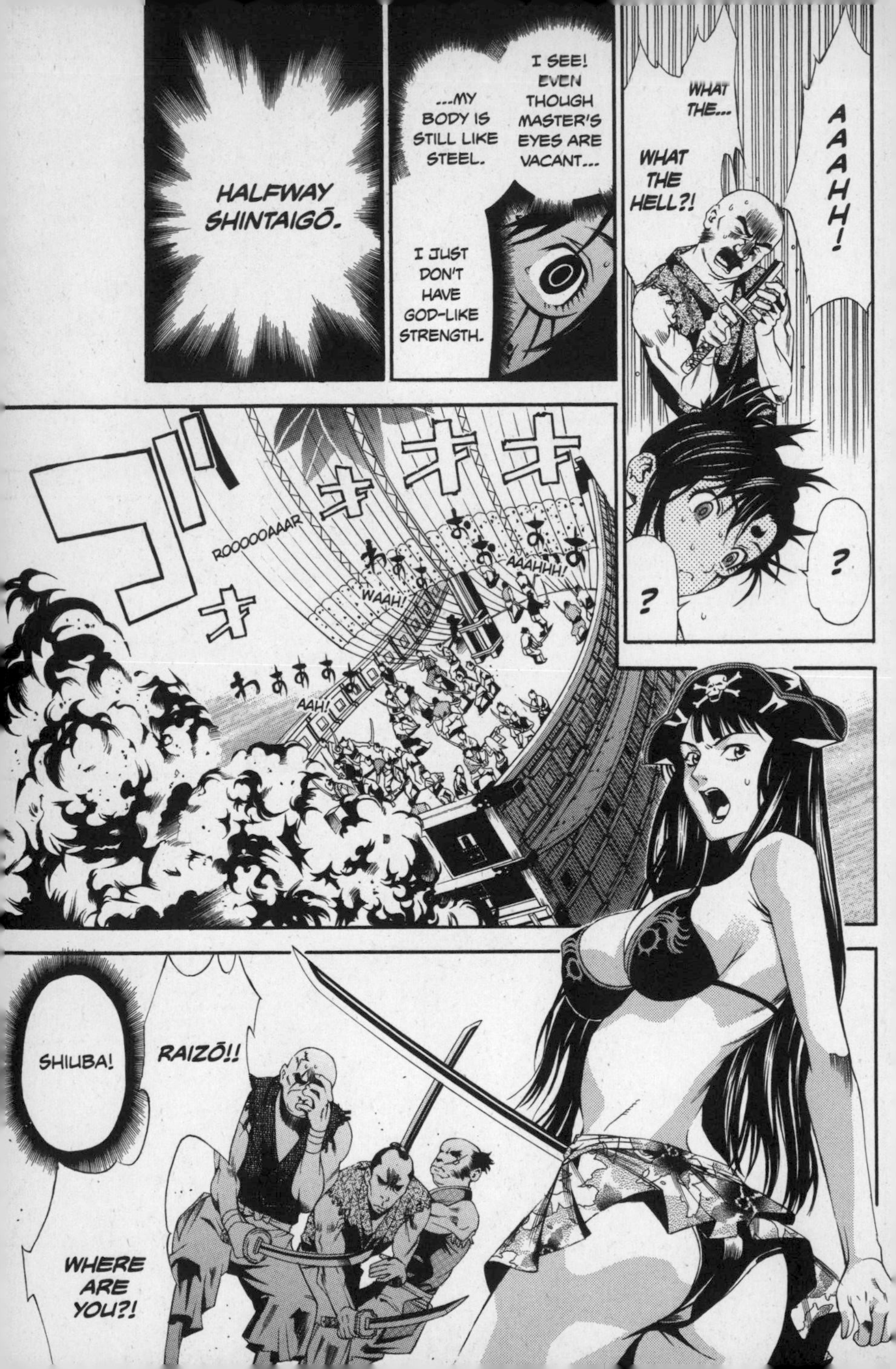
WHAT THE...
AAAAHH!
WHAT THE HELL?!
?
?
I SEE! EVEN THOUGH MASTER'S EYES ARE VACANT...
...MY BODY IS STILL LIKE STEEL.
I JUST DON'T HAVE GOD-LIKE STRENGTH.
HALFWAY SHINTAIGŌ.
ROOOOOAAAR
AAAHHH!
WAAH!
AAH!
RAIZŌ!!
SHIUBA!
WHERE ARE YOU?!

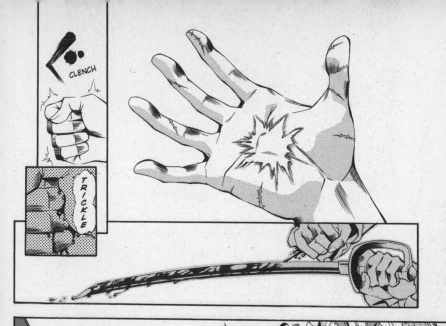

CLENCH

TRICKLE

SWISH

DRIP

DRIP

CHING

SHI....UBA.

WELL
DONE,
MEN.

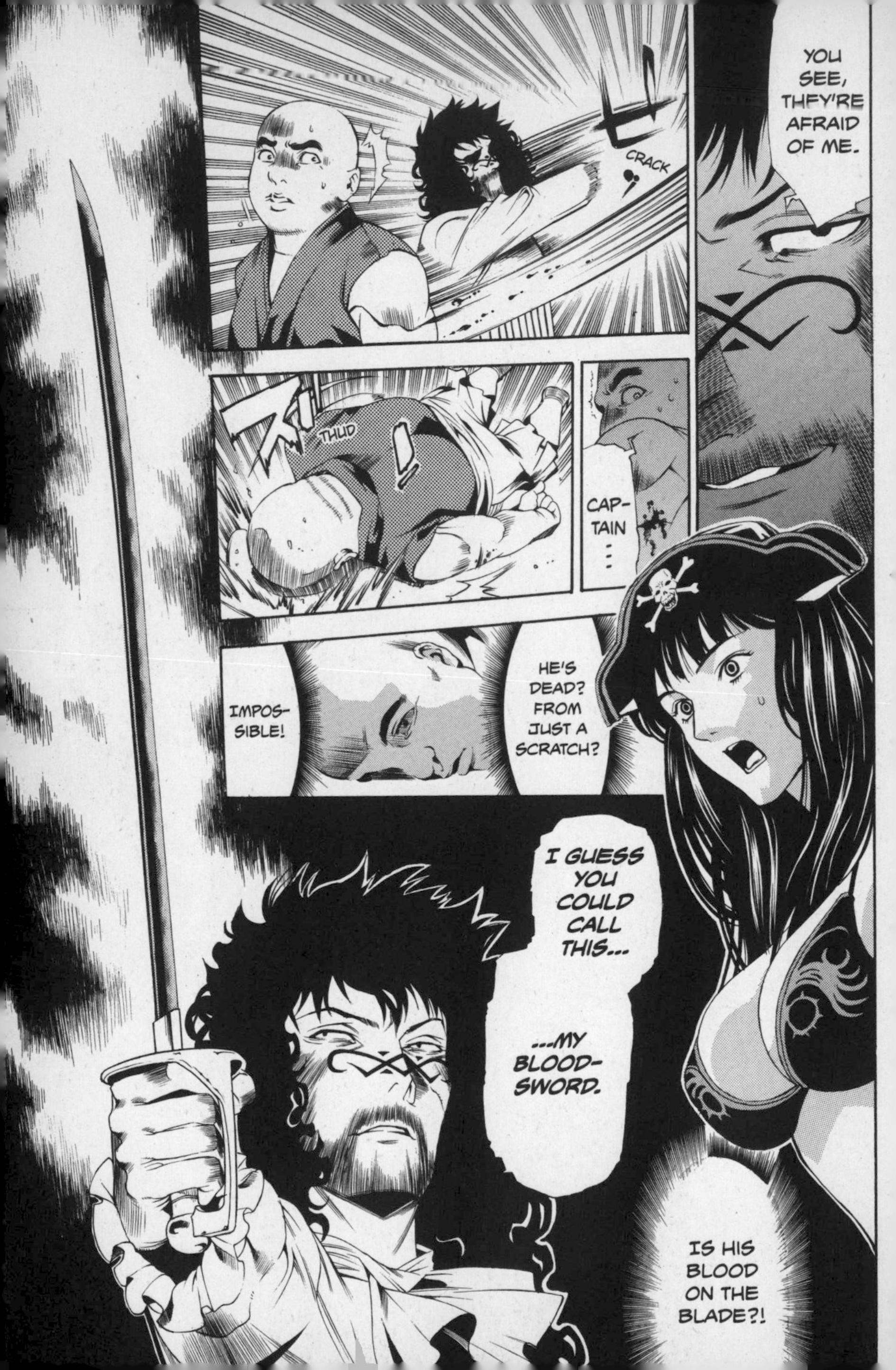
YOU SEE, THEY'RE AFRAID OF ME.
CRACK
CAP-TAIN ...
THUD
HE'S DEAD? FROM JUST A SCRATCH?
IMPOS-SIBLE!
I GUESS YOU COULD CALL THIS...
...MY BLOOD-SWORD.
IS HIS BLOOD ON THE BLADE?!

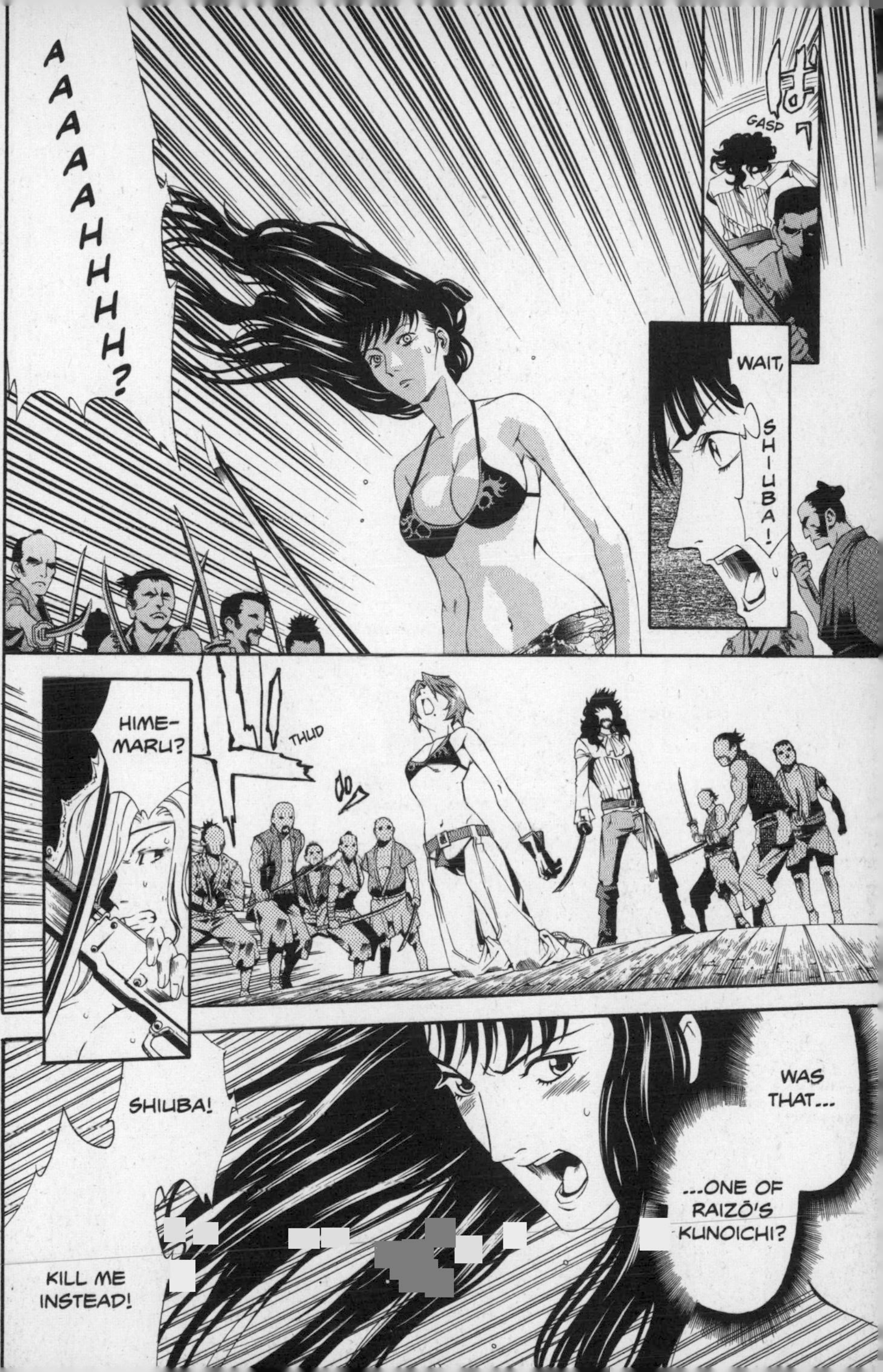
GASP
WAIT, SHIUBA!
AAAAAHHHH?
THUD
HIME-MARU?
WAS THAT...
...ONE OF RAIZŌ'S KUNOICHI?
SHIUBA!
KILL ME INSTEAD!

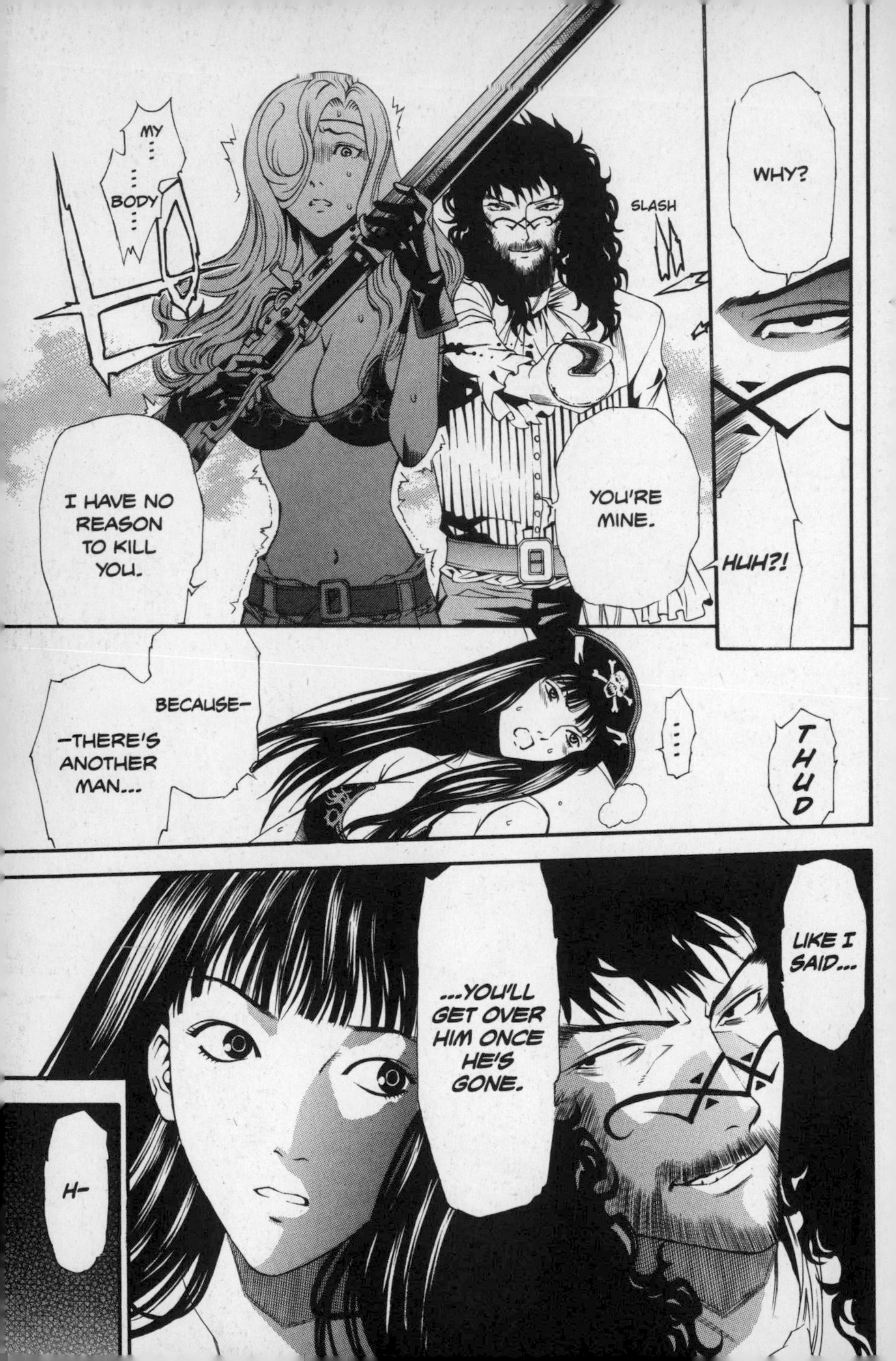
WHY?
HUH?!
SLASH
MY... ...BODY...
YOU'RE MINE.
I HAVE NO REASON TO KILL YOU.
THUD
......
BECAUSE—
—THERE'S ANOTHER MAN...
LIKE I SAID...
...YOU'LL GET OVER HIM ONCE HE'S GONE.
H-

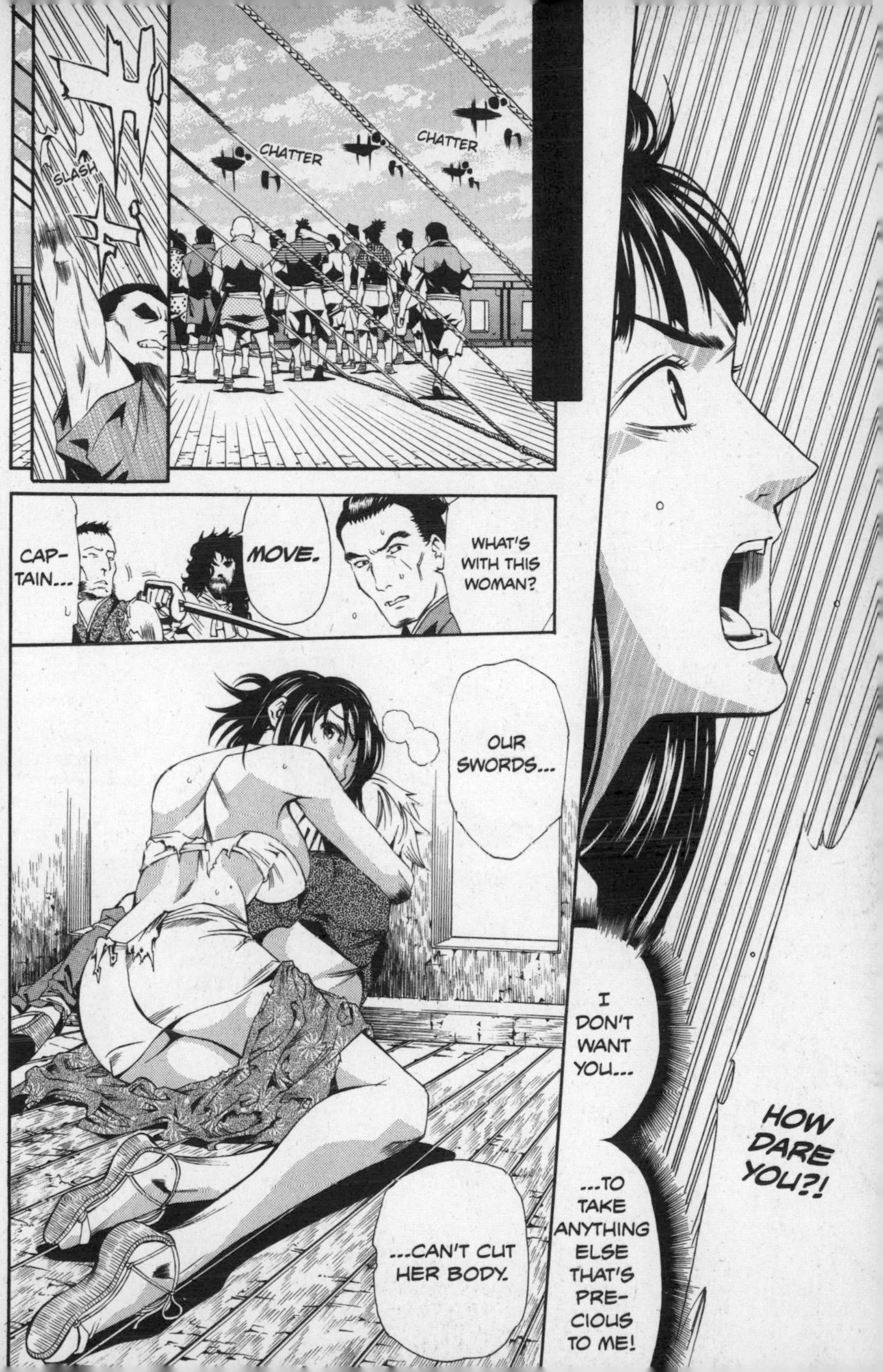
I DON'T WANT YOU...
...TO TAKE ANYTHING ELSE THAT'S PRECIOUS TO ME!
HOW DARE YOU?!
CHATTER
CHATTER
SLASH
WHAT'S WITH THIS WOMAN?
MOVE.
CAP-TAIN...
OUR SWORDS...
...CAN'T CUT HER BODY.

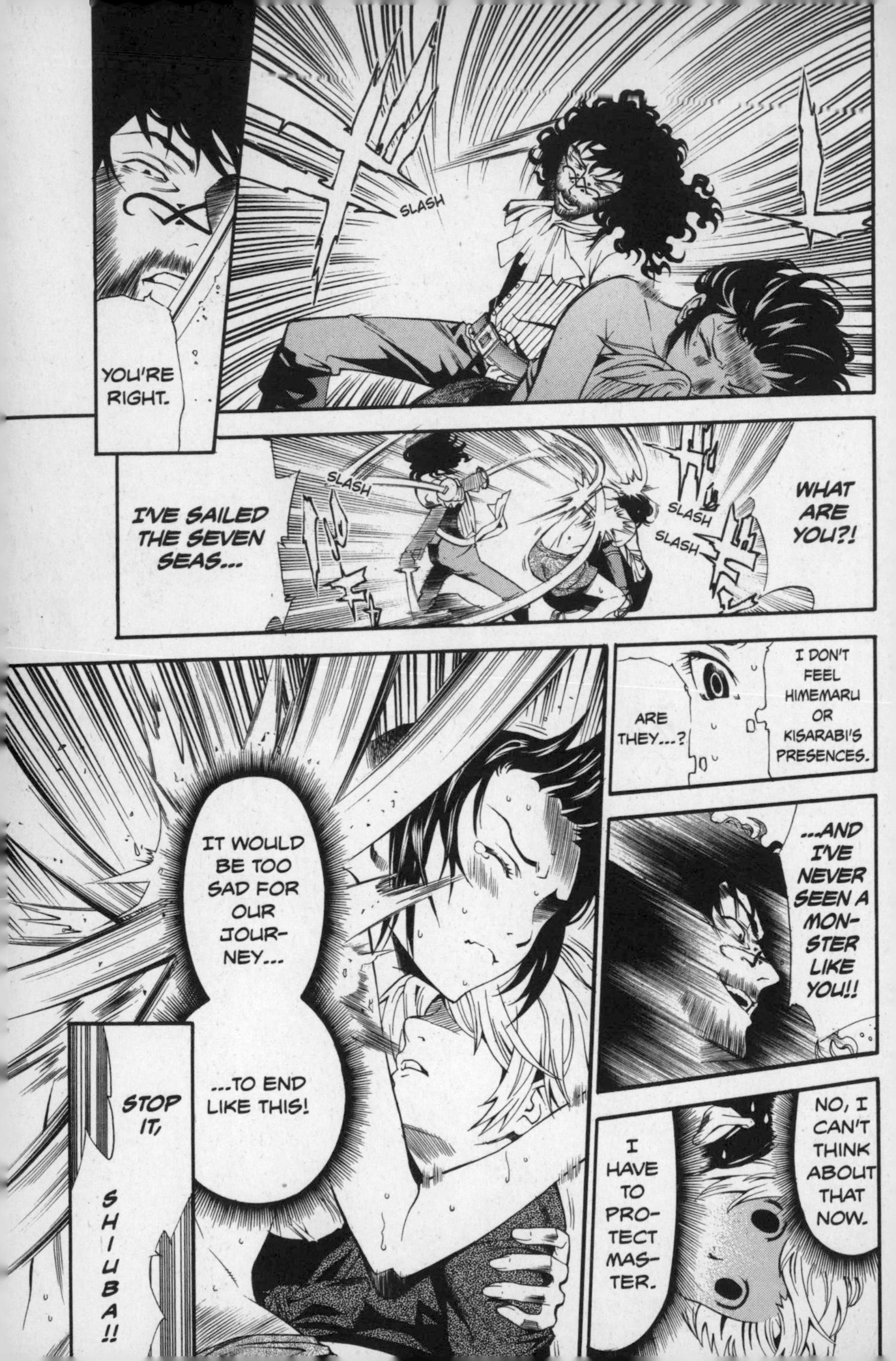
SLASH
YOU'RE RIGHT.
WHAT ARE YOU?!
SLASH
SLASH
SLASH
I'VE SAILED THE SEVEN SEAS...
I DON'T FEEL HIMEMARU OR KISARABI'S PRESENCES.
ARE THEY...?
...AND I'VE NEVER SEEN A MONSTER LIKE YOU!!
NO, I CAN'T THINK ABOUT THAT NOW.
I HAVE TO PROTECT MASTER.
IT WOULD BE TOO SAD FOR OUR JOURNEY...
...TO END LIKE THIS!
STOP IT,
SHIUBA!!

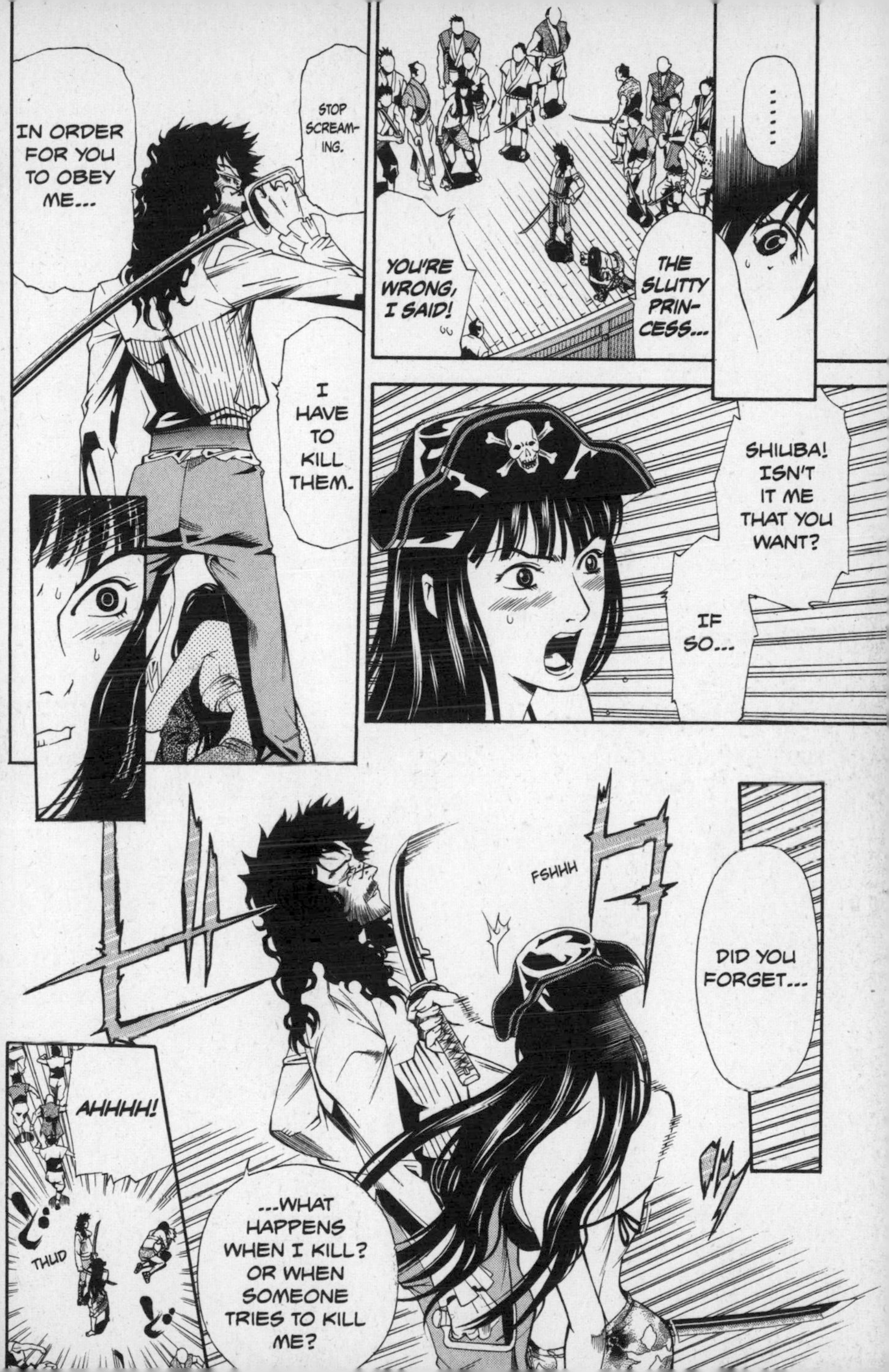
......
THE SLUTTY PRINCESS...
YOU'RE WRONG, I SAID!
SHIUBA! ISN'T IT ME THAT YOU WANT?
IF SO...
STOP SCREAMING.
IN ORDER FOR YOU TO OBEY ME...
I HAVE TO KILL THEM.
DID YOU FORGET...
FSHHH
...WHAT HAPPENS WHEN I KILL? OR WHEN SOMEONE TRIES TO KILL ME?
AHHHH!
THUD

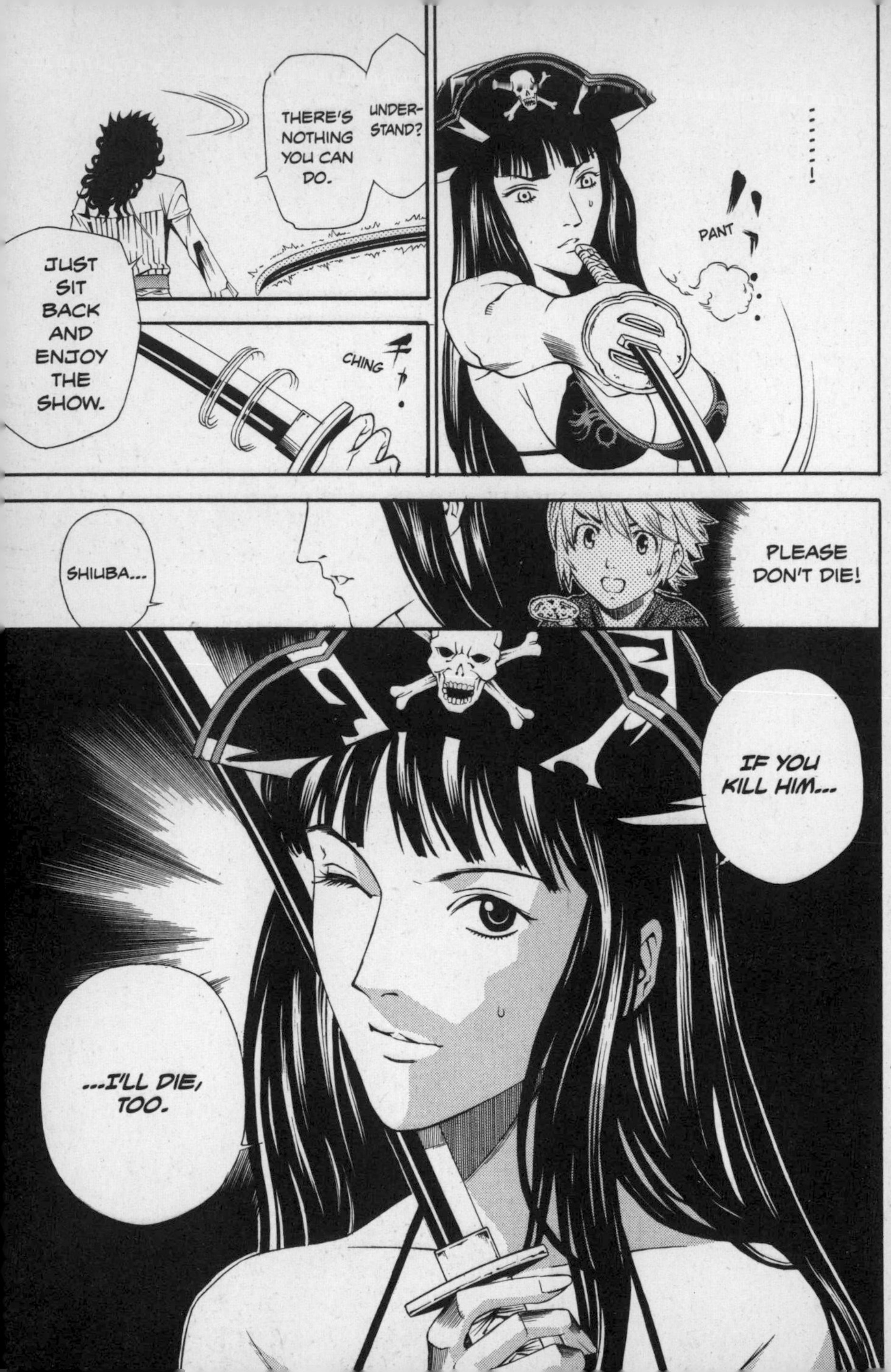
......!
PANT
UNDER-STAND?
THERE'S NOTHING YOU CAN DO.
JUST SIT BACK AND ENJOY THE SHOW.
CHING
PLEASE DON'T DIE!
SHIUBA...
IF YOU KILL HIM...
...I'LL DIE, TOO.

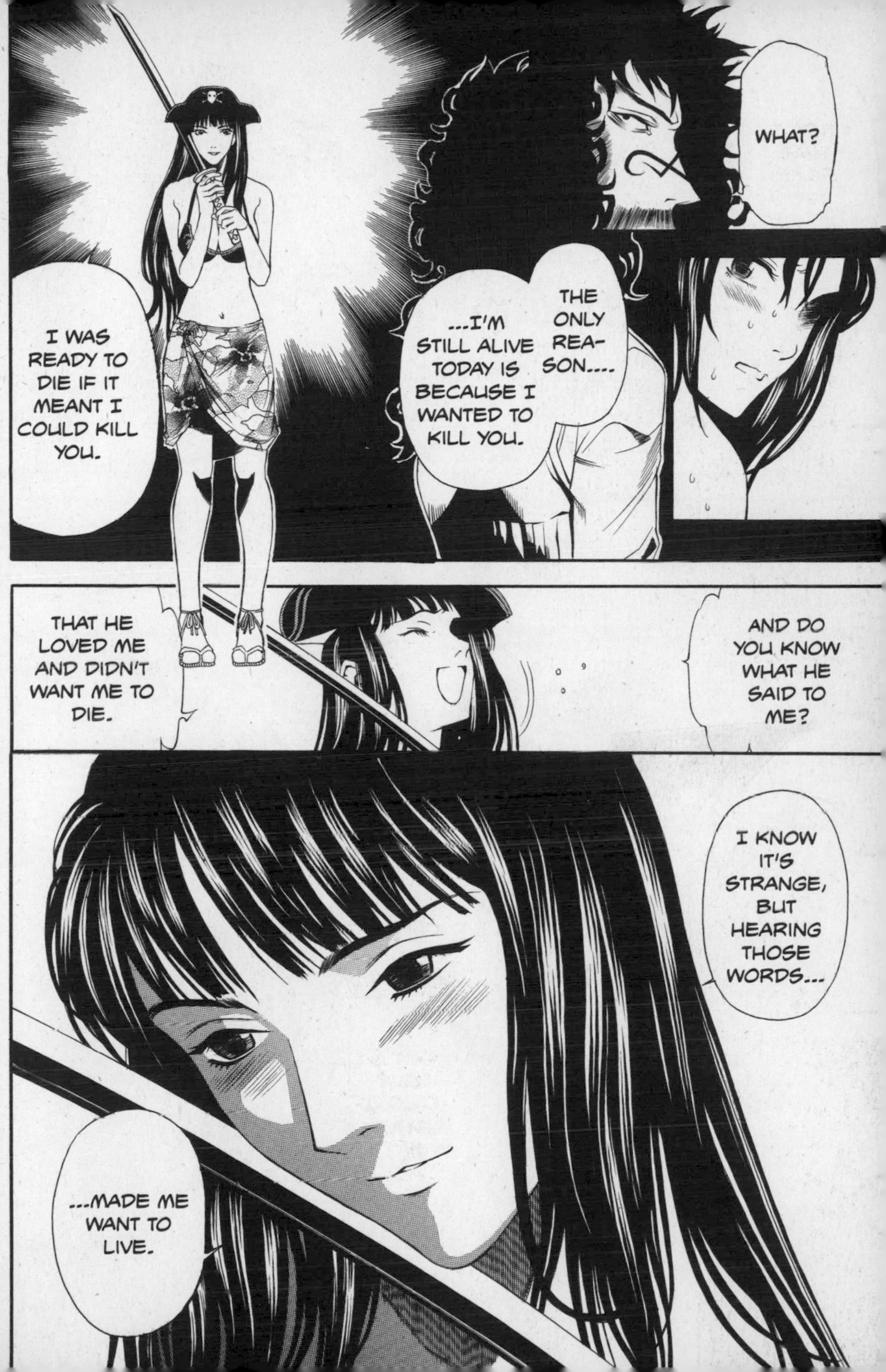
WHAT?
THE ONLY REASON....
...I'M STILL ALIVE TODAY IS BECAUSE I WANTED TO KILL YOU.
I WAS READY TO DIE IF IT MEANT I COULD KILL YOU.
AND DO YOU KNOW WHAT HE SAID TO ME?
THAT HE LOVED ME AND DIDN'T WANT ME TO DIE.
I KNOW IT'S STRANGE, BUT HEARING THOSE WORDS...
...MADE ME WANT TO LIVE.

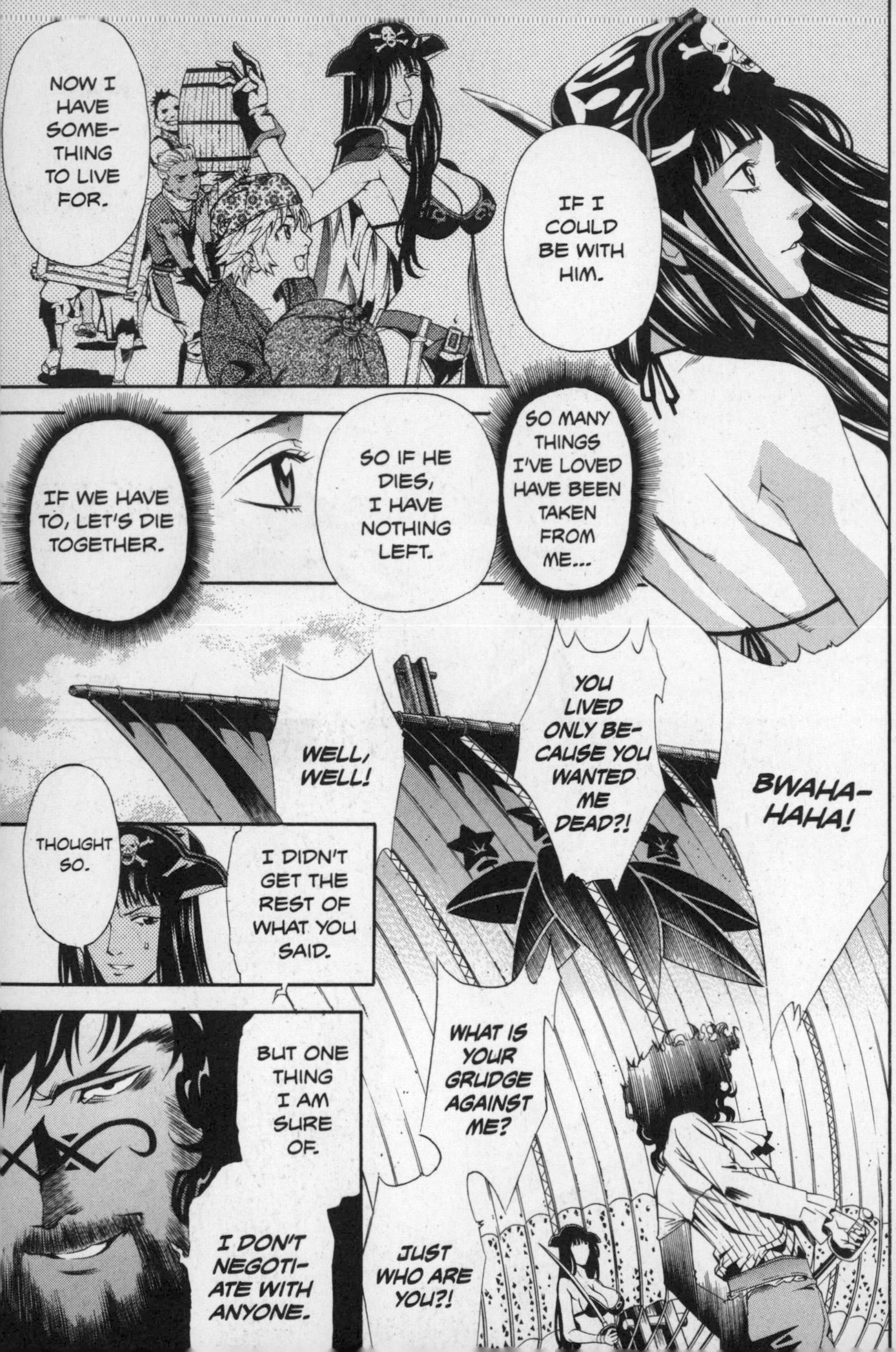
IF I COULD BE WITH HIM.
NOW I HAVE SOMETHING TO LIVE FOR.
SO MANY THINGS I'VE LOVED HAVE BEEN TAKEN FROM ME...
SO IF HE DIES, I HAVE NOTHING LEFT.
IF WE HAVE TO, LET'S DIE TOGETHER.
BWAHA-HAHA!
YOU LIVED ONLY BECAUSE YOU WANTED ME DEAD?!
WELL, WELL!
I DIDN'T GET THE REST OF WHAT YOU SAID.
THOUGHT SO.
WHAT IS YOUR GRUDGE AGAINST ME?
JUST WHO ARE YOU?!
BUT ONE THING I AM SURE OF.
I DON'T NEGOTIATE WITH ANYONE.

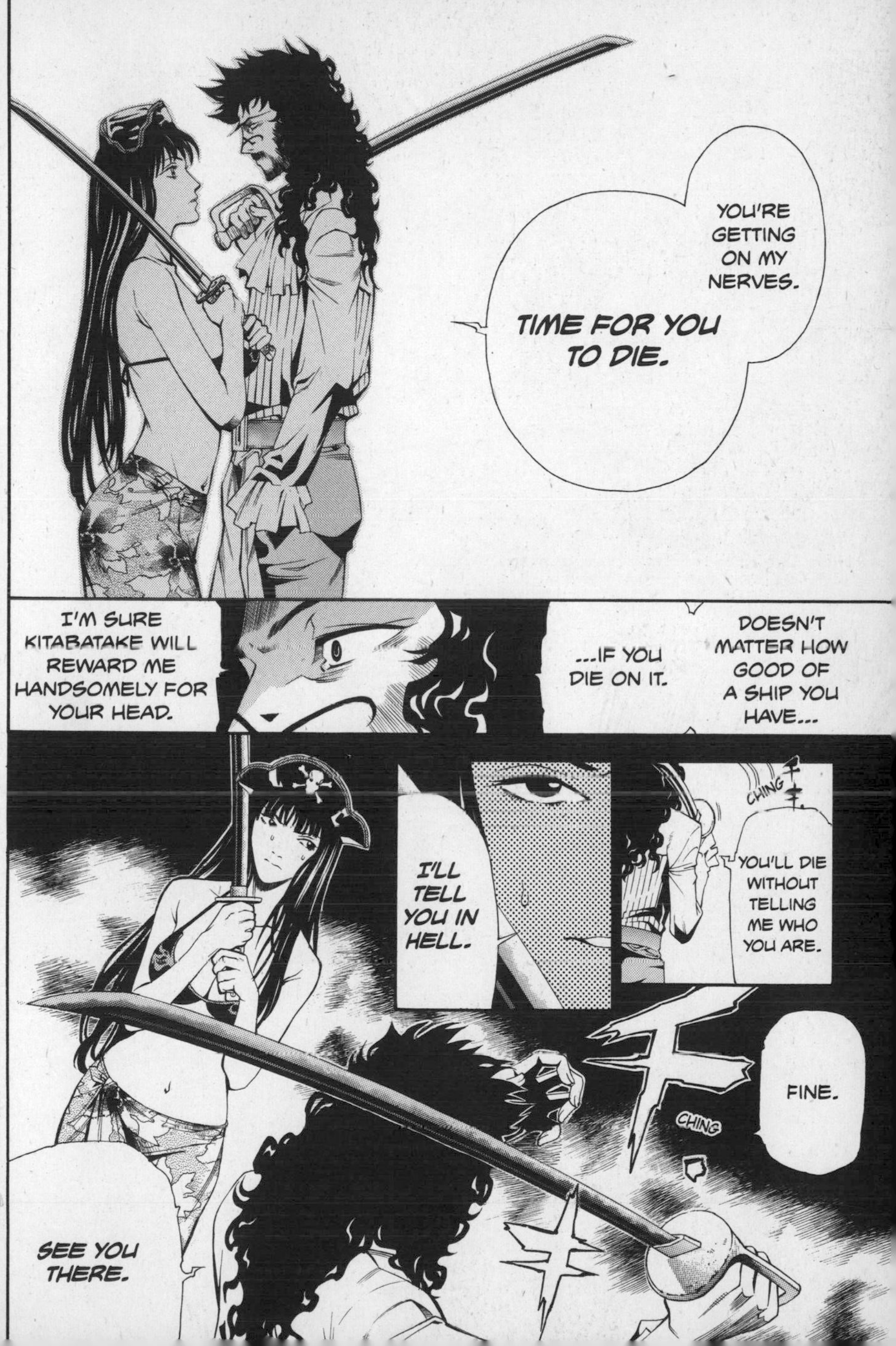
YOU'RE GETTING ON MY NERVES.
TIME FOR YOU TO DIE.
DOESN'T MATTER HOW GOOD OF A SHIP YOU HAVE...
...IF YOU DIE ON IT.
I'M SURE KITABATAKE WILL REWARD ME HANDSOMELY FOR YOUR HEAD.
CHING
YOU'LL DIE WITHOUT TELLING ME WHO YOU ARE.
I'LL TELL YOU IN HELL.
FINE.
CHING
SEE YOU THERE.

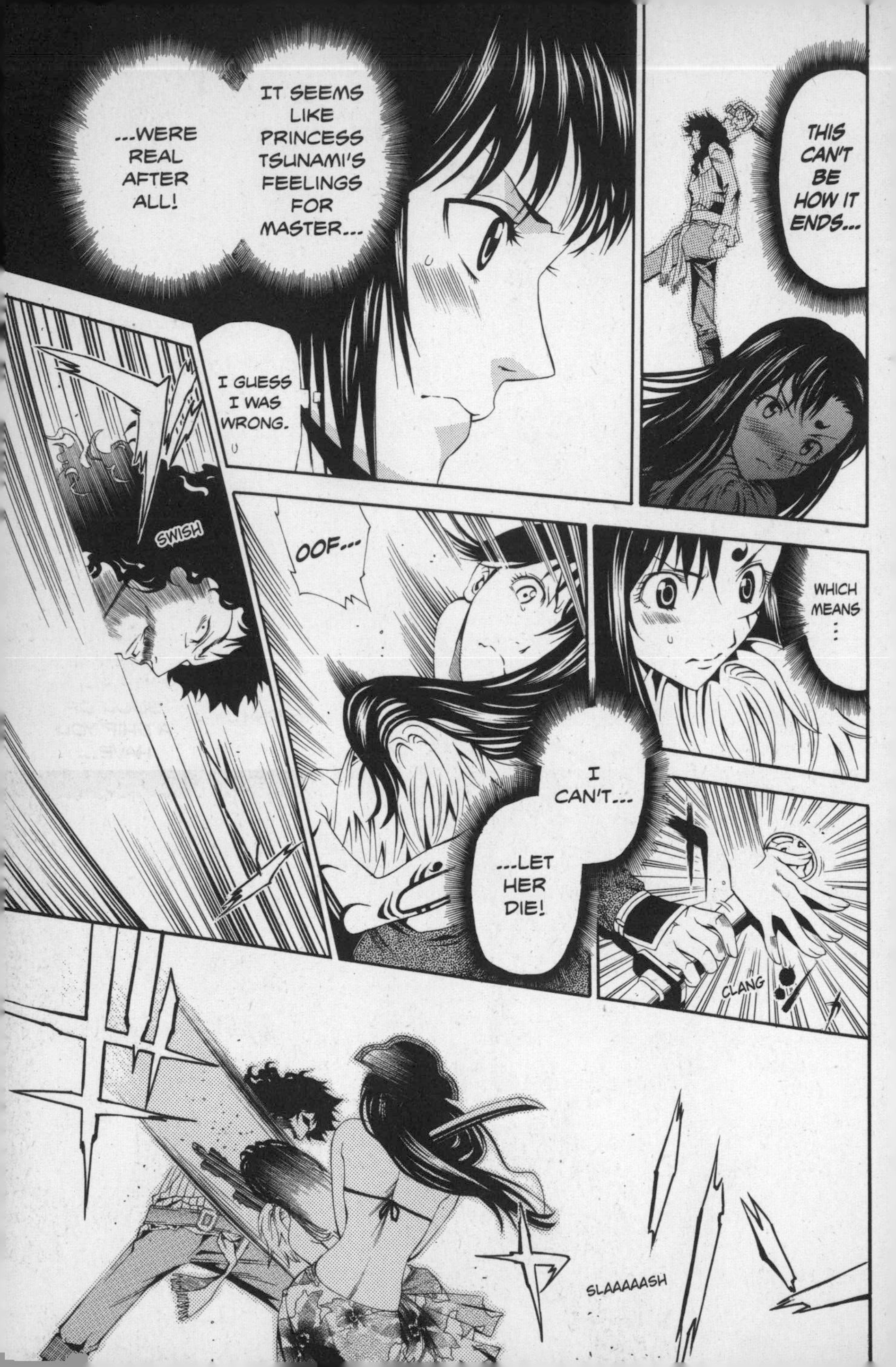
THIS CAN'T BE HOW IT ENDS...
IT SEEMS LIKE PRINCESS TSUNAMI'S FEELINGS FOR MASTER...
...WERE REAL AFTER ALL!
I GUESS I WAS WRONG.
WHICH MEANS ...
I CAN'T...
...LET HER DIE!
CLANG
OOF...
SWISH
SLAAAAASH

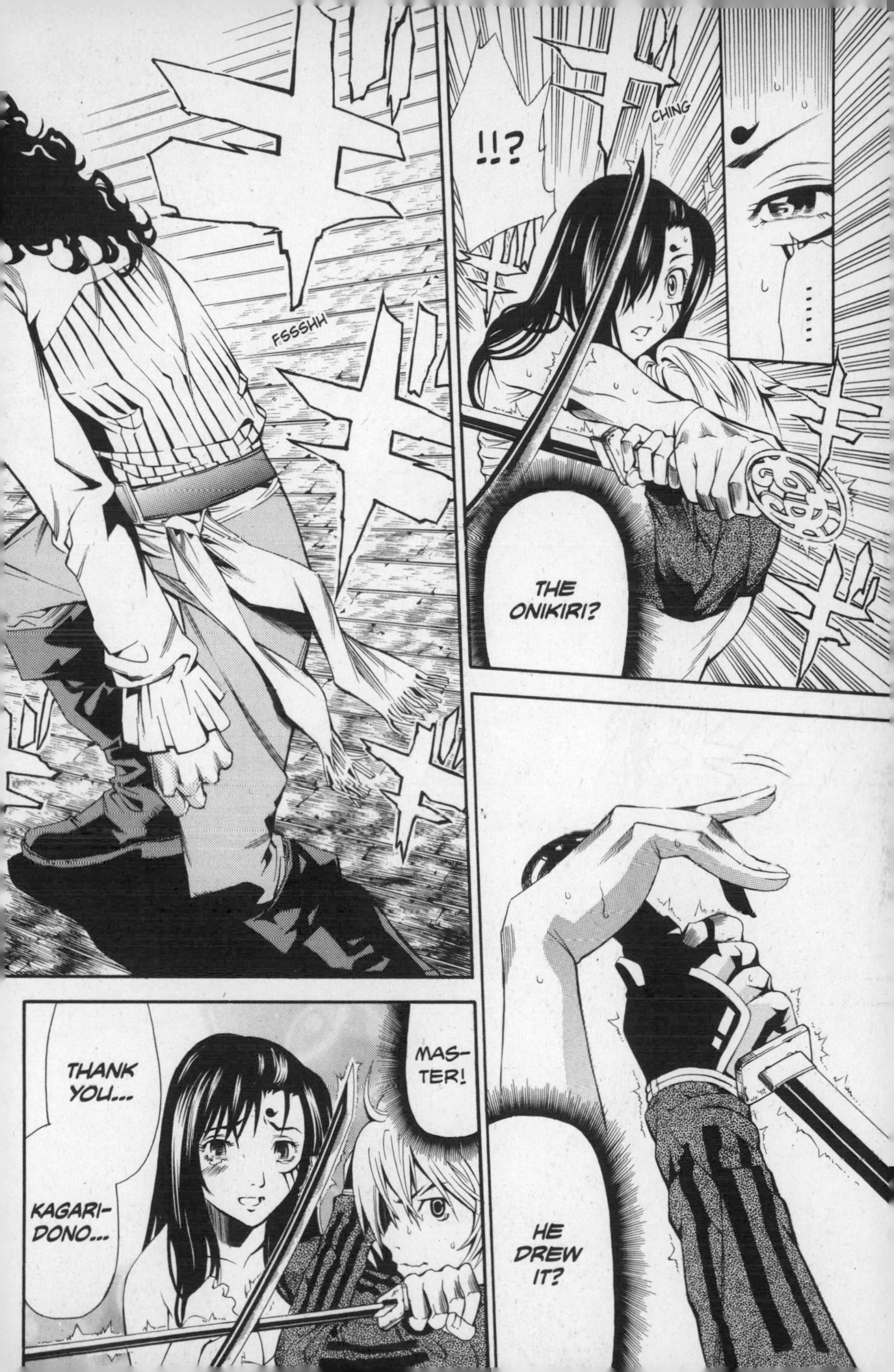
......
!!?
CHING
THE ONIKIRI?
FSSSHH
HE DREW IT?
MAS-TER!
THANK YOU...
KAGARI-DONO...

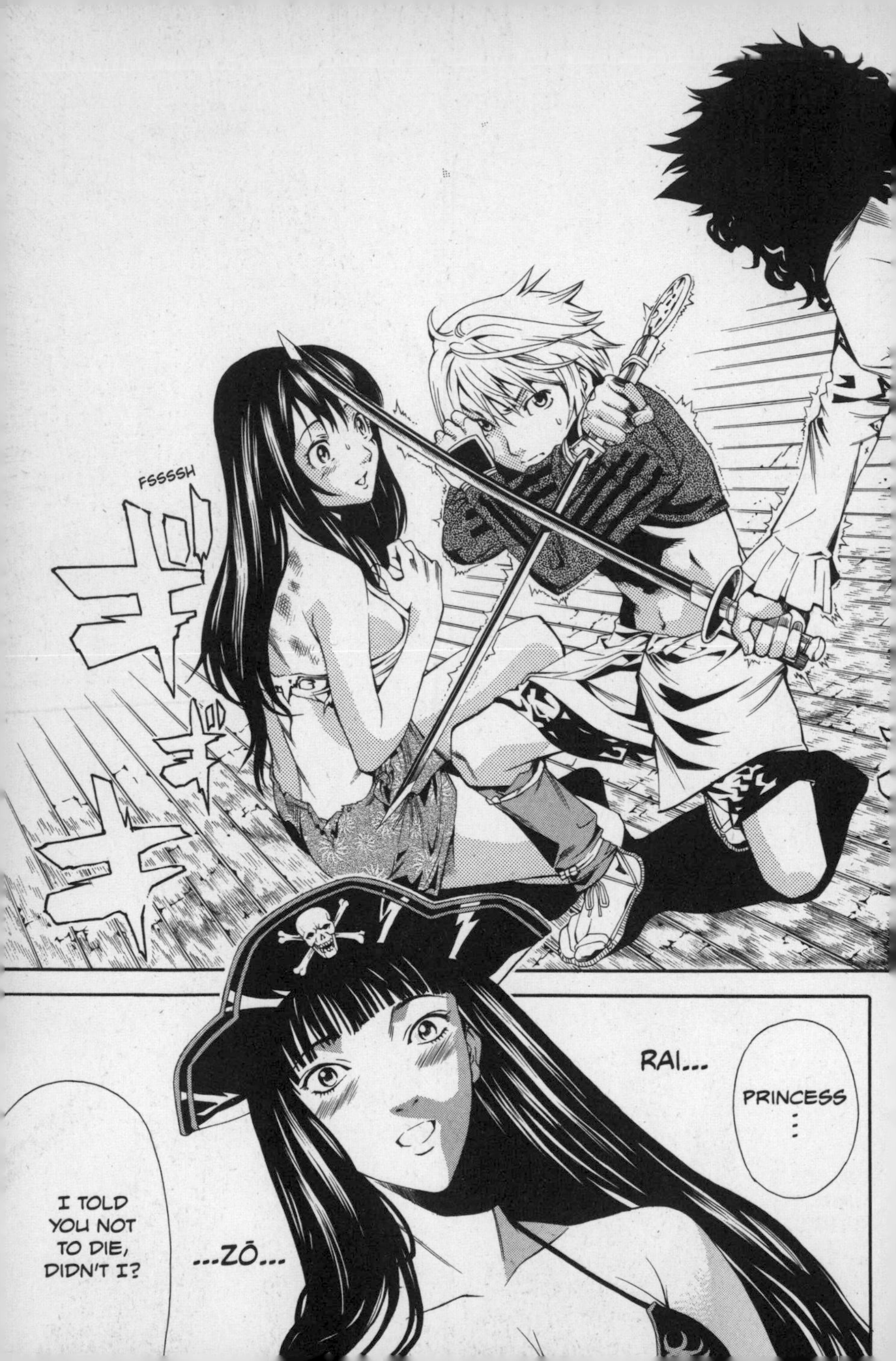
FSSSSH
PRINCESS
...
RAI...
...ZŌ...
I TOLD YOU NOT TO DIE, DIDN'T I?

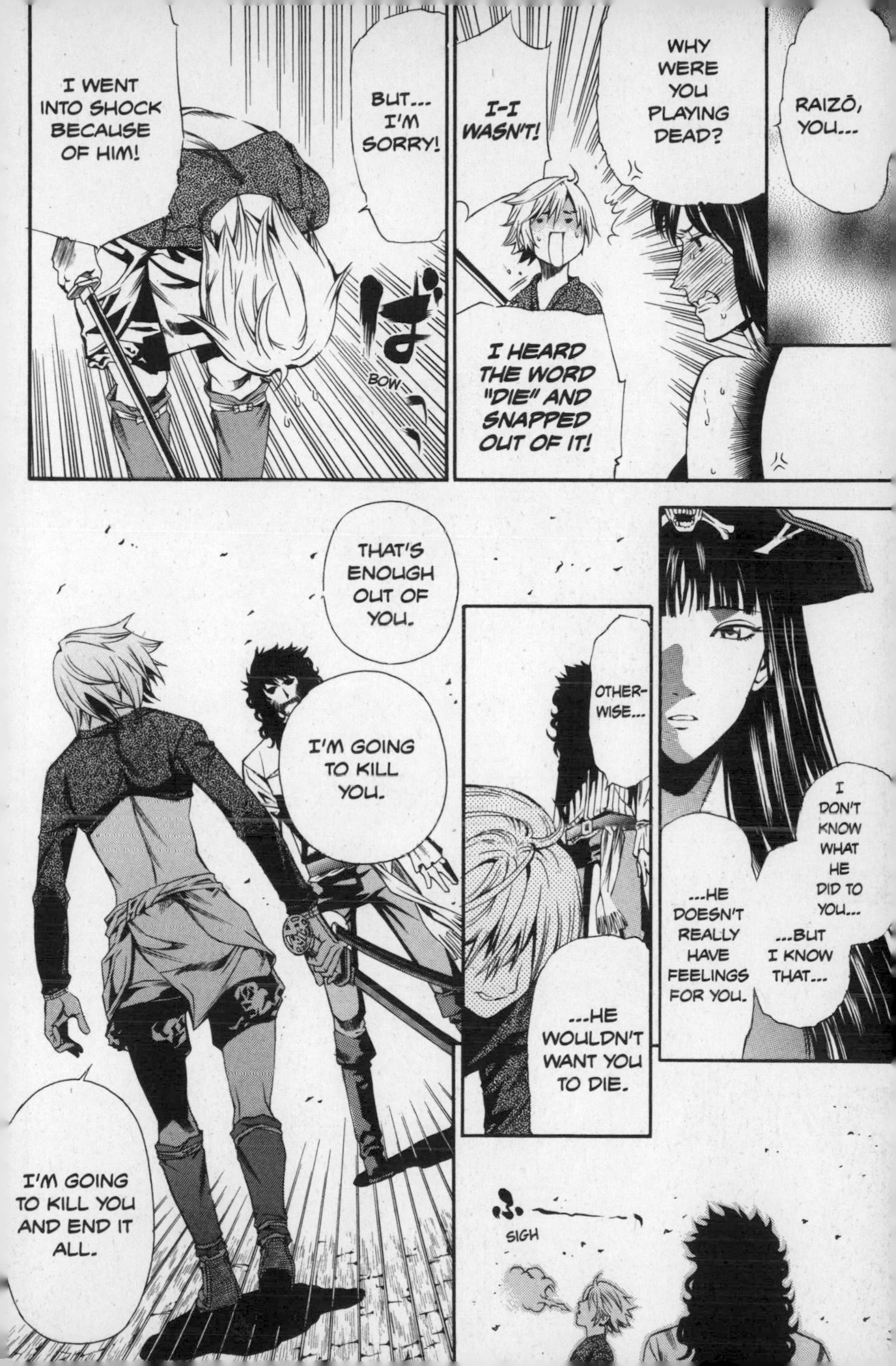
RAIZŌ, YOU...
WHY WERE YOU PLAYING DEAD?
I-I WASN'T!
I HEARD THE WORD "DIE" AND SNAPPED OUT OF IT!
BUT... I'M SORRY!
BOW
I WENT INTO SHOCK BECAUSE OF HIM!
I DON'T KNOW WHAT HE DID TO YOU...
...BUT I KNOW THAT...
...HE DOESN'T REALLY HAVE FEELINGS FOR YOU.
OTHER-WISE...
...HE WOULDN'T WANT YOU TO DIE.
SIGH
THAT'S ENOUGH OUT OF YOU.
I'M GOING TO KILL YOU.
I'M GOING TO KILL YOU AND END IT ALL.

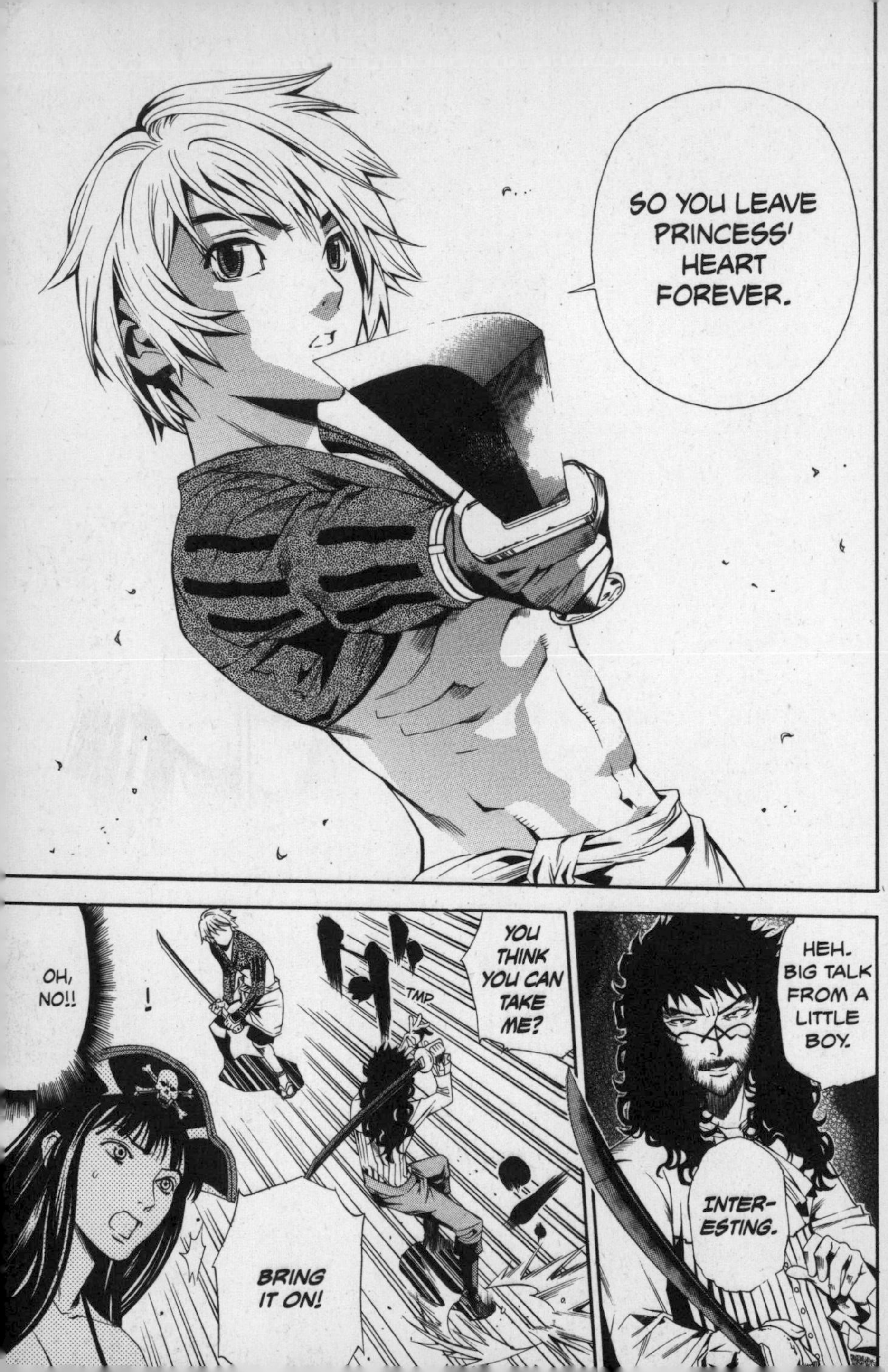
SO YOU LEAVE PRINCESS' HEART FOREVER.
HEH. BIG TALK FROM A LITTLE BOY.
INTER-ESTING.
YOU THINK YOU CAN TAKE ME?
TMP
!
OH, NO!!
BRING IT ON!

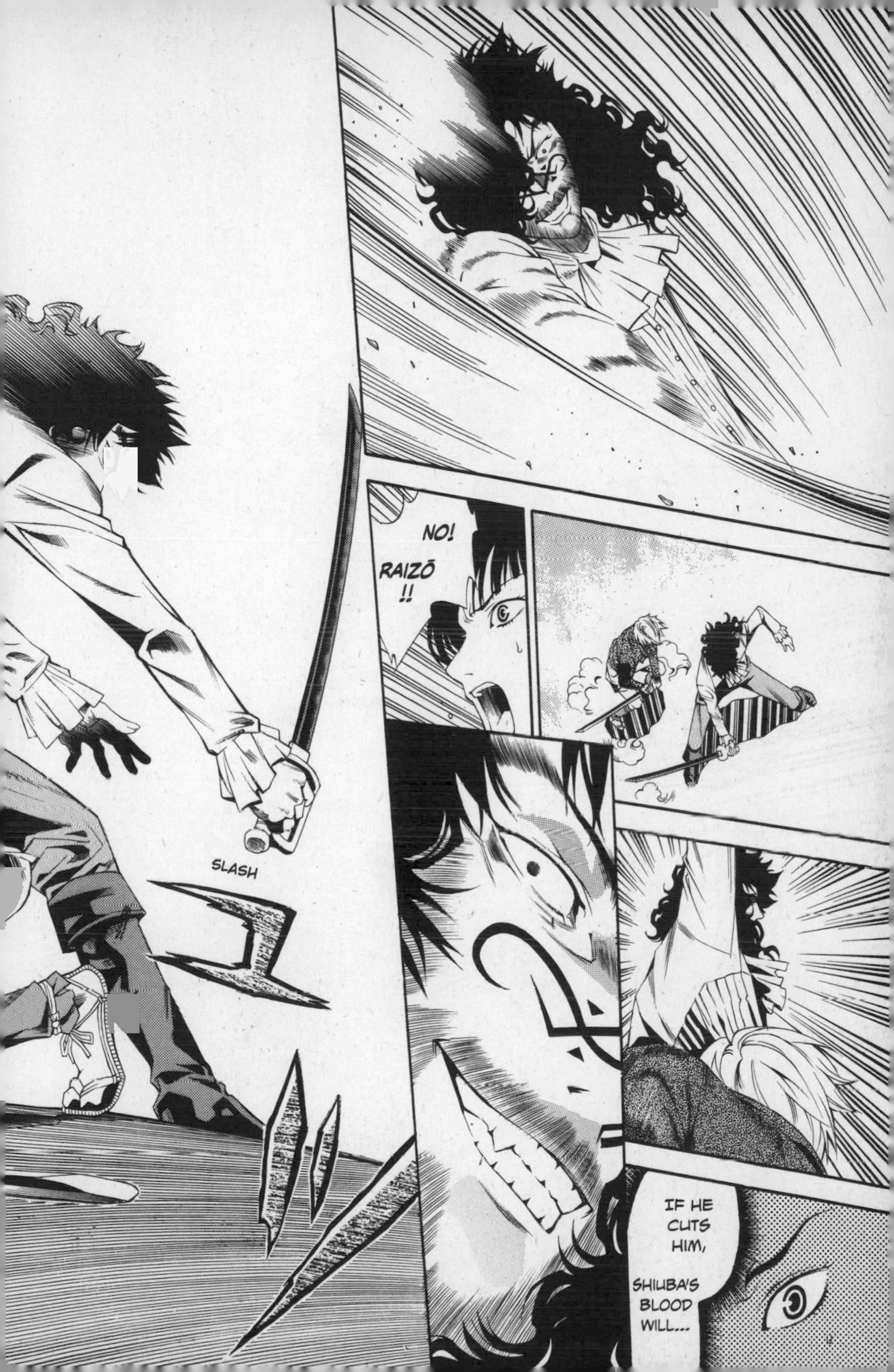
NO!
RAIZŌ!!
IF HE CUTS HIM,
SHIUBA'S BLOOD WILL...
SLASH

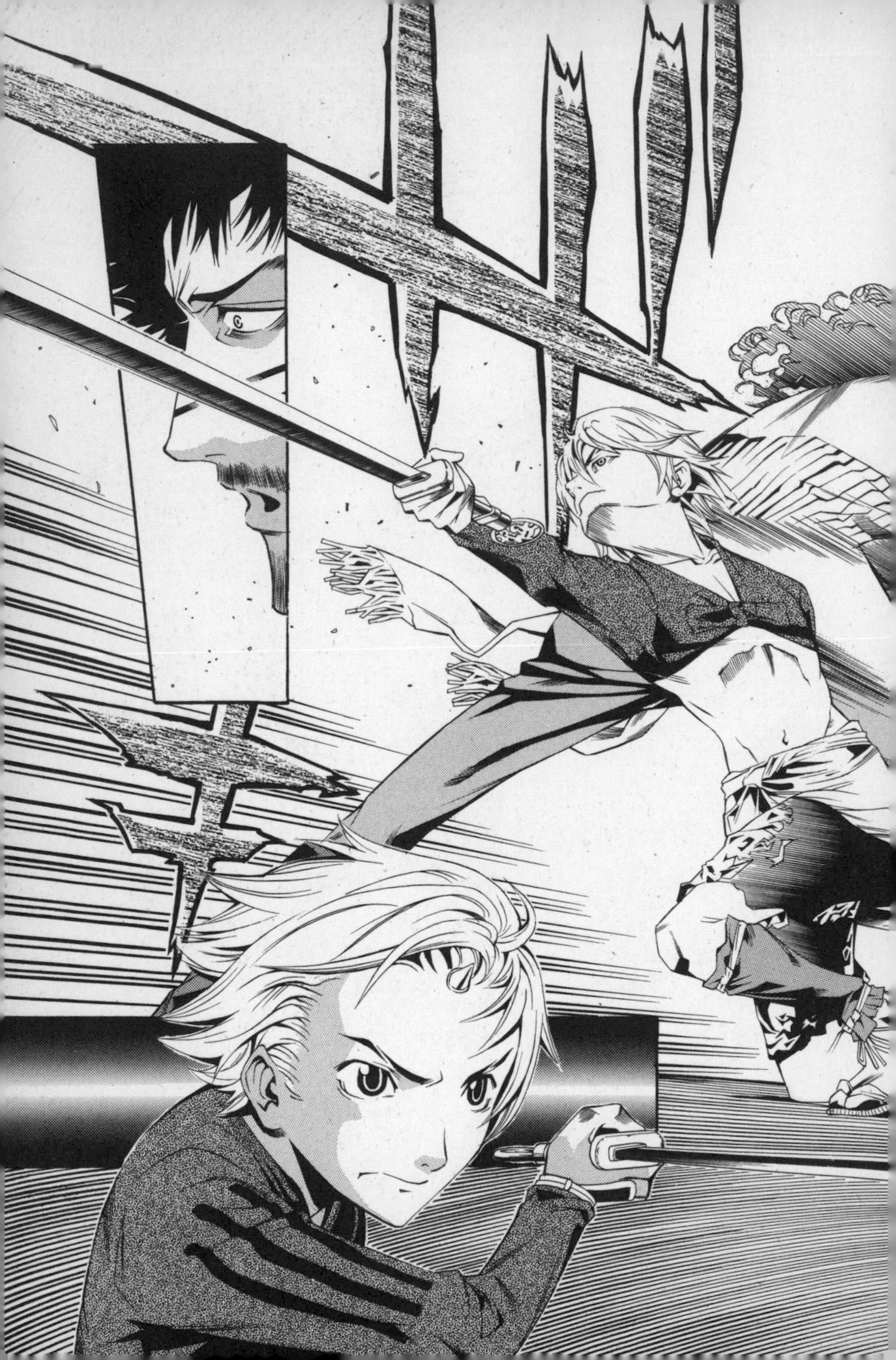

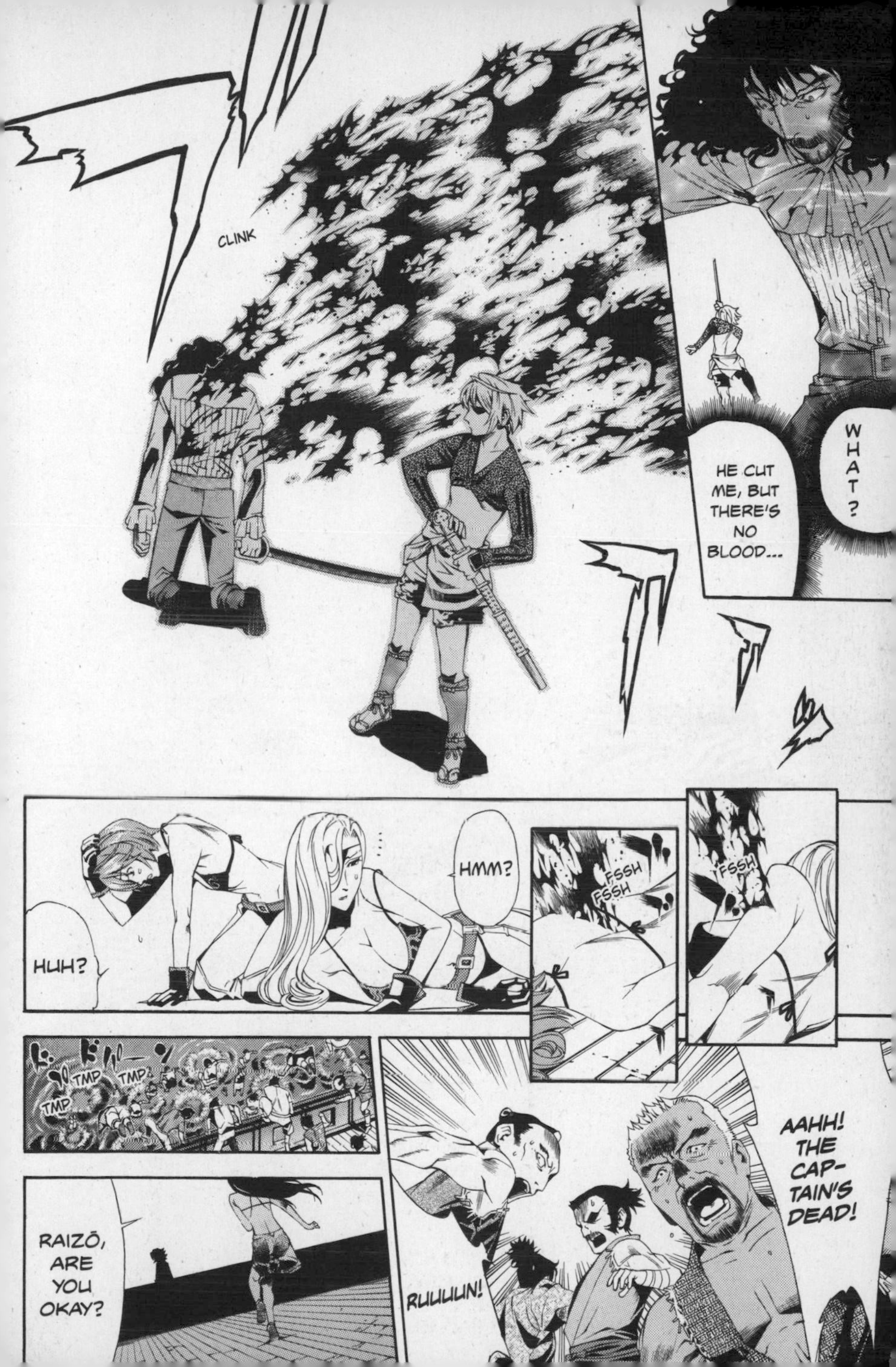
WHAT?
HE CUT ME, BUT THERE'S NO BLOOD...
CLINK
FSSH
FSSH FSSH
HMM?
HUH?
AAHH! THE CAP-TAIN'S DEAD!
RUUUUN!
TMP TMP TMP
RAIZŌ, ARE YOU OKAY?

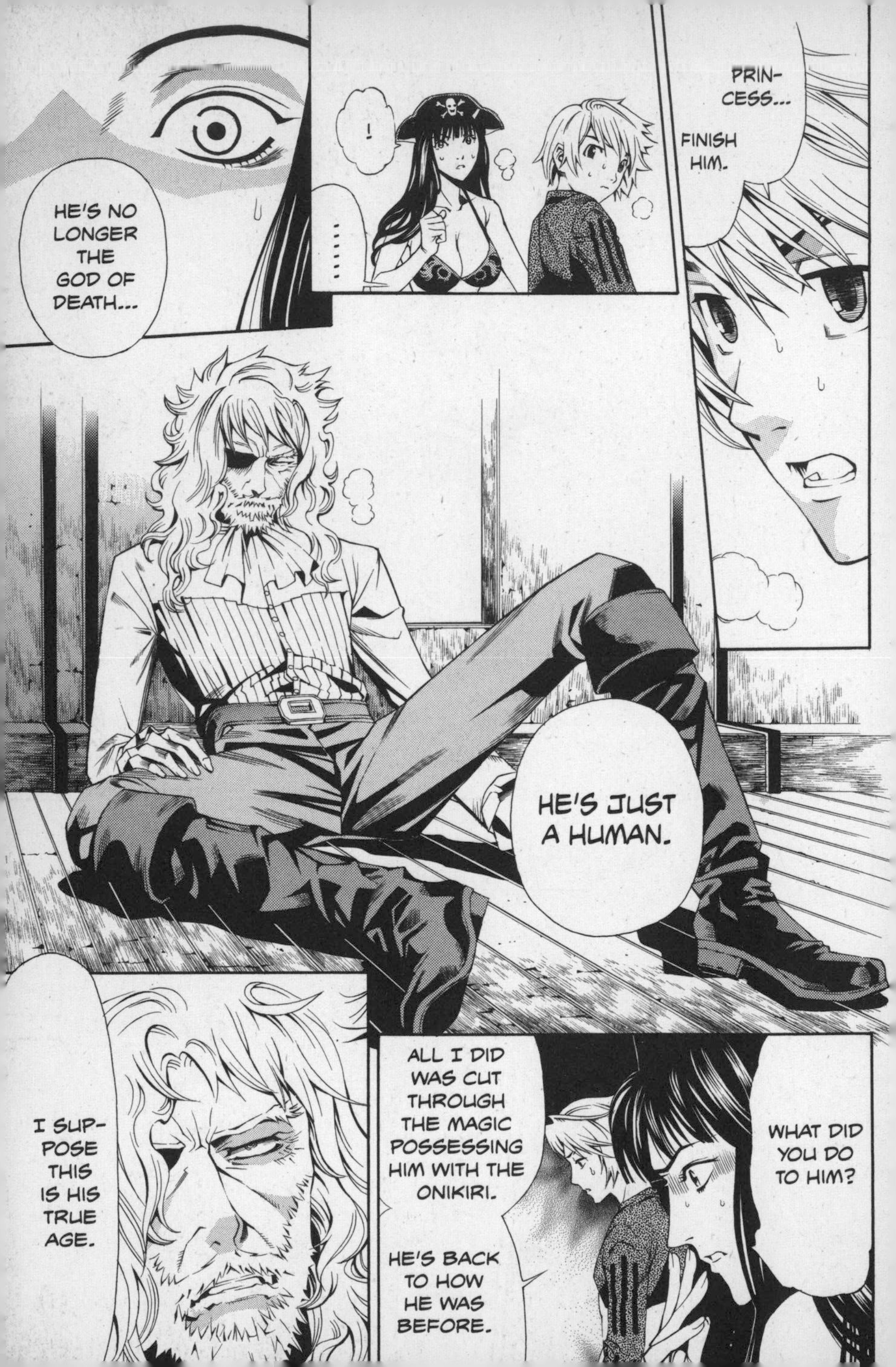
PRIN-CESS...
FINISH HIM.
!
......
HE'S NO LONGER THE GOD OF DEATH...
HE'S JUST A HUMAN.
WHAT DID YOU DO TO HIM?
ALL I DID WAS CUT THROUGH THE MAGIC POSSESSING HIM WITH THE ONIKIRI.
HE'S BACK TO HOW HE WAS BEFORE.
I SUP-POSE THIS IS HIS TRUE AGE.

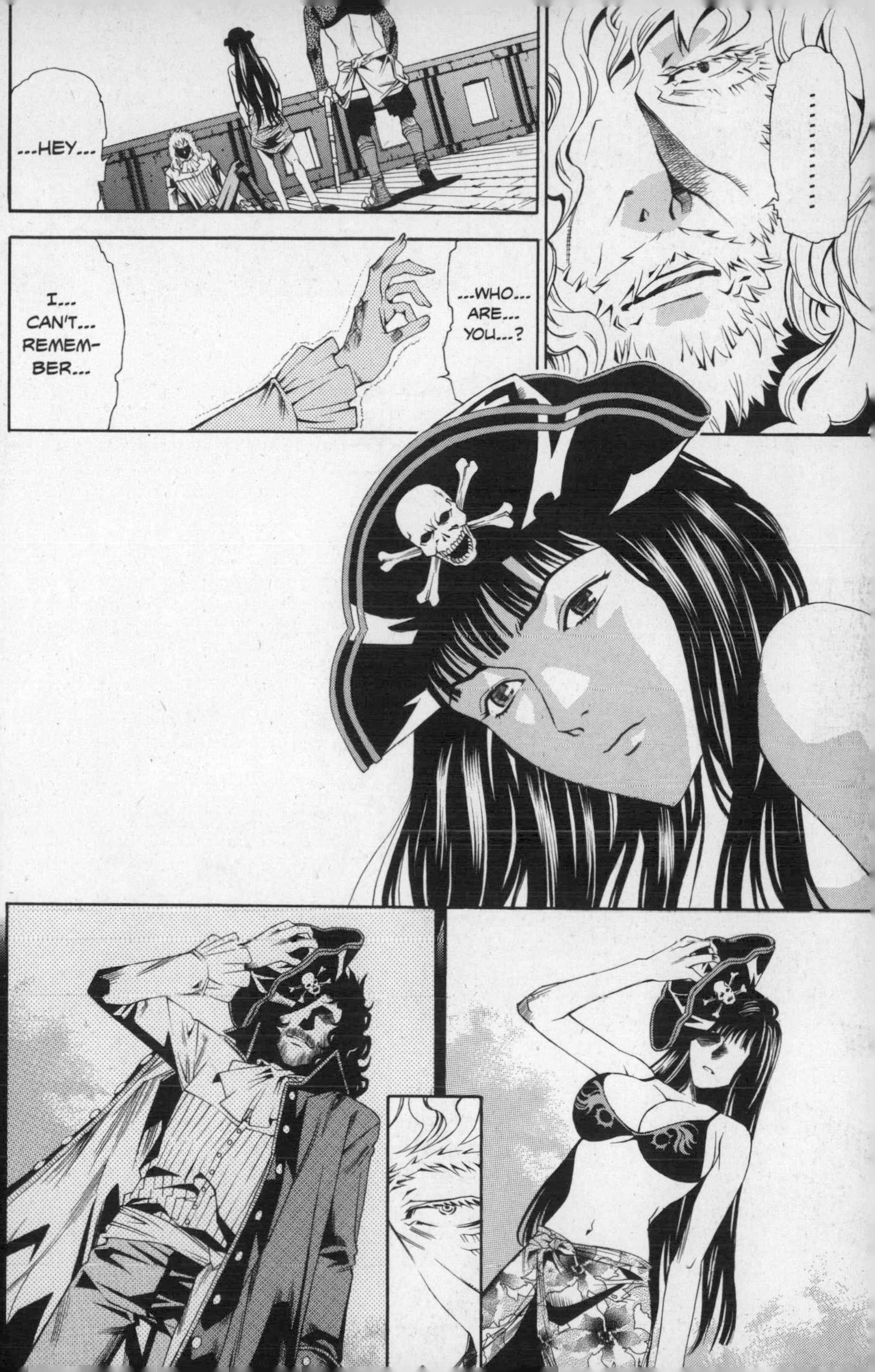
......
...HEY...
...WHO... ARE... YOU...?
I... CAN'T... REMEMBER...

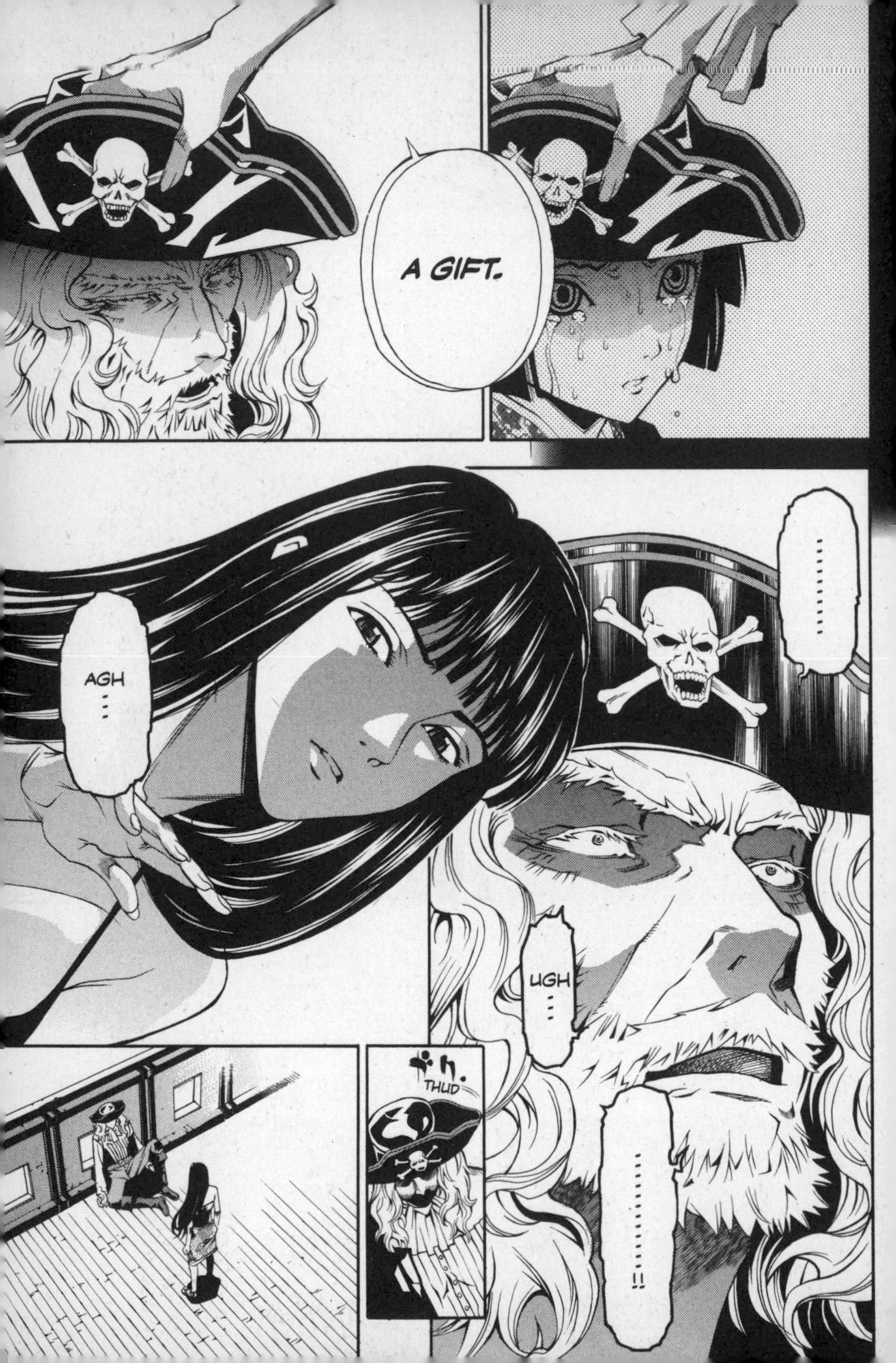
A GIFT.
......
AGH ...
UGH ...
......!!
THUD

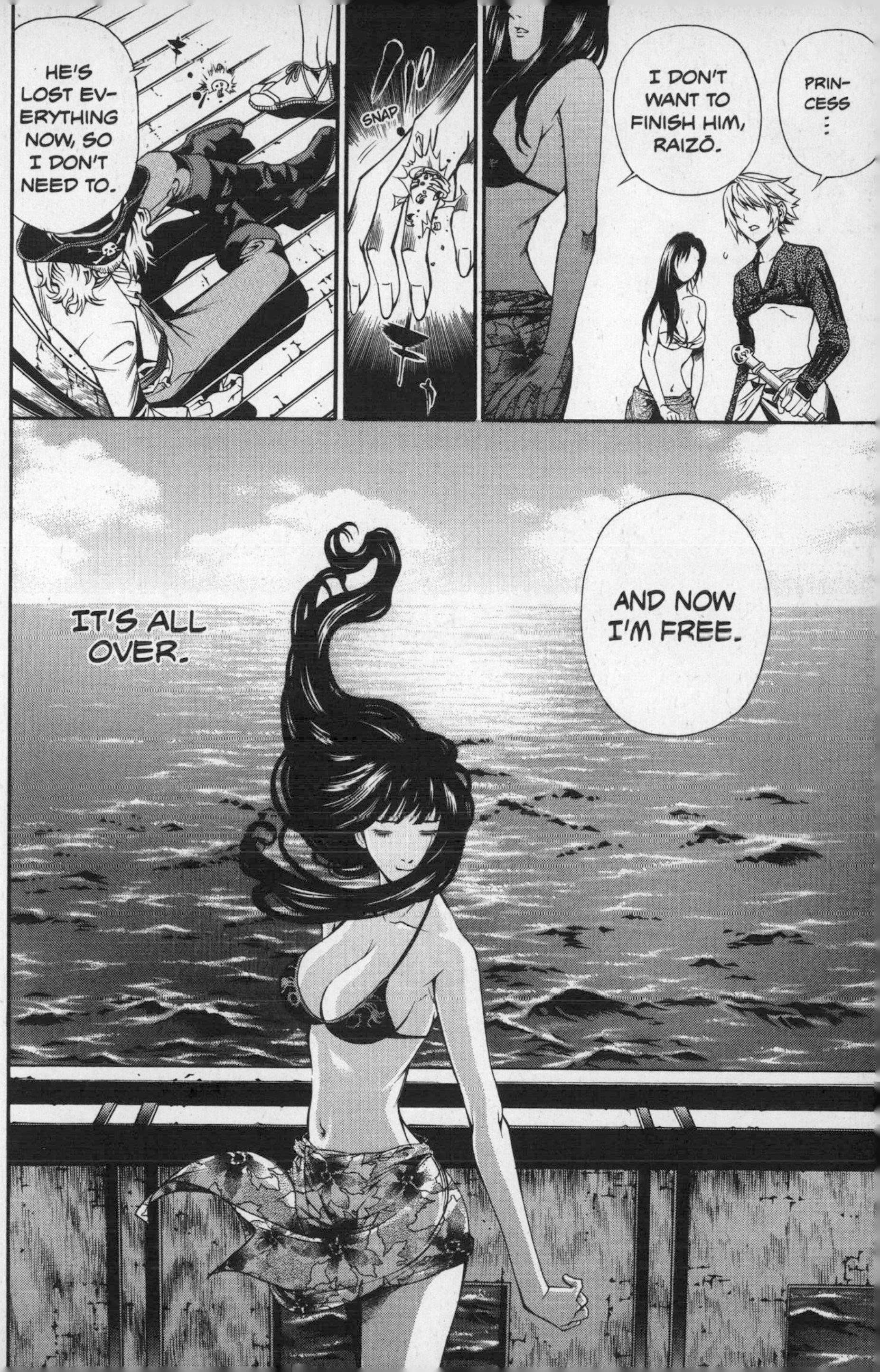
PRIN-CESS...
I DON'T WANT TO FINISH HIM, RAIZŌ.
SNAP
HE'S LOST EV-ERYTHING NOW, SO I DON'T NEED TO.
AND NOW I'M FREE.
IT'S ALL OVER.

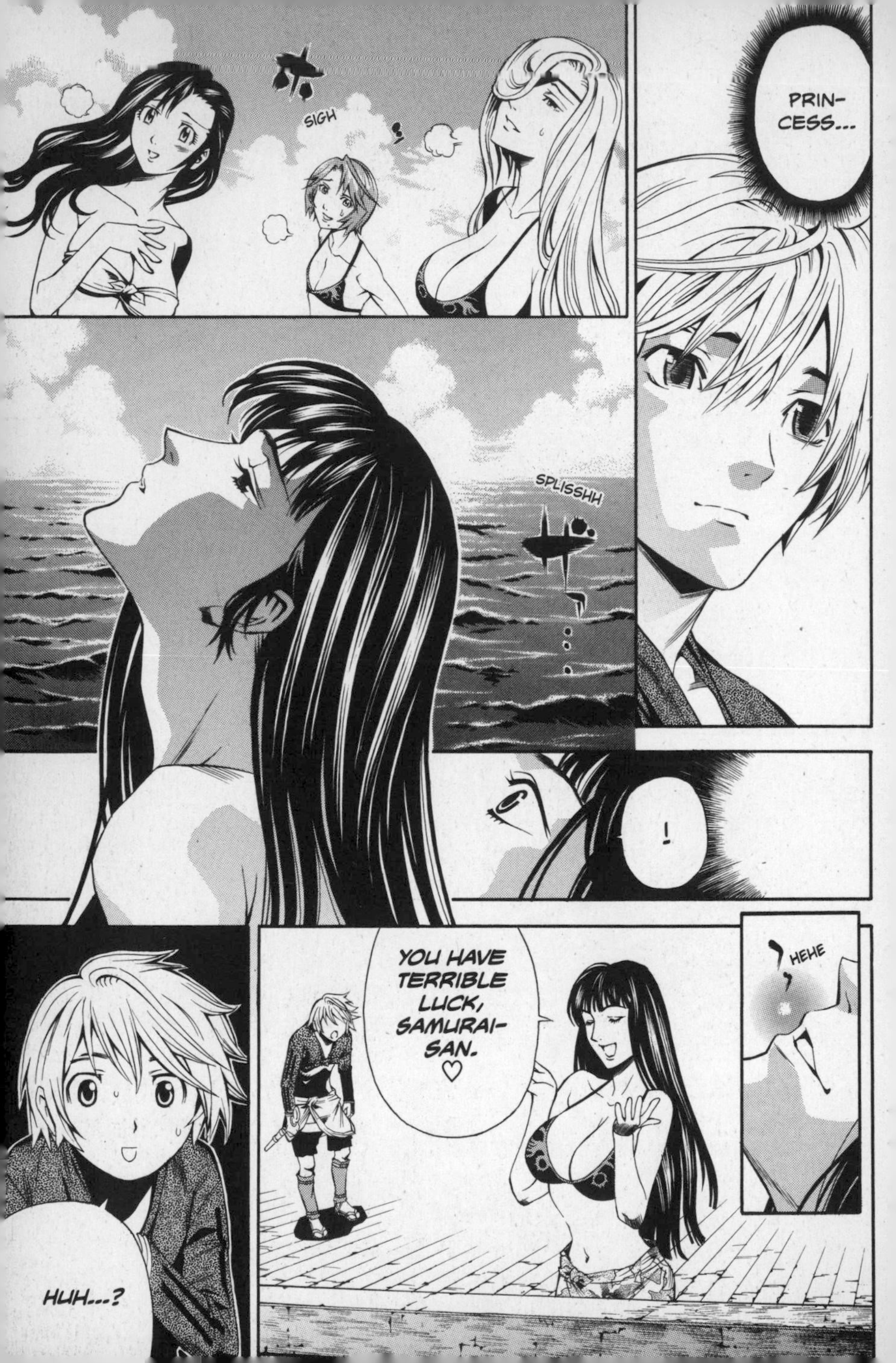
PRIN-
CESS...
SIGH
SPLISSHH
!
HEHE
YOU HAVE TERRIBLE LUCK, SAMURAI-SAN. ♡
HUH...?

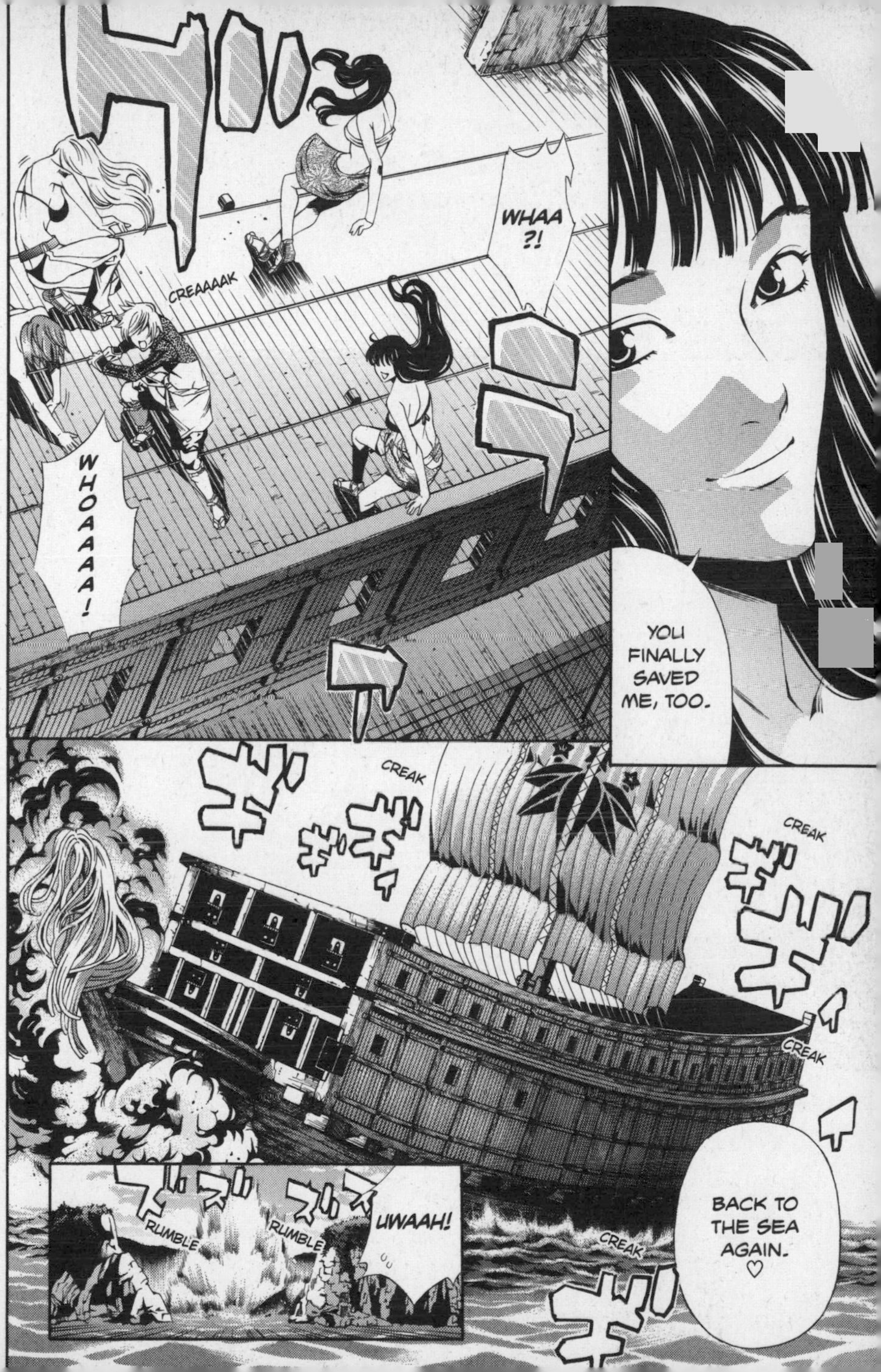
YOU FINALLY SAVED ME, TOO.
WHAA ?!
CREAAAAK
WHOAAAAA!
CREAK
CREAK
CREAK
BACK TO THE SEA AGAIN. ♡
CREAK
UWAAH!
RUMBLE
RUMBLE

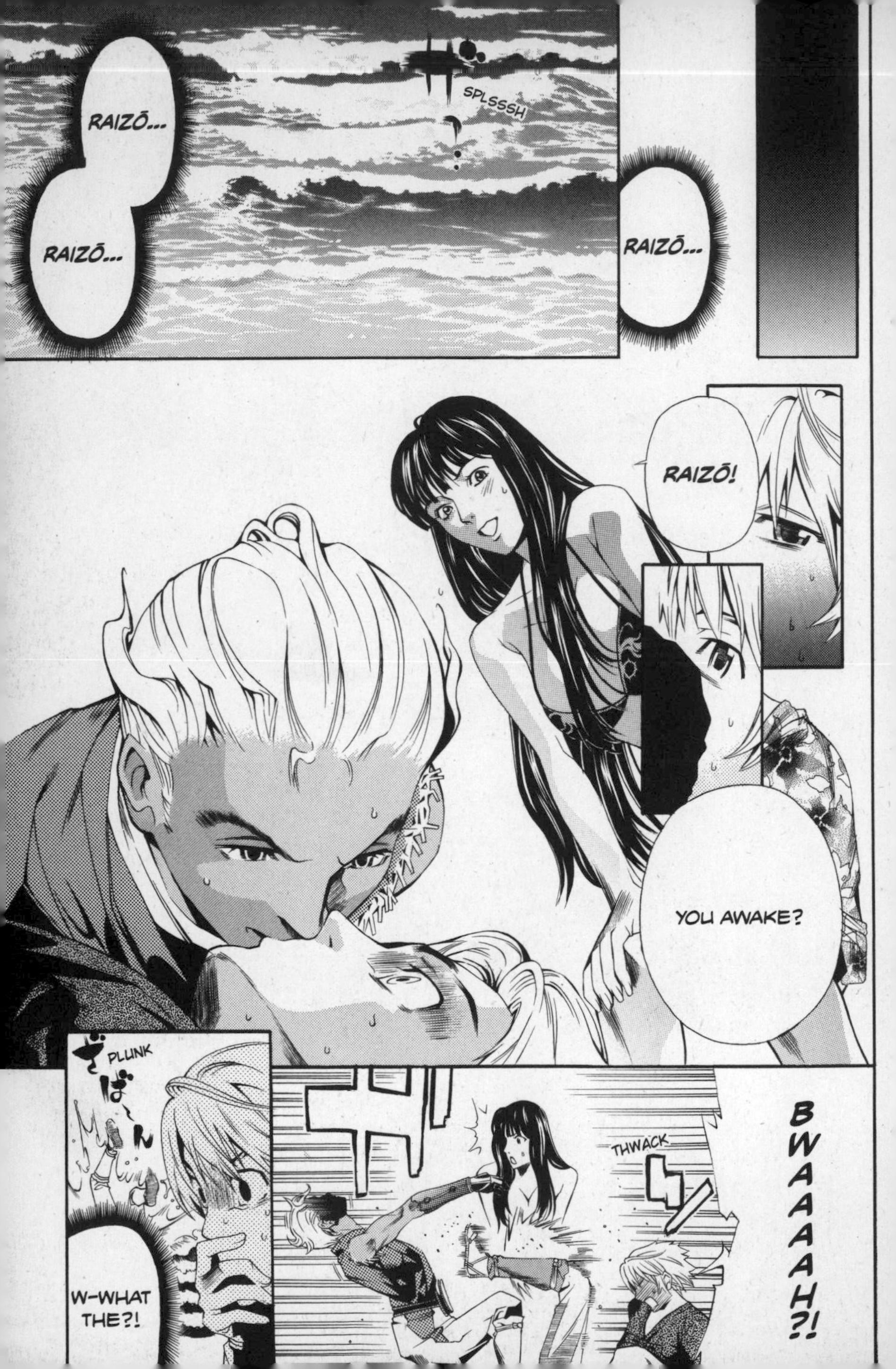
SPLSSSH
RAIZŌ...
RAIZŌ...
RAIZŌ...
RAIZŌ!
YOU AWAKE?
BWAAAAAH?!
THWACK
PLUNK
W-WHAT THE?!

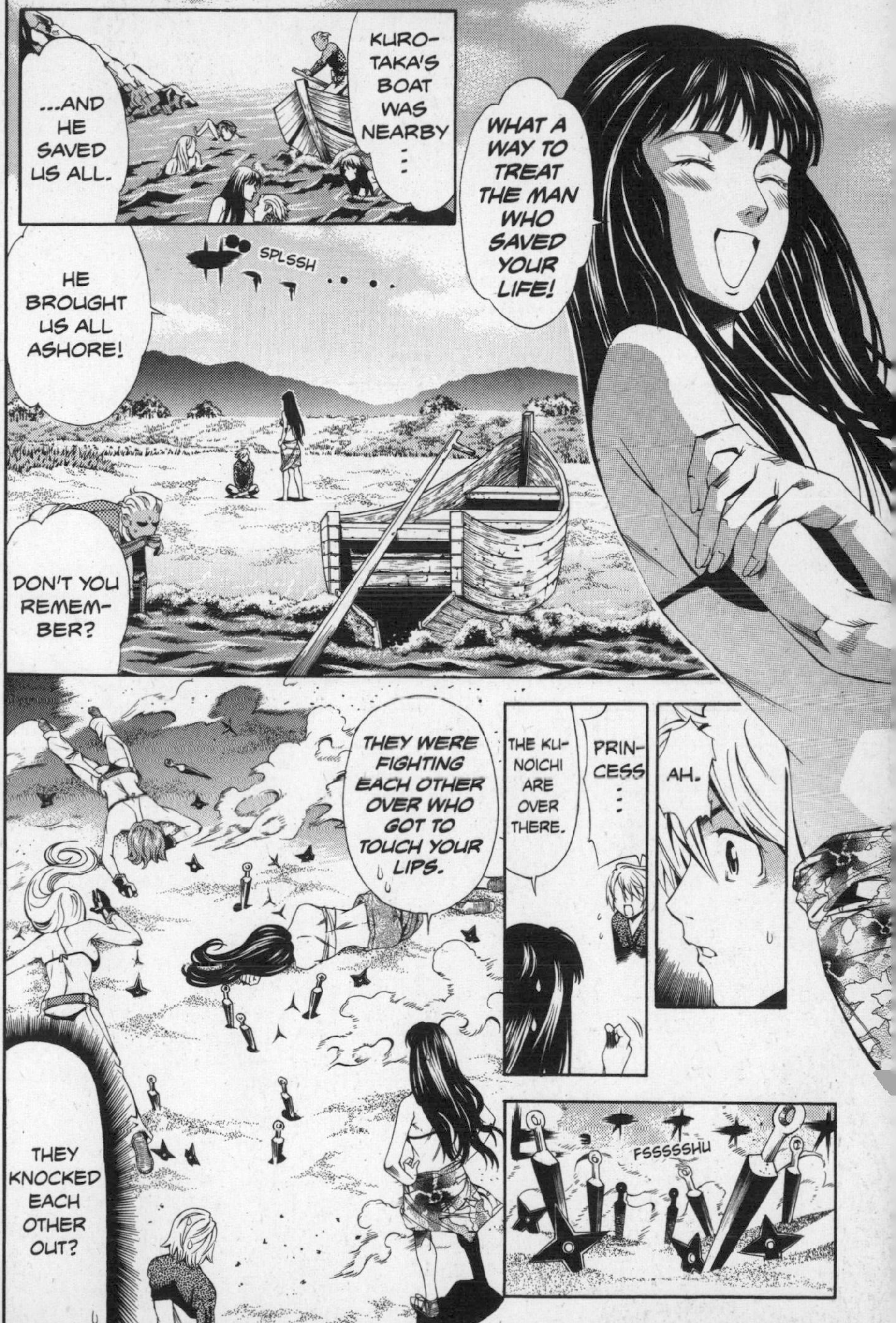
WHAT A WAY TO TREAT THE MAN WHO SAVED YOUR LIFE!
KURO-TAKA'S BOAT WAS NEARBY...
...AND HE SAVED US ALL.
SPLSSH
HE BROUGHT US ALL ASHORE!
DON'T YOU REMEM-BER?
AH.
PRIN-CESS...
THE KU-NOICHI ARE OVER THERE.
FSSSSSHU
THEY WERE FIGHTING EACH OTHER OVER WHO GOT TO TOUCH YOUR LIPS.
THEY KNOCKED EACH OTHER OUT?

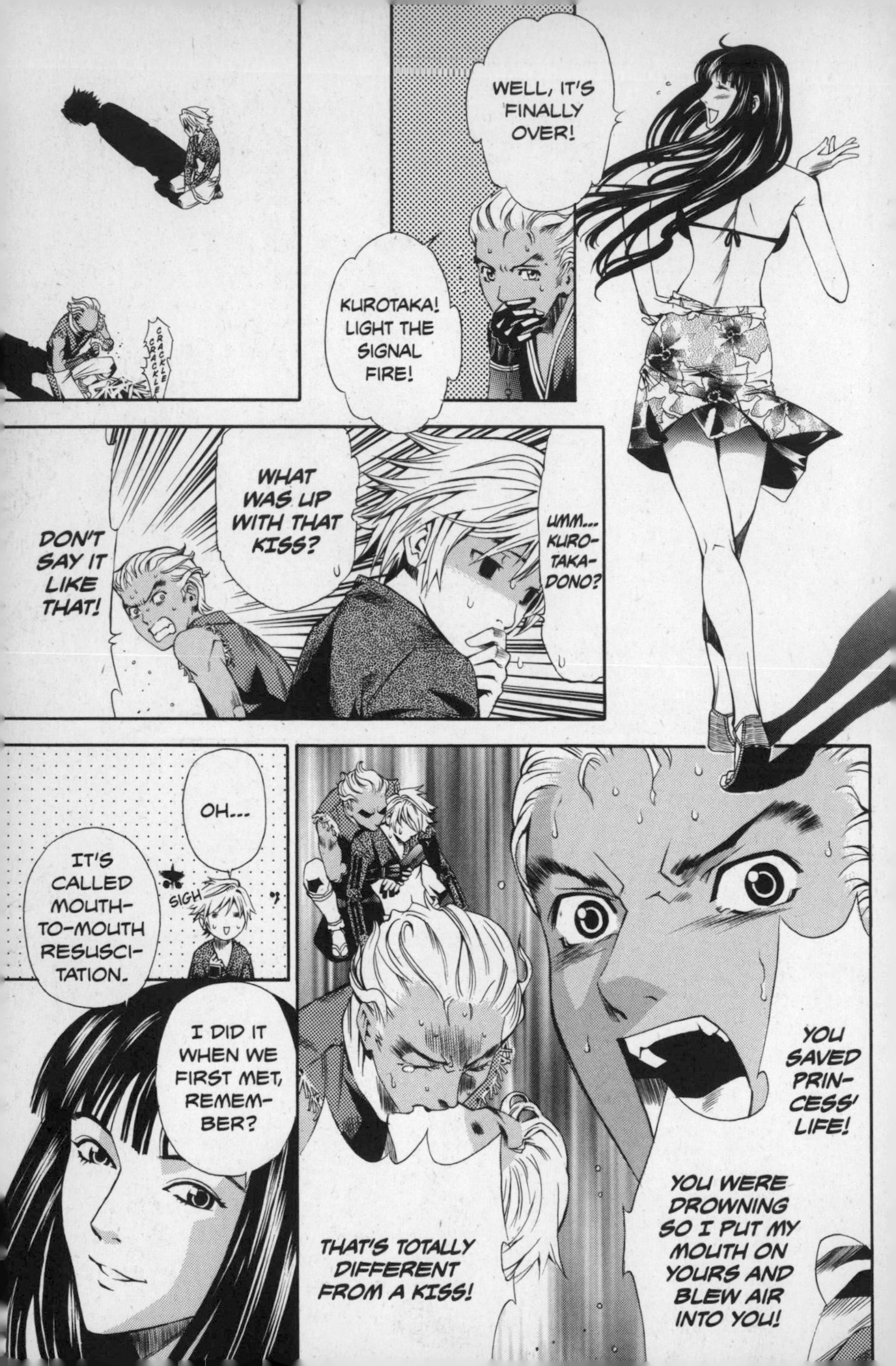
WELL, IT'S FINALLY OVER!
KUROTAKA! LIGHT THE SIGNAL FIRE!
CRACKLE CRACKLE
UMM... KURO-TAKA-DONO?
WHAT WAS UP WITH THAT KISS?
DON'T SAY IT LIKE THAT!
YOU SAVED PRIN-CESS' LIFE!
YOU WERE DROWNING SO I PUT MY MOUTH ON YOURS AND BLEW AIR INTO YOU!
THAT'S TOTALLY DIFFERENT FROM A KISS!
OH...
SIGH
IT'S CALLED MOUTH-TO-MOUTH RESUSCI-TATION.
I DID IT WHEN WE FIRST MET, REMEM-BER?

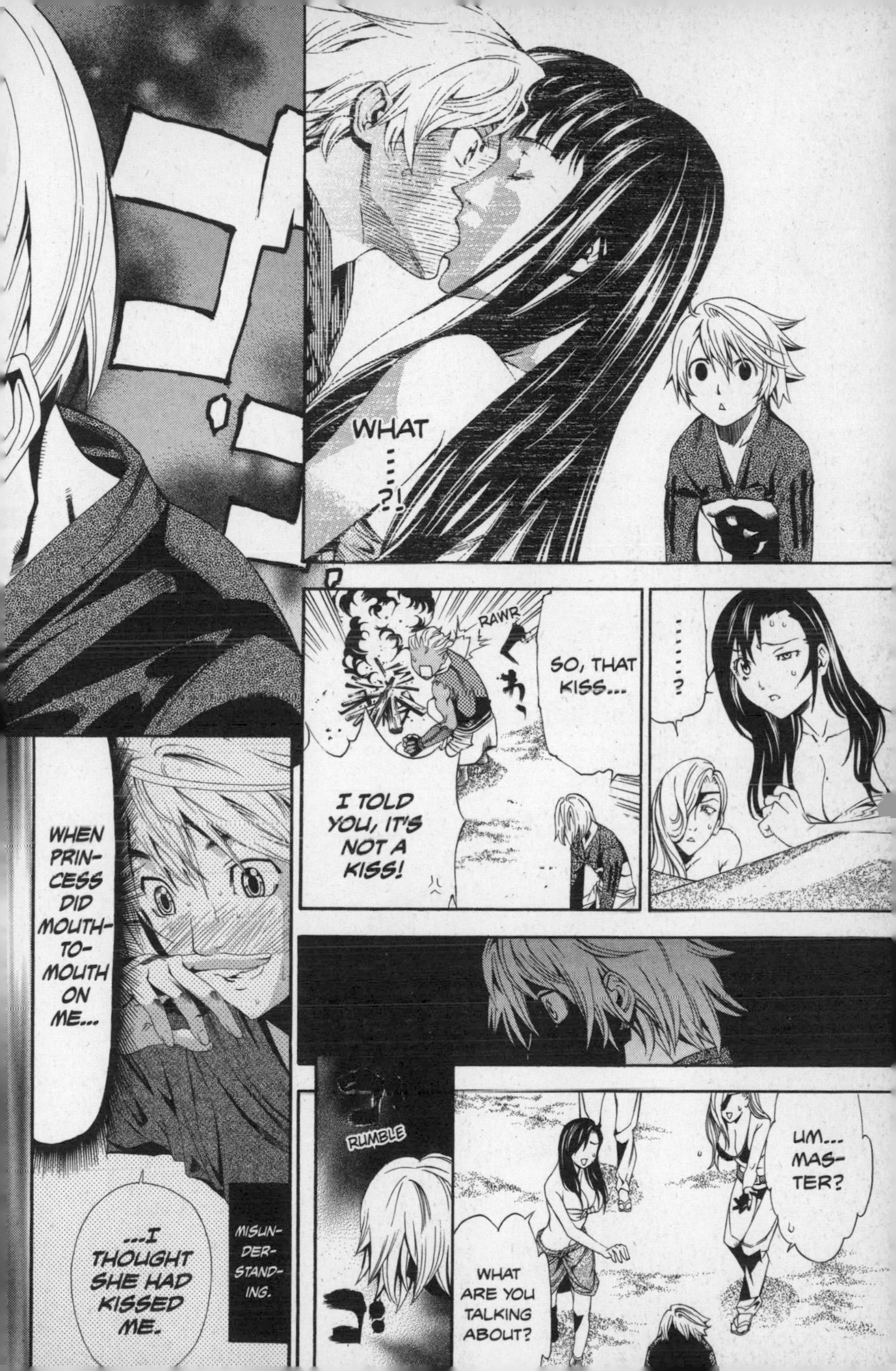
WHAT ...?!
......?
SO, THAT KISS...
RAWR
I TOLD YOU, IT'S NOT A KISS!
UM... MASTER?
RUMBLE
WHAT ARE YOU TALKING ABOUT?
WHEN PRINCESS DID MOUTH-TO-MOUTH ON ME...
...I THOUGHT SHE HAD KISSED ME.
MISUNDERSTANDING.

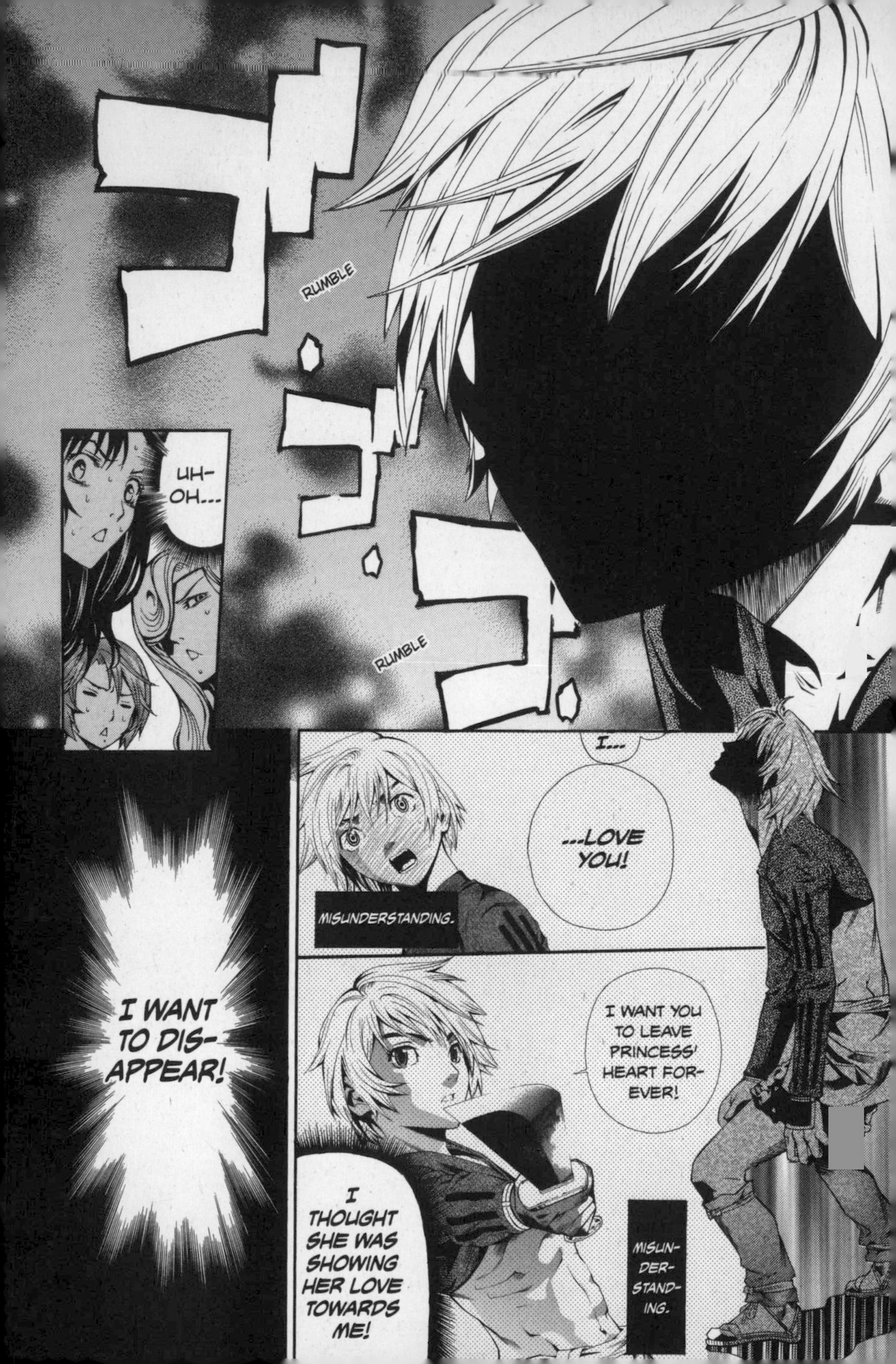
RUMBLE
RUMBLE
UH-OH...
I...
...LOVE YOU!
MISUNDERSTANDING.
I WANT YOU TO LEAVE PRINCESS' HEART FOREVER!
MISUNDERSTANDING.
I THOUGHT SHE WAS SHOWING HER LOVE TOWARDS ME!
I WANT TO DISAPPEAR!

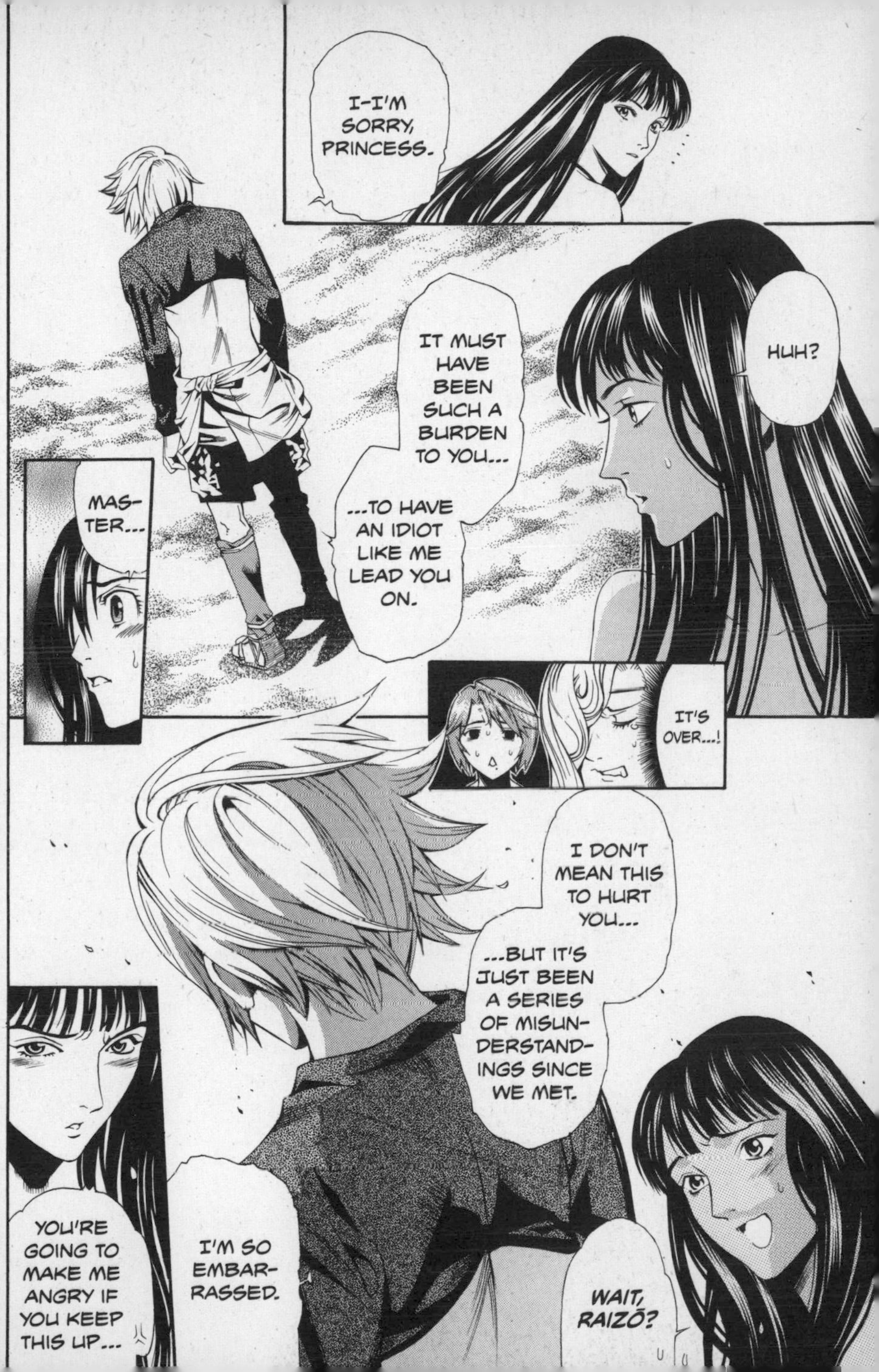
I-I'M SORRY, PRINCESS.
HUH?
IT MUST HAVE BEEN SUCH A BURDEN TO YOU...
...TO HAVE AN IDIOT LIKE ME LEAD YOU ON.
MAS-TER...
IT'S OVER...!
I DON'T MEAN THIS TO HURT YOU...
...BUT IT'S JUST BEEN A SERIES OF MISUN-DERSTAND-INGS SINCE WE MET.
WAIT, RAIZŌ?
I'M SO EMBAR-RASSED.
YOU'RE GOING TO MAKE ME ANGRY IF YOU KEEP THIS UP...

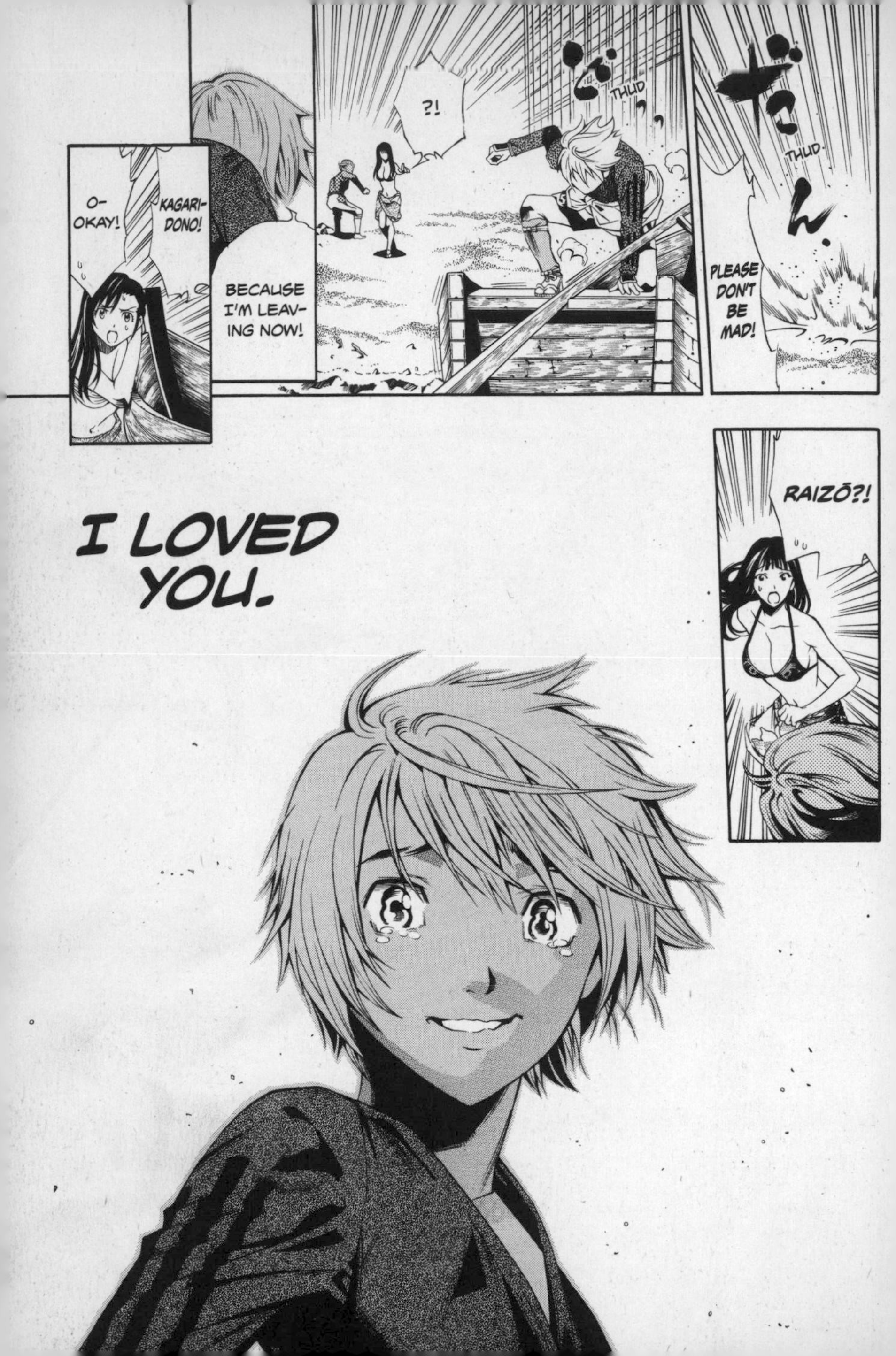
THUD
PLEASE DON'T BE MAD!
THUD
?!
KAGARI-DONO!
BECAUSE I'M LEAVING NOW!
O-OKAY!
RAIZŌ?!
I LOVED YOU.
...

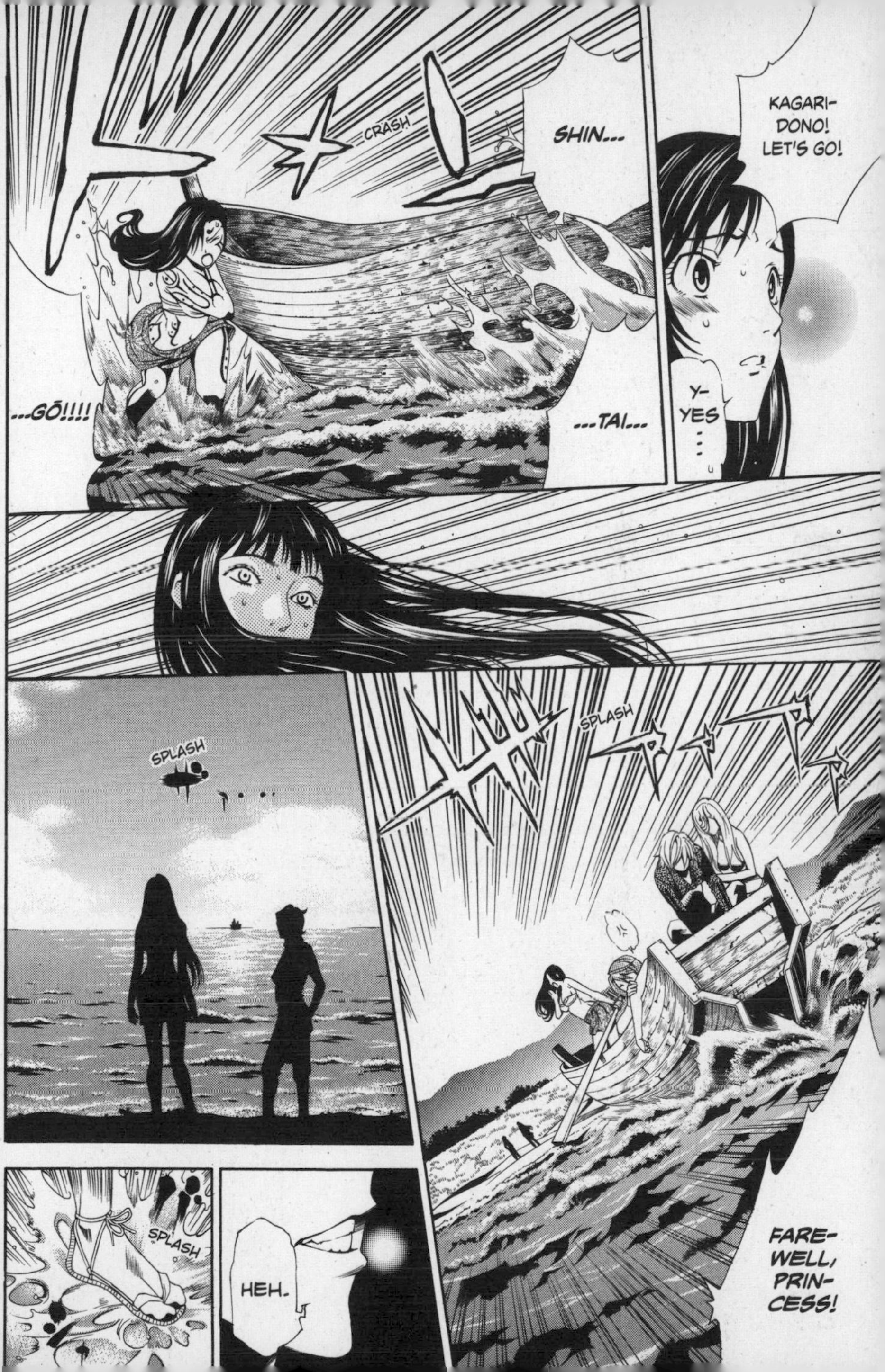
KAGARI-DONO! LET'S GO!
Y-YES ...
SHIN...
CRASH
...TAI...
...GŌ!!!!
SPLASH
FARE-WELL, PRIN-CESS!
SPLASH
HEH.
SPLASH

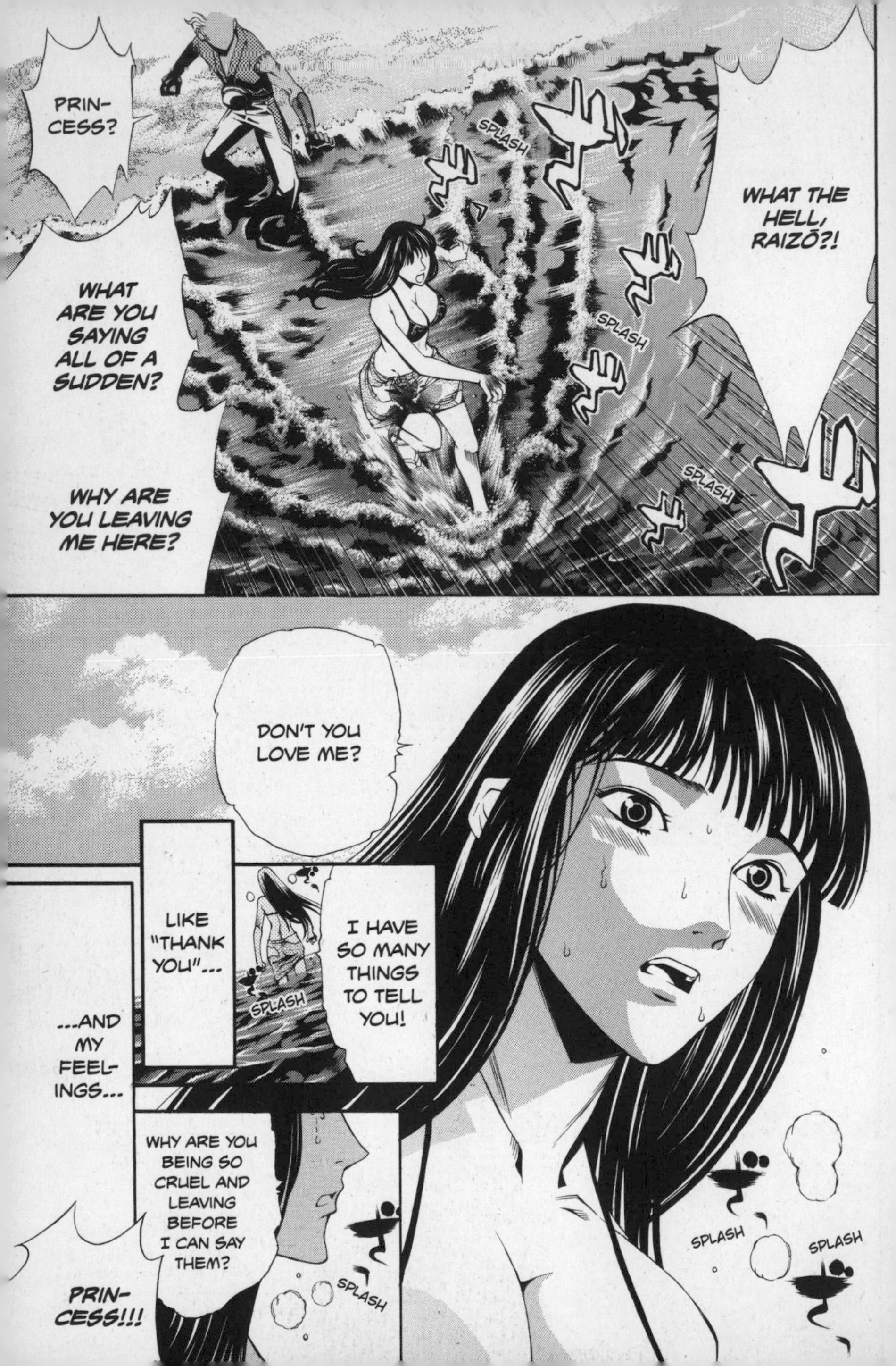
WHAT THE HELL, RAIZŌ?!
SPLASH
SPLASH
SPLASH
PRIN-CESS?
WHAT ARE YOU SAYING ALL OF A SUDDEN?
WHY ARE YOU LEAVING ME HERE?
DON'T YOU LOVE ME?
SPLASH
SPLASH
I HAVE SO MANY THINGS TO TELL YOU!
LIKE "THANK YOU"...
SPLASH
...AND MY FEEL-INGS...
WHY ARE YOU BEING SO CRUEL AND LEAVING BEFORE I CAN SAY THEM?
SPLASH
PRIN-CESS!!!

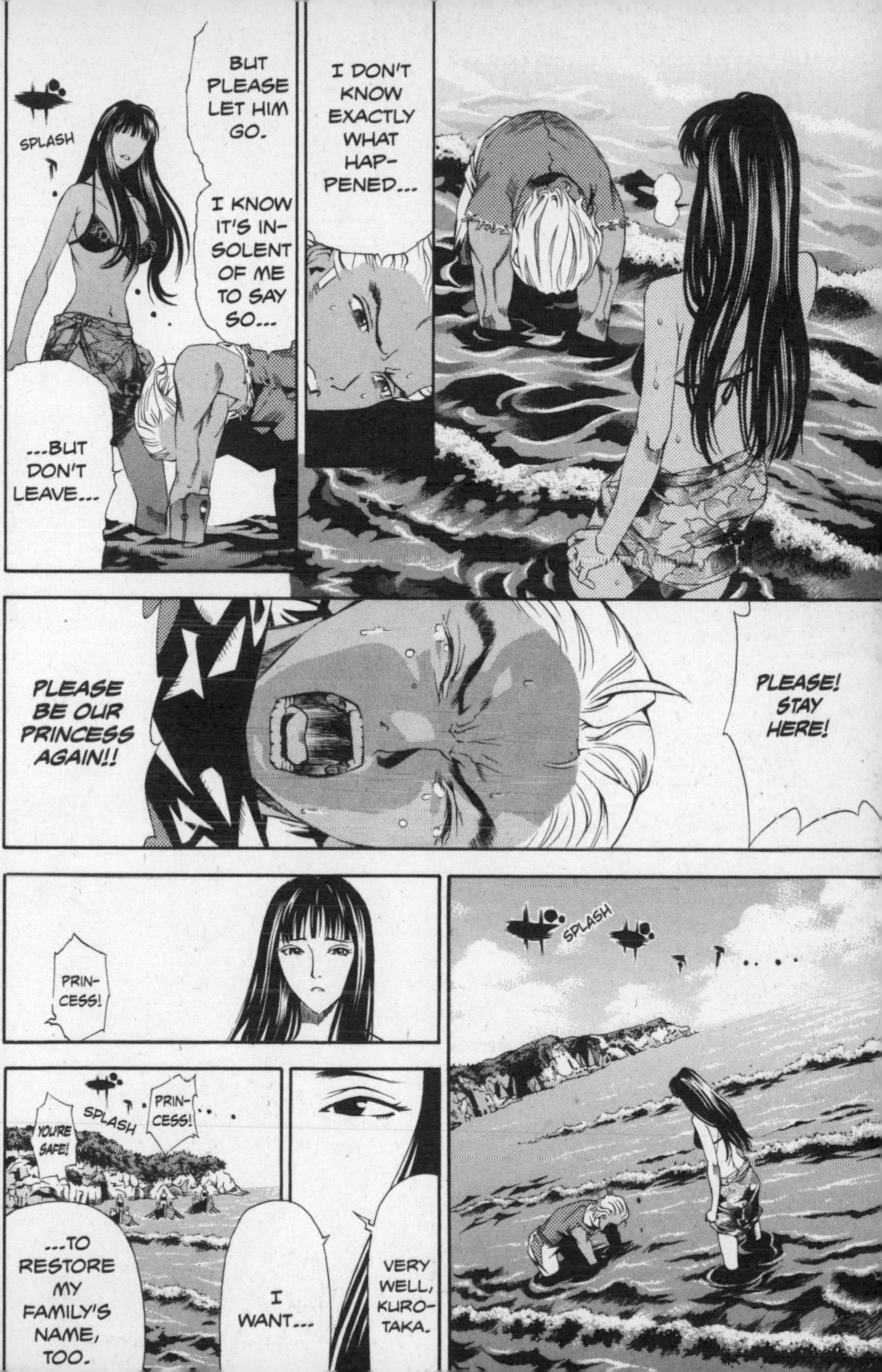
I DON'T KNOW EXACTLY WHAT HAP-PENED...
BUT PLEASE LET HIM GO.
I KNOW IT'S IN-SOLENT OF ME TO SAY SO...
SPLASH
...BUT DON'T LEAVE...
PLEASE! STAY HERE!
PLEASE BE OUR PRINCESS AGAIN!!
SPLASH
PRIN-CESS!
VERY WELL, KURO-TAKA.
I WANT...
PRIN-CESS!
YOU'RE SAFE!
SPLASH
...TO RESTORE MY FAMILY'S NAME, TOO.

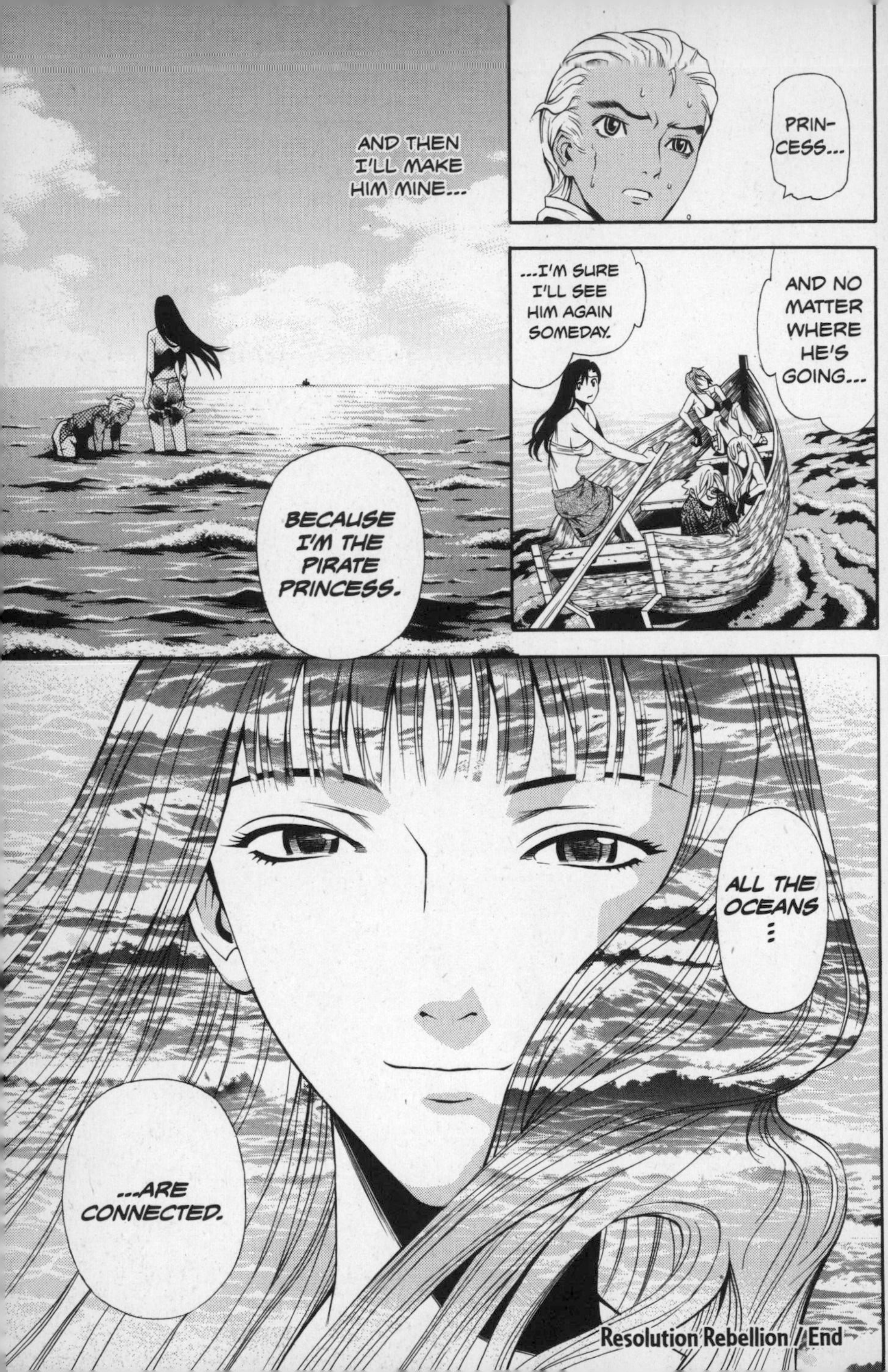
PRIN-CESS...
AND NO MATTER WHERE HE'S GOING...
...I'M SURE I'LL SEE HIM AGAIN SOMEDAY.
AND THEN I'LL MAKE HIM MINE...
BECAUSE I'M THE PIRATE PRINCESS.
ALL THE OCEANS ...
...ARE CONNECTED.
Resolution Rebellion / End

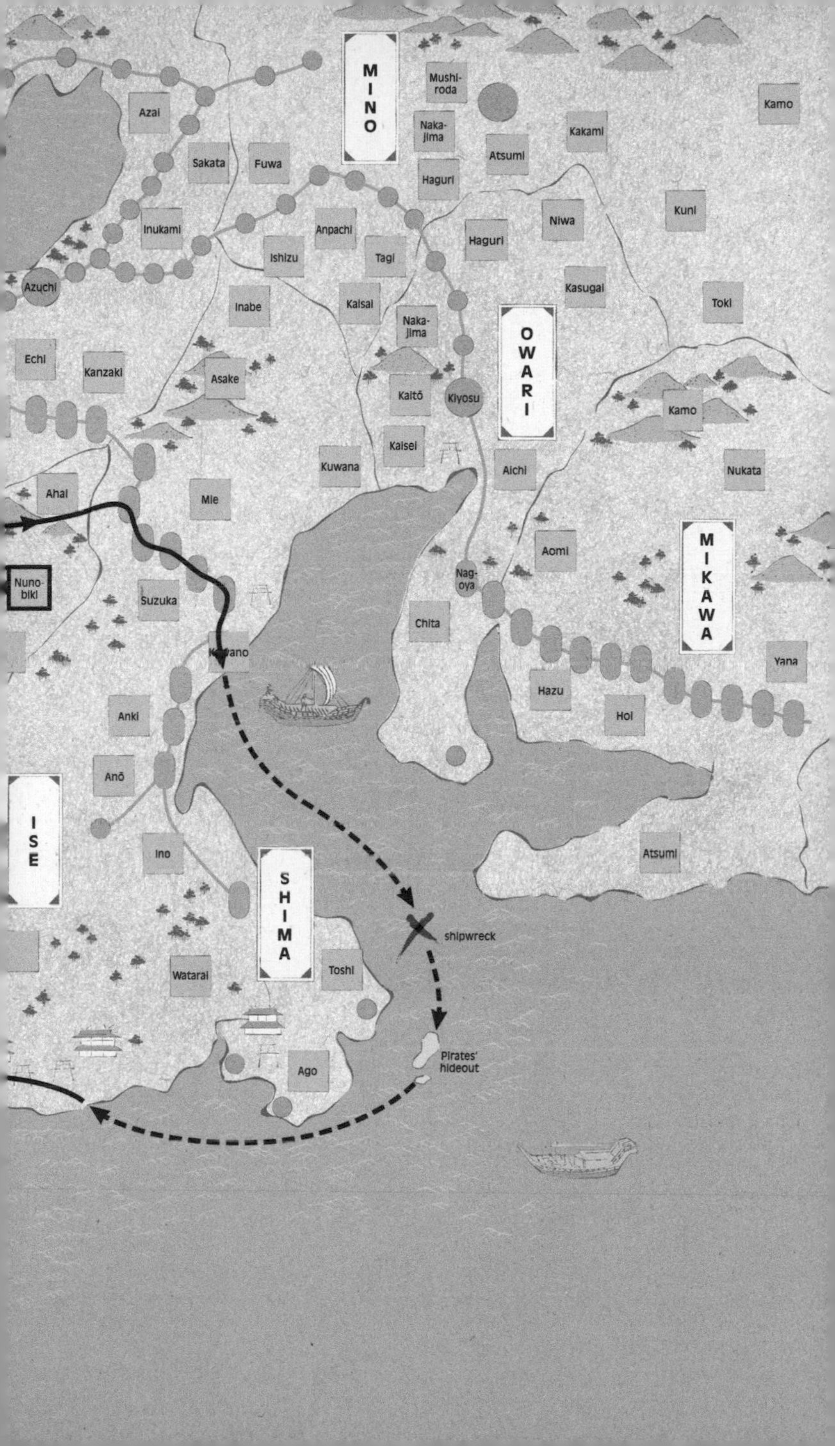
MINO
OWARI
MIKAWA
ISE
SHIMA
Mushi-roda
Naka-jima
Atsumi
Kakami
Kamo
Azai
Sakata
Fuwa
Haguri
Niwa
Kuni
Inukami
Anpachi
Ishizu
Tagi
Haguri
Azuchi
Inabe
Kaisai
Kasugai
Toki
Naka-jima
Echi
Kanzaki
Asake
Kaitō
Kiyosu
Kamo
Kaisei
Kuwana
Aichi
Nukata
Ahai
Mie
Aomi
Nunobiki
Suzuka
Nag-oya
Chita
Kuwano
Yana
Hazu
Hoi
Anki
Anō
Ino
Atsumi
shipwreck
Watarai
Toshi
Ago
Pirates' hideout

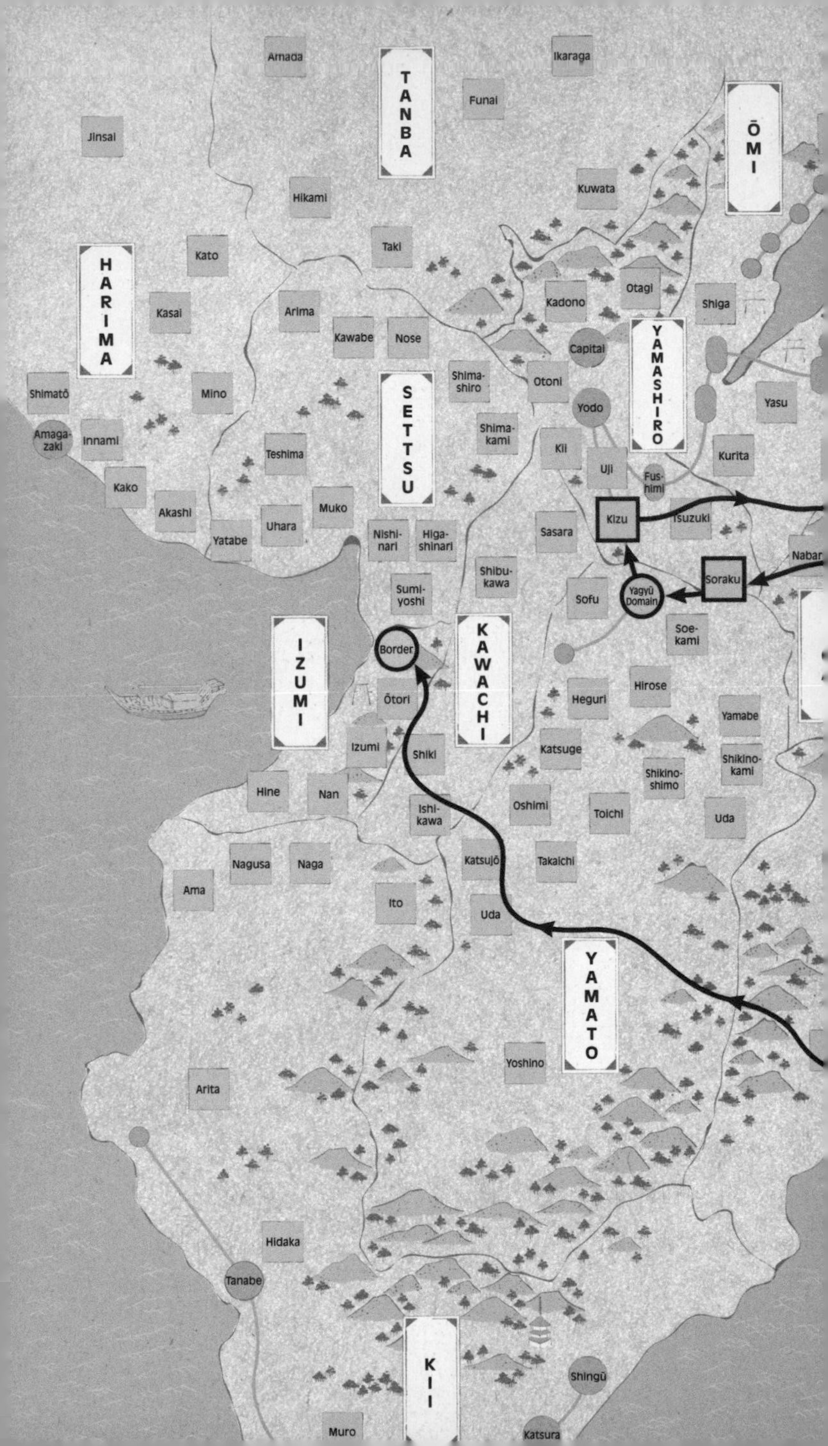

Amada
TANBA
Ikaraga
Funai
ŌMI
Jinsai
Hikami
Kuwata
HARIMA
Kato
Taki
Otagi
Kasai
Arima
Kadono
Shiga
Kawabe
Nose
Capital
YAMASHIRO
Shimatō
Mino
Shima-shiro
Otoni
Yodo
Yasu
SETTSU
Amaga-zaki
Innami
Shima-kami
Teshima
Kii
Uji
Kurita
Fus-himi
Kako
Muko
Akashi
Kizu
Isuzuki
Uhara
Yatabe
Nishi-nari
Higa-shinari
Sasara
Nabar
Shibu-kawa
Soraku
Sumi-yoshi
Sofu
Yagyū Domain
IZUMI
KAWACHI
Soe-kami
Border
Hirose
Ōtori
Heguri
Yamabe
Izumi
Shiki
Katsuge
Shikino-kami
Shikino-shimo
Hine
Nan
Oshimi
Toichi
Uda
Ishi-kawa
Nagusa
Naga
Katsujō
Takaichi
Ama
Ito
Uda
YAMATO
Yoshino
Arita
Hidaka
Tanabe
KII
Shingū
Muro
Katsura

Ninja Girls

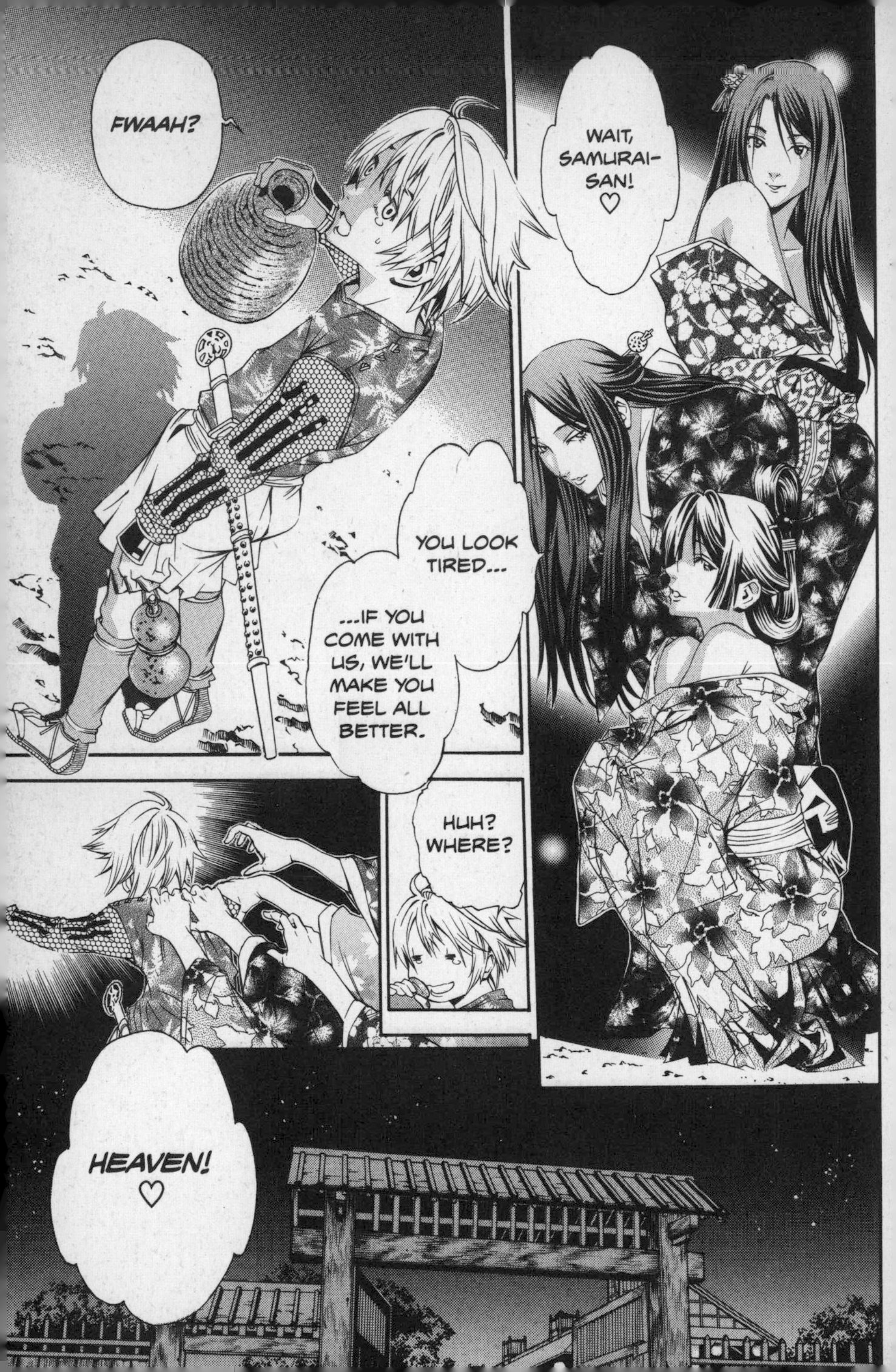
WAIT, SAMURAI-SAN! ♡
YOU LOOK TIRED...
...IF YOU COME WITH US, WE'LL MAKE YOU FEEL ALL BETTER.
FWAAH?
HUH? WHERE?
HEAVEN! ♡

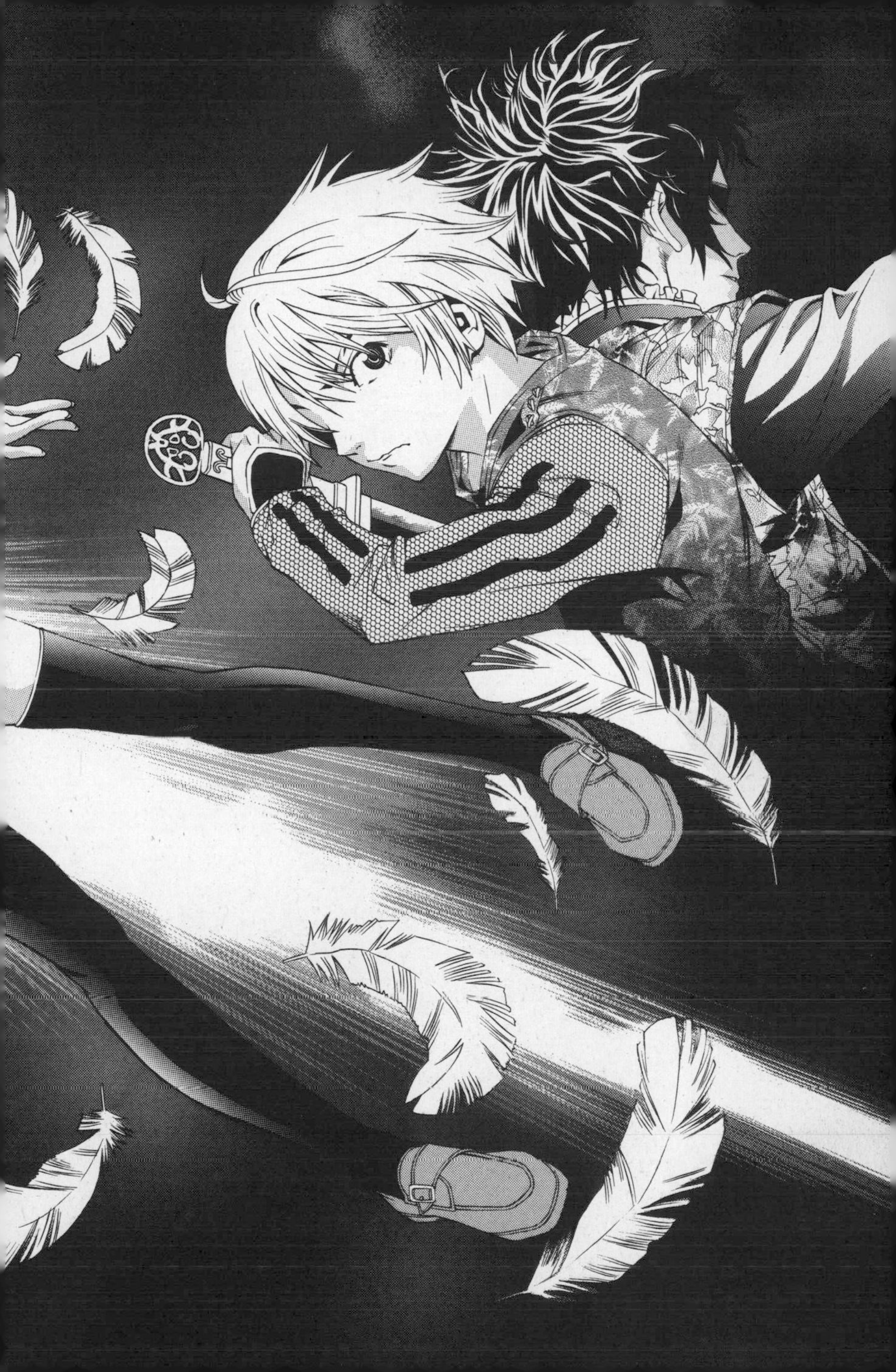

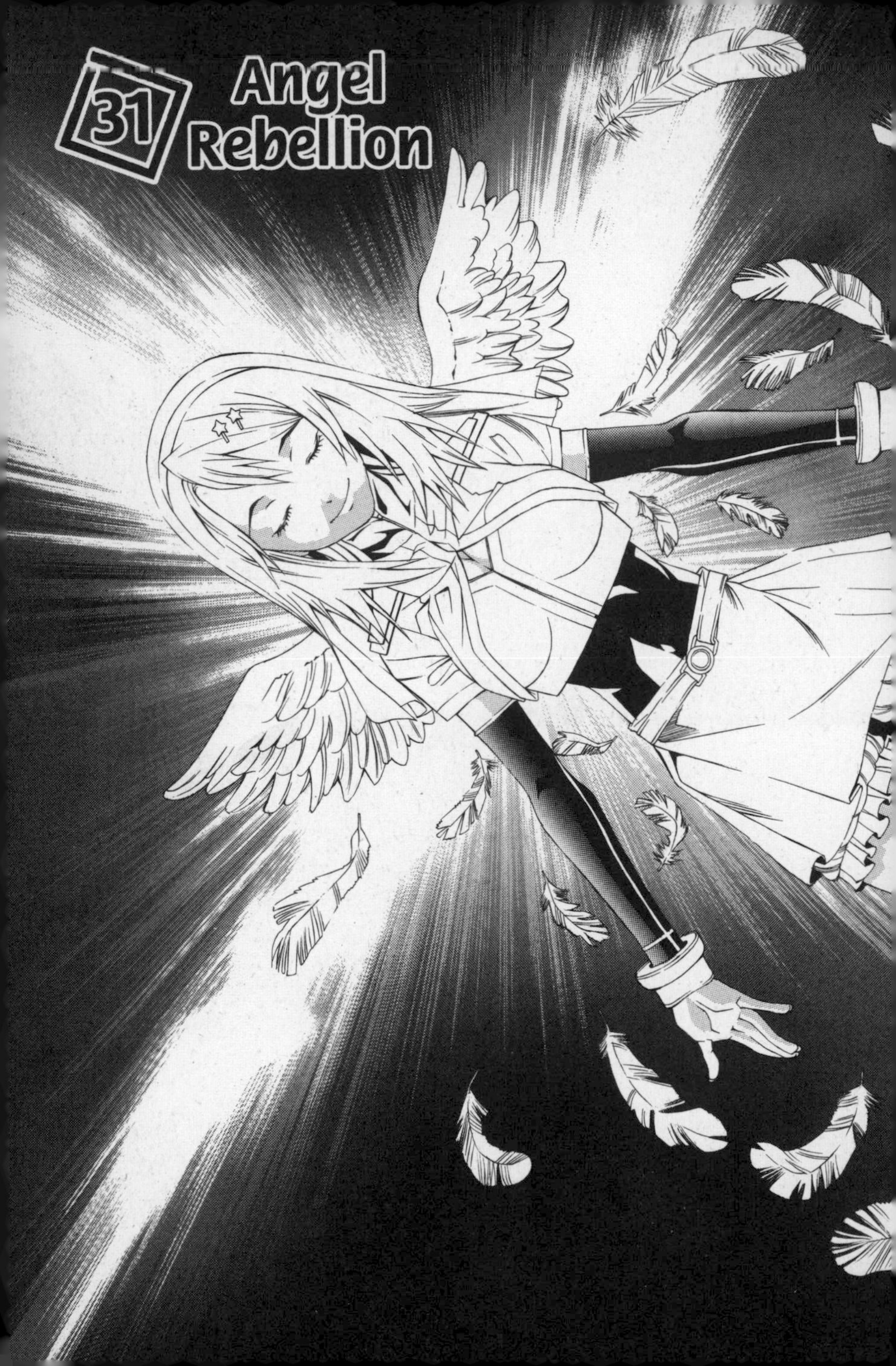
31
Angel
Rebellion

Ninja Girls

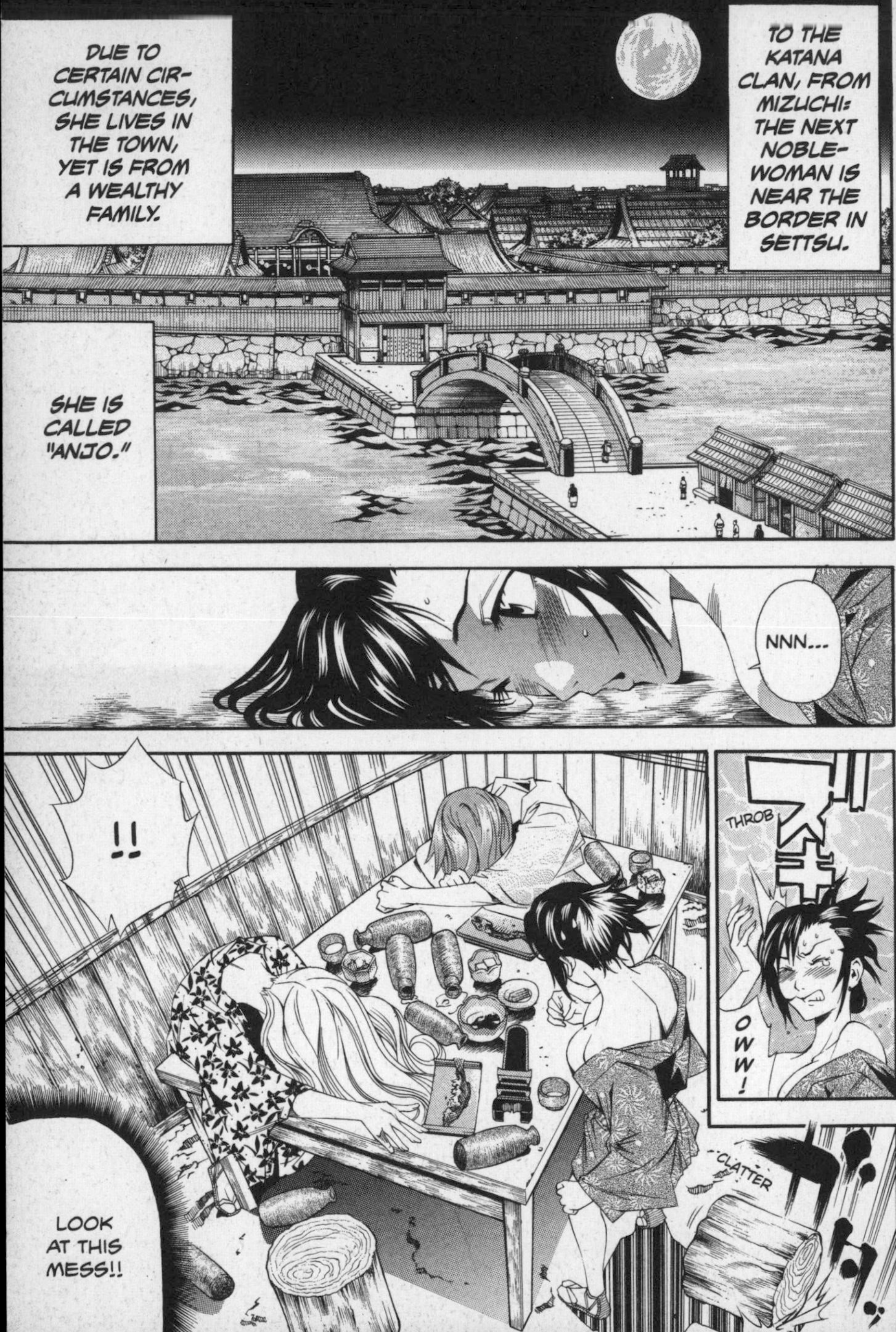
TO THE KATANA CLAN, FROM MIZUCHI: THE NEXT NOBLE-WOMAN IS NEAR THE BORDER IN SETTSU.
DUE TO CERTAIN CIR-CUMSTANCES, SHE LIVES IN THE TOWN, YET IS FROM A WEALTHY FAMILY.
SHE IS CALLED "ANJO."
NNN...
THROB
OWW!
CLATTER
!!
LOOK AT THIS MESS!!

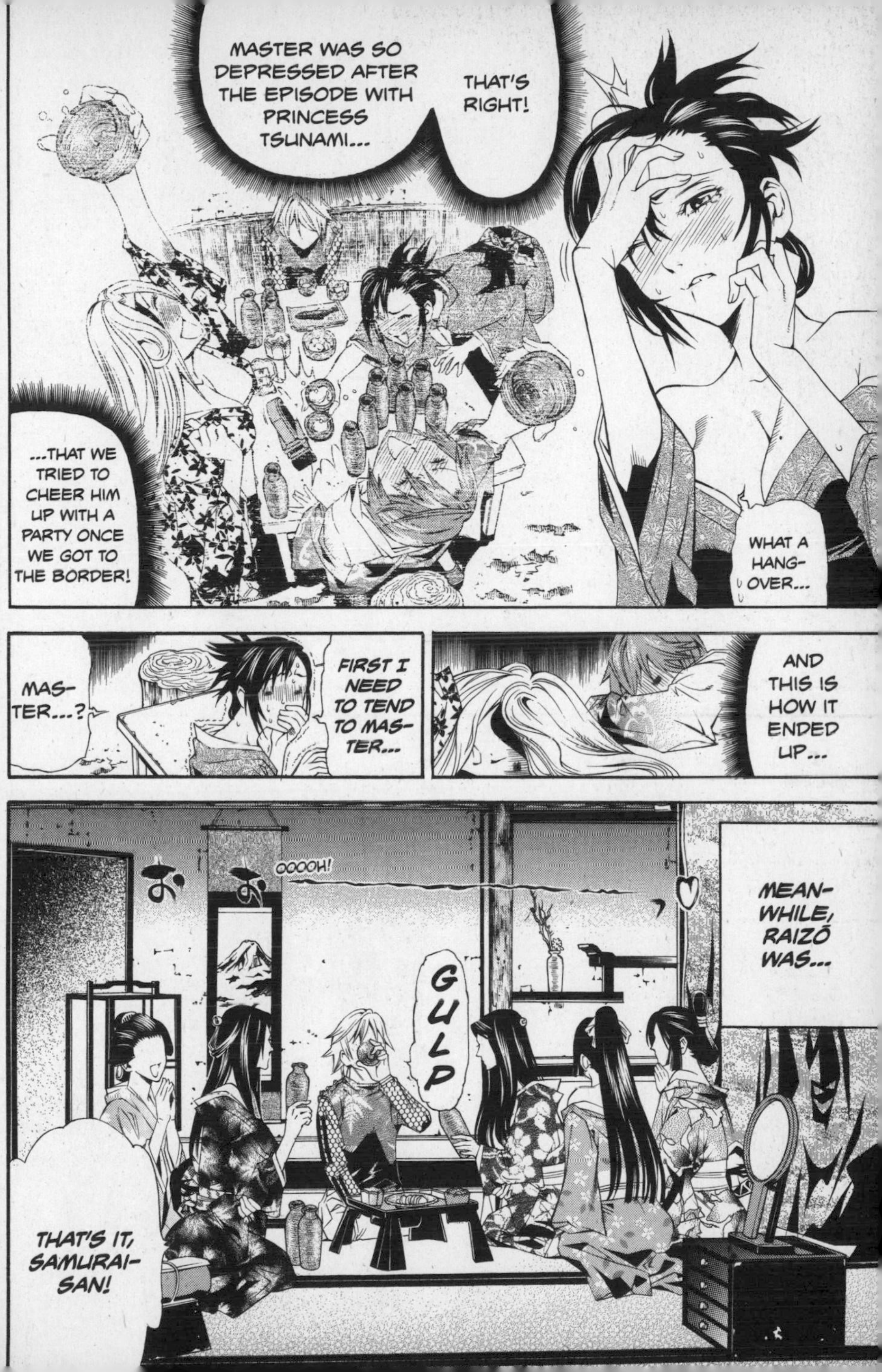
THAT'S RIGHT!
MASTER WAS SO DEPRESSED AFTER THE EPISODE WITH PRINCESS TSUNAMI...
...THAT WE TRIED TO CHEER HIM UP WITH A PARTY ONCE WE GOT TO THE BORDER!
WHAT A HANG-OVER...
AND THIS IS HOW IT ENDED UP...
FIRST I NEED TO TEND TO MAS-TER...
MAS-TER...?
MEAN-WHILE, RAIZŌ WAS...
GULP
OOOOH!
THAT'S IT, SAMURAI-SAN!

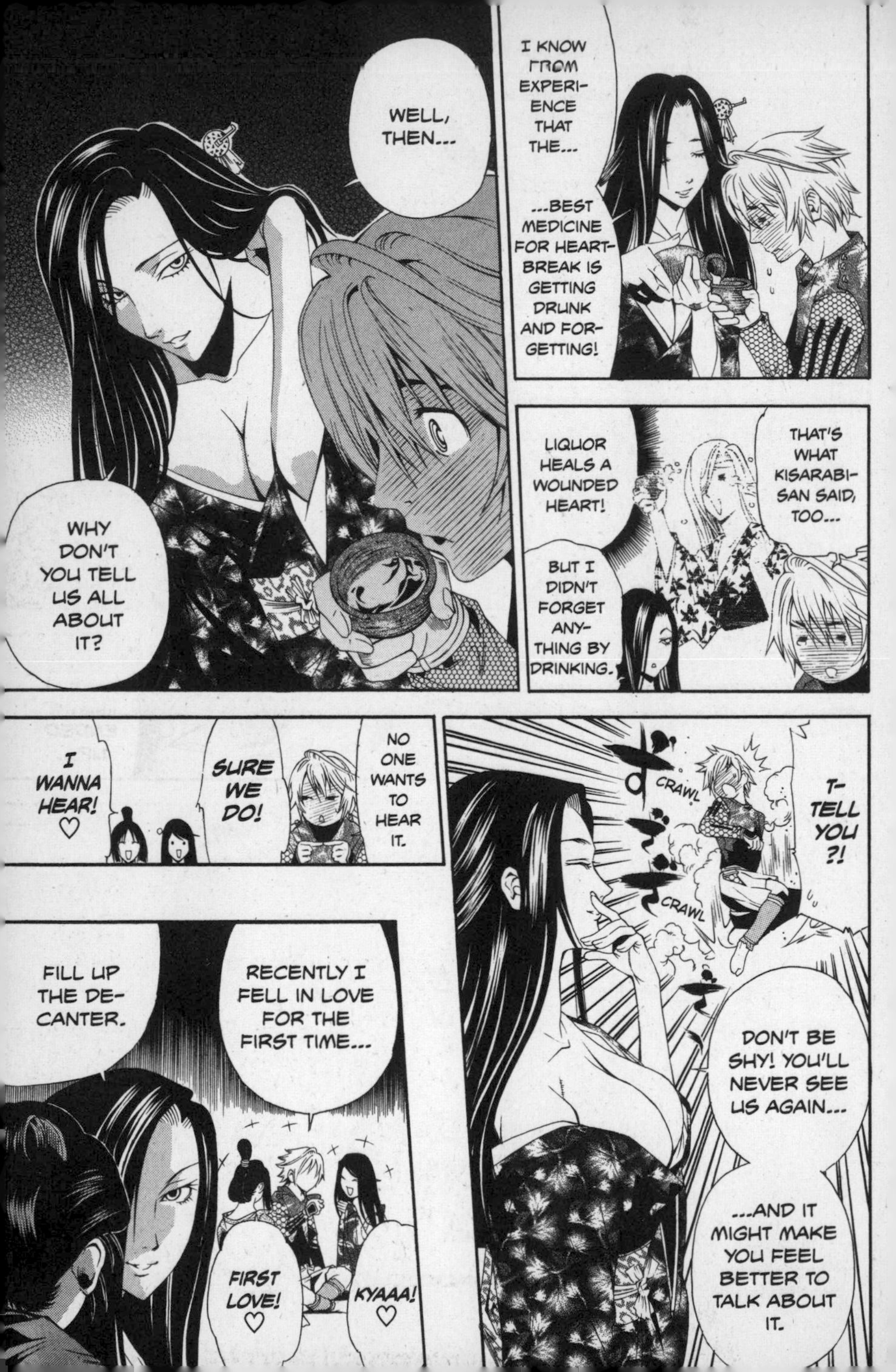
I KNOW FROM EXPERIENCE THAT THE...
...BEST MEDICINE FOR HEARTBREAK IS GETTING DRUNK AND FORGETTING!
THAT'S WHAT KISARABI-SAN SAID, TOO...
LIQUOR HEALS A WOUNDED HEART!
BUT I DIDN'T FORGET ANYTHING BY DRINKING.
WELL, THEN...
WHY DON'T YOU TELL US ALL ABOUT IT?
T-TELL YOU?!
CRAWL
CRAWL
DON'T BE SHY! YOU'LL NEVER SEE US AGAIN...
...AND IT MIGHT MAKE YOU FEEL BETTER TO TALK ABOUT IT.
NO ONE WANTS TO HEAR IT.
SURE WE DO!
I WANNA HEAR! ♡
RECENTLY I FELL IN LOVE FOR THE FIRST TIME...
FILL UP THE DECANTER.
KYAAA! ♡
FIRST LOVE! ♡

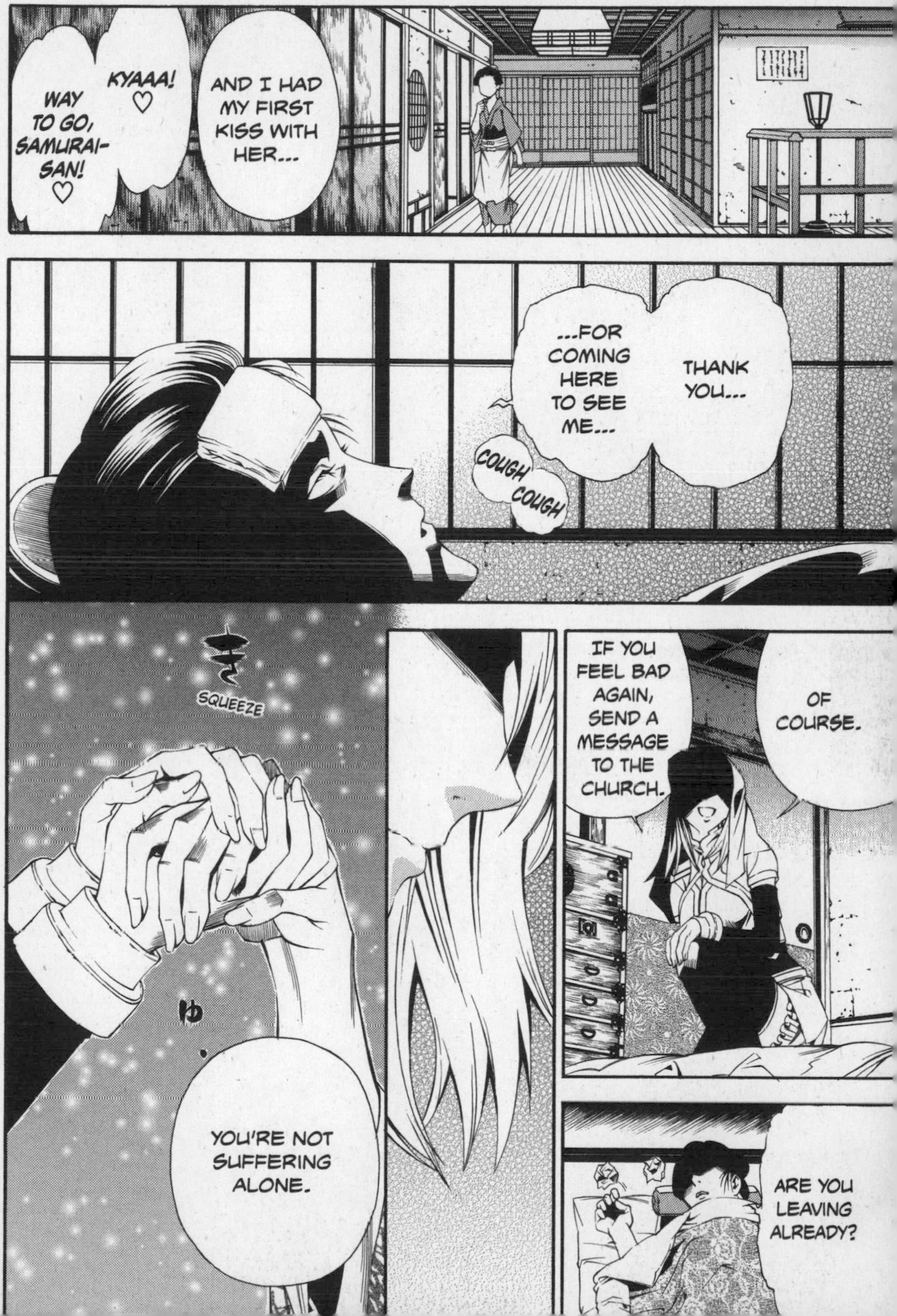
AND I HAD MY FIRST KISS WITH HER...
KYAAA! ♡
WAY TO GO, SAMURAI-SAN! ♡
THANK YOU...
...FOR COMING HERE TO SEE ME...
COUGH COUGH
OF COURSE.
IF YOU FEEL BAD AGAIN, SEND A MESSAGE TO THE CHURCH.
ARE YOU LEAVING ALREADY?
SQUEEZE
YOU'RE NOT SUFFERING ALONE.

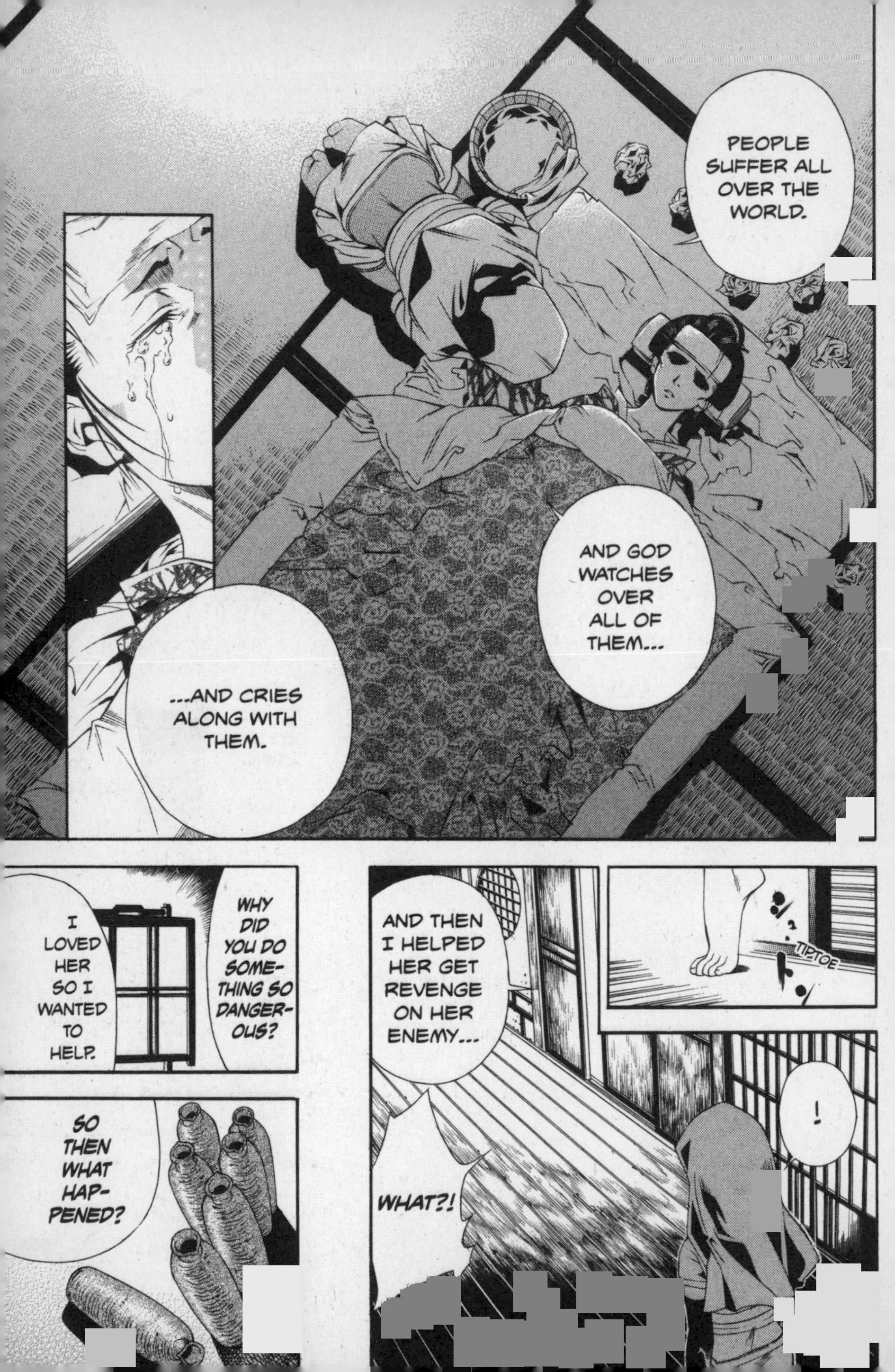
PEOPLE SUFFER ALL OVER THE WORLD.
AND GOD WATCHES OVER ALL OF THEM...
...AND CRIES ALONG WITH THEM.
TIPTOE
AND THEN I HELPED HER GET REVENGE ON HER ENEMY...
!
WHAT?!
WHY DID YOU DO SOME-THING SO DANGER-OUS?
I LOVED HER SO I WANTED TO HELP.
SO THEN WHAT HAP-PENED?

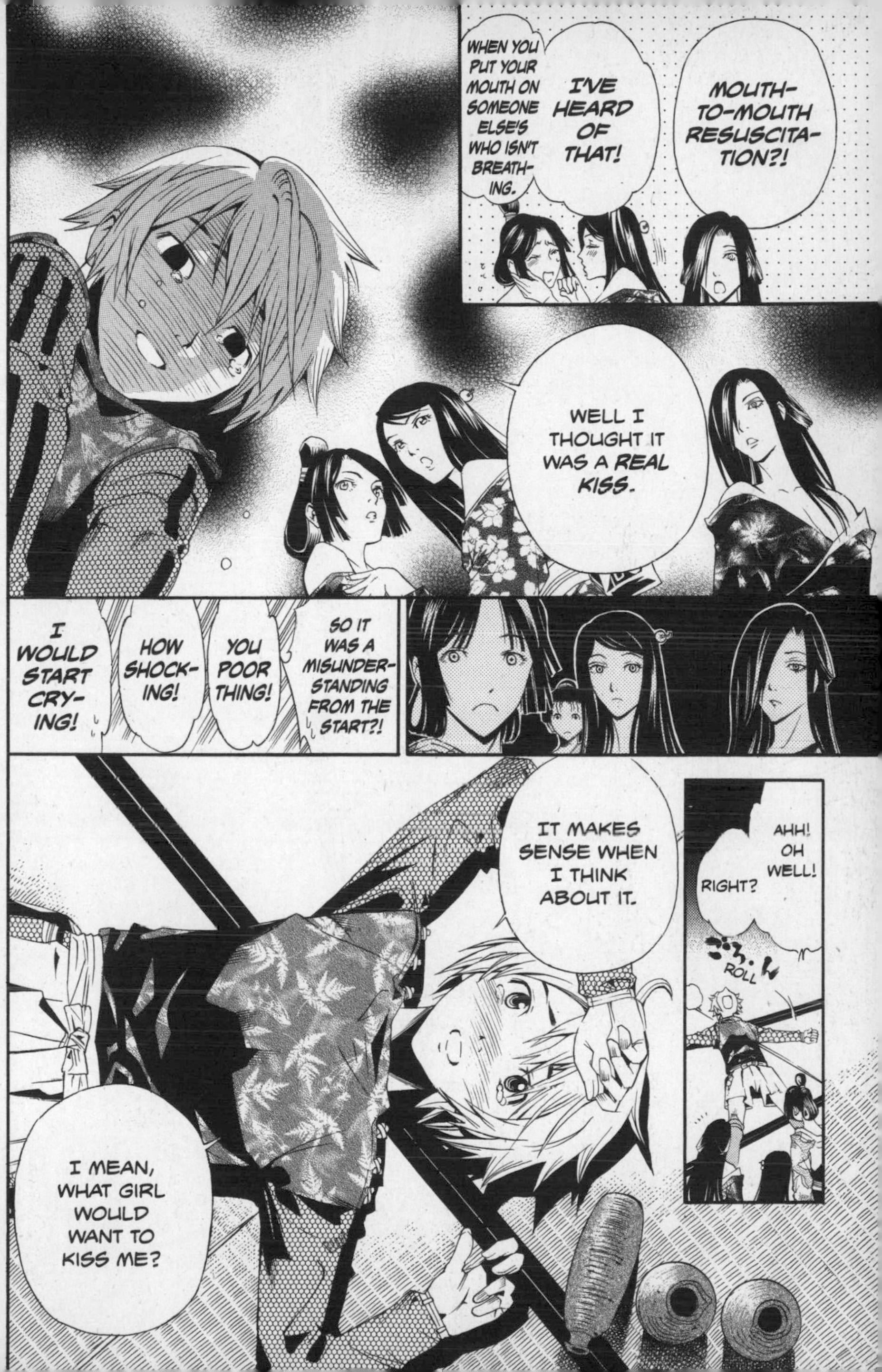
MOUTH-TO-MOUTH RESUSCITATION?!
I'VE HEARD OF THAT!
WHEN YOU PUT YOUR MOUTH ON SOMEONE ELSE'S WHO ISN'T BREATHING.
WELL I THOUGHT IT WAS A REAL KISS.
SO IT WAS A MISUNDERSTANDING FROM THE START?!
YOU POOR THING!
HOW SHOCKING!
I WOULD START CRYING!
AHH! OH WELL!
RIGHT?
ROLL
IT MAKES SENSE WHEN I THINK ABOUT IT.
I MEAN, WHAT GIRL WOULD WANT TO KISS ME?

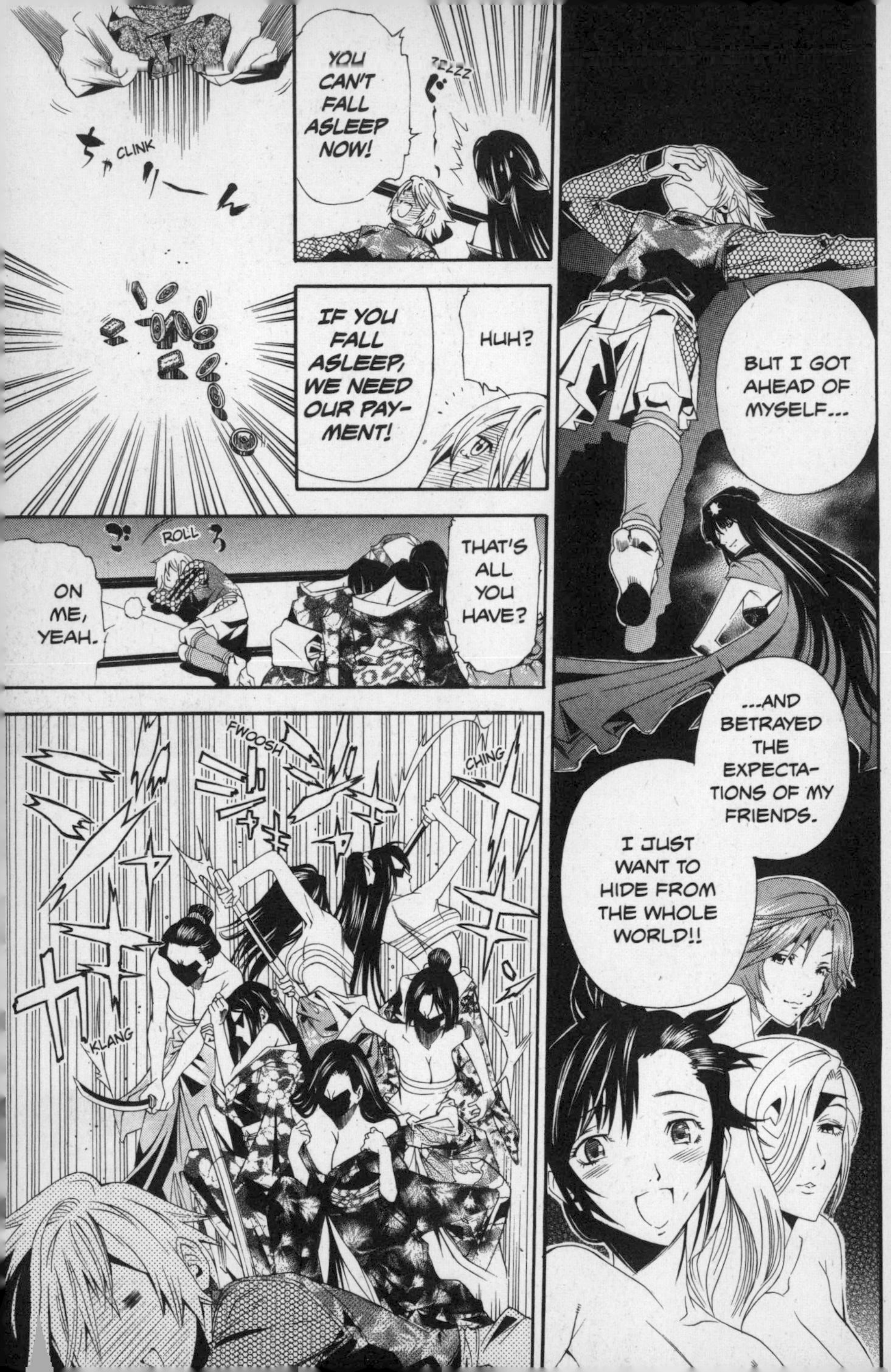
BUT I GOT AHEAD OF MYSELF...
...AND BETRAYED THE EXPECTATIONS OF MY FRIENDS.
I JUST WANT TO HIDE FROM THE WHOLE WORLD!!
YOU CAN'T FALL ASLEEP NOW!
ZZZZ
CLINK
HUH?
IF YOU FALL ASLEEP, WE NEED OUR PAYMENT!
THAT'S ALL YOU HAVE?
ROLL
ON ME, YEAH.
CHING
FWOOSH
KLANG

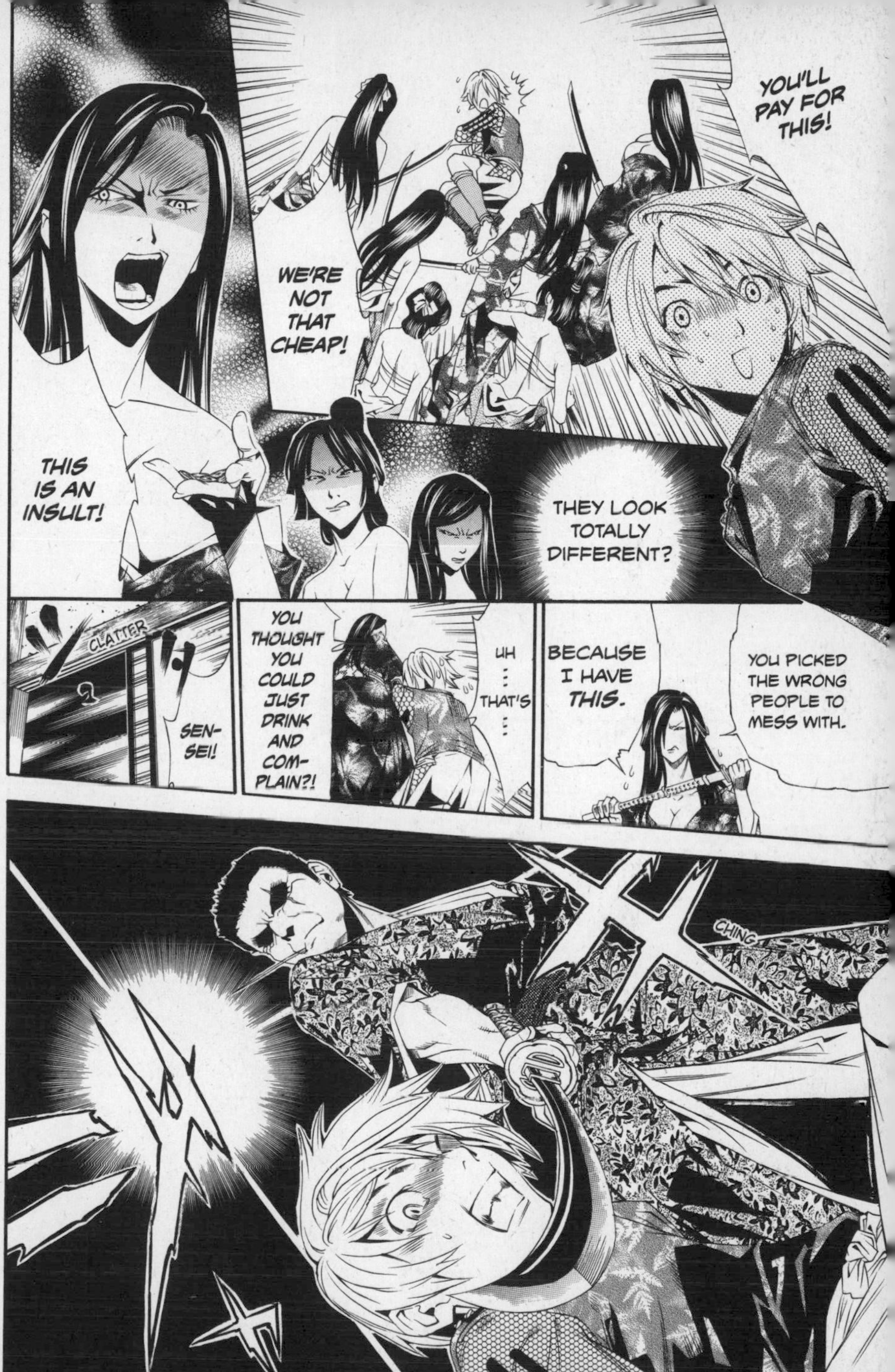
YOU'LL PAY FOR THIS!
WE'RE NOT THAT CHEAP!
THEY LOOK TOTALLY DIFFERENT?
THIS IS AN INSULT!
YOU PICKED THE WRONG PEOPLE TO MESS WITH.
BECAUSE I HAVE *THIS*.
UH... THAT'S...
YOU THOUGHT YOU COULD JUST DRINK AND COM-PLAIN?!
CLATTER
SEN-SEI!
CHING

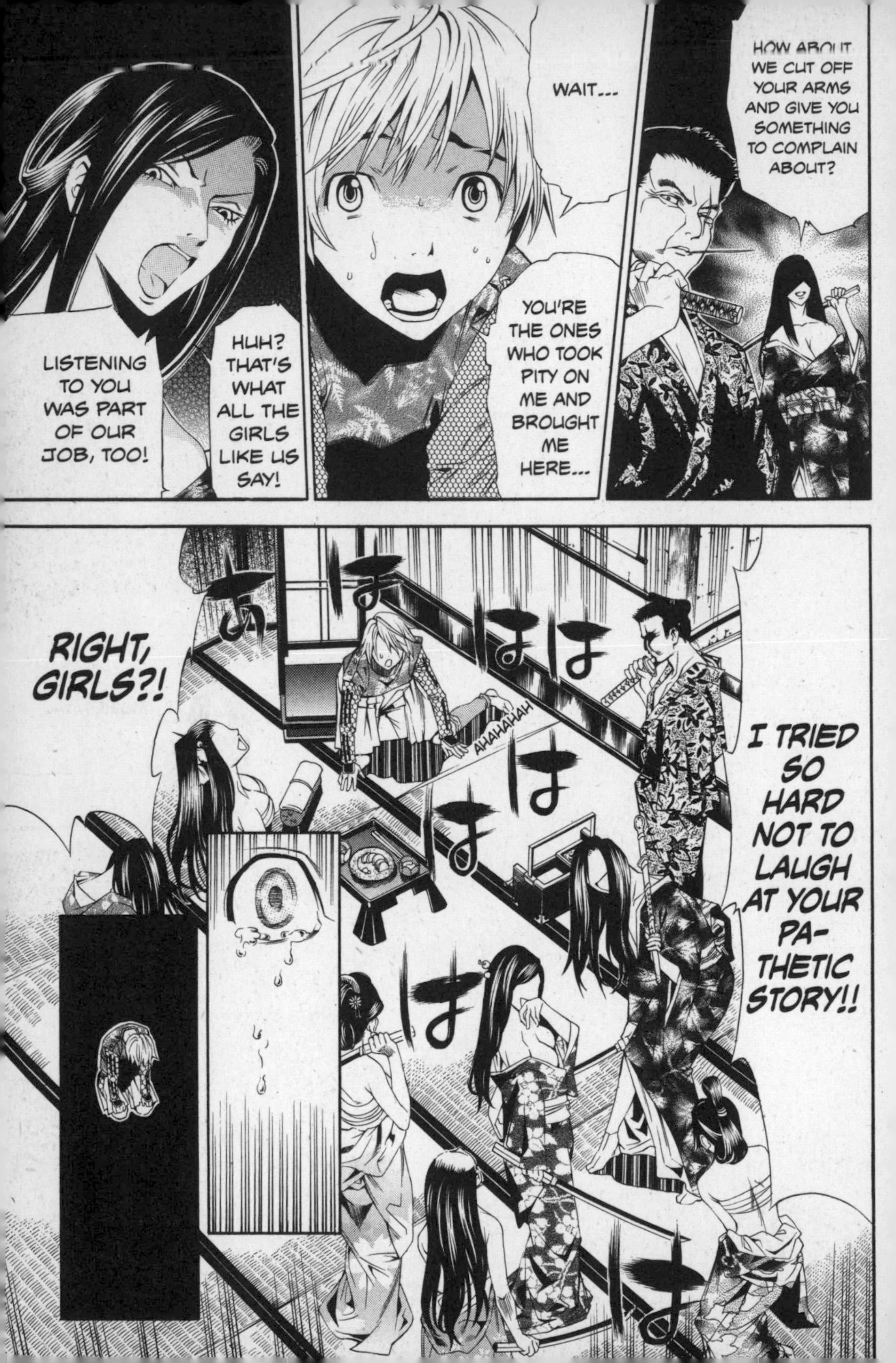
HOW ABOUT WE CUT OFF YOUR ARMS AND GIVE YOU SOMETHING TO COMPLAIN ABOUT?
WAIT...
YOU'RE THE ONES WHO TOOK PITY ON ME AND BROUGHT ME HERE...
HUH? THAT'S WHAT ALL THE GIRLS LIKE US SAY!
LISTENING TO YOU WAS PART OF OUR JOB, TOO!
I TRIED SO HARD NOT TO LAUGH AT YOUR PA-THETIC STORY!!
RIGHT, GIRLS?!
AHAHAHAH

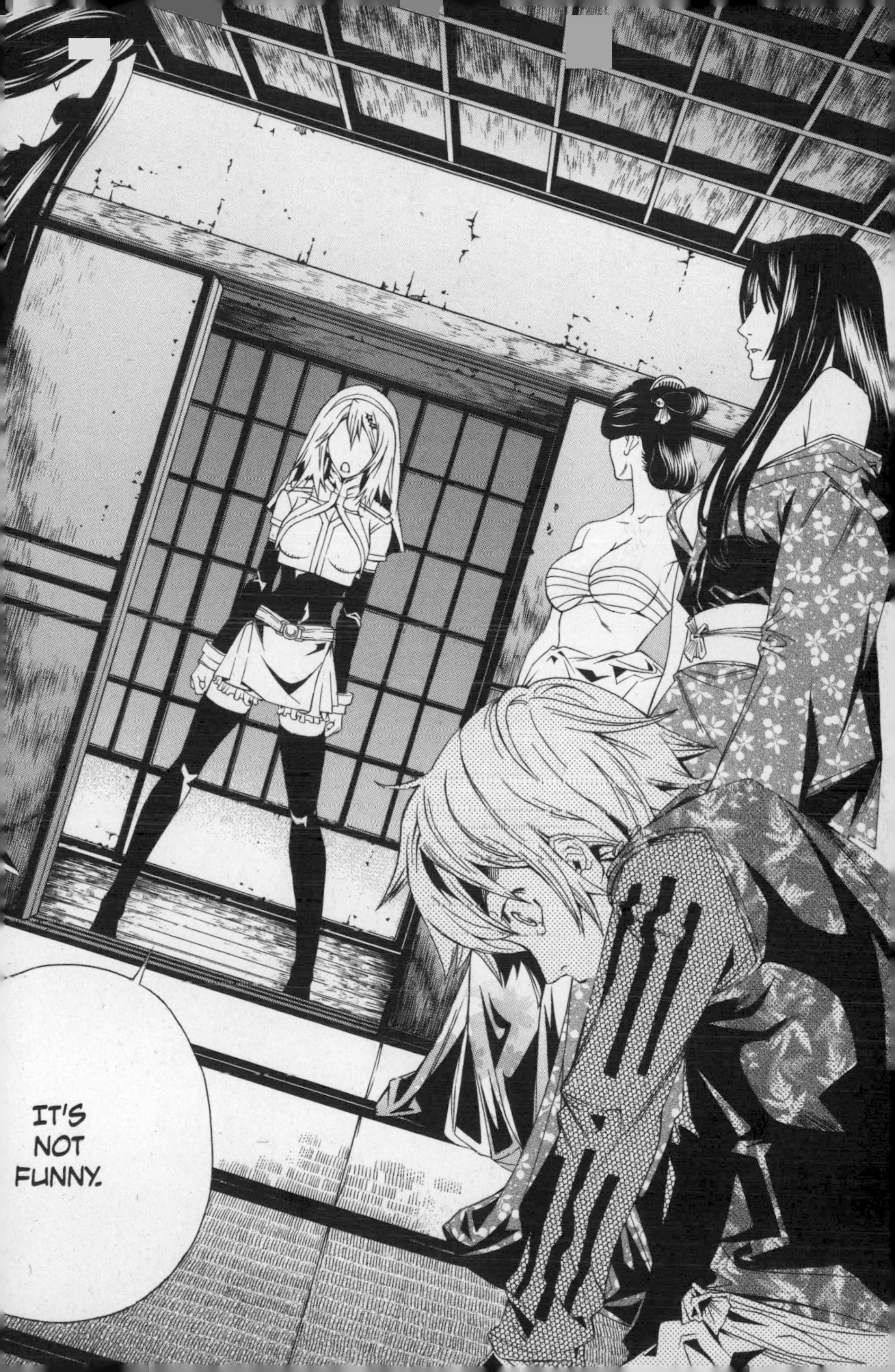
IT'S NOT FUNNY.

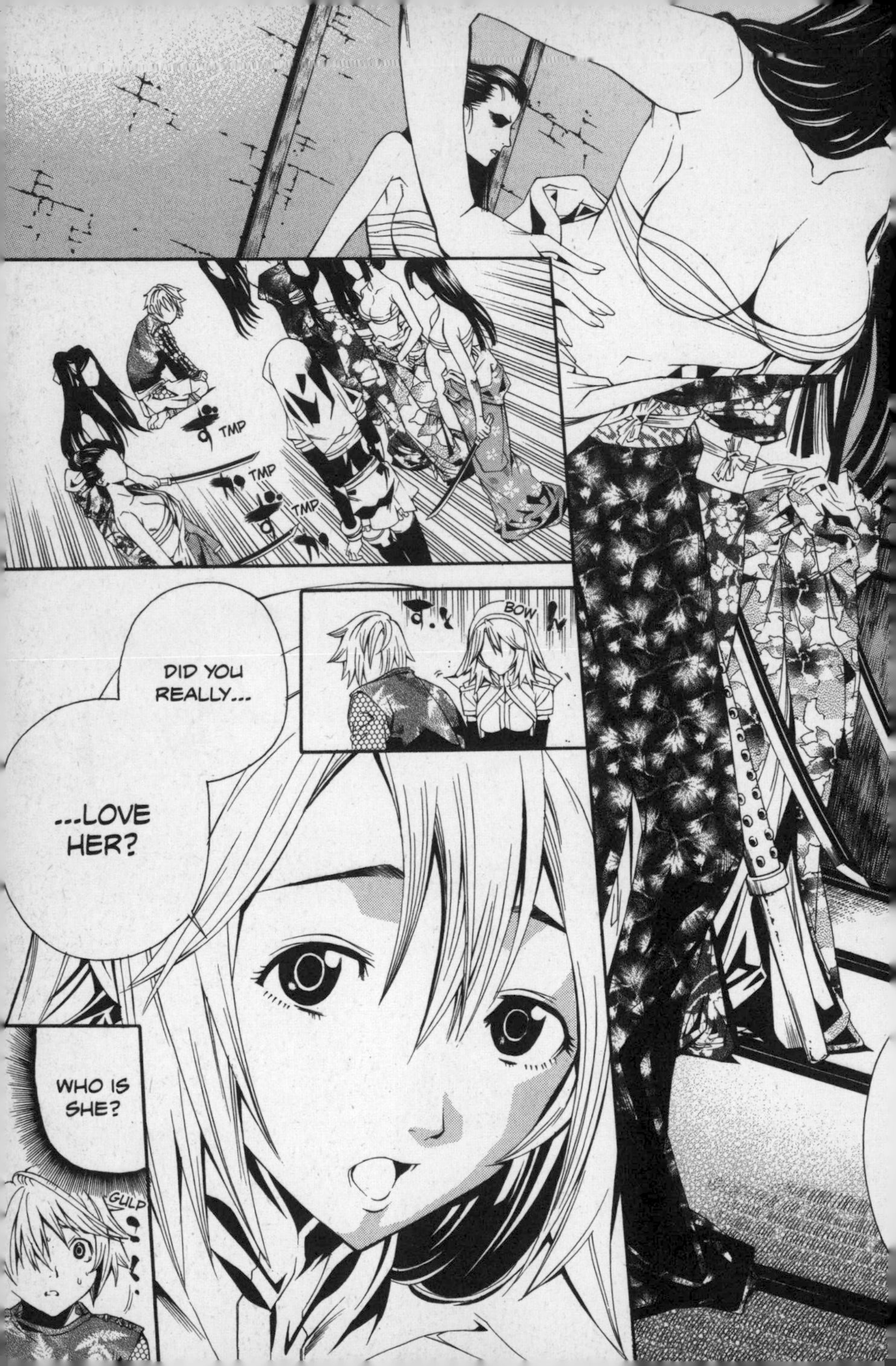
TMP
TMP
TMP
BOW
DID YOU REALLY...
...LOVE HER?
WHO IS SHE?
GULP

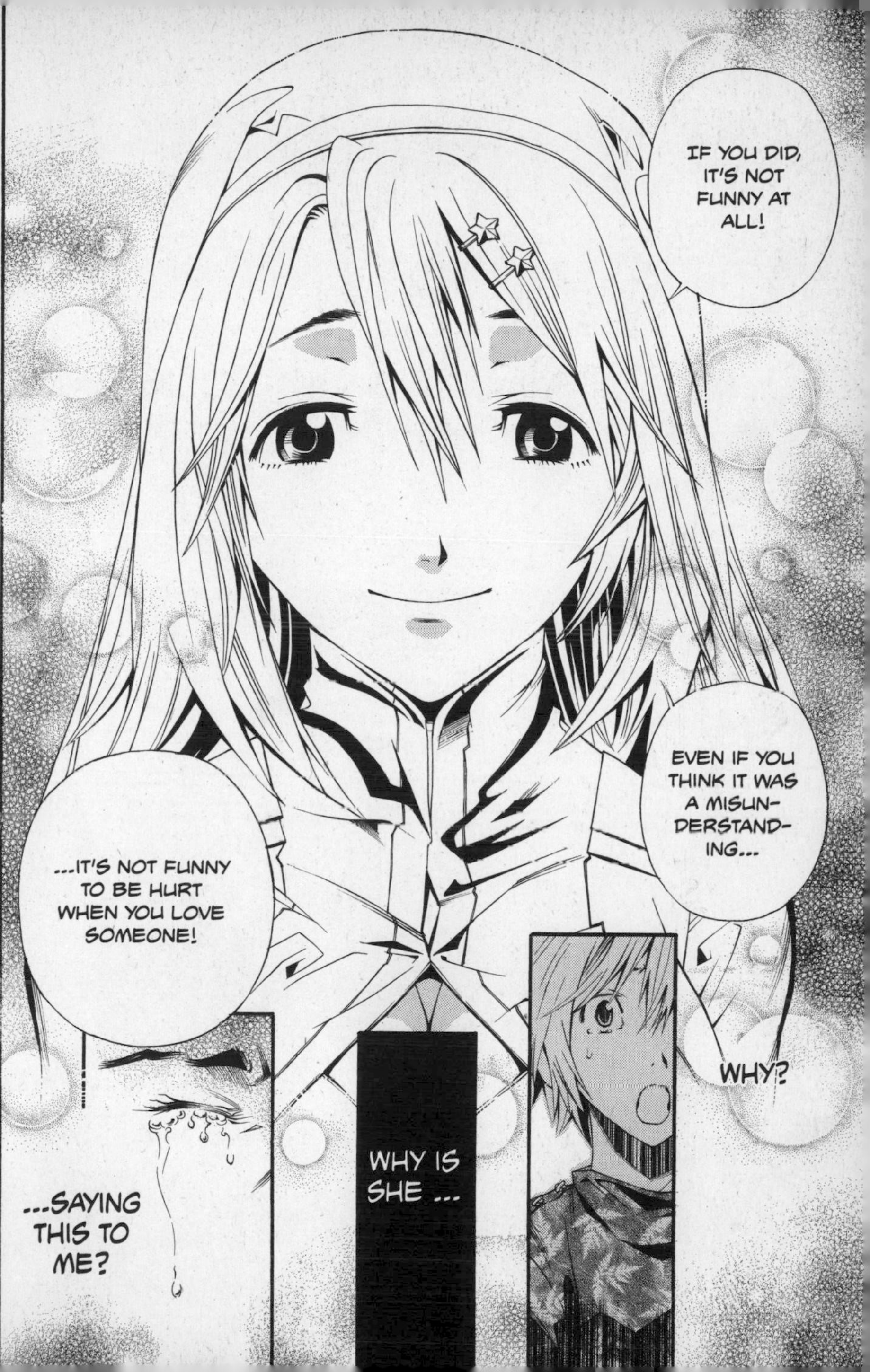

IF YOU DID, IT'S NOT FUNNY AT ALL!
EVEN IF YOU THINK IT WAS A MISUNDER-STANDING...
...IT'S NOT FUNNY TO BE HURT WHEN YOU LOVE SOMEONE!
WHY?
WHY IS SHE ...
...SAYING THIS TO ME?

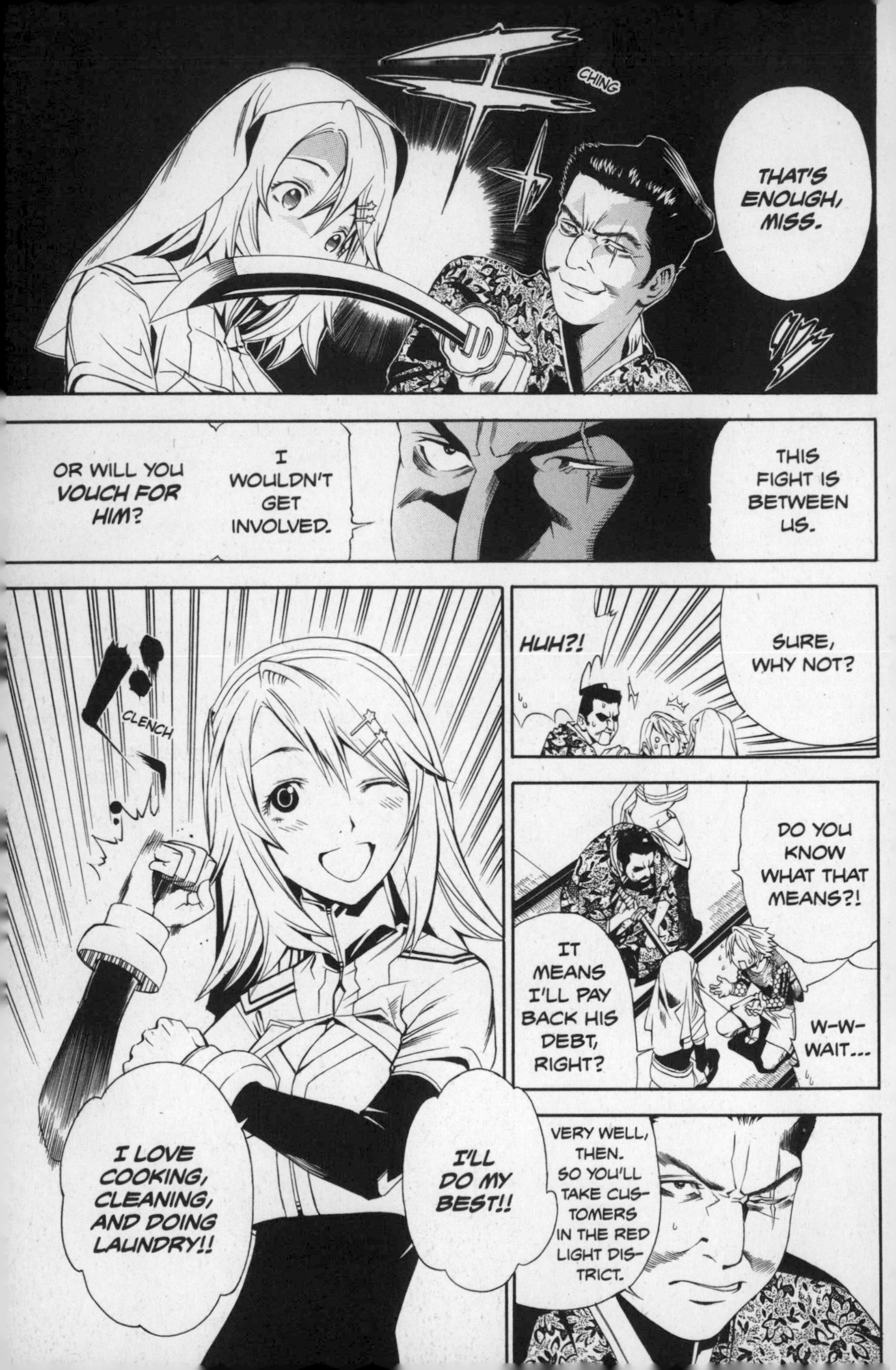
CHING
THAT'S ENOUGH, MISS.
THIS FIGHT IS BETWEEN US.
I WOULDN'T GET INVOLVED.
OR WILL YOU VOUCH FOR HIM?
SURE, WHY NOT?
HUH?!
DO YOU KNOW WHAT THAT MEANS?!
W-W-WAIT...
IT MEANS I'LL PAY BACK HIS DEBT, RIGHT?
VERY WELL, THEN. SO YOU'LL TAKE CUS-TOMERS IN THE RED LIGHT DIS-TRICT.
CLENCH
I'LL DO MY BEST!!
I LOVE COOKING, CLEANING, AND DOING LAUNDRY!!

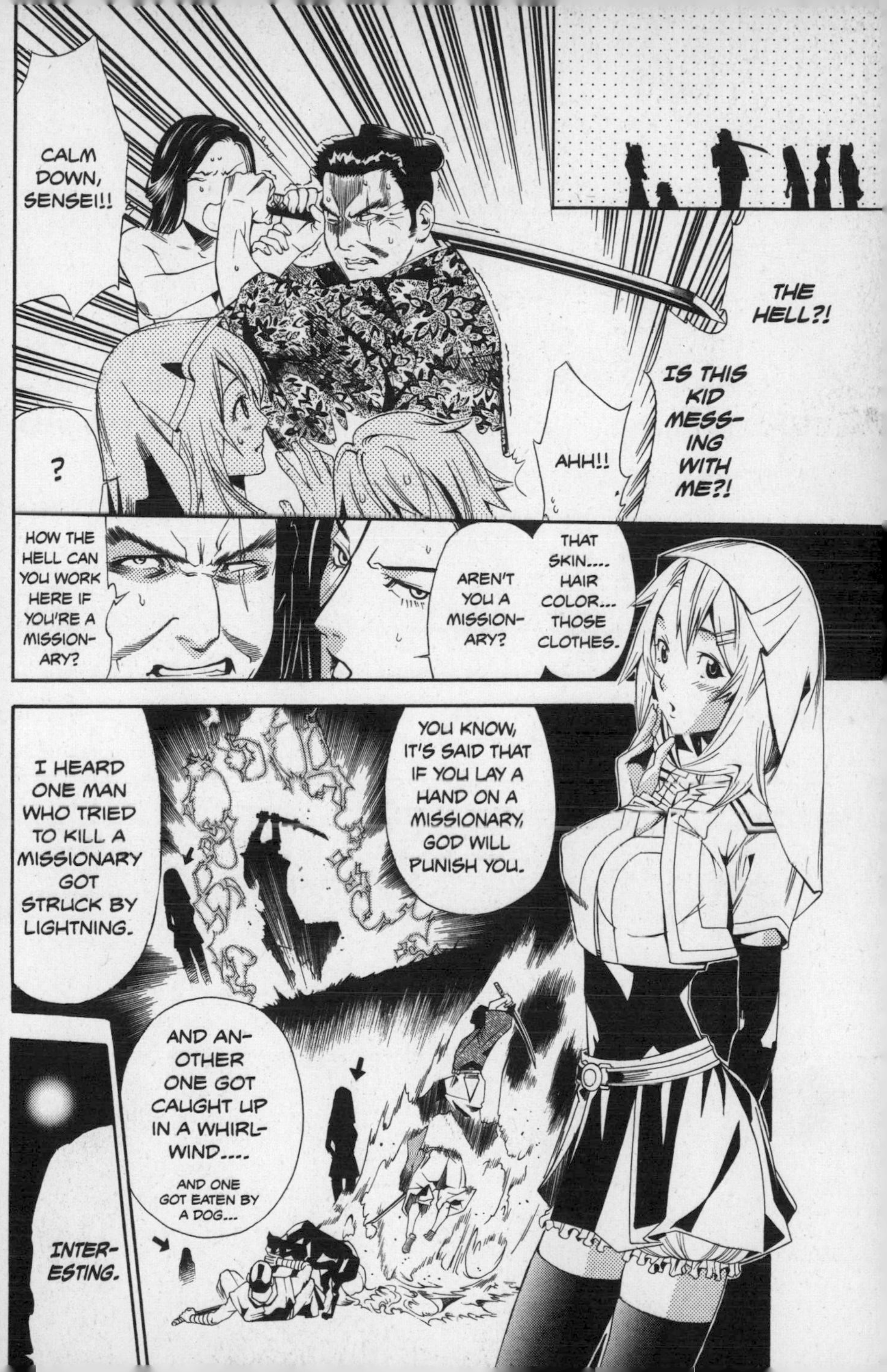
THE HELL?!
IS THIS KID MESS-ING WITH ME?!
AHH!!
CALM DOWN, SENSEI!!
?
THAT SKIN.... HAIR COLOR... THOSE CLOTHES.
AREN'T YOU A MISSION-ARY?
HOW THE HELL CAN YOU WORK HERE IF YOU'RE A MISSION-ARY?
YOU KNOW, IT'S SAID THAT IF YOU LAY A HAND ON A MISSIONARY, GOD WILL PUNISH YOU.
I HEARD ONE MAN WHO TRIED TO KILL A MISSIONARY GOT STRUCK BY LIGHTNING.
AND AN-OTHER ONE GOT CAUGHT UP IN A WHIRL-WIND....
AND ONE GOT EATEN BY A DOG...
INTER-ESTING.

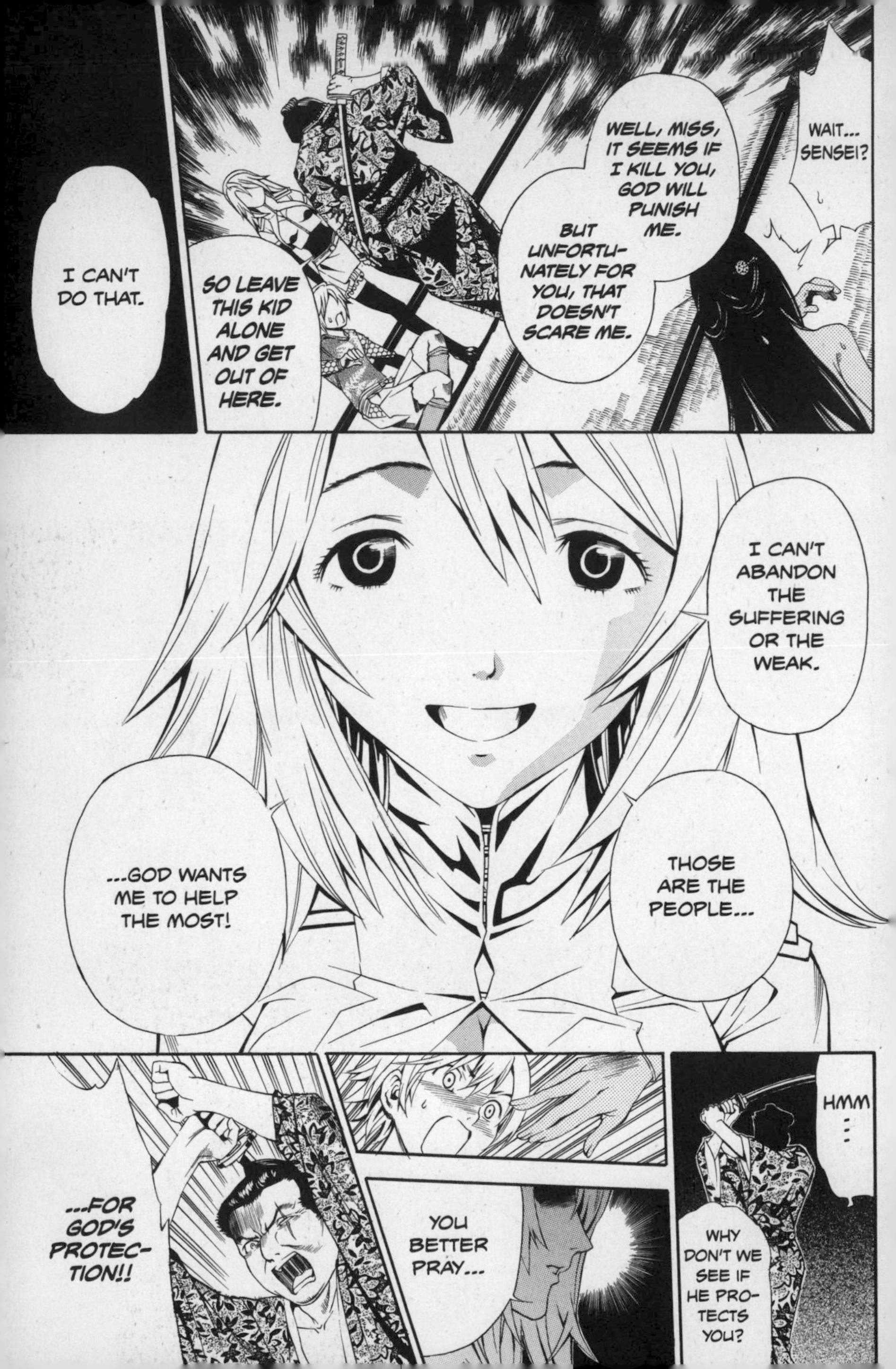
WAIT... SENSEI?
WELL, MISS, IT SEEMS IF I KILL YOU, GOD WILL PUNISH ME.
BUT UNFORTUNATELY FOR YOU, THAT DOESN'T SCARE ME.
SO LEAVE THIS KID ALONE AND GET OUT OF HERE.
I CAN'T DO THAT.
I CAN'T ABANDON THE SUFFERING OR THE WEAK.
THOSE ARE THE PEOPLE...
...GOD WANTS ME TO HELP THE MOST!
HMM...
WHY DON'T WE SEE IF HE PROTECTS YOU?
YOU BETTER PRAY...
...FOR GOD'S PROTECTION!!

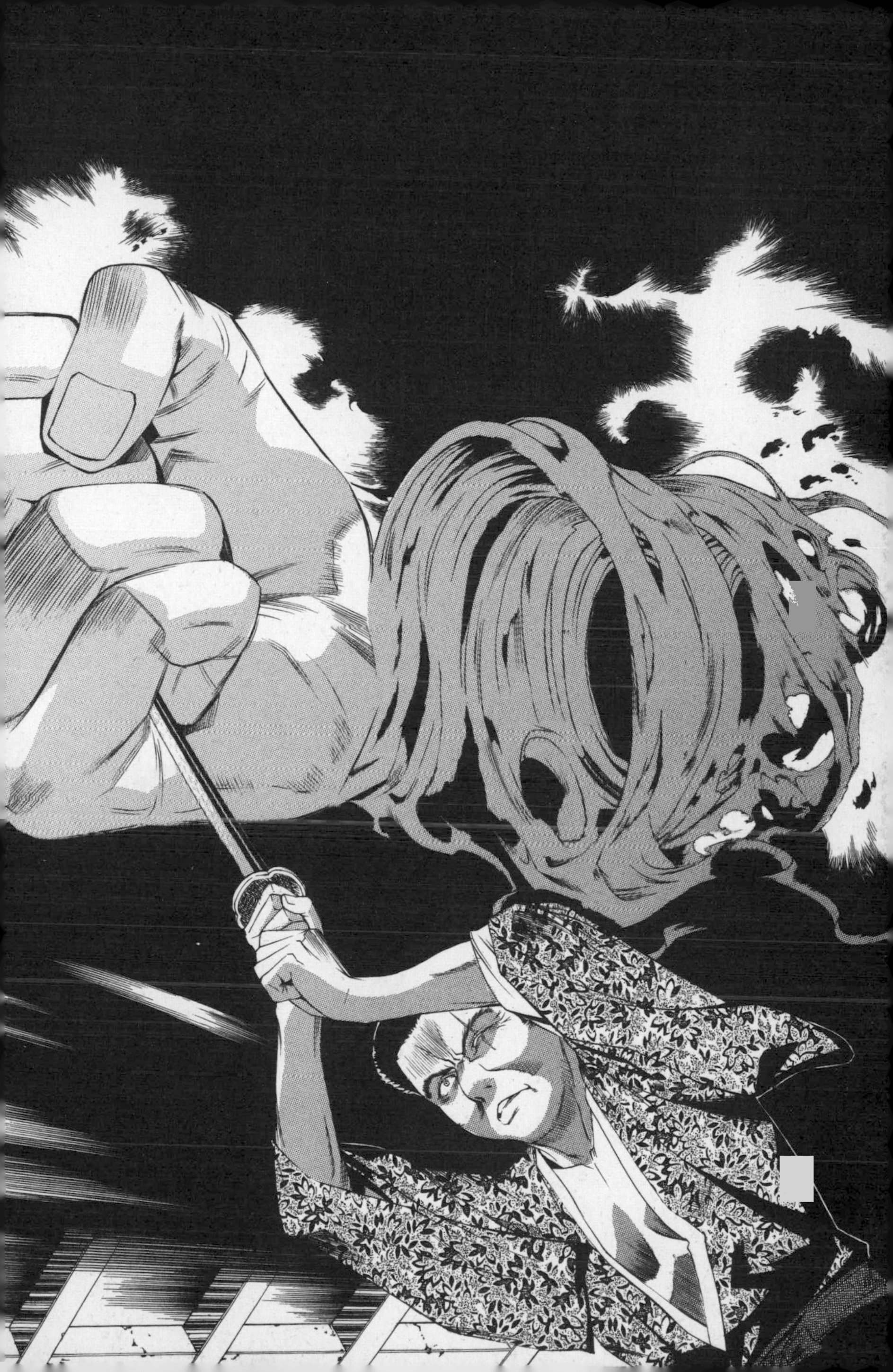

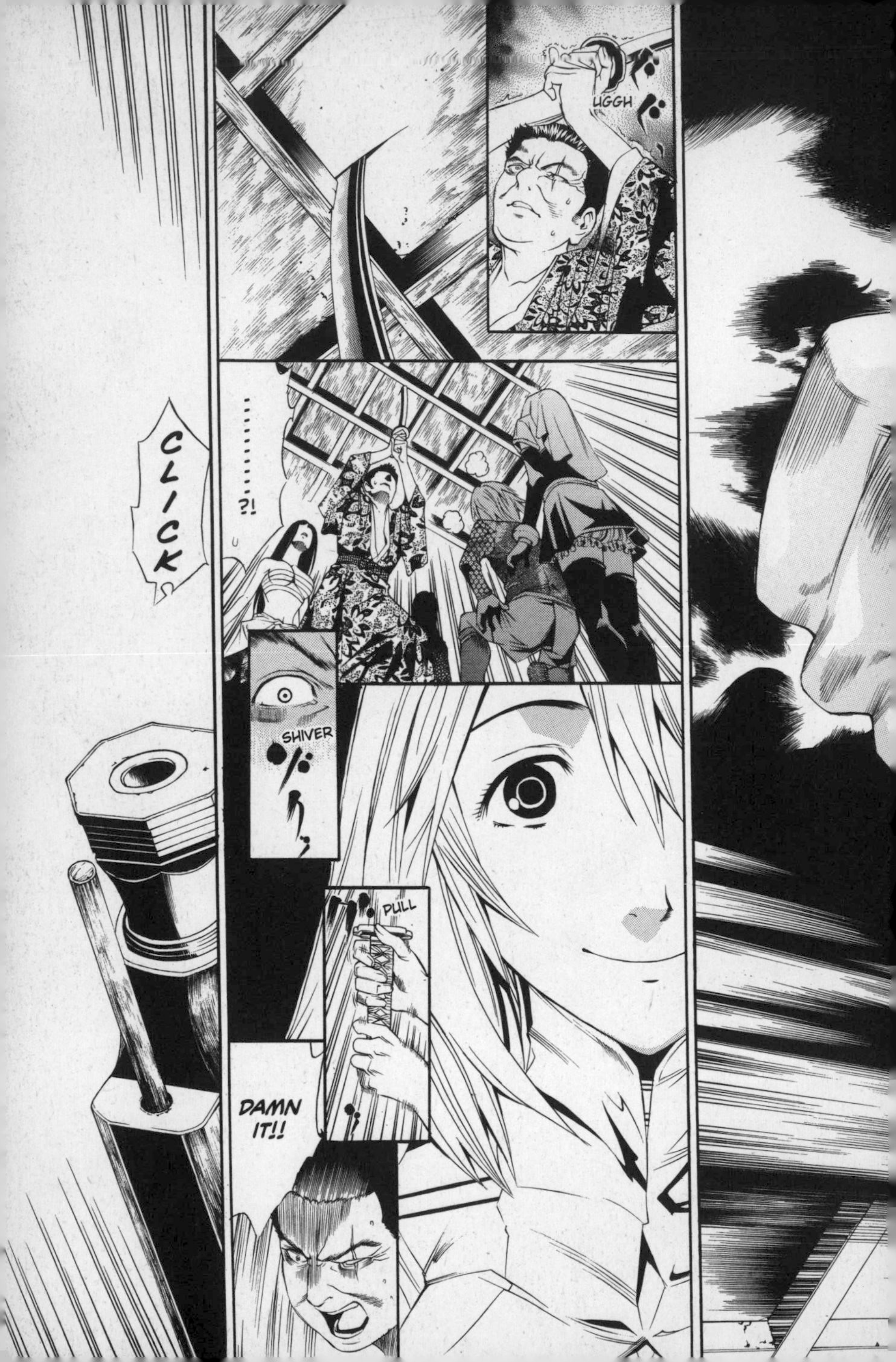
UGGH
......
?!
CLICK
SHIVER
PULL
DAMN IT!!

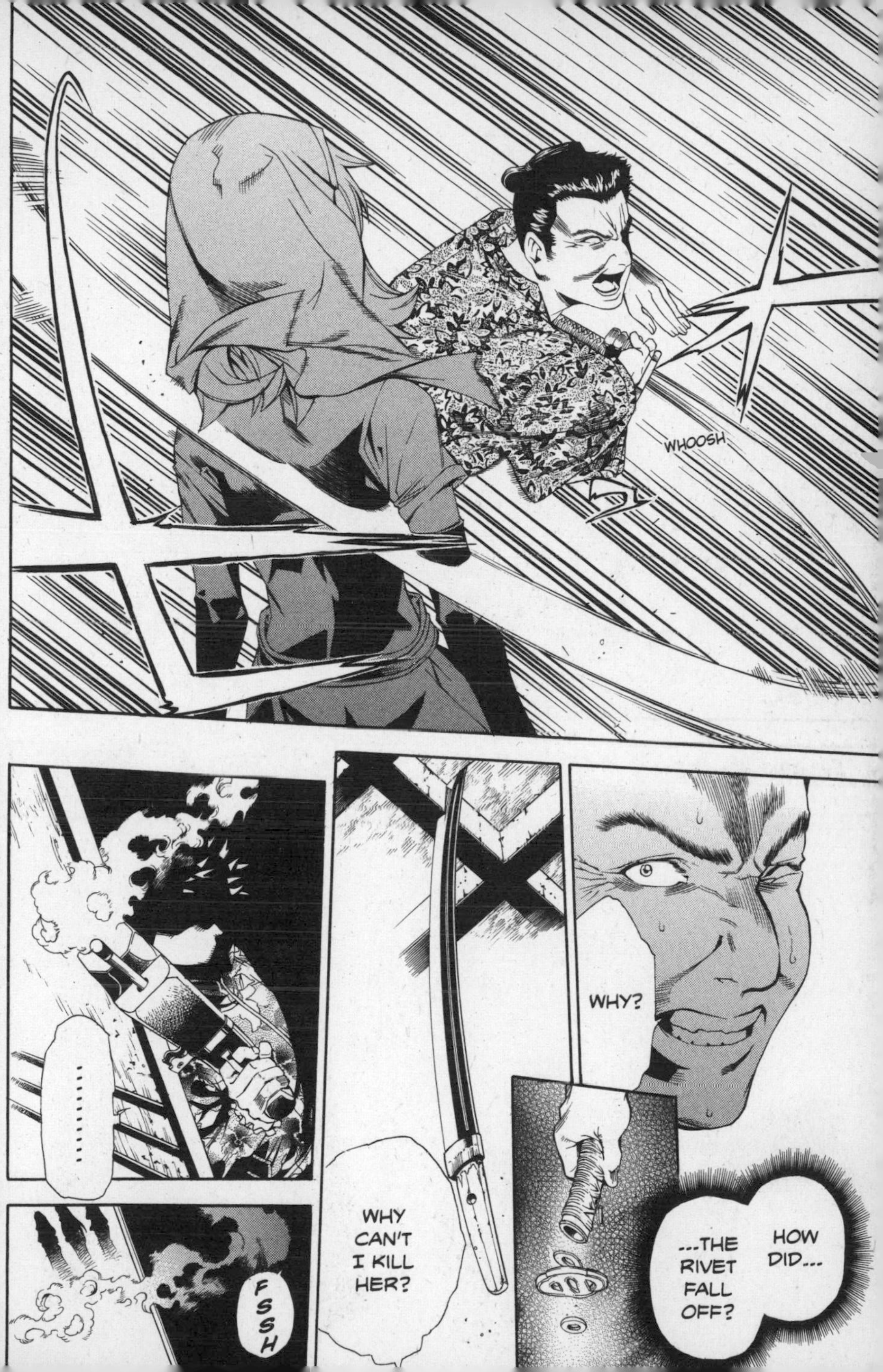
WHOOSH
WHY?
HOW DID...
...THE RIVET FALL OFF?
WHY CAN'T I KILL HER?
......
FSSH

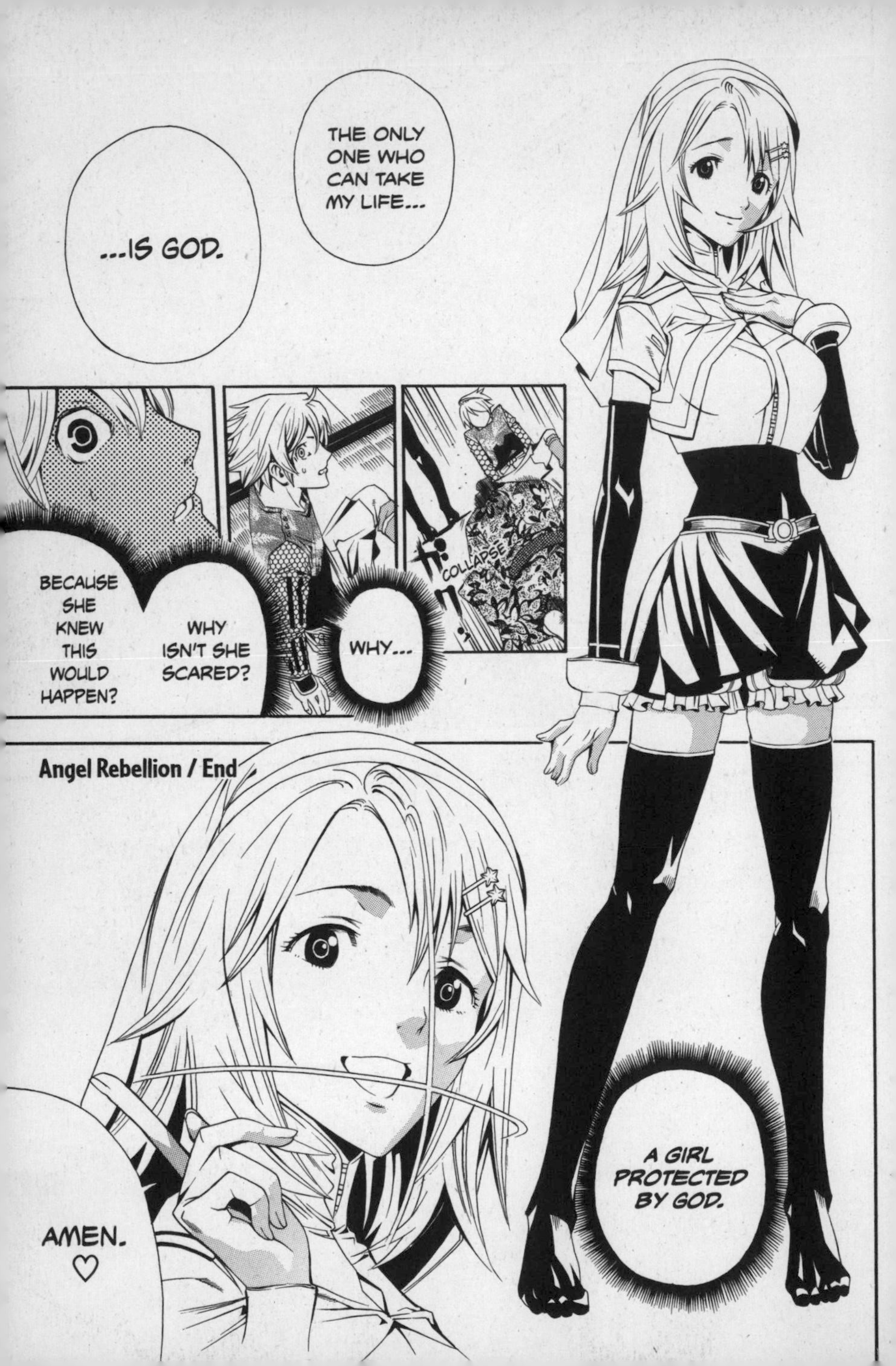
THE ONLY ONE WHO CAN TAKE MY LIFE...
...IS GOD.
A GIRL PROTECTED BY GOD.
COLLAPSE
WHY...
WHY ISN'T SHE SCARED?
BECAUSE SHE KNEW THIS WOULD HAPPEN?
Angel Rebellion / End
AMEN. ♡

Ninja Girls

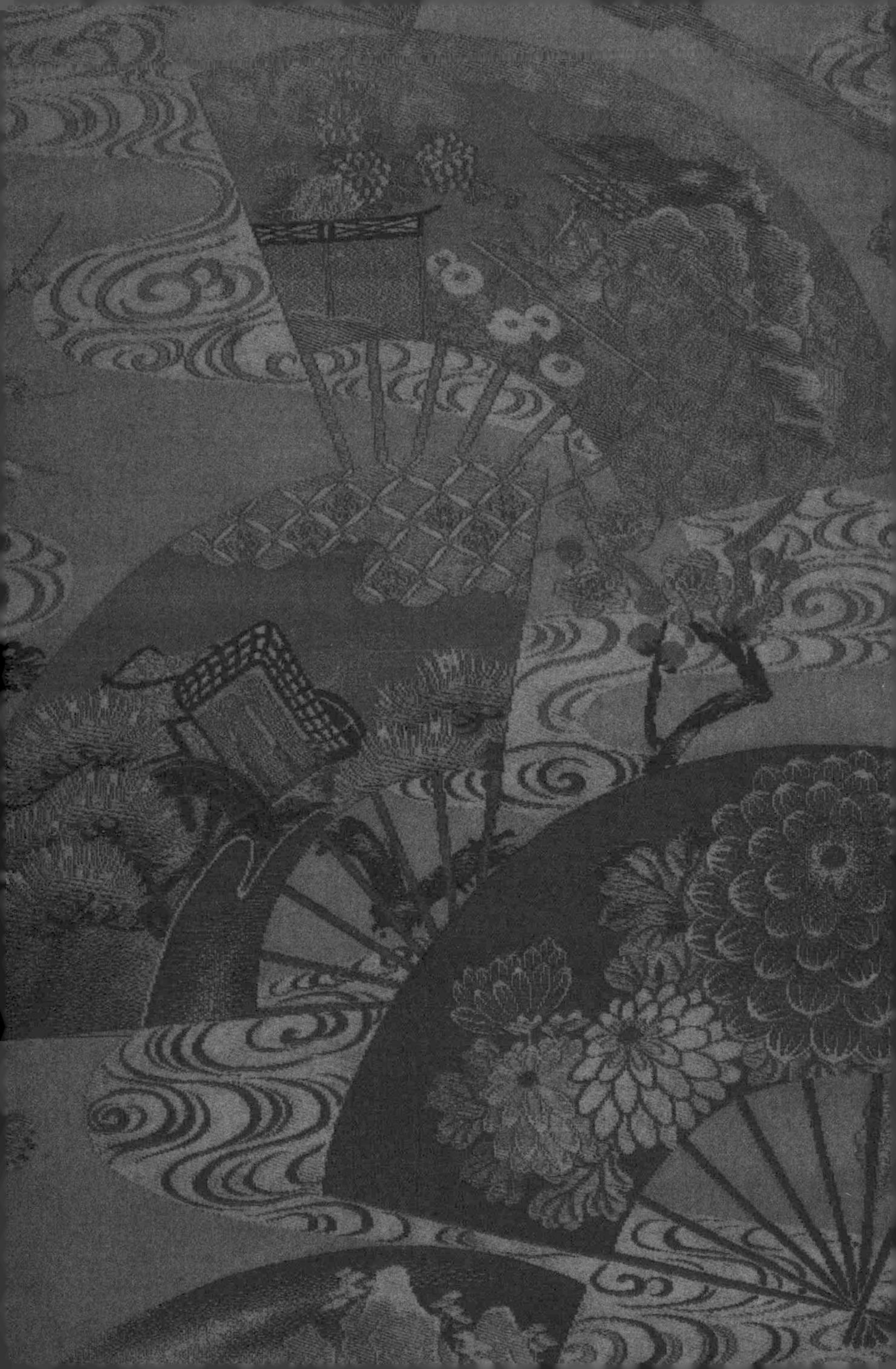

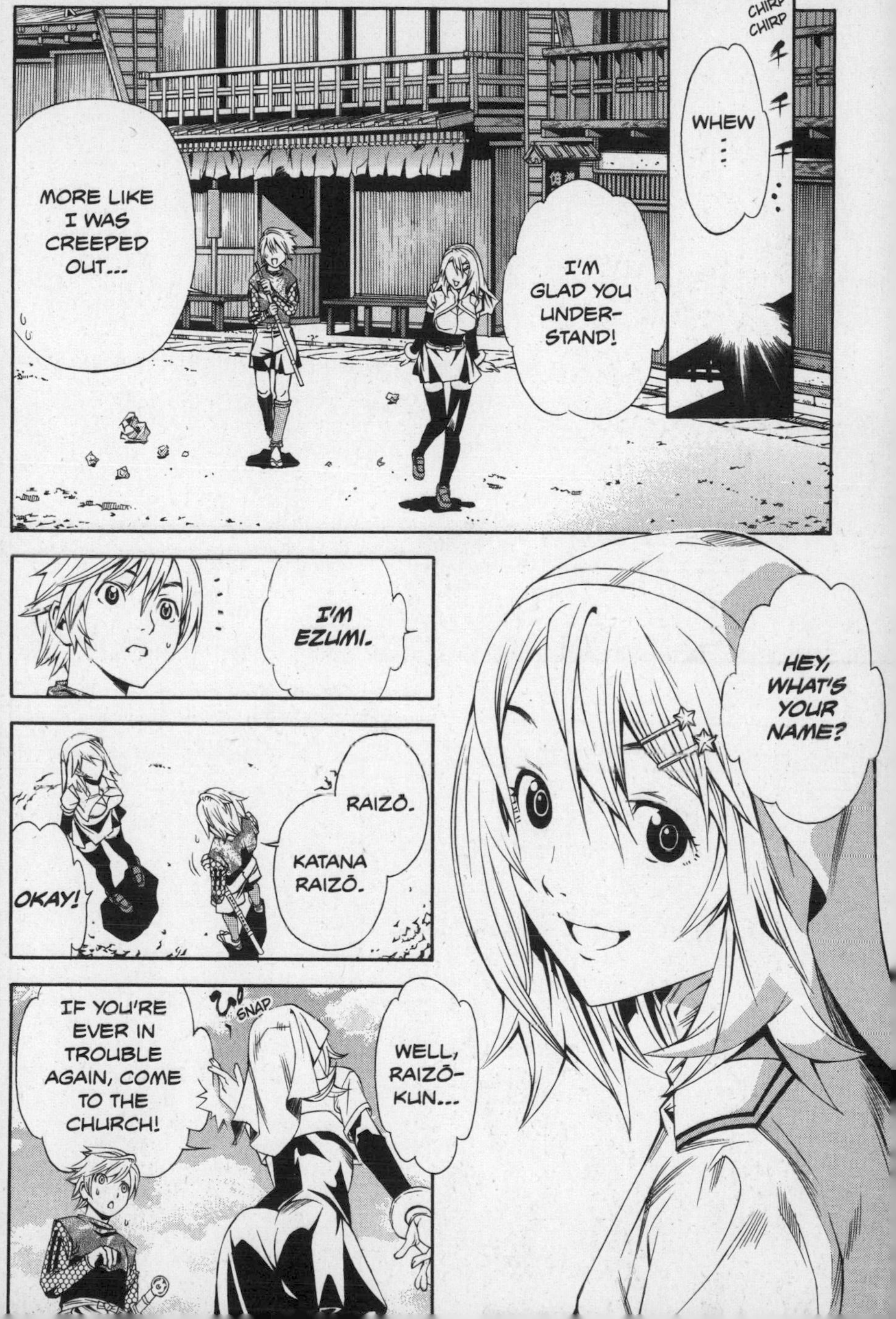
CHIRP CHIRP
WHEW...
I'M GLAD YOU UNDER-STAND!
MORE LIKE I WAS CREEPED OUT...
HEY, WHAT'S YOUR NAME?
I'M EZUMI.
RAIZŌ.
KATANA RAIZŌ.
OKAY!
WELL, RAIZŌ-KUN...
SNAP
IF YOU'RE EVER IN TROUBLE AGAIN, COME TO THE CHURCH!

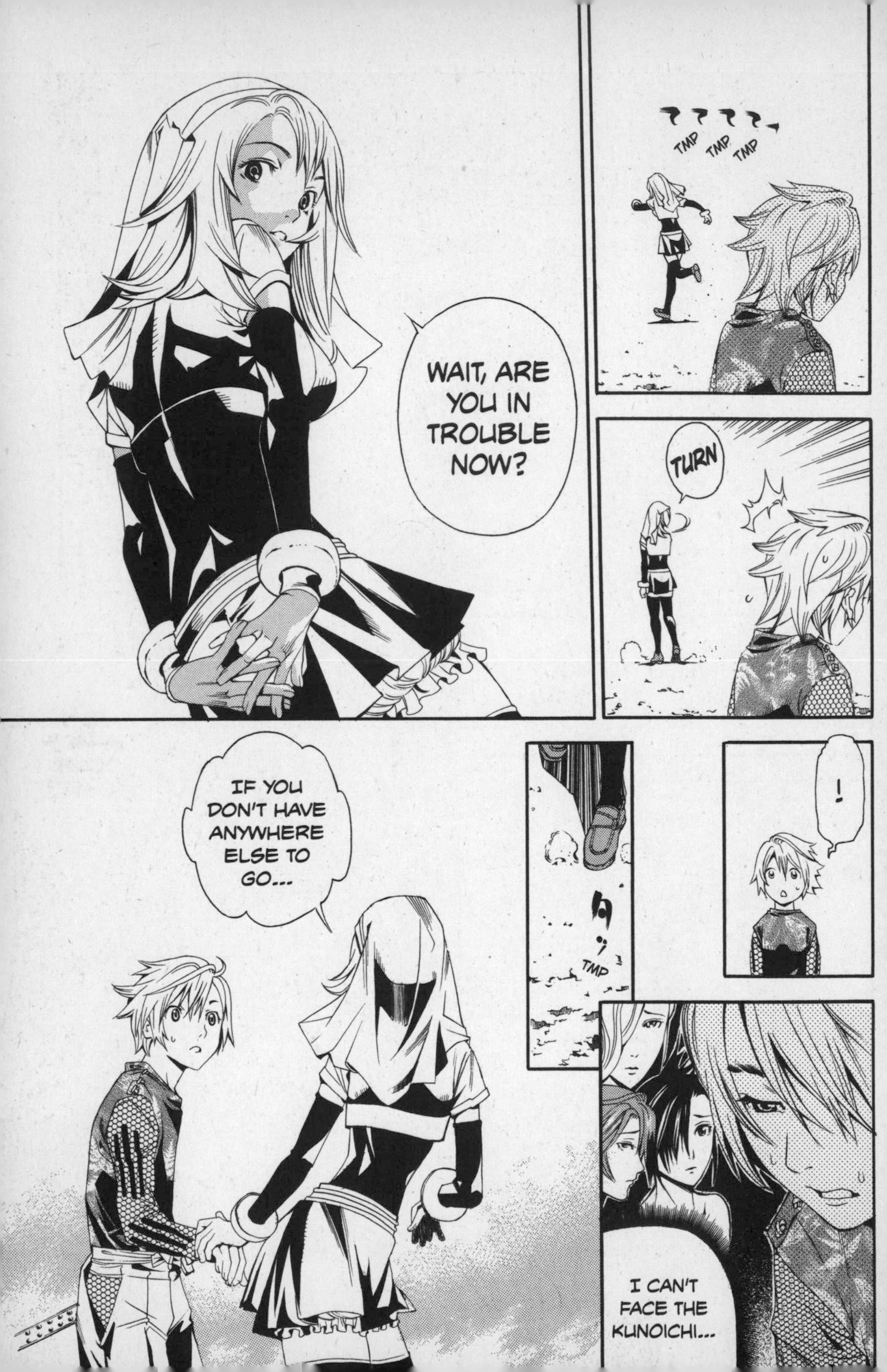
TMP TMP TMP
TURN
WAIT, ARE YOU IN TROUBLE NOW?
!
TMP
I CAN'T FACE THE KUNOICHI...
IF YOU DON'T HAVE ANYWHERE ELSE TO GO...

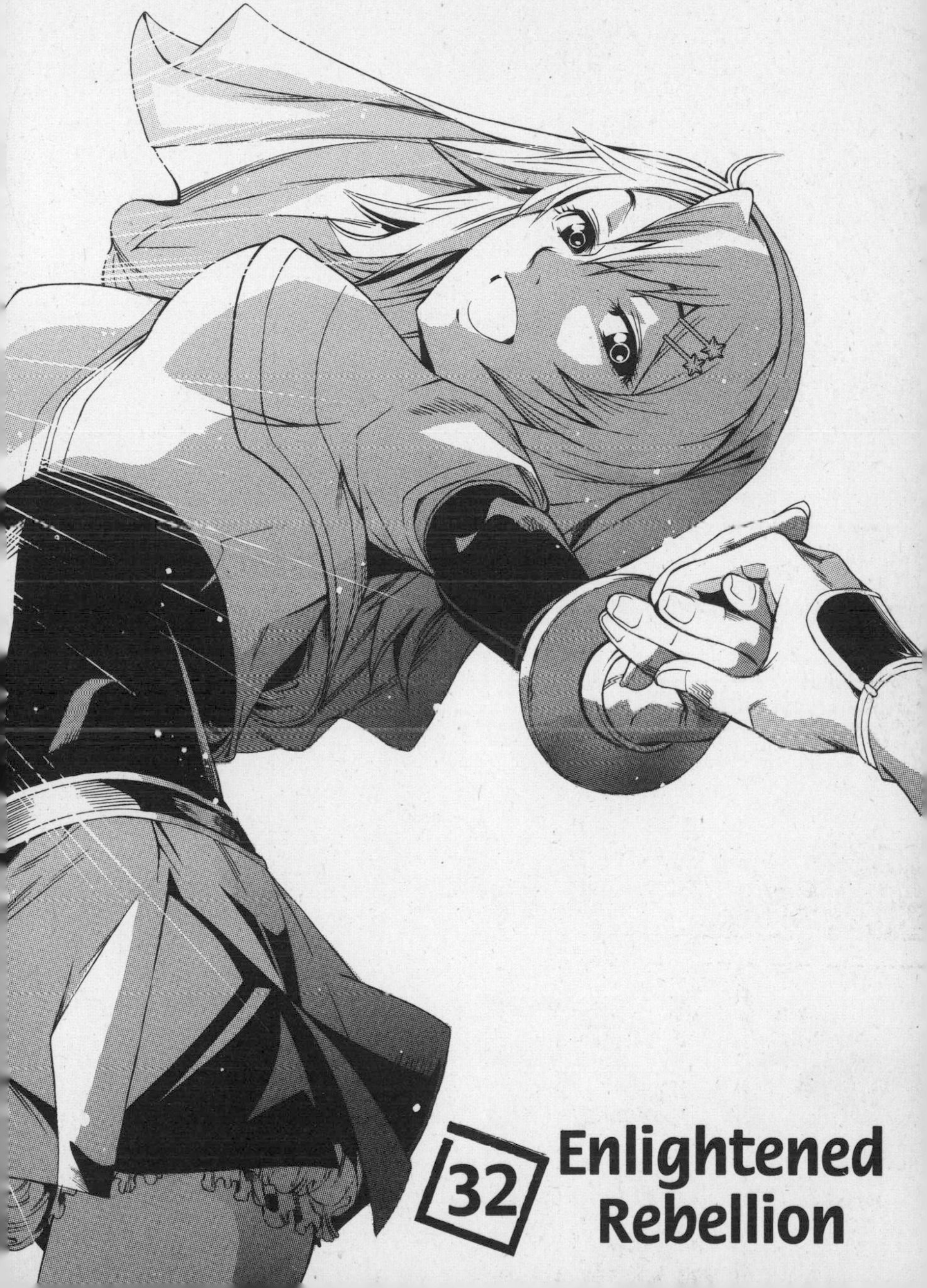

32 Enlightened Rebellion

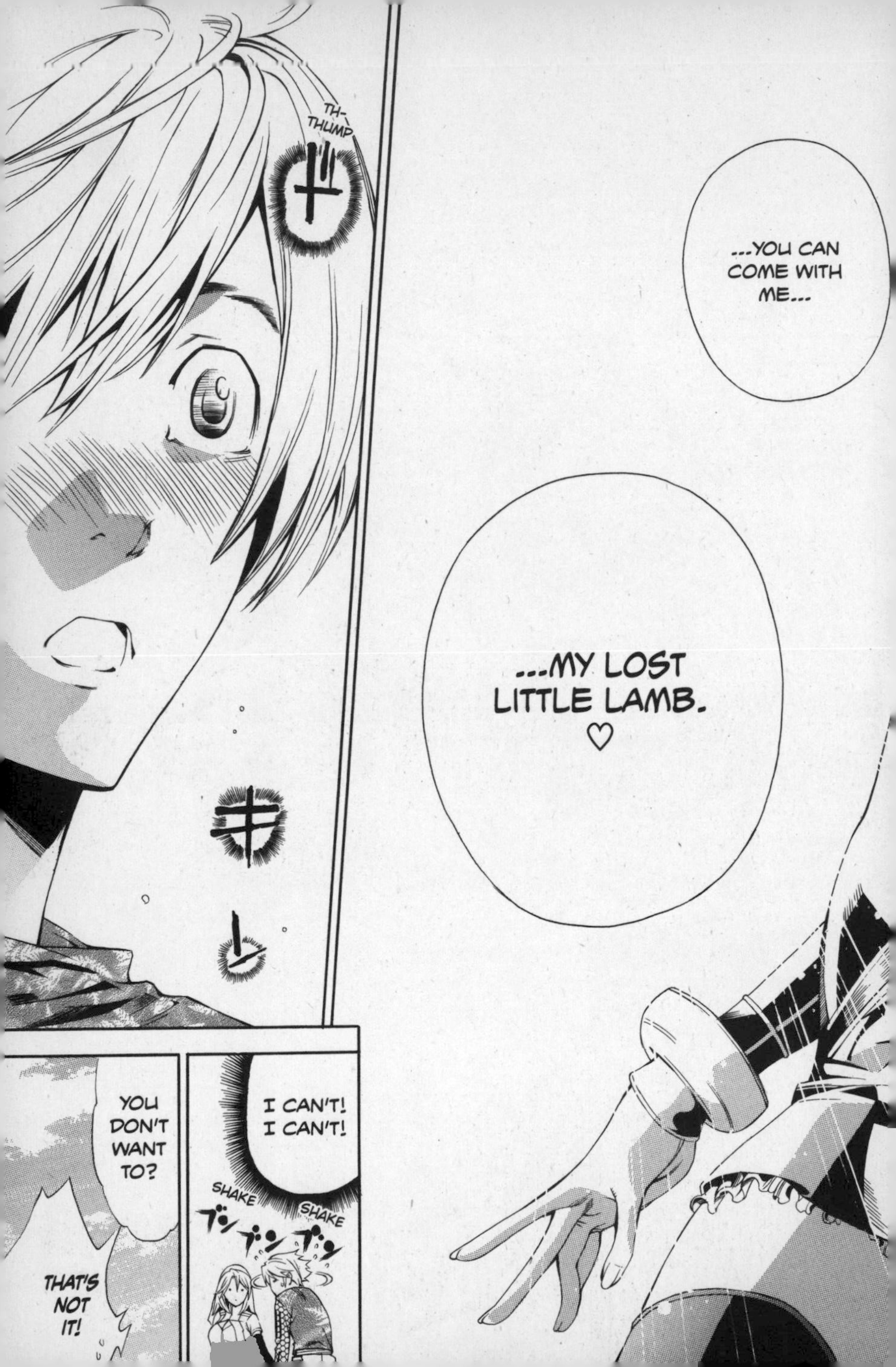
...YOU CAN COME WITH ME...
...MY LOST LITTLE LAMB. ♡
TH-THUMP
I CAN'T! I CAN'T!
SHAKE
SHAKE
YOU DON'T WANT TO?
THAT'S NOT IT!

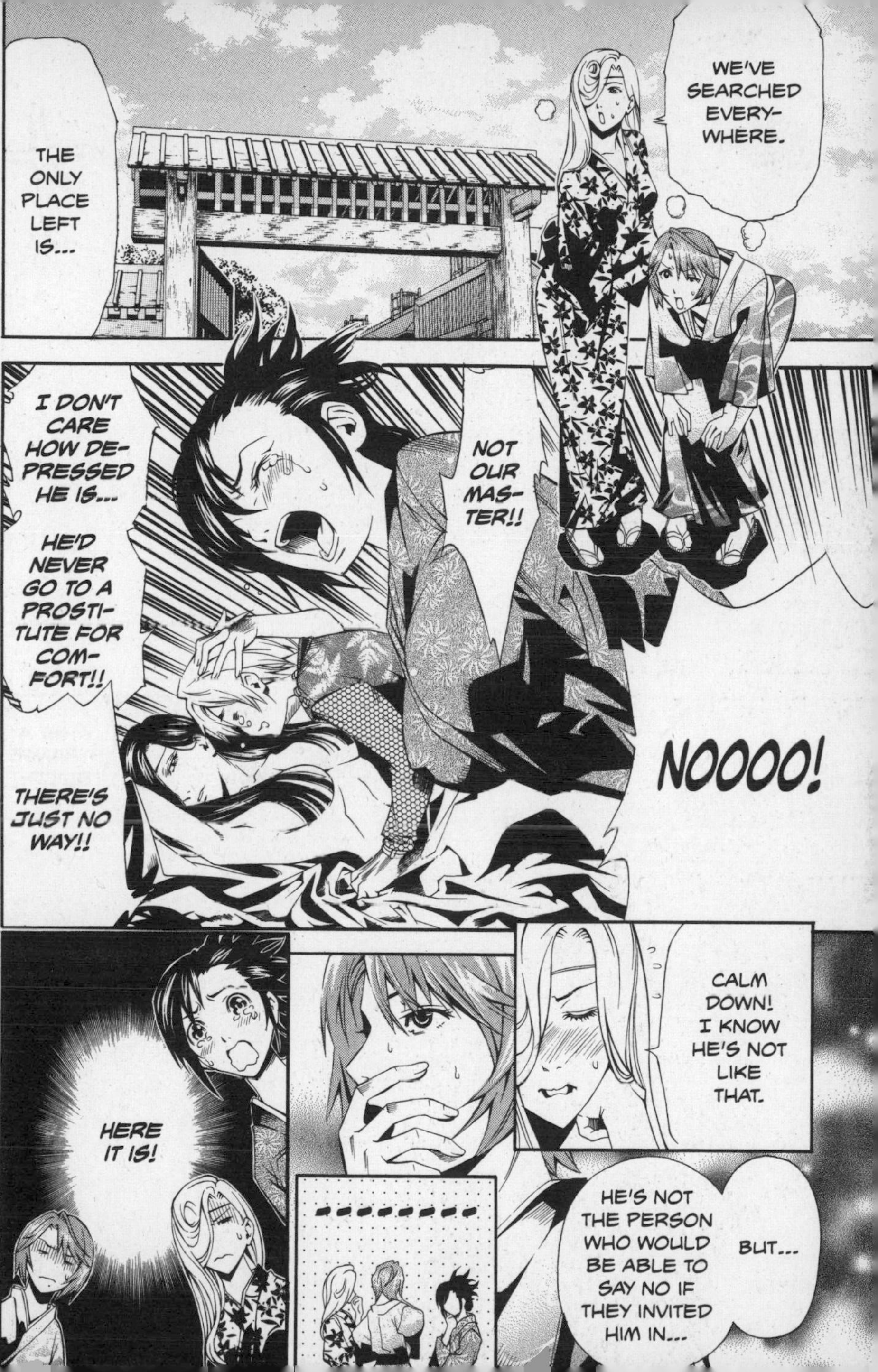
WE'VE SEARCHED EVERYWHERE.
THE ONLY PLACE LEFT IS...
NOT OUR MASTER!!
NOOOO!
I DON'T CARE HOW DEPRESSED HE IS...
HE'D NEVER GO TO A PROSTITUTE FOR COMFORT!!
THERE'S JUST NO WAY!!
CALM DOWN! I KNOW HE'S NOT LIKE THAT.
BUT...
HE'S NOT THE PERSON WHO WOULD BE ABLE TO SAY NO IF THEY INVITED HIM IN...
....
HERE IT IS!

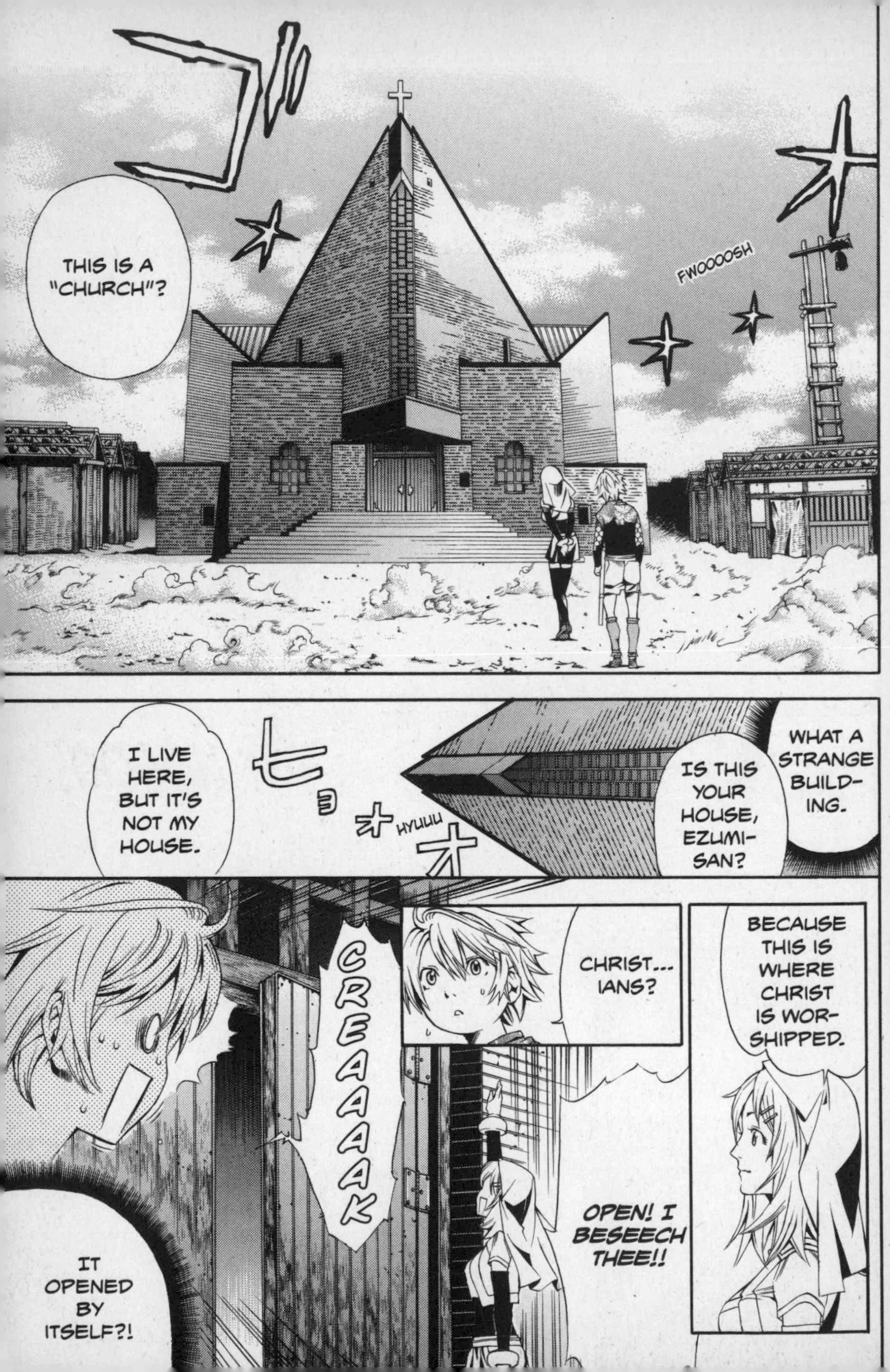
FWOOOOSH
THIS IS A "CHURCH"?
WHAT A STRANGE BUILD-ING.
IS THIS YOUR HOUSE, EZUMI-SAN?
HYUUU
I LIVE HERE, BUT IT'S NOT MY HOUSE.
BECAUSE THIS IS WHERE CHRIST IS WOR-SHIPPED.
CHRIST... IANS?
OPEN! I BESEECH THEE!!
CREAAAAK
IT OPENED BY ITSELF?!

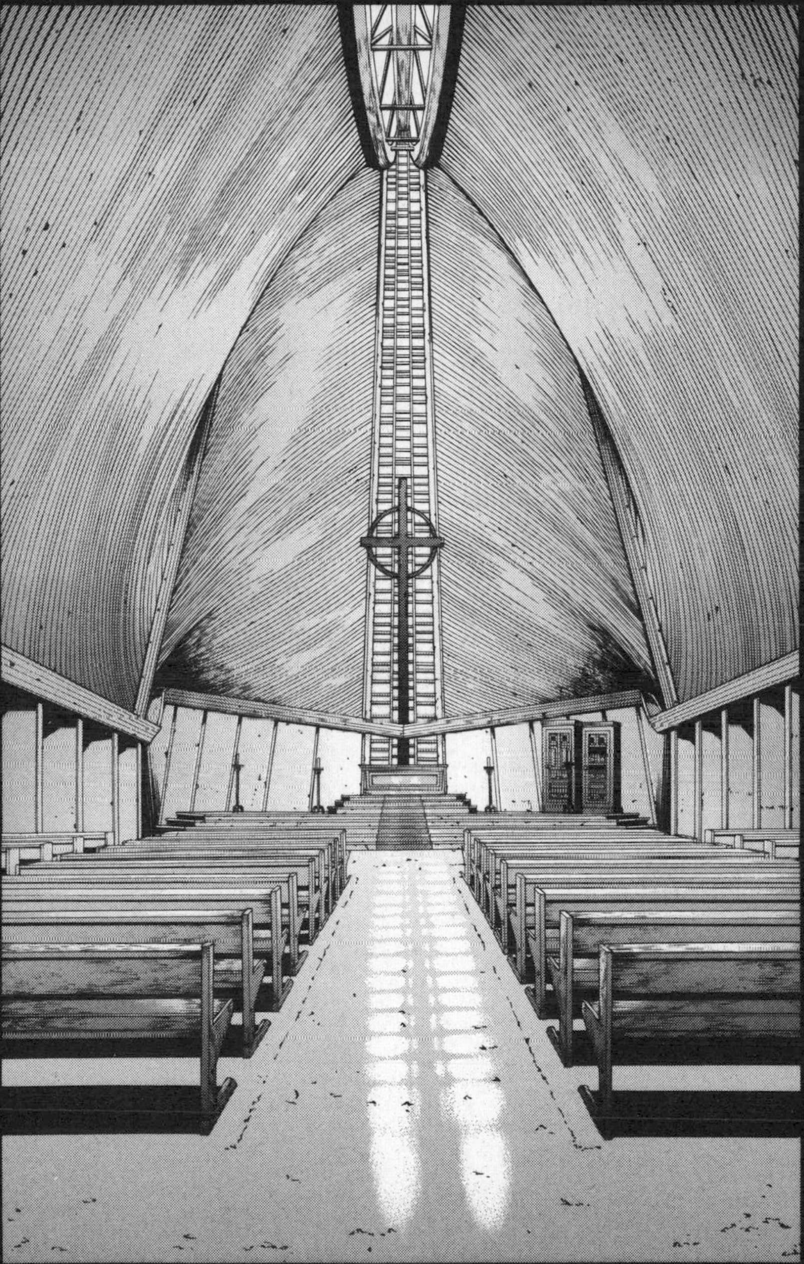

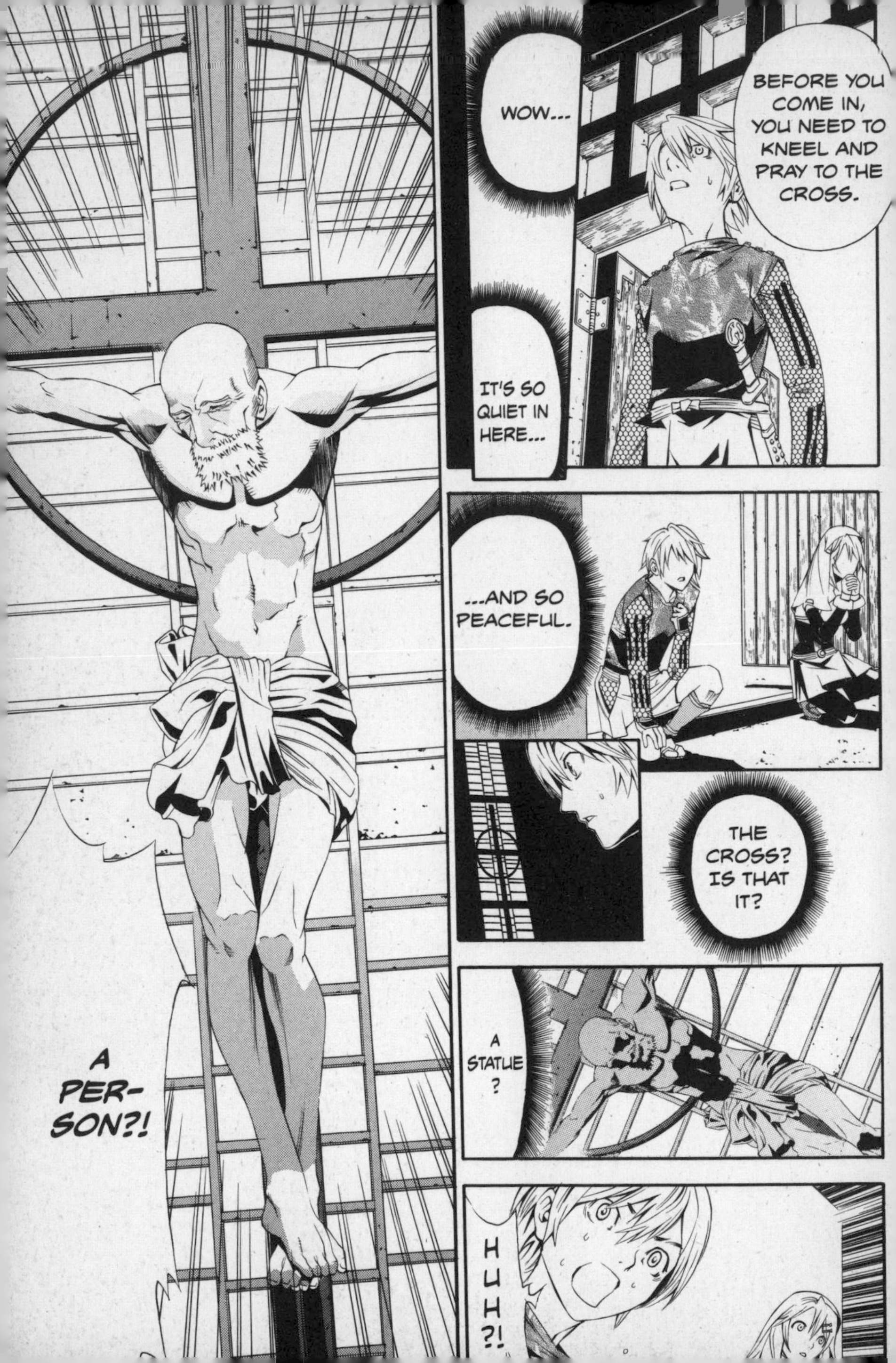
BEFORE YOU COME IN, YOU NEED TO KNEEL AND PRAY TO THE CROSS.
WOW...
IT'S SO QUIET IN HERE...
...AND SO PEACEFUL.
THE CROSS? IS THAT IT?
A STATUE?
HUH?!
A PER-SON?!

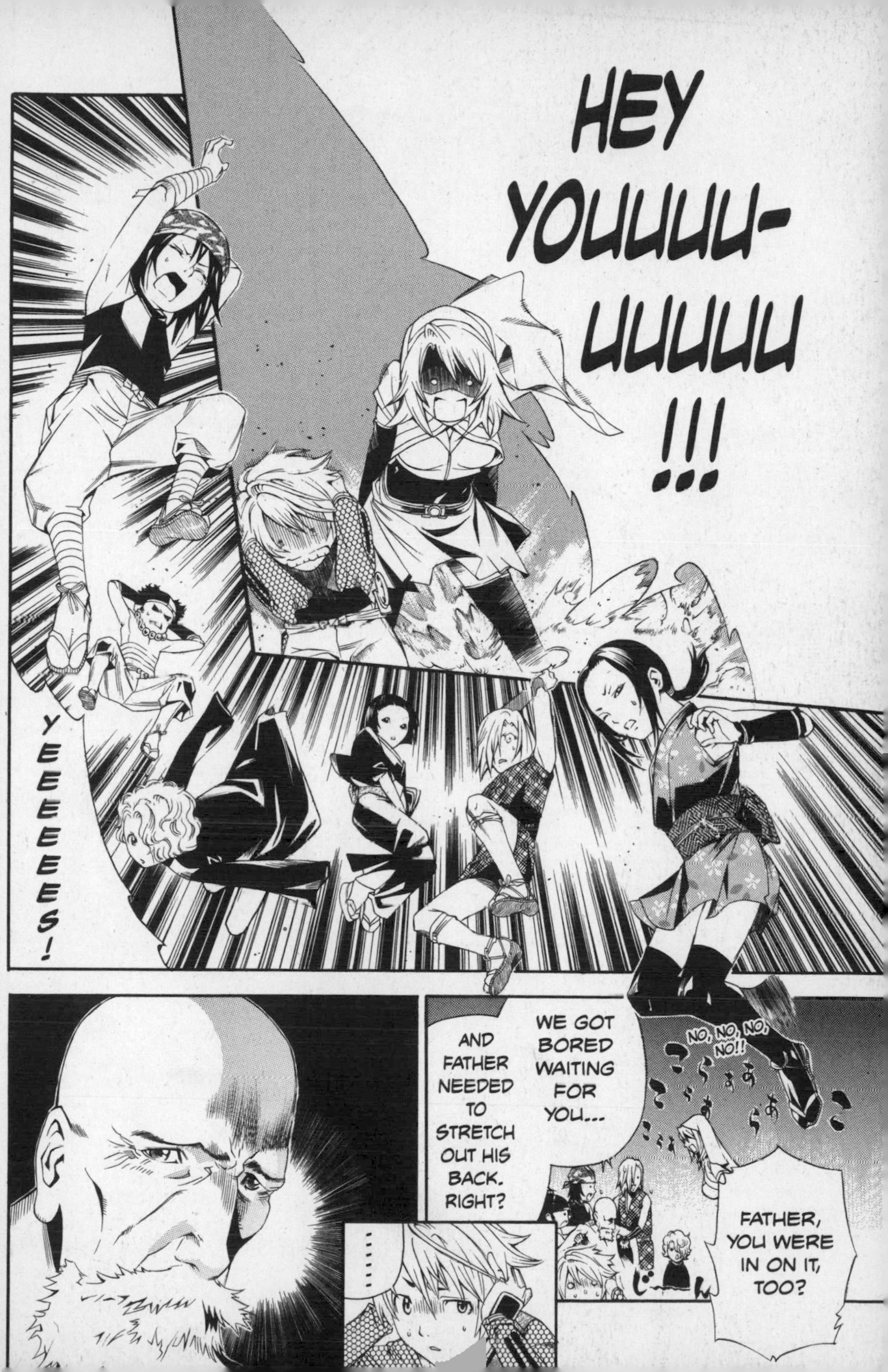
HEY YOUUUU-UUUUU!!!
YEEEEEES!
NO, NO, NO, NO!!
WE GOT BORED WAITING FOR YOU...
AND FATHER NEEDED TO STRETCH OUT HIS BACK. RIGHT?
FATHER, YOU WERE IN ON IT, TOO?
......

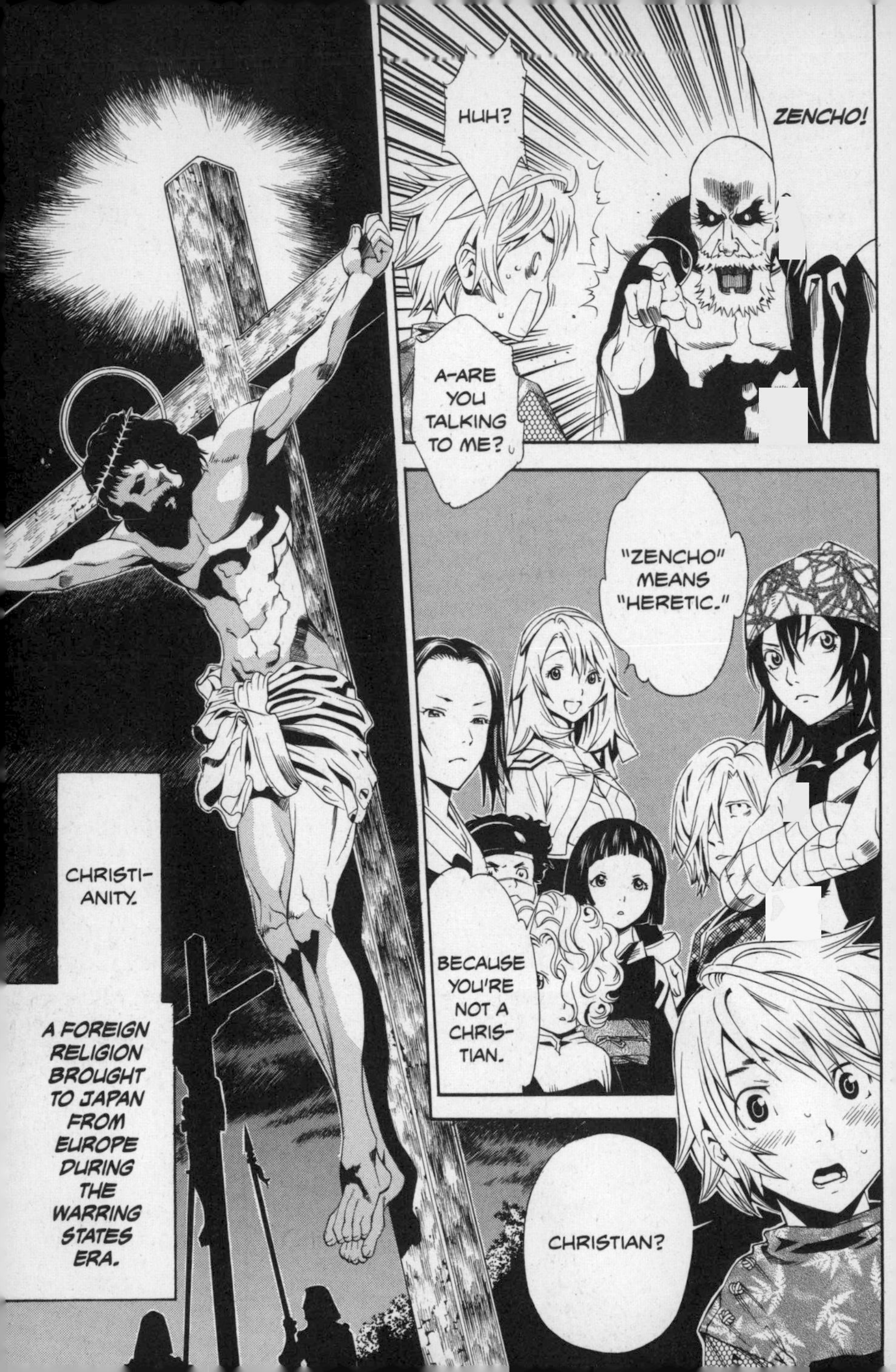
ZENCHO!
HUH?
A-ARE YOU TALKING TO ME?
"ZENCHO" MEANS "HERETIC."
BECAUSE YOU'RE NOT A CHRIS-TIAN.
CHRISTIAN?
CHRISTI-ANITY.
A FOREIGN RELIGION BROUGHT TO JAPAN FROM EUROPE DURING THE WARRING STATES ERA.

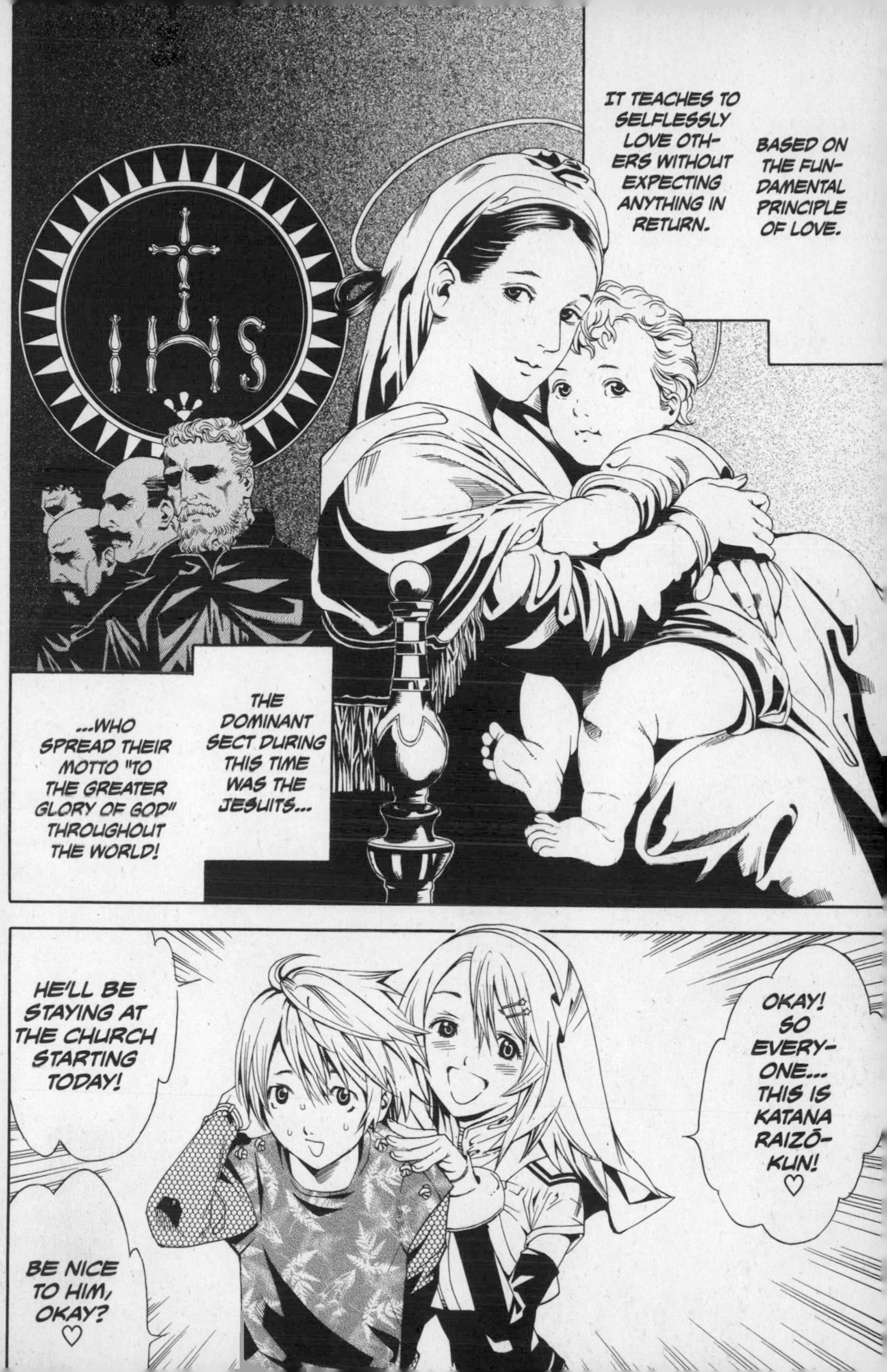
BASED ON THE FUNDAMENTAL PRINCIPLE OF LOVE.
IT TEACHES TO SELFLESSLY LOVE OTHERS WITHOUT EXPECTING ANYTHING IN RETURN.
THE DOMINANT SECT DURING THIS TIME WAS THE JESUITS...
...WHO SPREAD THEIR MOTTO "TO THE GREATER GLORY OF GOD" THROUGHOUT THE WORLD!
OKAY! SO EVERYONE... THIS IS KATANA RAIZŌ-KUN! ♡
HE'LL BE STAYING AT THE CHURCH STARTING TODAY!
BE NICE TO HIM, OKAY? ♡

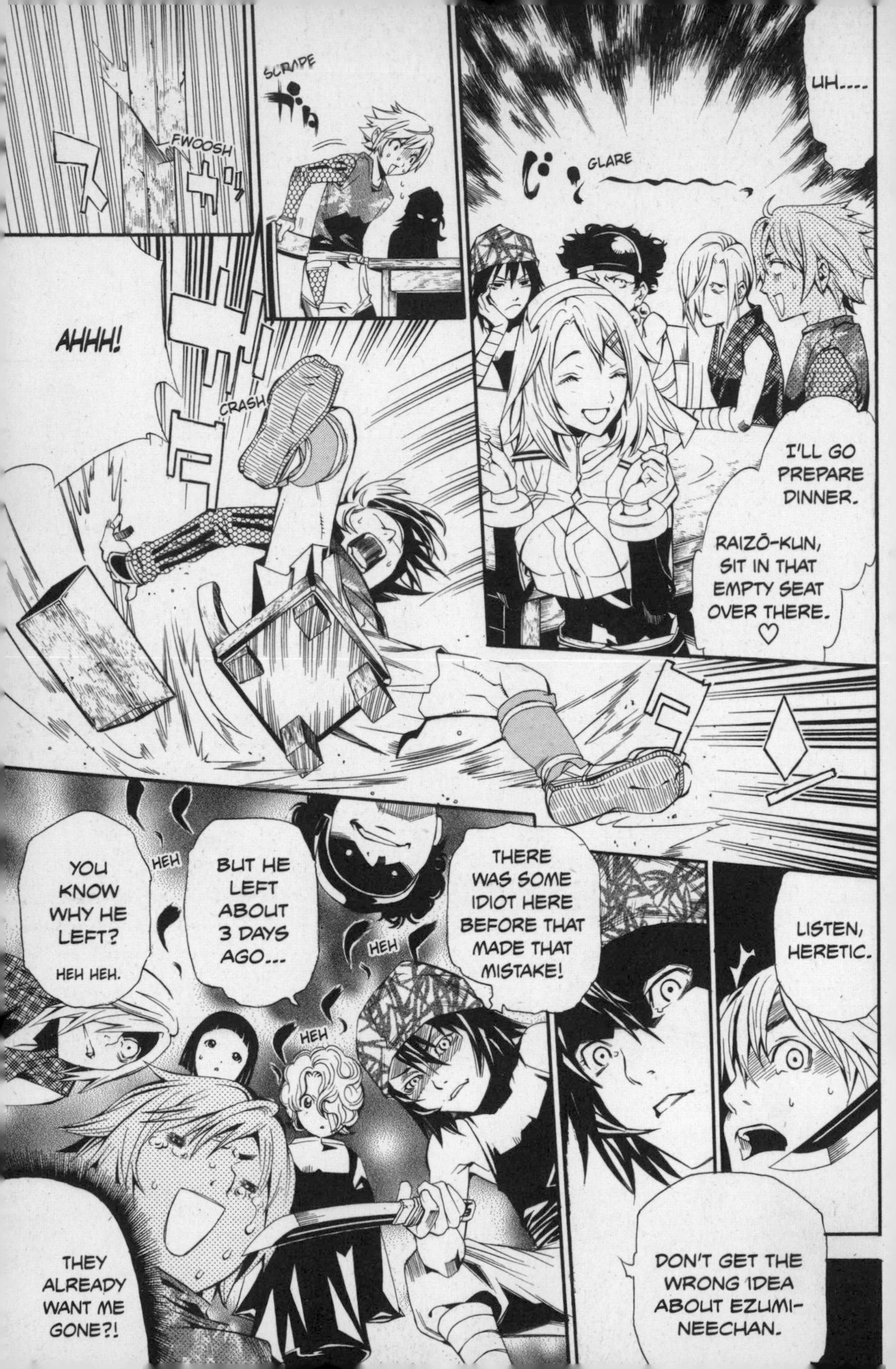
UH....
GLARE
I'LL GO PREPARE DINNER.
RAIZŌ-KUN, SIT IN THAT EMPTY SEAT OVER THERE. ♡
SCRAPE
FWOOSH
AHHH!
CRASH
LISTEN, HERETIC.
DON'T GET THE WRONG IDEA ABOUT EZUMI-NEECHAN.
THERE WAS SOME IDIOT HERE BEFORE THAT MADE THAT MISTAKE!
HEH
BUT HE LEFT ABOUT 3 DAYS AGO...
HEH
YOU KNOW WHY HE LEFT?
HEH HEH.
HEH
THEY ALREADY WANT ME GONE?!

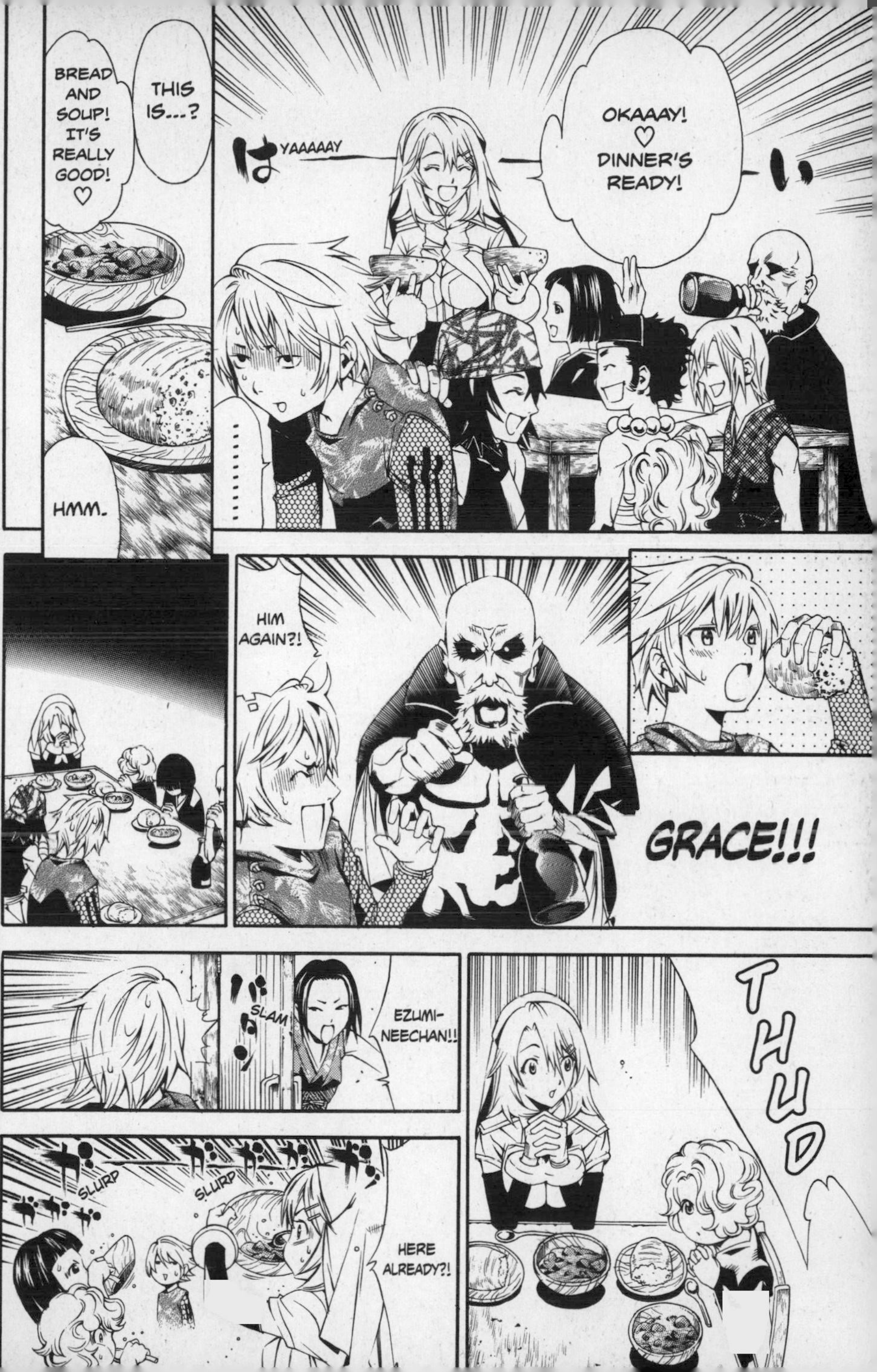
OKAAAY! ♡ DINNER'S READY!
YAAAAAY
......
THIS IS...?
BREAD AND SOUP! IT'S REALLY GOOD! ♡
HMM.
GRACE!!!
HIM AGAIN?!
THUD
EZUMI-NEECHAN!!
SLAM
HERE ALREADY?!
SLURP
SLURP

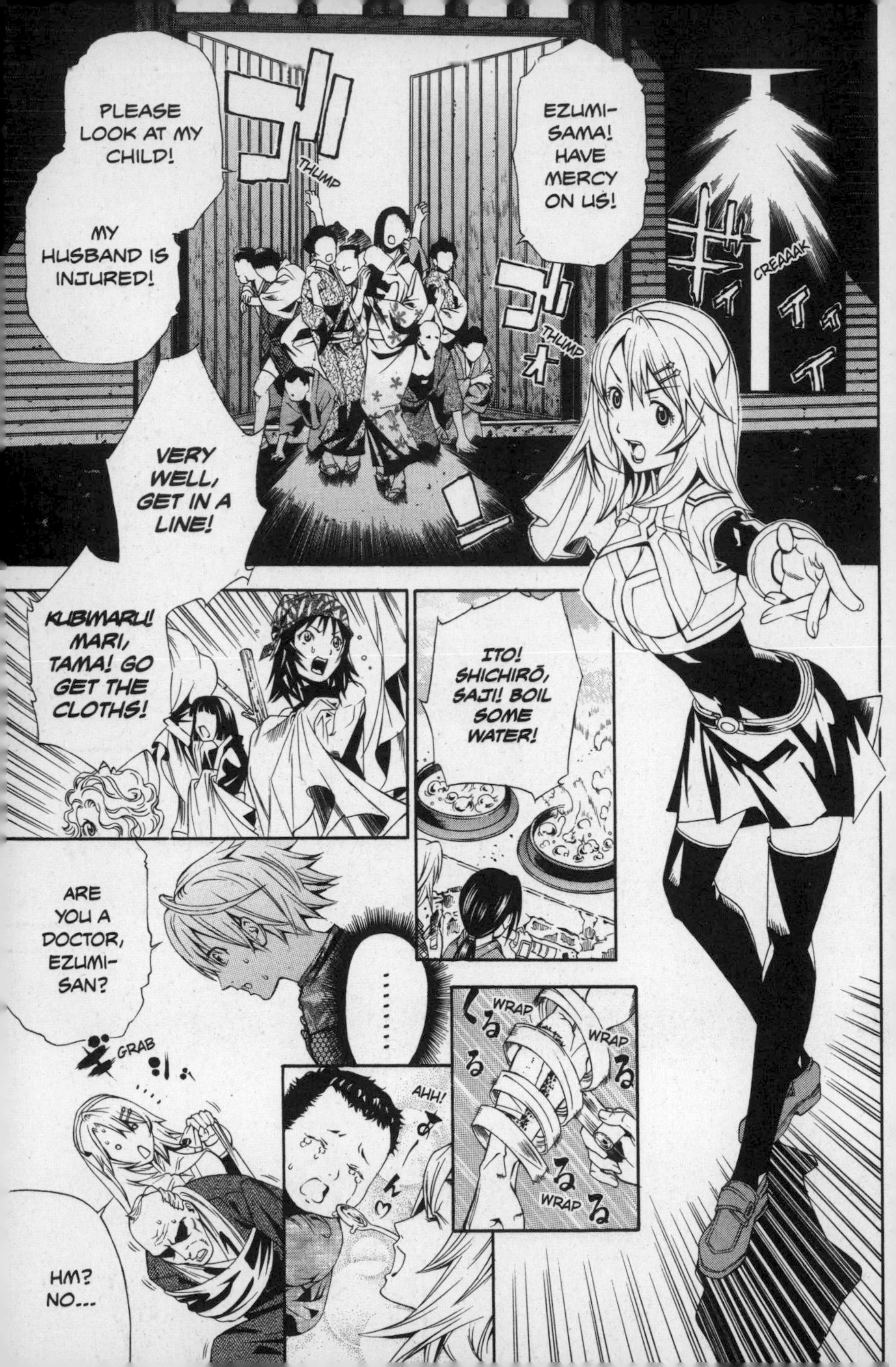
EZUMI-SAMA! HAVE MERCY ON US!
CREAAAK
THUMP
PLEASE LOOK AT MY CHILD!
THUMP
MY HUSBAND IS INJURED!
VERY WELL, GET IN A LINE!
ITO! SHICHIRŌ, SAJI! BOIL SOME WATER!
KUBIMARU! MARI, TAMA! GO GET THE CLOTHS!
WRAP
WRAP
WRAP
......
ARE YOU A DOCTOR, EZUMI-SAN?
AHH!
GRAB
HM? NO...

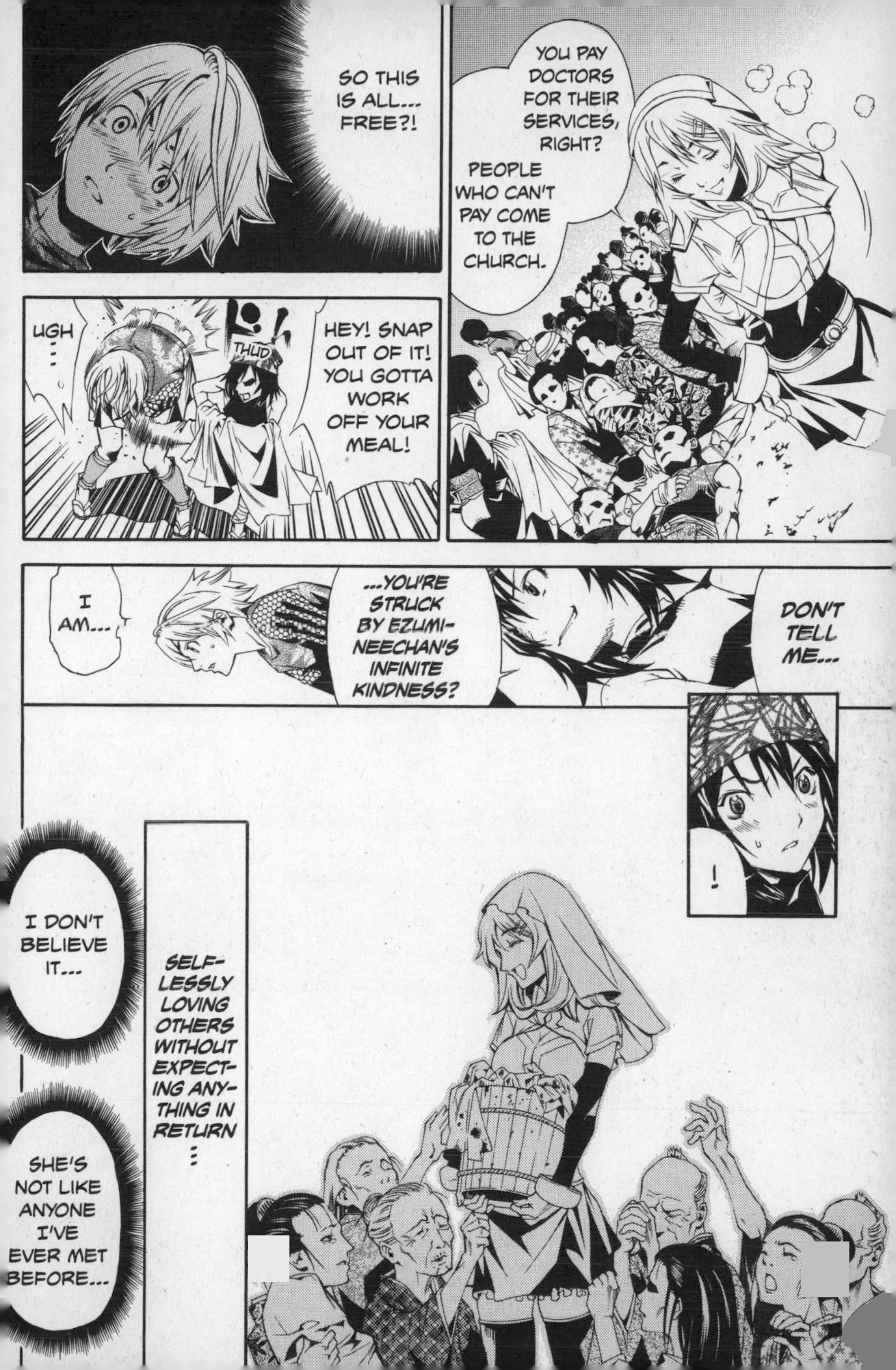
YOU PAY DOCTORS FOR THEIR SERVICES, RIGHT?
PEOPLE WHO CAN'T PAY COME TO THE CHURCH.
SO THIS IS ALL... FREE?!
HEY! SNAP OUT OF IT! YOU GOTTA WORK OFF YOUR MEAL!
THUD
UGH...
DON'T TELL ME...
...YOU'RE STRUCK BY EZUMI-NEECHAN'S INFINITE KINDNESS?
I AM...
!
SELF-LESSLY LOVING OTHERS WITHOUT EXPECT-ING ANY-THING IN RETURN...
I DON'T BELIEVE IT...
SHE'S NOT LIKE ANYONE I'VE EVER MET BEFORE...

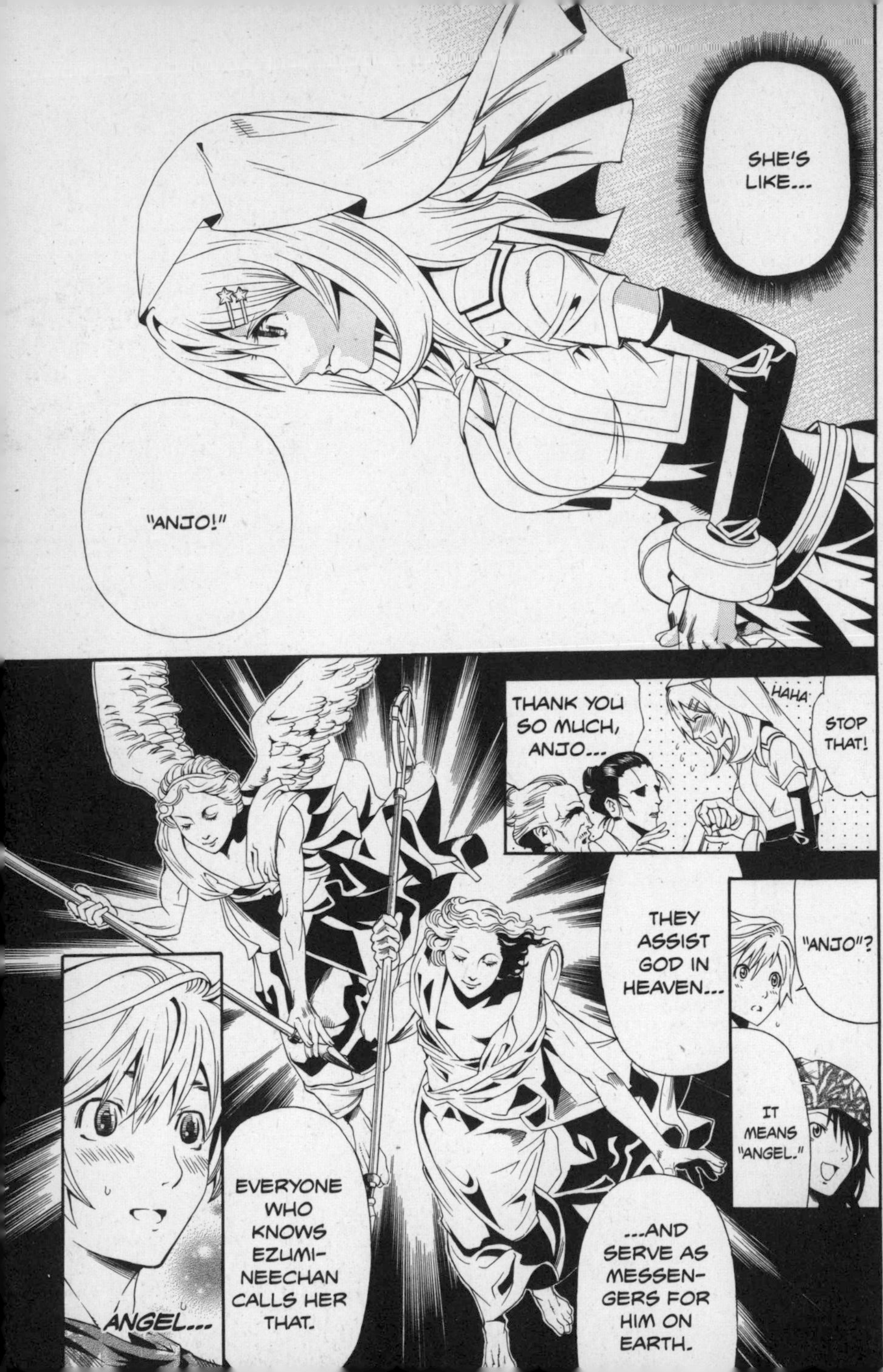
SHE'S LIKE...
"ANJO!"
STOP THAT!
HAHA
THANK YOU SO MUCH, ANJO...
"ANJO"?
IT MEANS "ANGEL."
THEY ASSIST GOD IN HEAVEN...
...AND SERVE AS MESSENGERS FOR HIM ON EARTH.
EVERYONE WHO KNOWS EZUMI-NEECHAN CALLS HER THAT.
ANGEL...

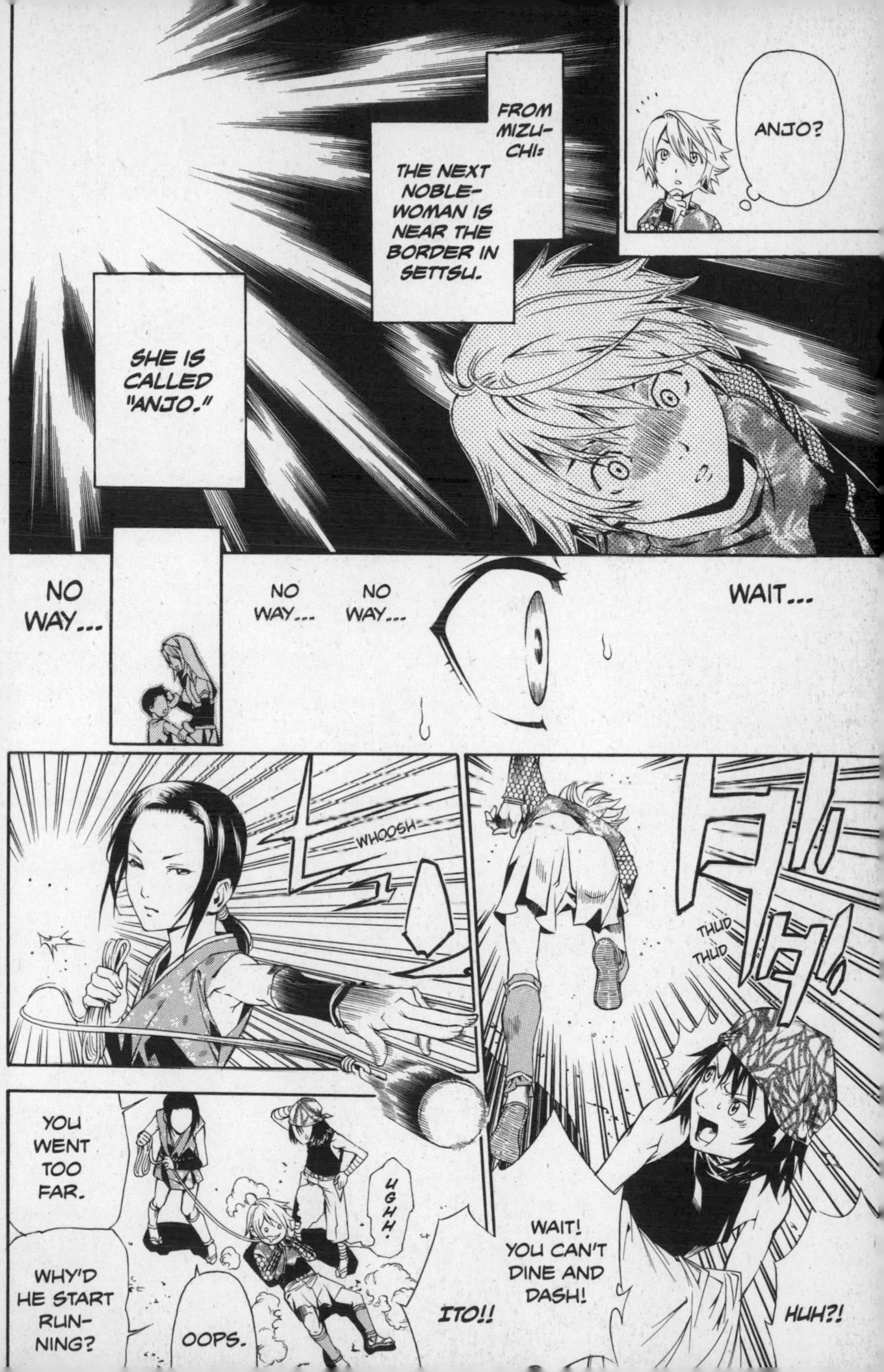

ANJO?
FROM MIZUCHI:
THE NEXT NOBLEWOMAN IS NEAR THE BORDER IN SETTSU.
SHE IS CALLED "ANJO."
WAIT...
NO WAY... NO WAY...
NO WAY...
THUD THUD
HUH?!
WAIT! YOU CAN'T DINE AND DASH!
WHOOSH
ITO!!
UGHH.
YOU WENT TOO FAR.
WHY'D HE START RUNNING?
OOPS.

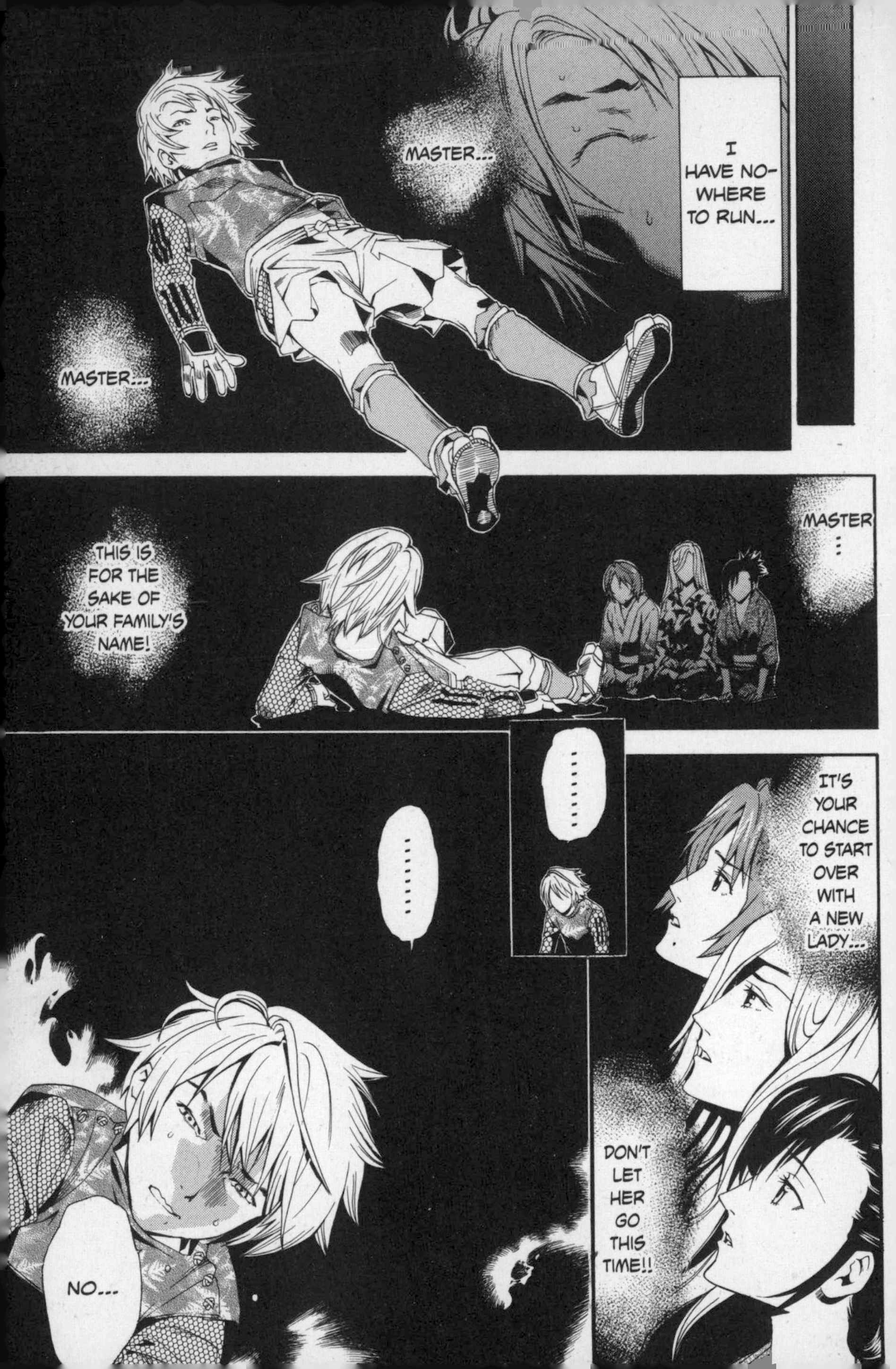

I HAVE NO-WHERE TO RUN...
MASTER...
MASTER...
MASTER ...
THIS IS FOR THE SAKE OF YOUR FAMILY'S NAME!
IT'S YOUR CHANCE TO START OVER WITH A NEW LADY...
DON'T LET HER GO THIS TIME!!
......
......
NO...

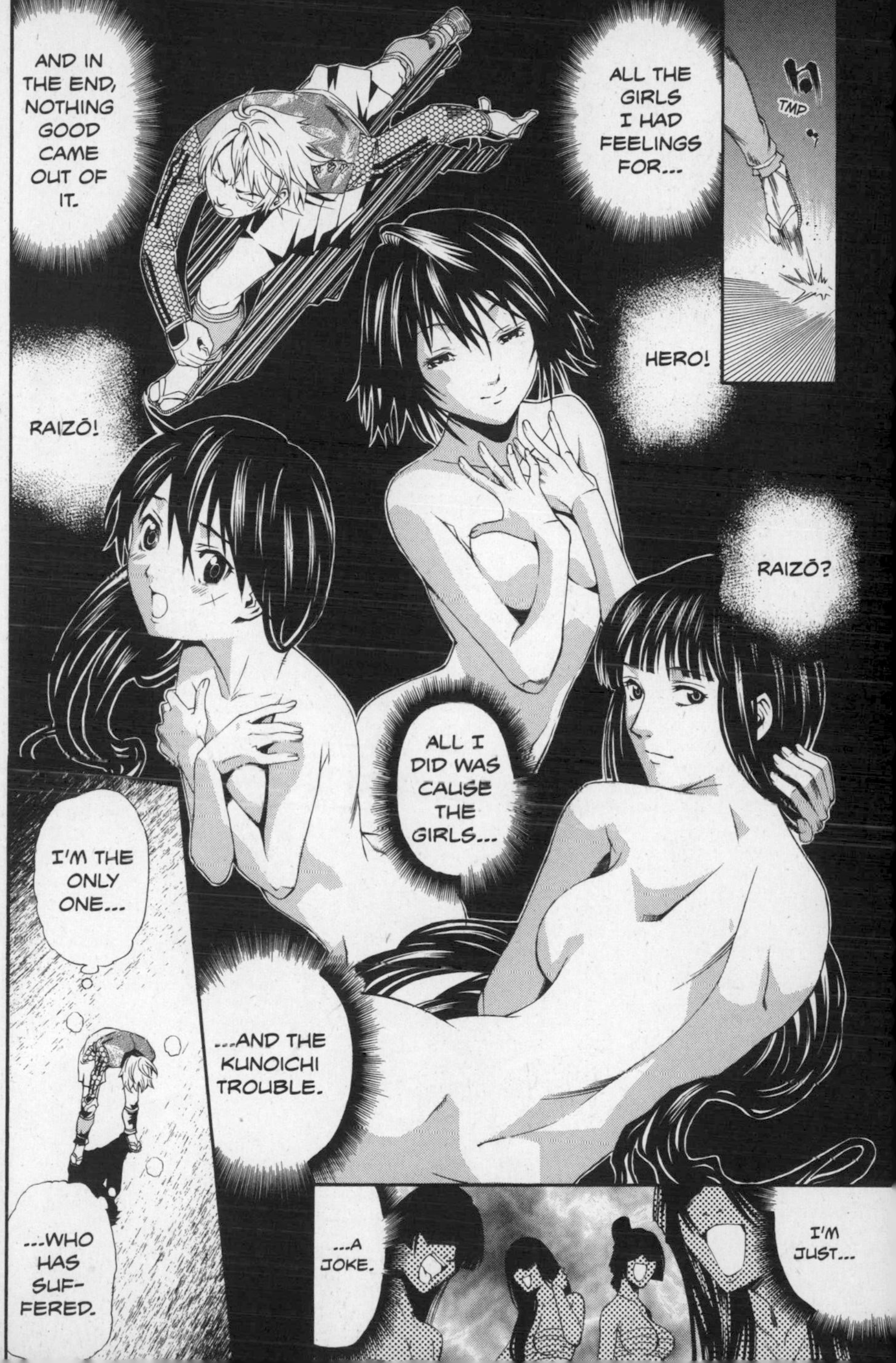
TMP
ALL THE GIRLS I HAD FEELINGS FOR...
AND IN THE END, NOTHING GOOD CAME OUT OF IT.
HERO!
RAIZŌ!
RAIZŌ?
ALL I DID WAS CAUSE THE GIRLS...
...AND THE KUNOICHI TROUBLE.
I'M JUST...
...A JOKE.
I'M THE ONLY ONE...
...WHO HAS SUF-FERED.

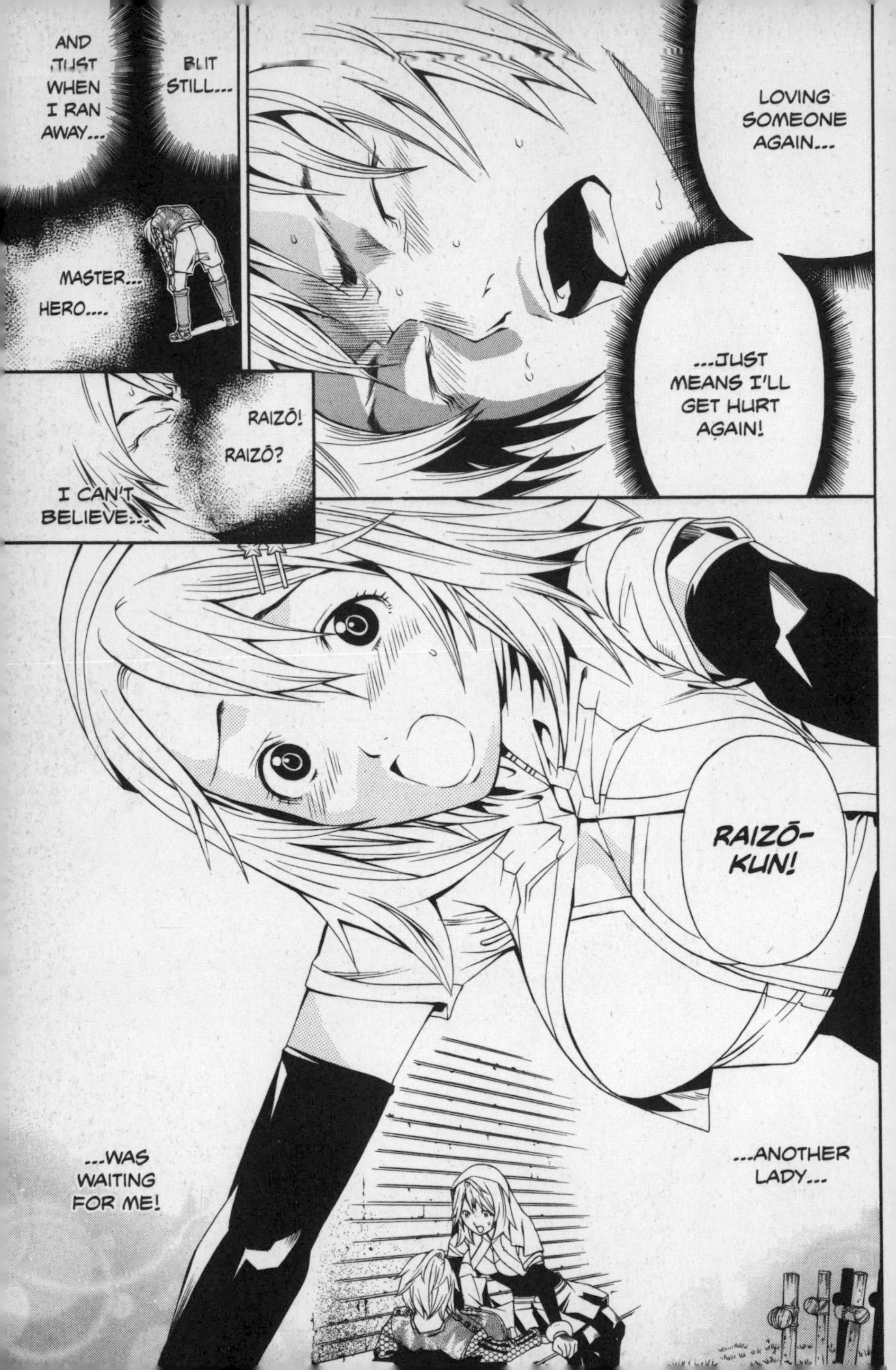
LOVING SOMEONE AGAIN...
...JUST MEANS I'LL GET HURT AGAIN!
BUT STILL...
AND JUST WHEN I RAN AWAY...
MASTER...
HERO....
RAIZŌ!
RAIZŌ?
I CAN'T BELIEVE...
RAIZŌ-KUN!
...ANOTHER LADY...
...WAS WAITING FOR ME!

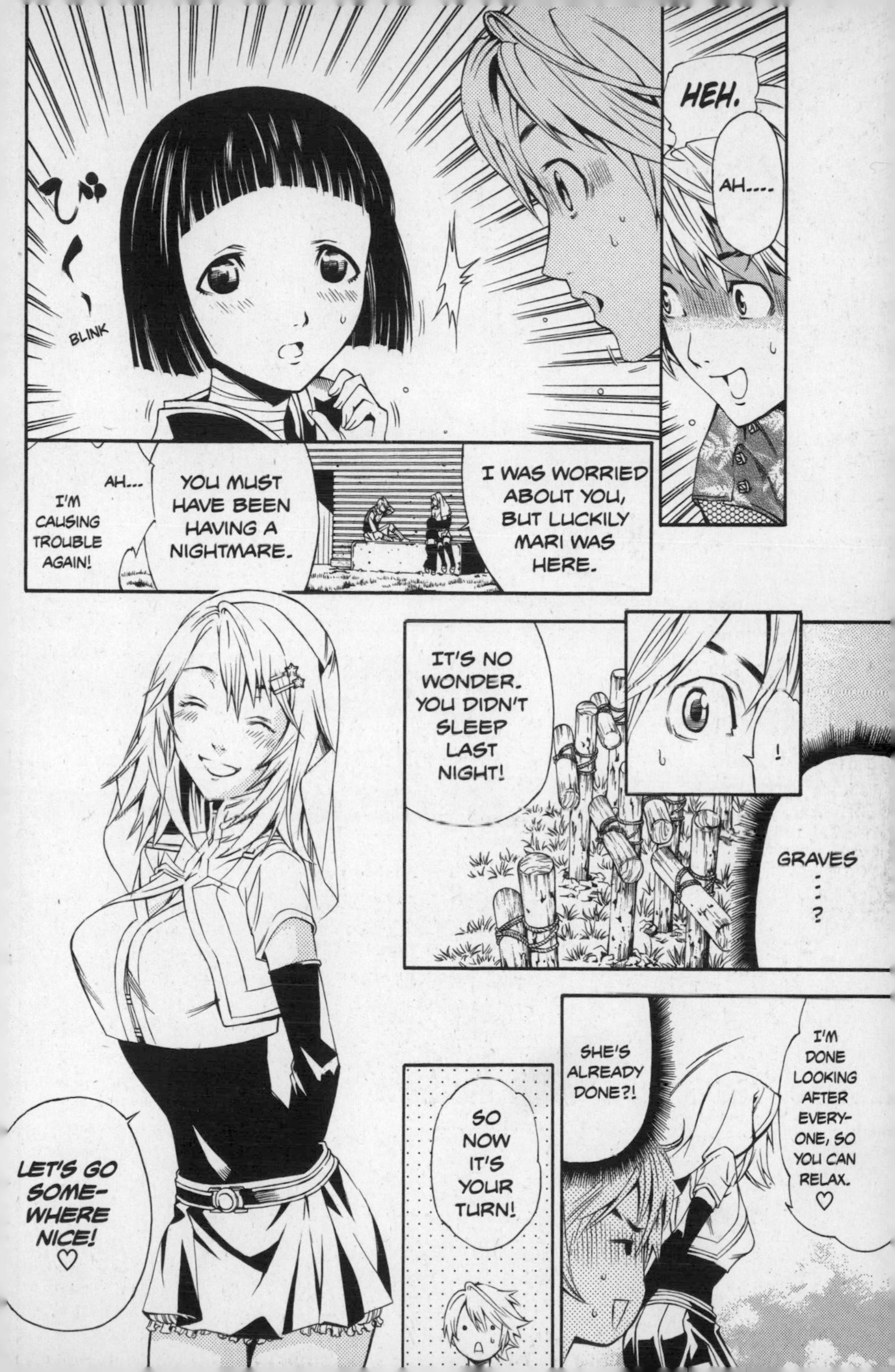
HEH.
AH....
BLINK
I WAS WORRIED ABOUT YOU, BUT LUCKILY MARI WAS HERE.
YOU MUST HAVE BEEN HAVING A NIGHTMARE.
AH...
I'M CAUSING TROUBLE AGAIN!
!
GRAVES ...?
IT'S NO WONDER. YOU DIDN'T SLEEP LAST NIGHT!
I'M DONE LOOKING AFTER EVERY-ONE, SO YOU CAN RELAX. ♡
SHE'S ALREADY DONE?!
SO NOW IT'S YOUR TURN!
LET'S GO SOME-WHERE NICE! ♡

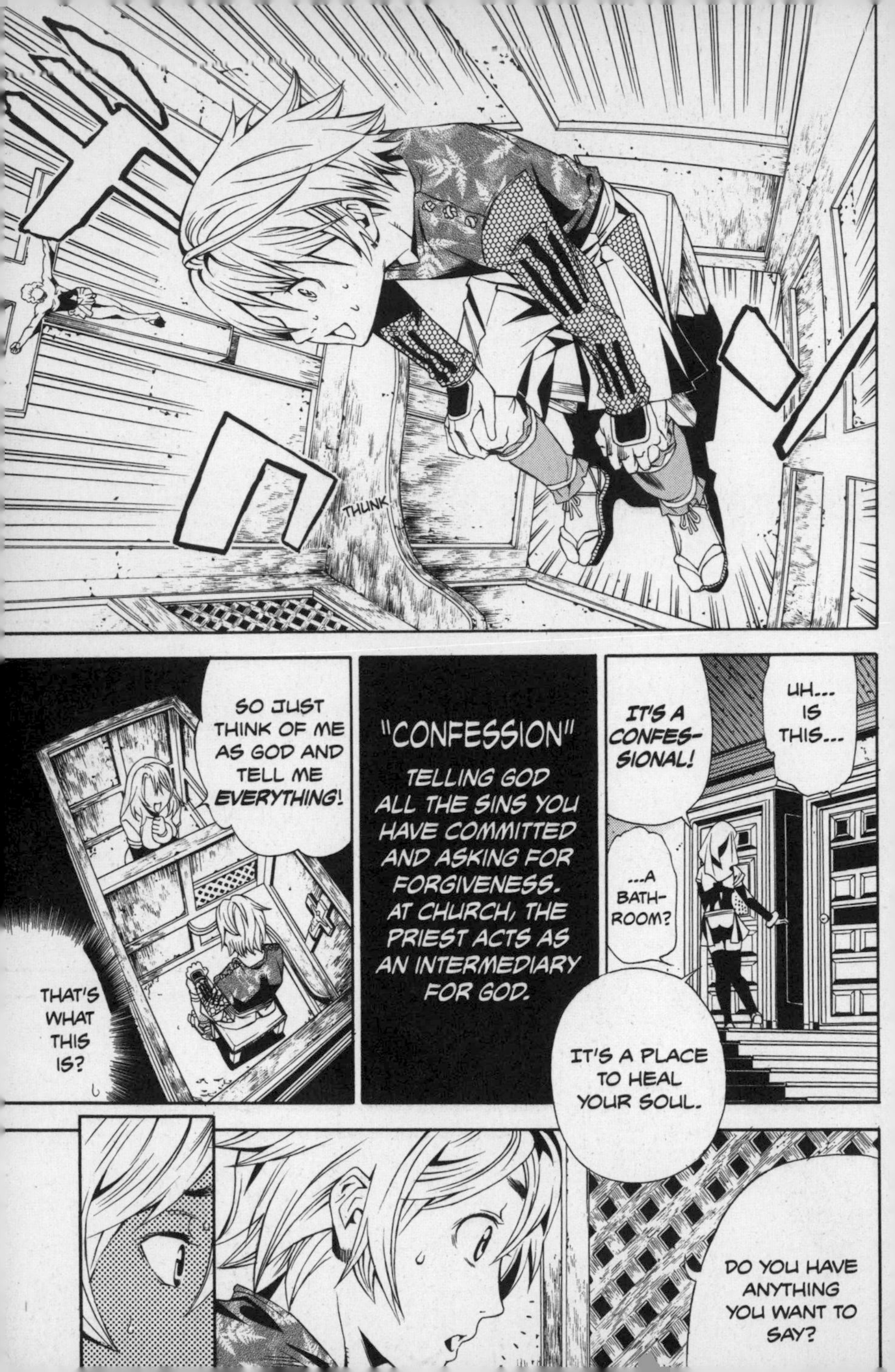
THUNK
UH... IS THIS...
...A BATH-ROOM?
IT'S A CONFES-SIONAL!
IT'S A PLACE TO HEAL YOUR SOUL.
"CONFESSION"
TELLING GOD ALL THE SINS YOU HAVE COMMITTED AND ASKING FOR FORGIVENESS. AT CHURCH, THE PRIEST ACTS AS AN INTERMEDIARY FOR GOD.
SO JUST THINK OF ME AS GOD AND TELL ME EVERYTHING!
THAT'S WHAT THIS IS?
DO YOU HAVE ANYTHING YOU WANT TO SAY?

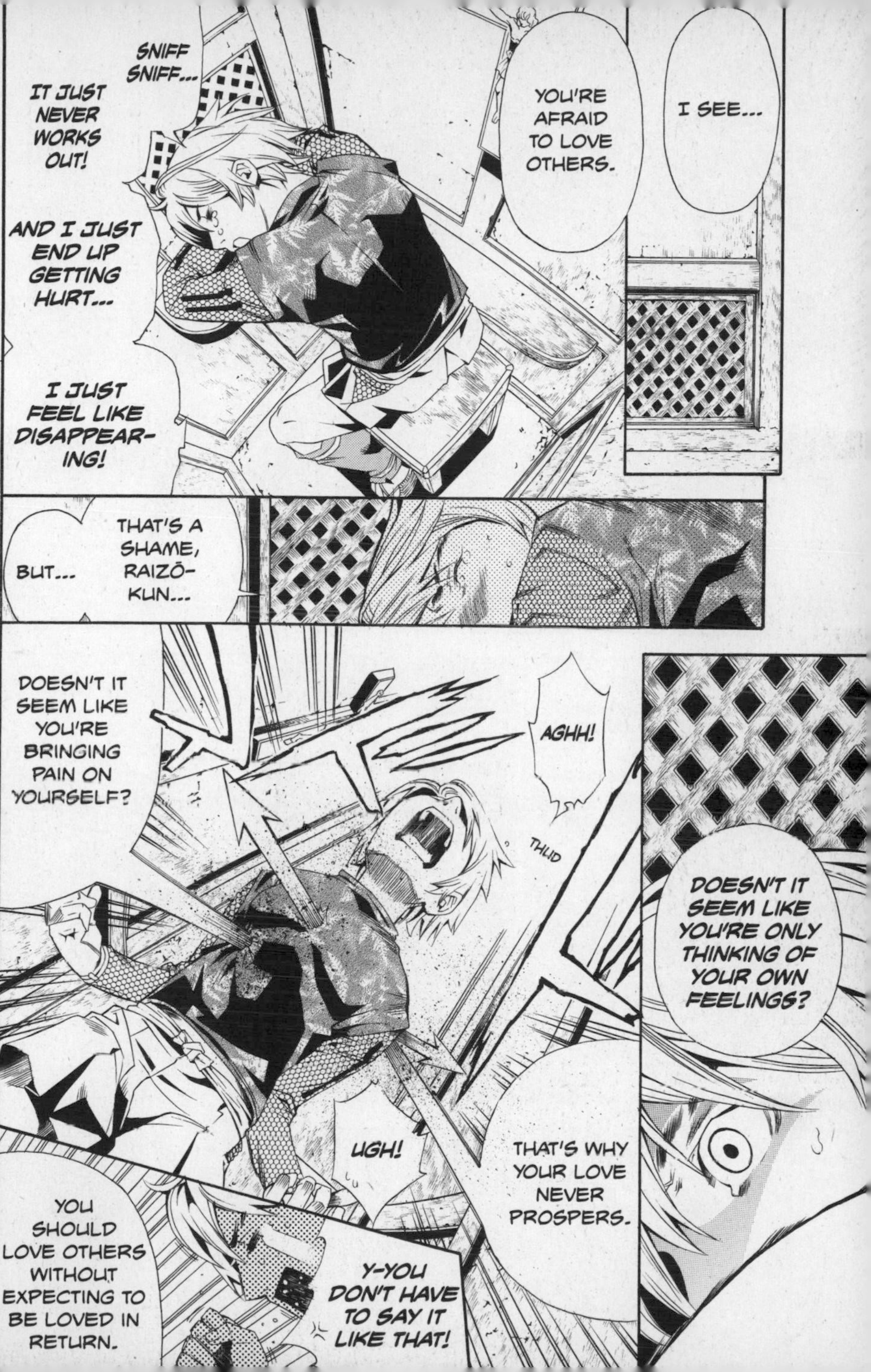
I SEE...
YOU'RE AFRAID TO LOVE OTHERS.
SNIFF SNIFF...
IT JUST NEVER WORKS OUT!
AND I JUST END UP GETTING HURT...
I JUST FEEL LIKE DISAPPEARING!
THAT'S A SHAME, RAIZŌ-KUN...
BUT...
DOESN'T IT SEEM LIKE YOU'RE ONLY THINKING OF YOUR OWN FEELINGS?
AGHH!
DOESN'T IT SEEM LIKE YOU'RE BRINGING PAIN ON YOURSELF?
THUD
THAT'S WHY YOUR LOVE NEVER PROSPERS.
UGH!
Y-YOU DON'T HAVE TO SAY IT LIKE THAT!
YOU SHOULD LOVE OTHERS WITHOUT EXPECTING TO BE LOVED IN RETURN.

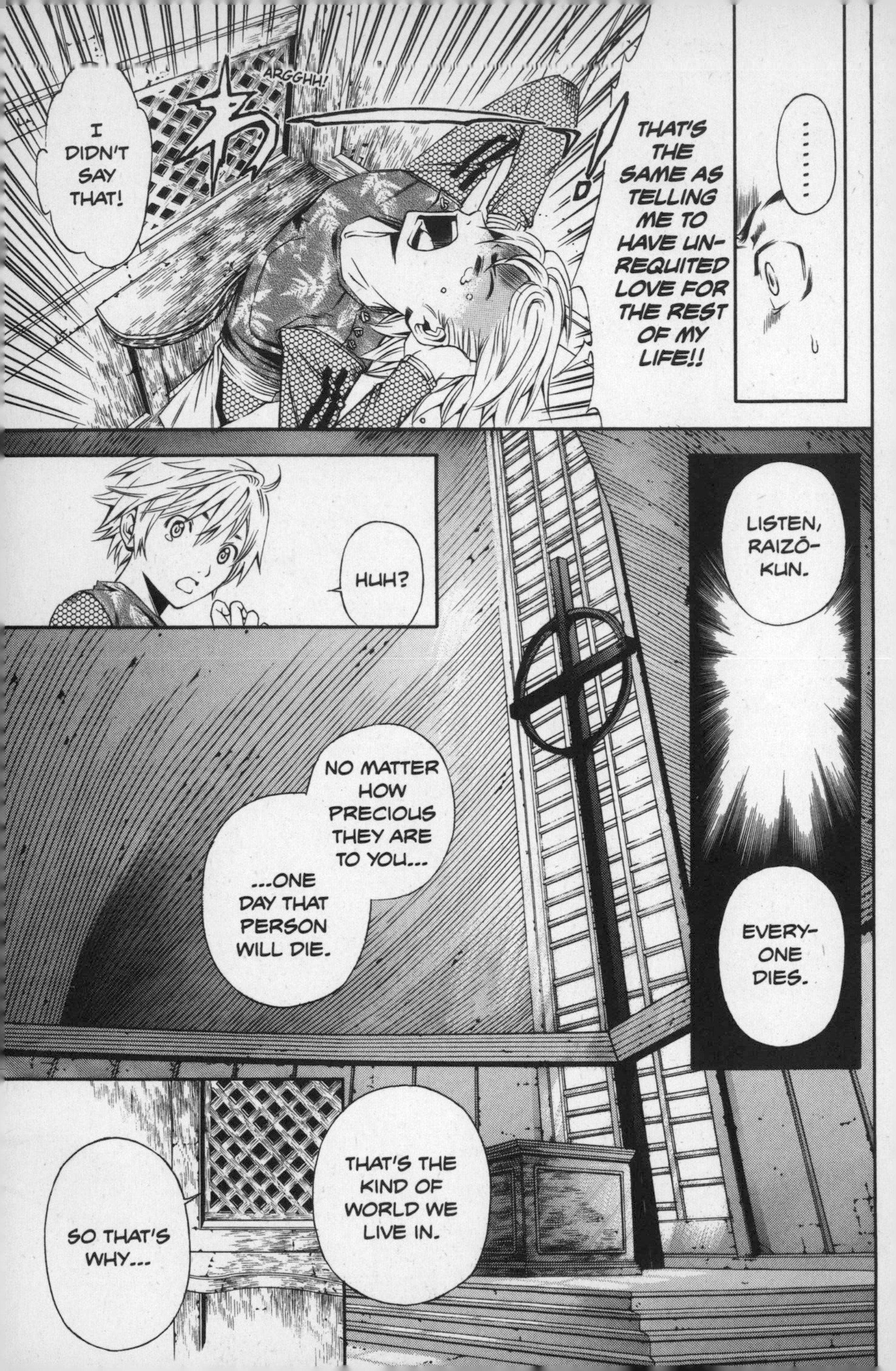
......
THAT'S THE SAME AS TELLING ME TO HAVE UN-REQUITED LOVE FOR THE REST OF MY LIFE!!
ARGGHH!
I DIDN'T SAY THAT!
LISTEN, RAIZŌ-KUN.
EVERY-ONE DIES.
HUH?
NO MATTER HOW PRECIOUS THEY ARE TO YOU...
...ONE DAY THAT PERSON WILL DIE.
THAT'S THE KIND OF WORLD WE LIVE IN.
SO THAT'S WHY...

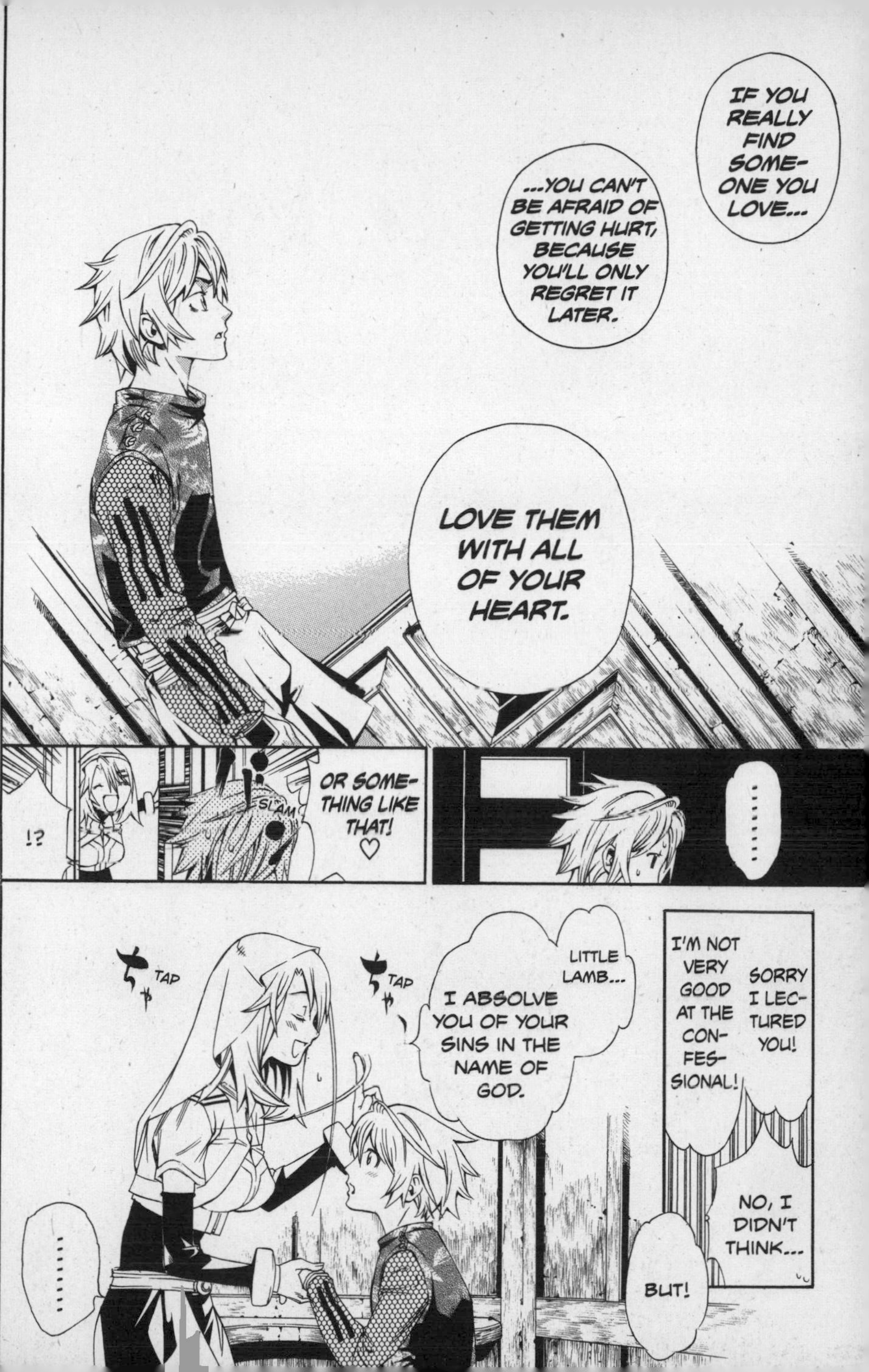
IF YOU REALLY FIND SOME-ONE YOU LOVE...
...YOU CAN'T BE AFRAID OF GETTING HURT, BECAUSE YOU'LL ONLY REGRET IT LATER.
LOVE THEM WITH ALL OF YOUR HEART.
....
OR SOME-THING LIKE THAT! ♡
SLAM
!?
SORRY I LEC-TURED YOU!
I'M NOT VERY GOOD AT THE CON-FES-SIONAL!
LITTLE LAMB...
I ABSOLVE YOU OF YOUR SINS IN THE NAME OF GOD.
TAP
TAP
NO, I DIDN'T THINK...
BUT!
....

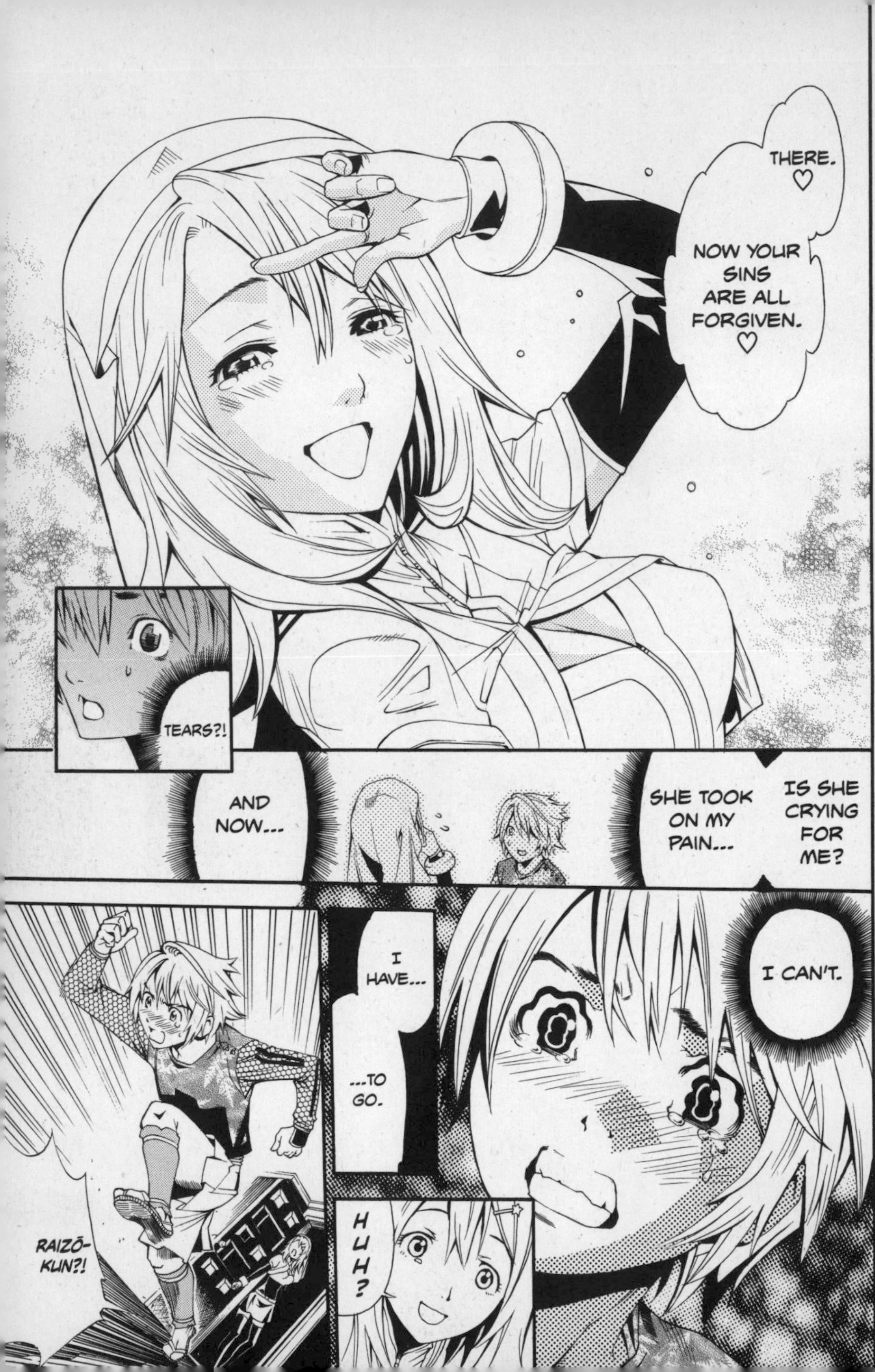
THERE. ♡
NOW YOUR SINS ARE ALL FORGIVEN. ♡
TEARS?!
IS SHE CRYING FOR ME?
SHE TOOK ON MY PAIN...
AND NOW...
I CAN'T.
I HAVE...
...TO GO.
HUH?
RAIZŌ-KUN?!

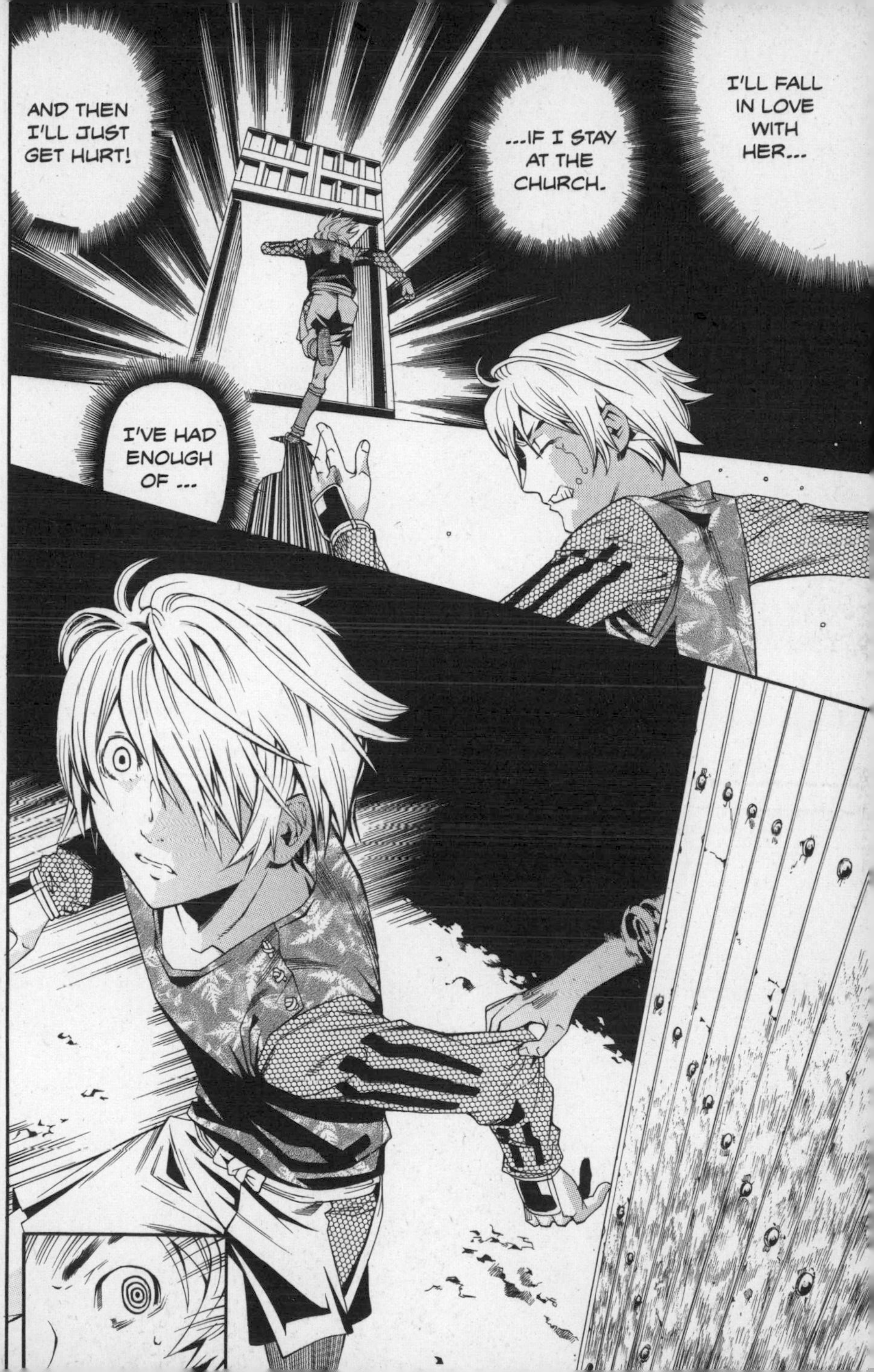
I'LL FALL IN LOVE WITH HER...
...IF I STAY AT THE CHURCH.
AND THEN I'LL JUST GET HURT!
I'VE HAD ENOUGH OF ...

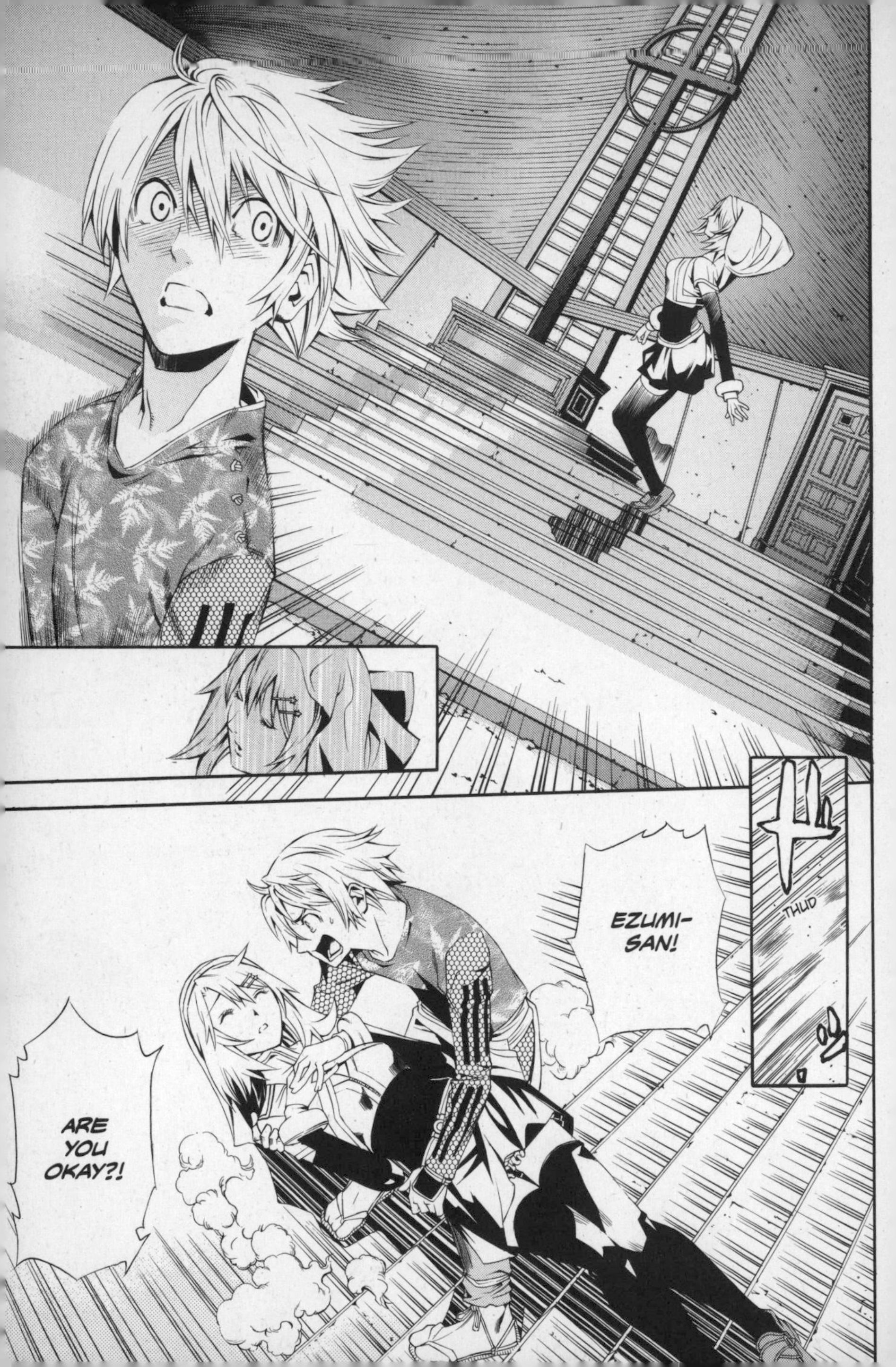
THUD
EZUMI-SAN!
ARE YOU OKAY?!

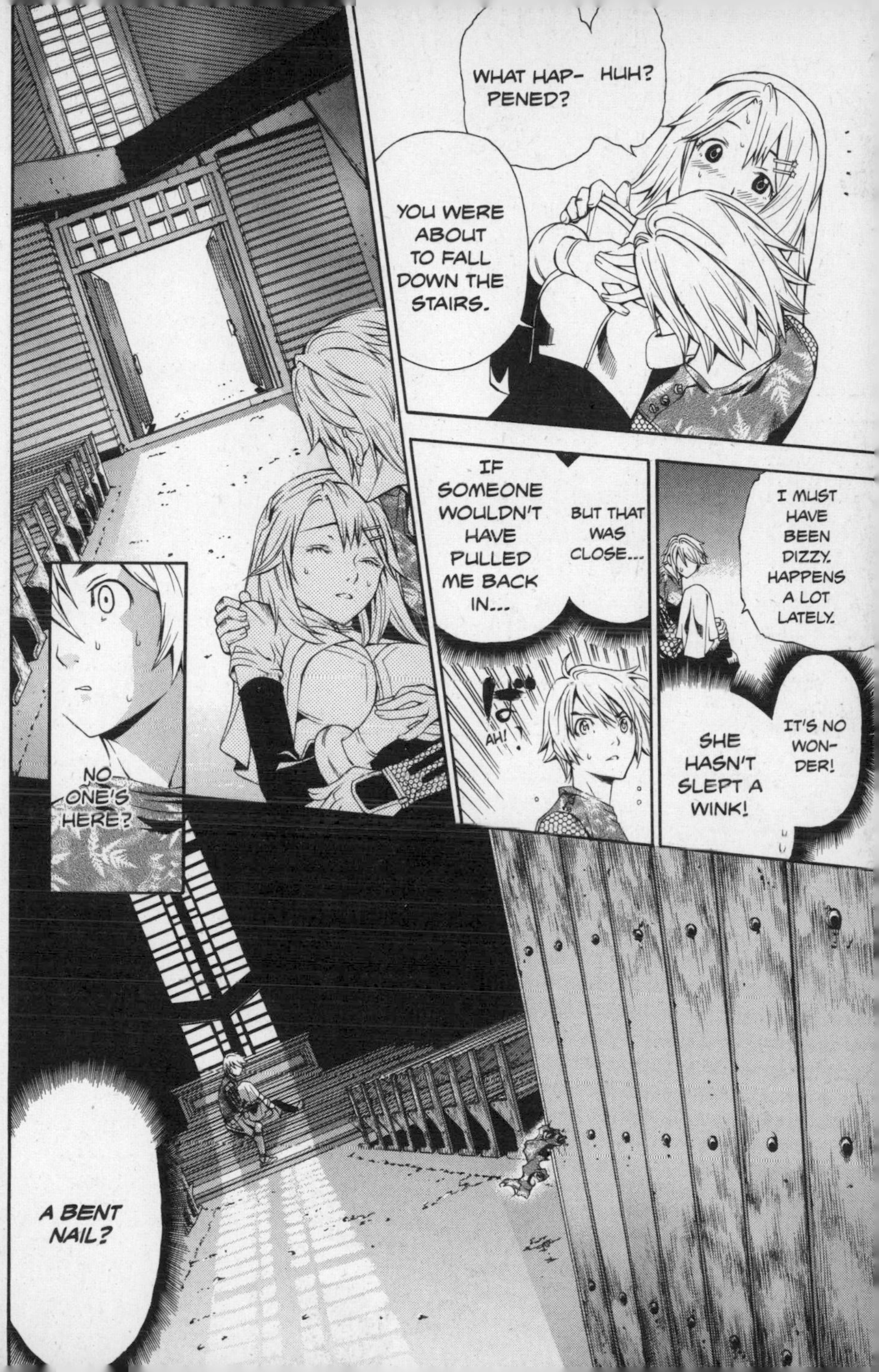
HUH?
WHAT HAP- PENED?
YOU WERE ABOUT TO FALL DOWN THE STAIRS.
I MUST HAVE BEEN DIZZY. HAPPENS A LOT LATELY.
IT'S NO WON- DER!
SHE HASN'T SLEPT A WINK!
BUT THAT WAS CLOSE...
IF SOMEONE WOULDN'T HAVE PULLED ME BACK IN...
AH!
NO ONE'S HERE?
A BENT NAIL?

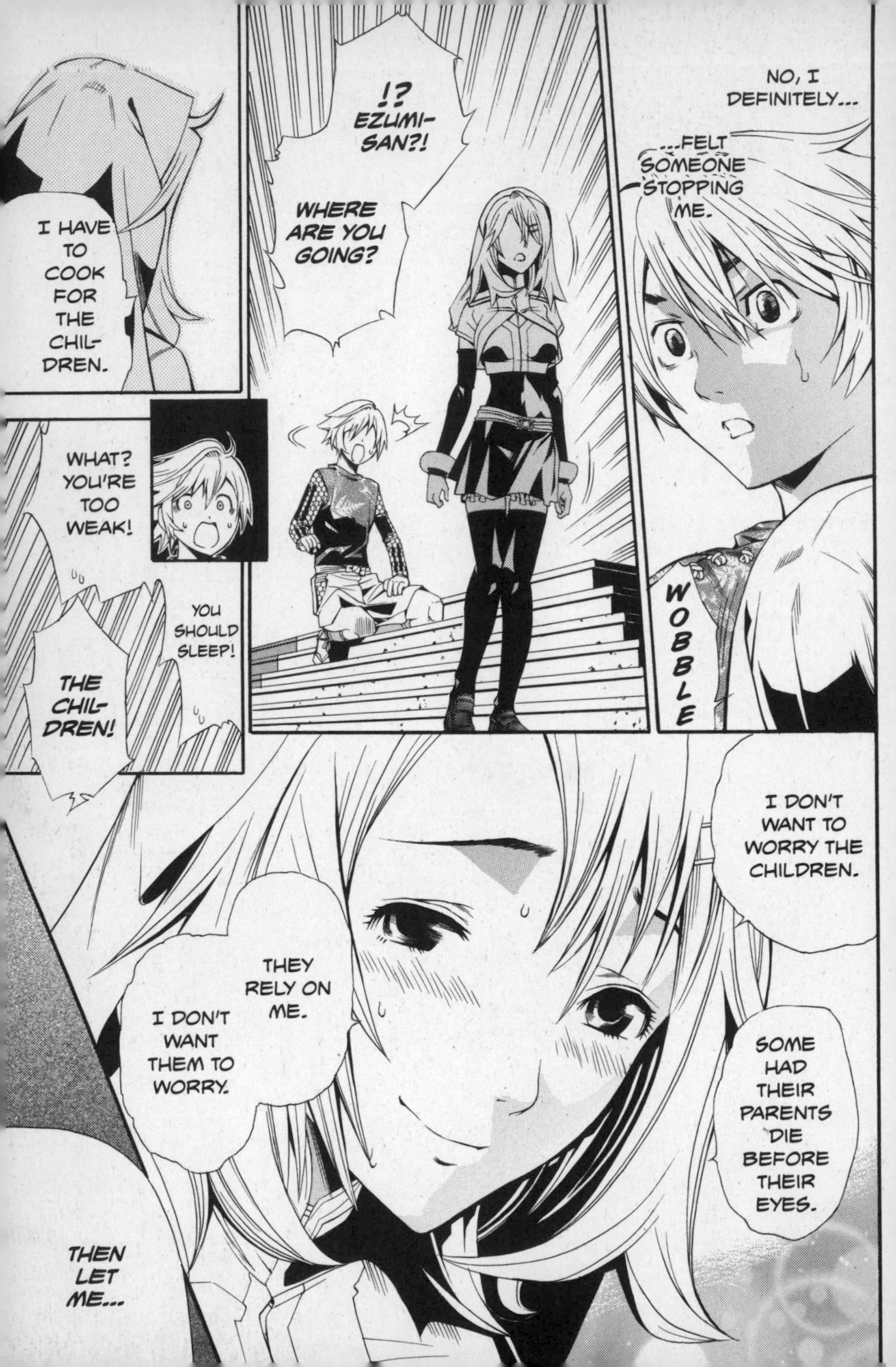
NO, I DEFINITELY...
...FELT SOMEONE STOPPING ME.
WOBBLE
!? EZUMI-SAN?!
WHERE ARE YOU GOING?
I HAVE TO COOK FOR THE CHIL-DREN.
WHAT? YOU'RE TOO WEAK!
YOU SHOULD SLEEP!
THE CHIL-DREN!
I DON'T WANT TO WORRY THE CHILDREN.
SOME HAD THEIR PARENTS DIE BEFORE THEIR EYES.
THEY RELY ON ME.
I DON'T WANT THEM TO WORRY.
THEN LET ME...

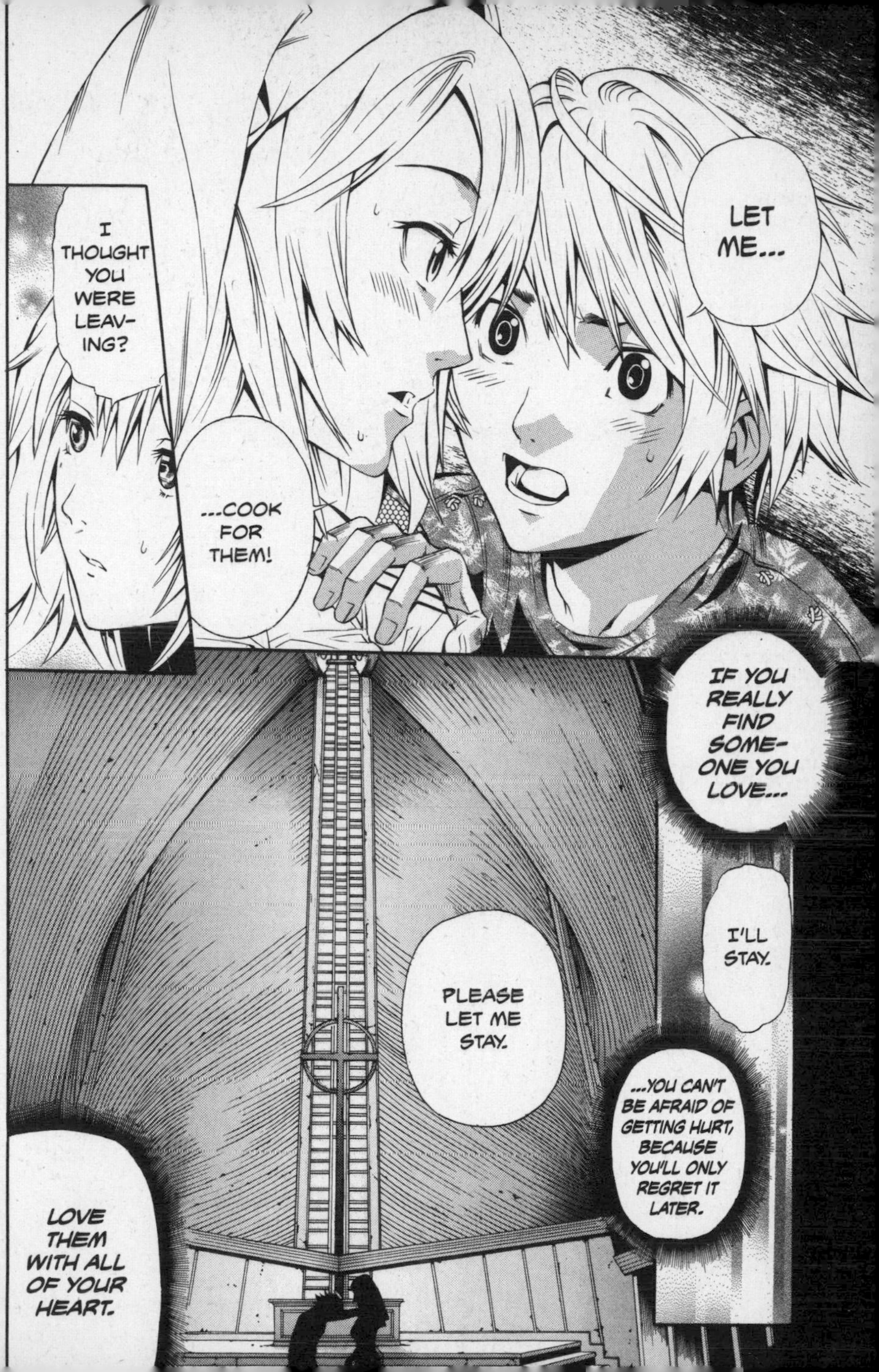
LET ME...
...COOK FOR THEM!
I THOUGHT YOU WERE LEAV-ING?
IF YOU REALLY FIND SOME-ONE YOU LOVE...
I'LL STAY.
PLEASE LET ME STAY.
...YOU CAN'T BE AFRAID OF GETTING HURT, BECAUSE YOU'LL ONLY REGRET IT LATER.
LOVE THEM WITH ALL OF YOUR HEART.

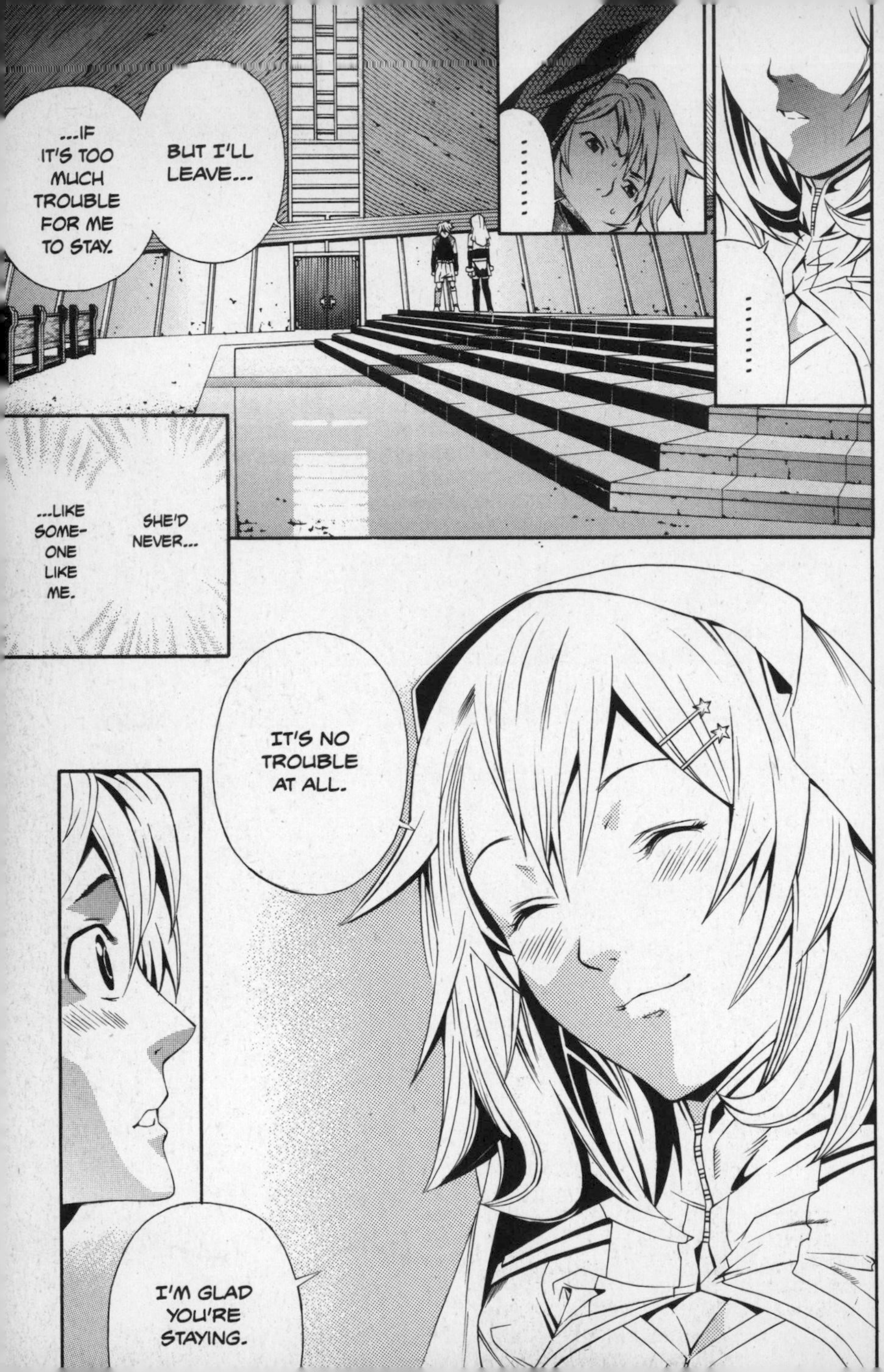
......
......
BUT I'LL LEAVE...
...IF IT'S TOO MUCH TROUBLE FOR ME TO STAY.
SHE'D NEVER...
...LIKE SOME-ONE LIKE ME.
IT'S NO TROUBLE AT ALL.
I'M GLAD YOU'RE STAYING.

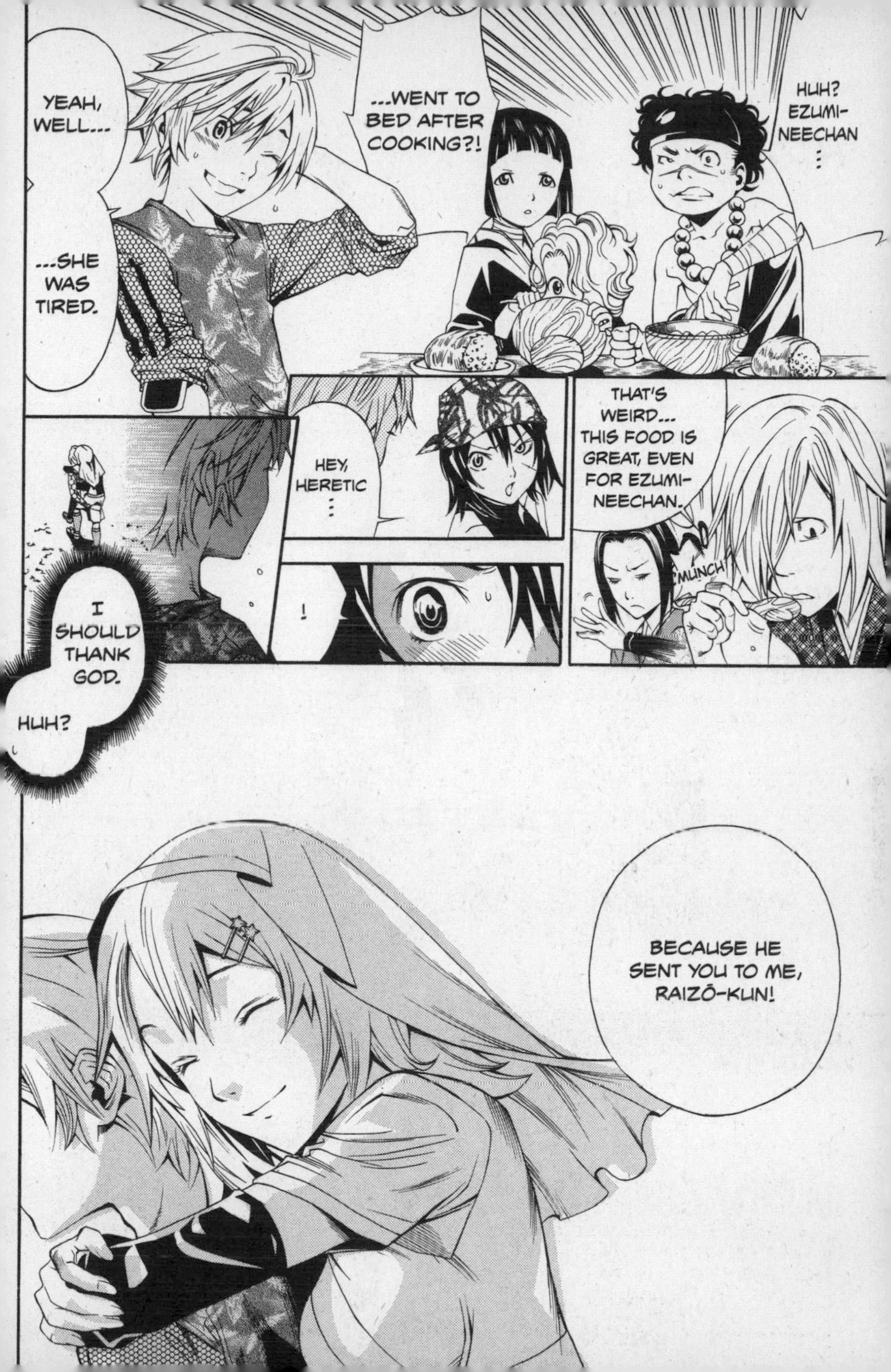
HUH? EZUMI-NEECHAN ...
...WENT TO BED AFTER COOKING?!
YEAH, WELL...
...SHE WAS TIRED.
THAT'S WEIRD... THIS FOOD IS GREAT, EVEN FOR EZUMI-NEECHAN..
MUNCH
HEY, HERETIC ...
!
I SHOULD THANK GOD.
HUH?
BECAUSE HE SENT YOU TO ME, RAIZŌ-KUN!

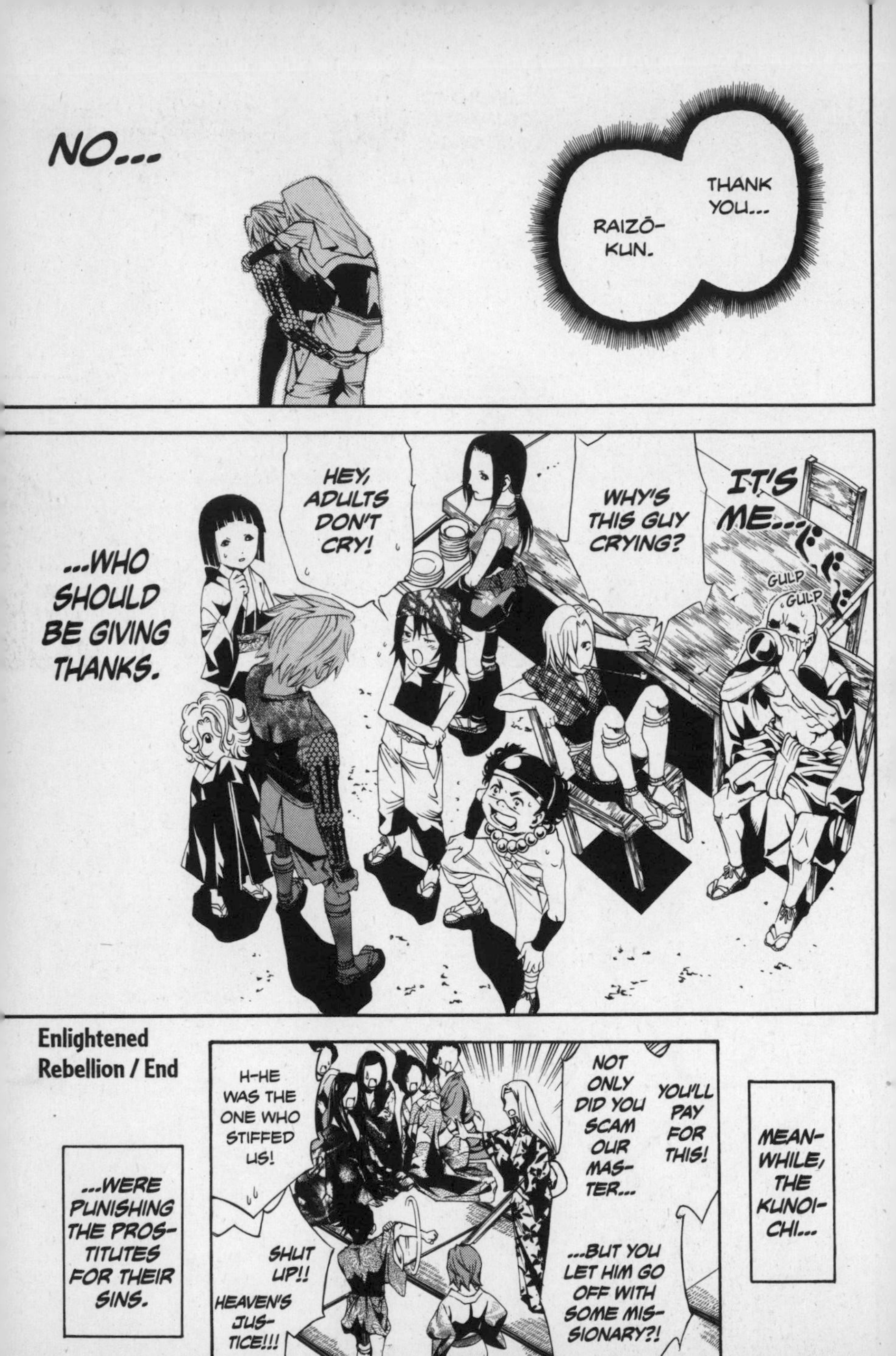
THANK YOU... RAIZŌ-KUN.
NO...
IT'S ME...
GULP GULP
WHY'S THIS GUY CRYING?
HEY, ADULTS DON'T CRY!
...WHO SHOULD BE GIVING THANKS.
MEANWHILE, THE KUNOICHI...
YOU'LL PAY FOR THIS!
NOT ONLY DID YOU SCAM OUR MASTER...
H-HE WAS THE ONE WHO STIFFED US!
...BUT YOU LET HIM GO OFF WITH SOME MISSIONARY?!
SHUT UP!! HEAVEN'S JUSTICE!!!
...WERE PUNISHING THE PROSTITUTES FOR THEIR SINS.
Enlightened Rebellion / End

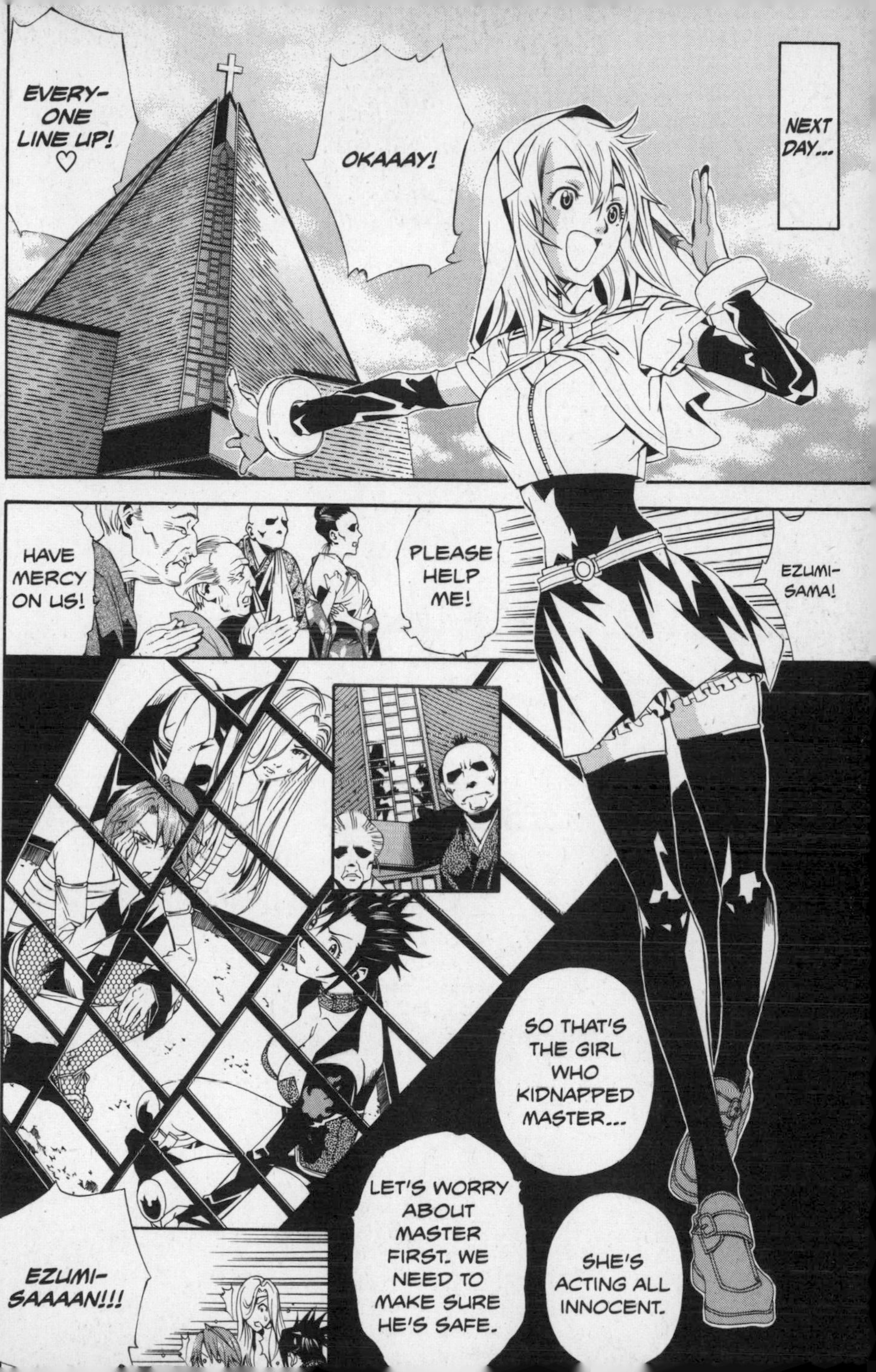
NEXT DAY...
OKAAAY!
EVERY-ONE LINE UP! ♡
EZUMI-SAMA!
PLEASE HELP ME!
HAVE MERCY ON US!
SO THAT'S THE GIRL WHO KIDNAPPED MASTER...
SHE'S ACTING ALL INNOCENT.
LET'S WORRY ABOUT MASTER FIRST. WE NEED TO MAKE SURE HE'S SAFE.
EZUMI-SAAAAN!!!

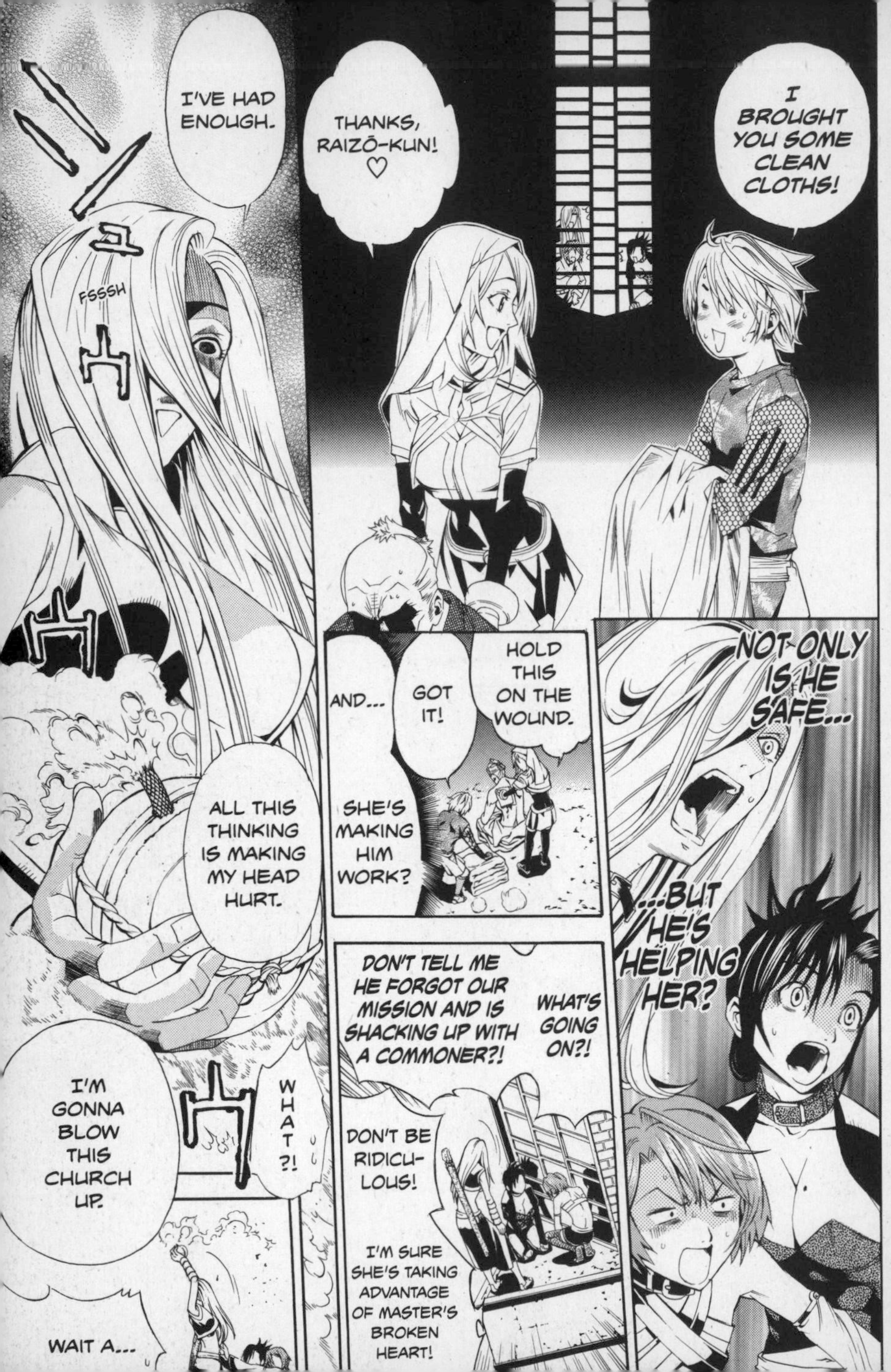
I BROUGHT YOU SOME CLEAN CLOTHS!
THANKS, RAIZŌ-KUN! ♡
NOT ONLY IS HE SAFE...
...BUT HE'S HELPING HER?
HOLD THIS ON THE WOUND.
GOT IT!
AND...
SHE'S MAKING HIM WORK?
WHAT'S GOING ON?!
DON'T TELL ME HE FORGOT OUR MISSION AND IS SHACKING UP WITH A COMMONER?!
DON'T BE RIDICULOUS!
I'M SURE SHE'S TAKING ADVANTAGE OF MASTER'S BROKEN HEART!
I'VE HAD ENOUGH.
FSSSH
ALL THIS THINKING IS MAKING MY HEAD HURT.
I'M GONNA BLOW THIS CHURCH UP.
WHAT?!
WAIT A...

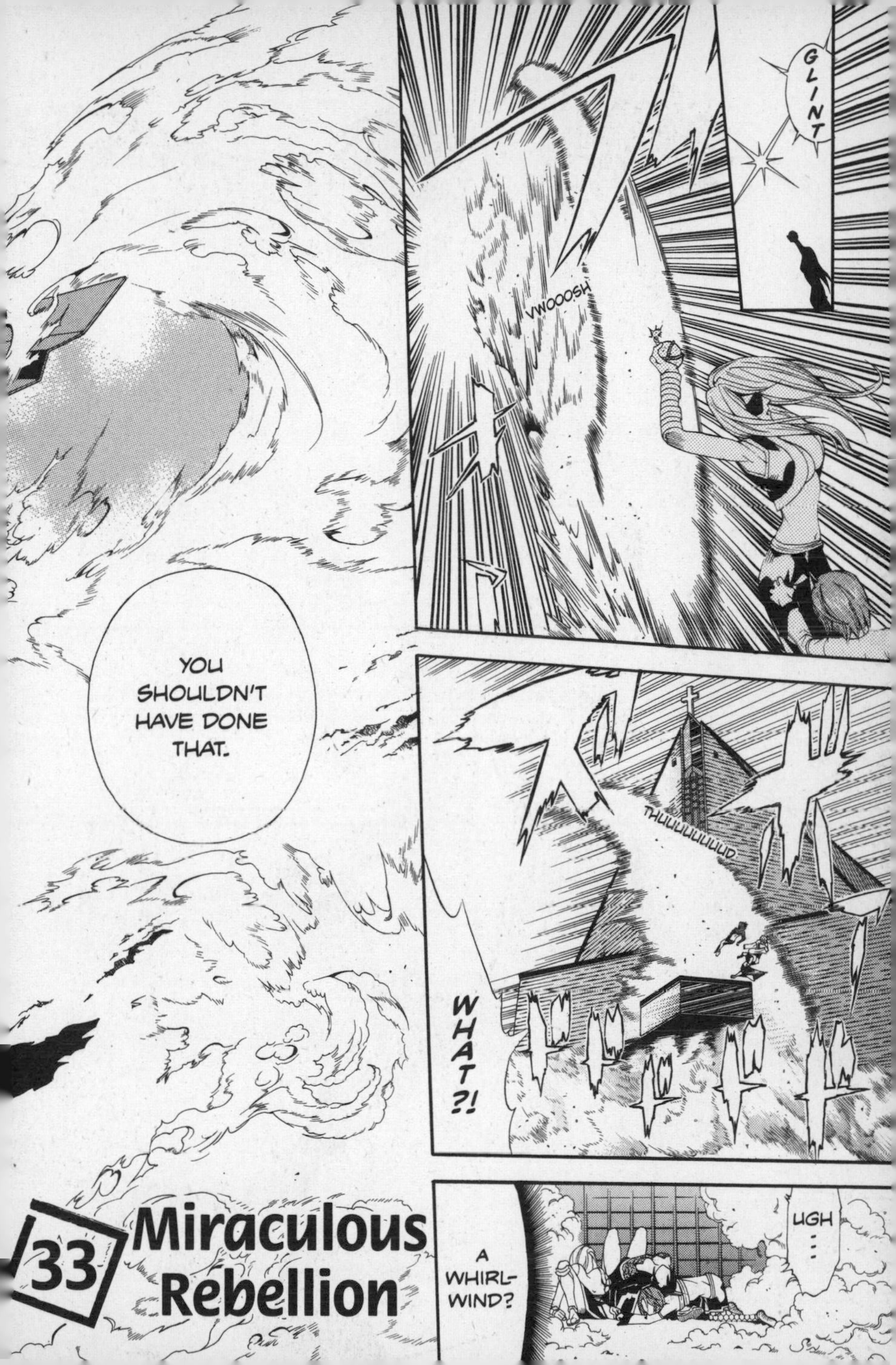
GLINT
VWOOOSH
THUUUUUUUUD
WHAT?!
UGH...
A WHIRLWIND?
YOU SHOULDN'T HAVE DONE THAT.
33 Miraculous Rebellion

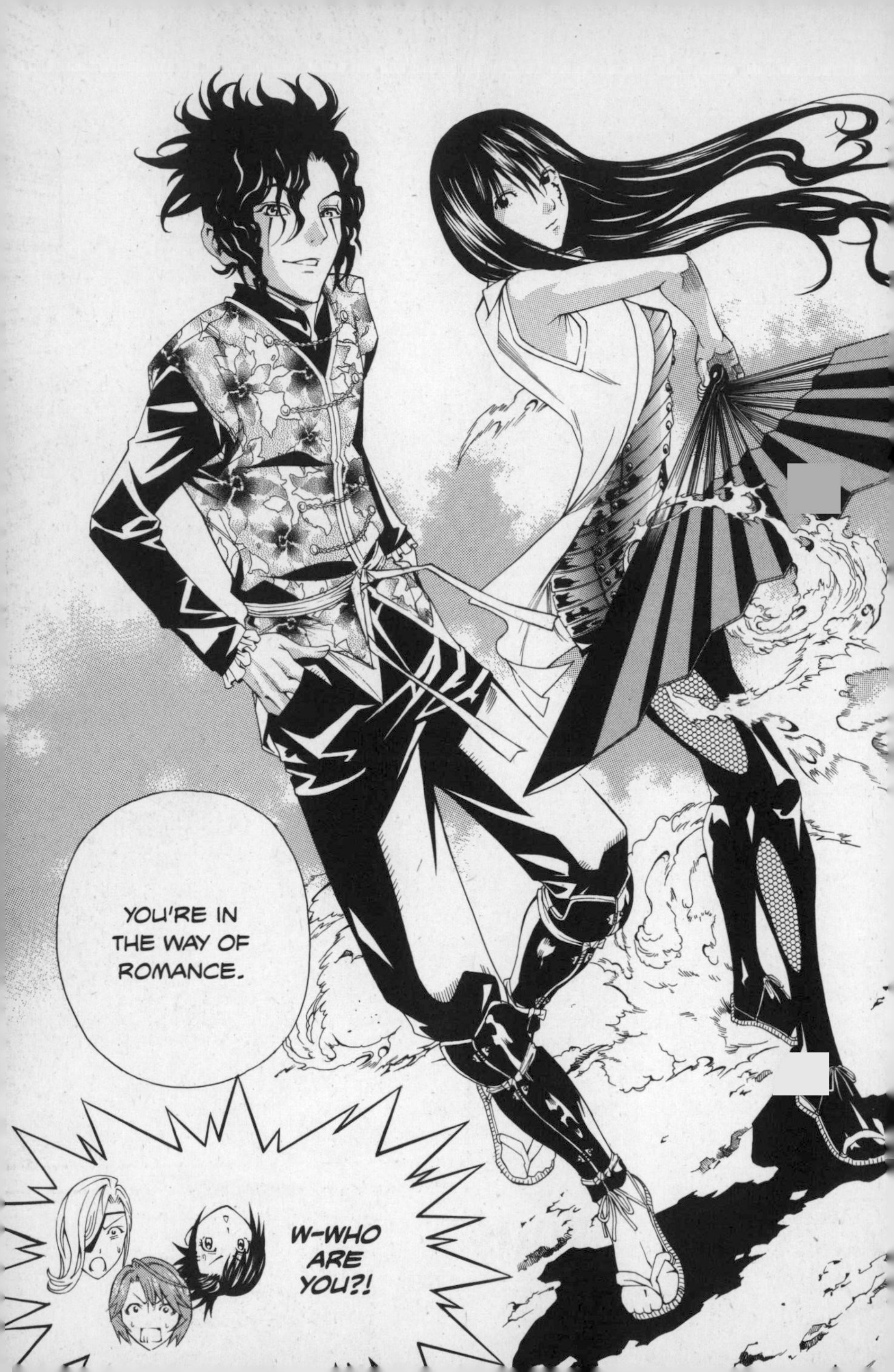
YOU'RE IN THE WAY OF ROMANCE.
W-WHO ARE YOU?!

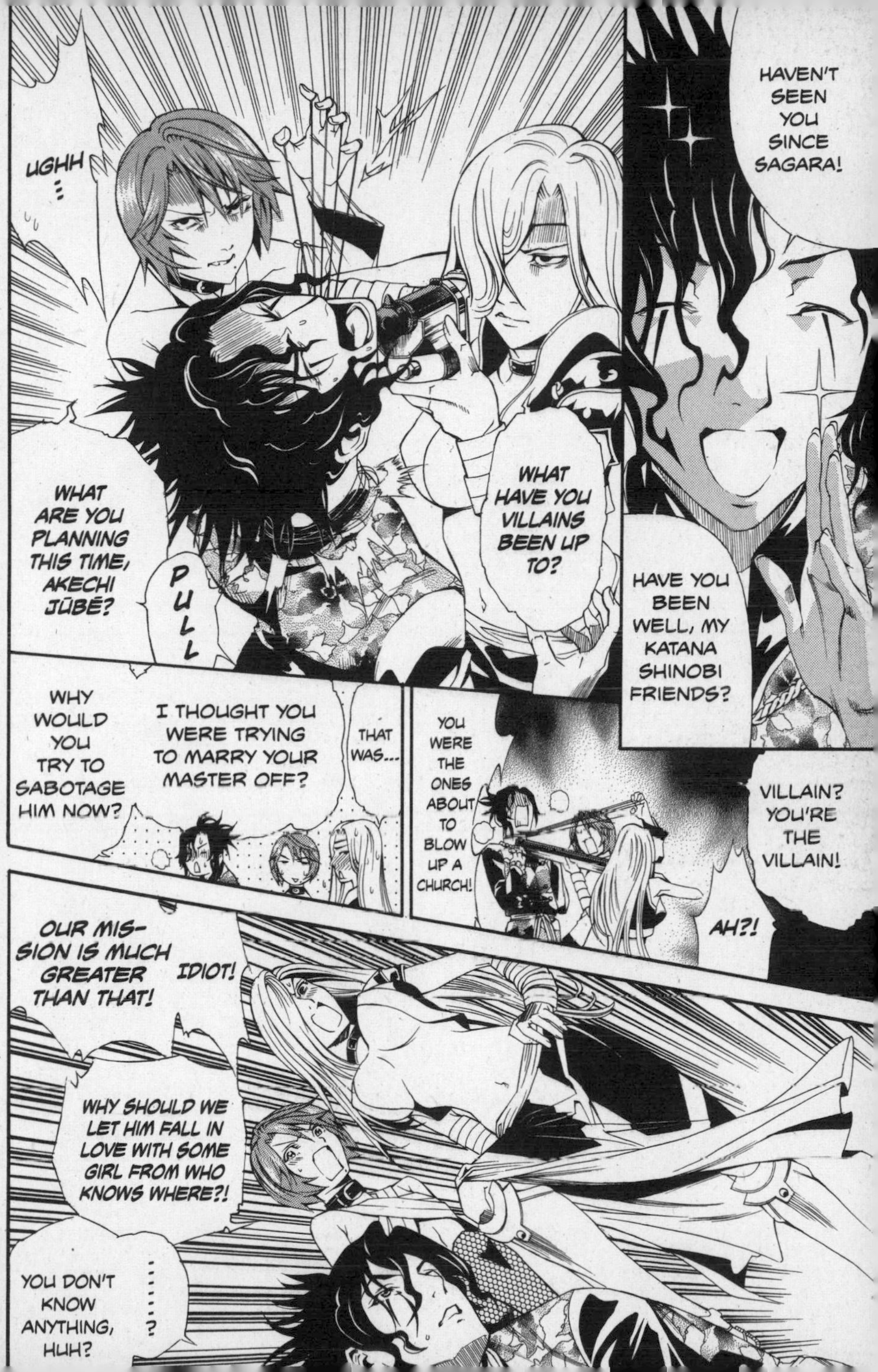
HAVEN'T SEEN YOU SINCE SAGARA!
HAVE YOU BEEN WELL, MY KATANA SHINOBI FRIENDS?
WHAT HAVE YOU VILLAINS BEEN UP TO?
UGHH …
WHAT ARE YOU PLANNING THIS TIME, AKECHI JŪBĒ?
PULL
VILLAIN? YOU'RE THE VILLAIN!
AH?!
YOU WERE THE ONES ABOUT TO BLOW UP A CHURCH!
THAT WAS...
I THOUGHT YOU WERE TRYING TO MARRY YOUR MASTER OFF?
WHY WOULD YOU TRY TO SABOTAGE HIM NOW?
IDIOT!
OUR MISSION IS MUCH GREATER THAN THAT!
WHY SHOULD WE LET HIM FALL IN LOVE WITH SOME GIRL FROM WHO KNOWS WHERE?!
......?
YOU DON'T KNOW ANYTHING, HUH?

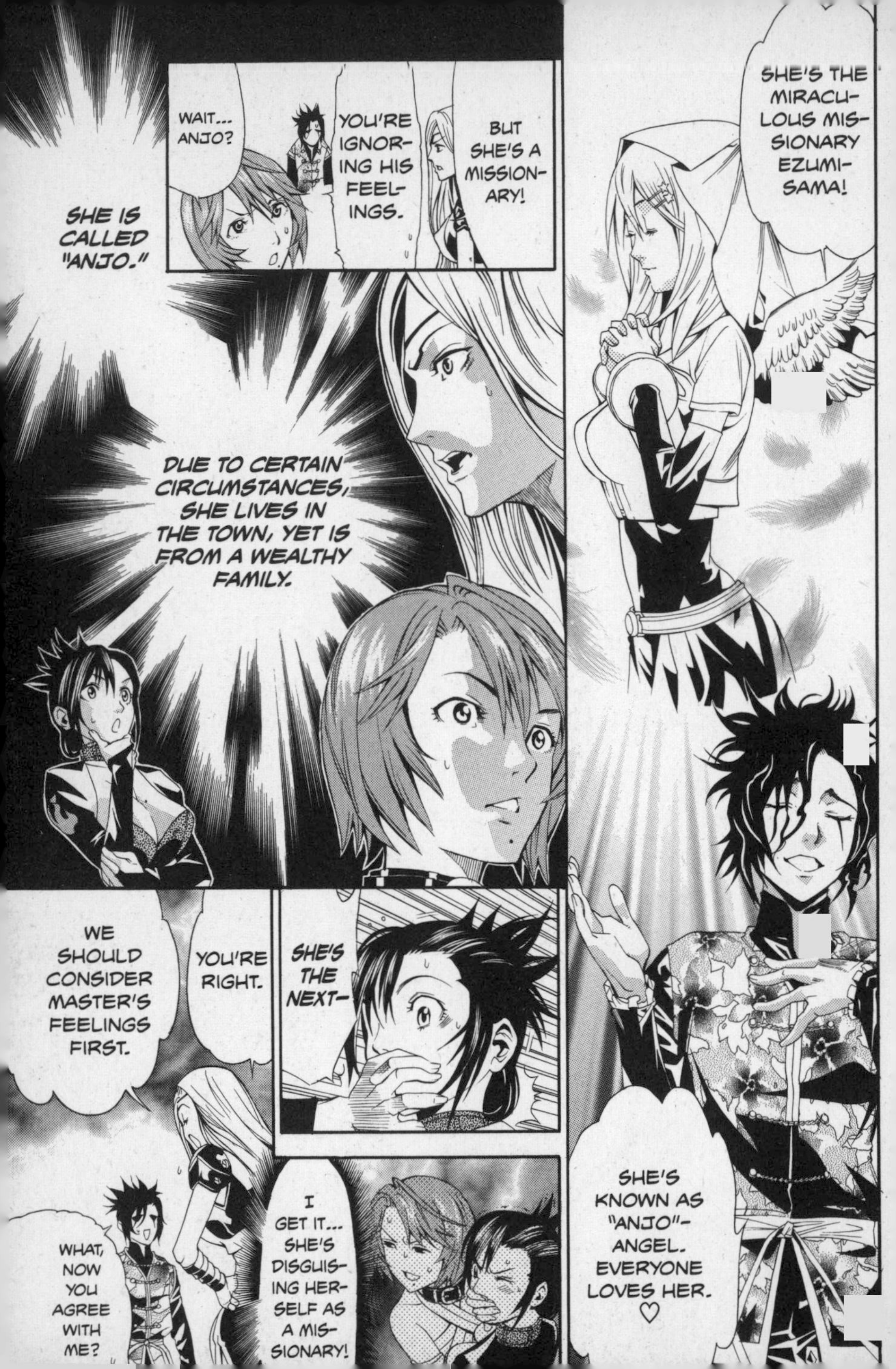

SHE'S THE MIRACULOUS MISSIONARY EZUMI-SAMA!
SHE'S KNOWN AS "ANJO"- ANGEL. EVERYONE LOVES HER. ♡
BUT SHE'S A MISSIONARY!
YOU'RE IGNORING HIS FEELINGS.
WAIT... ANJO?
SHE IS CALLED "ANJO."
DUE TO CERTAIN CIRCUMSTANCES, SHE LIVES IN THE TOWN, YET IS FROM A WEALTHY FAMILY.
SHE'S THE NEXT—
YOU'RE RIGHT.
WE SHOULD CONSIDER MASTER'S FEELINGS FIRST.
I GET IT... SHE'S DISGUISING HERSELF AS A MISSIONARY!
WHAT, NOW YOU AGREE WITH ME?

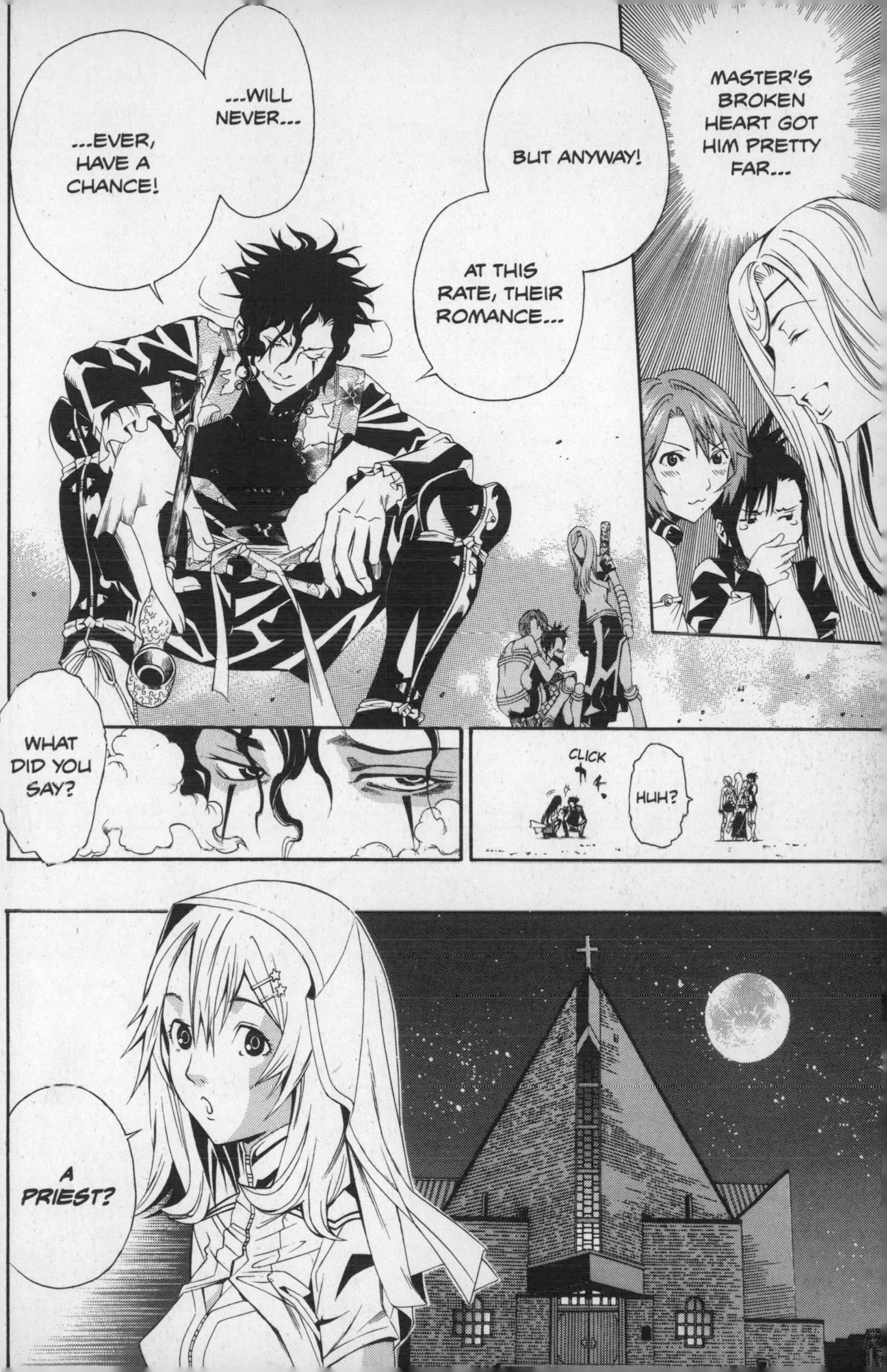
MASTER'S BROKEN HEART GOT HIM PRETTY FAR...
BUT ANYWAY!
AT THIS RATE, THEIR ROMANCE...
...WILL NEVER...
...EVER, HAVE A CHANCE!
CLICK
HUH?
WHAT DID YOU SAY?
A PRIEST?

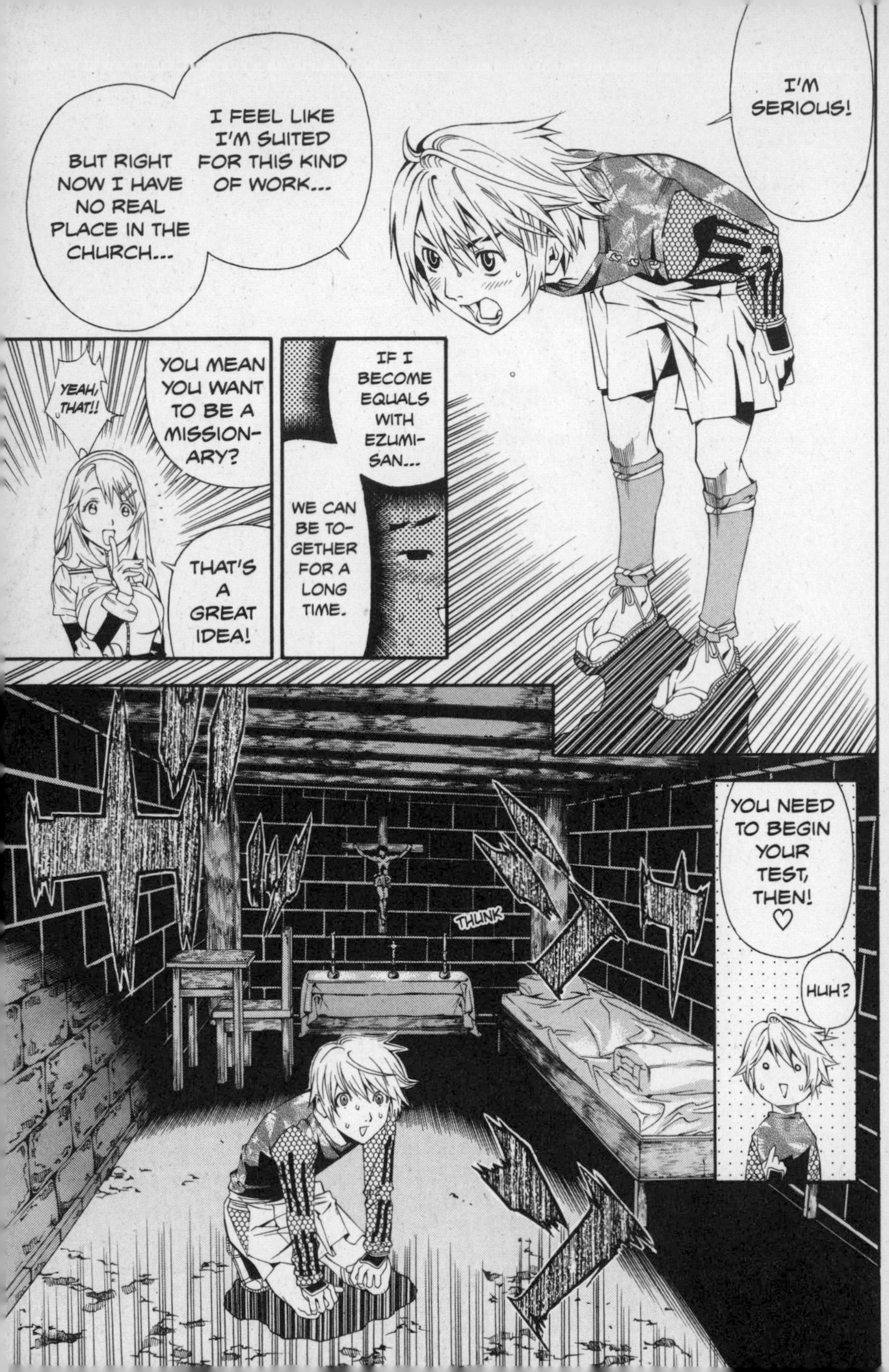
I'M SERIOUS!
I FEEL LIKE I'M SUITED FOR THIS KIND OF WORK... BUT RIGHT NOW I HAVE NO REAL PLACE IN THE CHURCH...
IF I BECOME EQUALS WITH EZUMI-SAN...
WE CAN BE TOGETHER FOR A LONG TIME.
YOU MEAN YOU WANT TO BE A MISSIONARY?
YEAH, THAT!!
THAT'S A GREAT IDEA!
YOU NEED TO BEGIN YOUR TEST, THEN! ♡
HUH?
THUNK

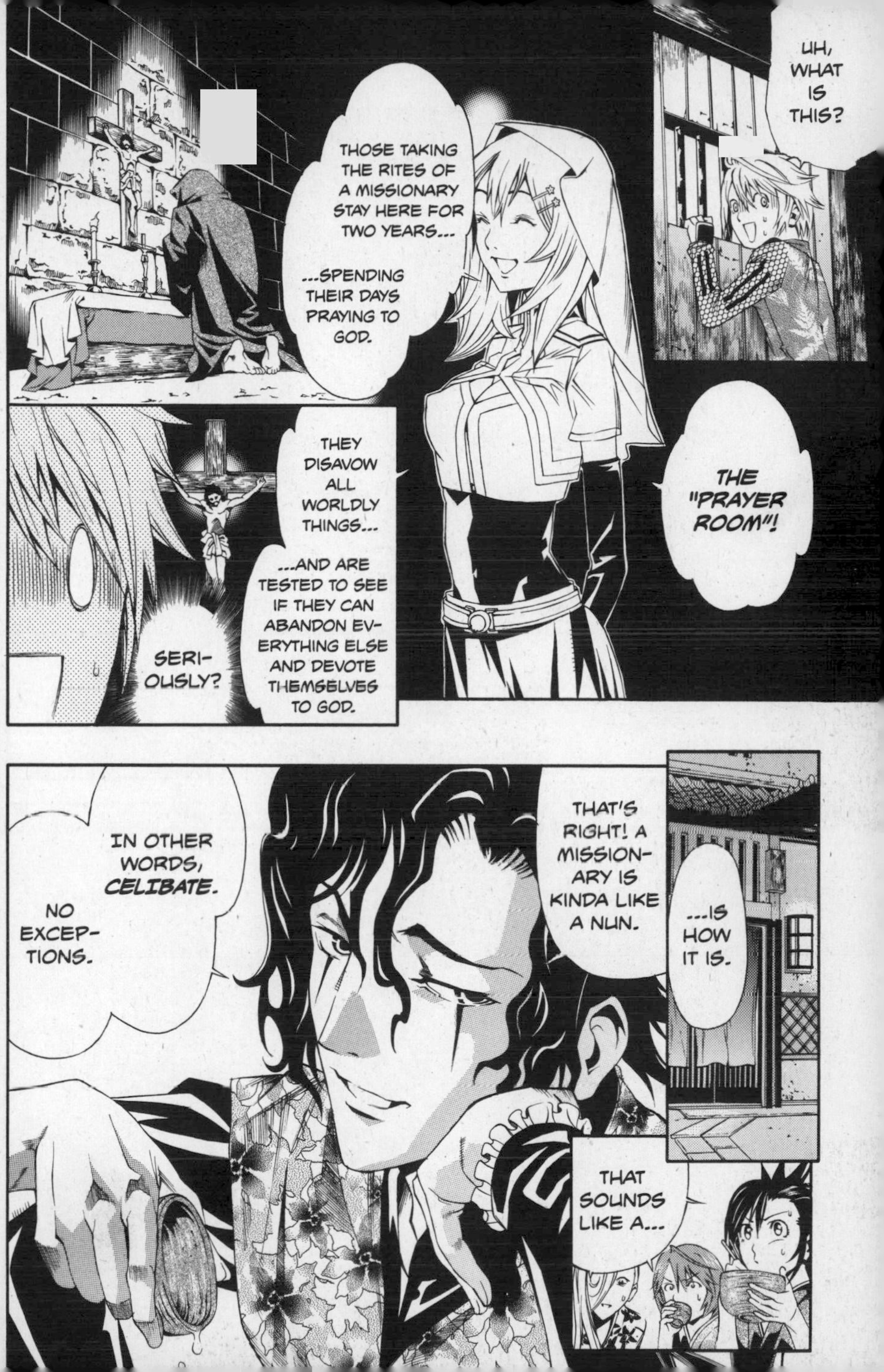
UH, WHAT IS THIS?
THE "PRAYER ROOM"!
THOSE TAKING THE RITES OF A MISSIONARY STAY HERE FOR TWO YEARS...
...SPENDING THEIR DAYS PRAYING TO GOD.
THEY DISAVOW ALL WORLDLY THINGS...
...AND ARE TESTED TO SEE IF THEY CAN ABANDON EV-ERYTHING ELSE AND DEVOTE THEMSELVES TO GOD.
SERI-OUSLY?
THAT'S RIGHT! A MISSION-ARY IS KINDA LIKE A NUN.
...IS HOW IT IS.
THAT SOUNDS LIKE A...
IN OTHER WORDS, CELIBATE.
NO EXCEP-TIONS.

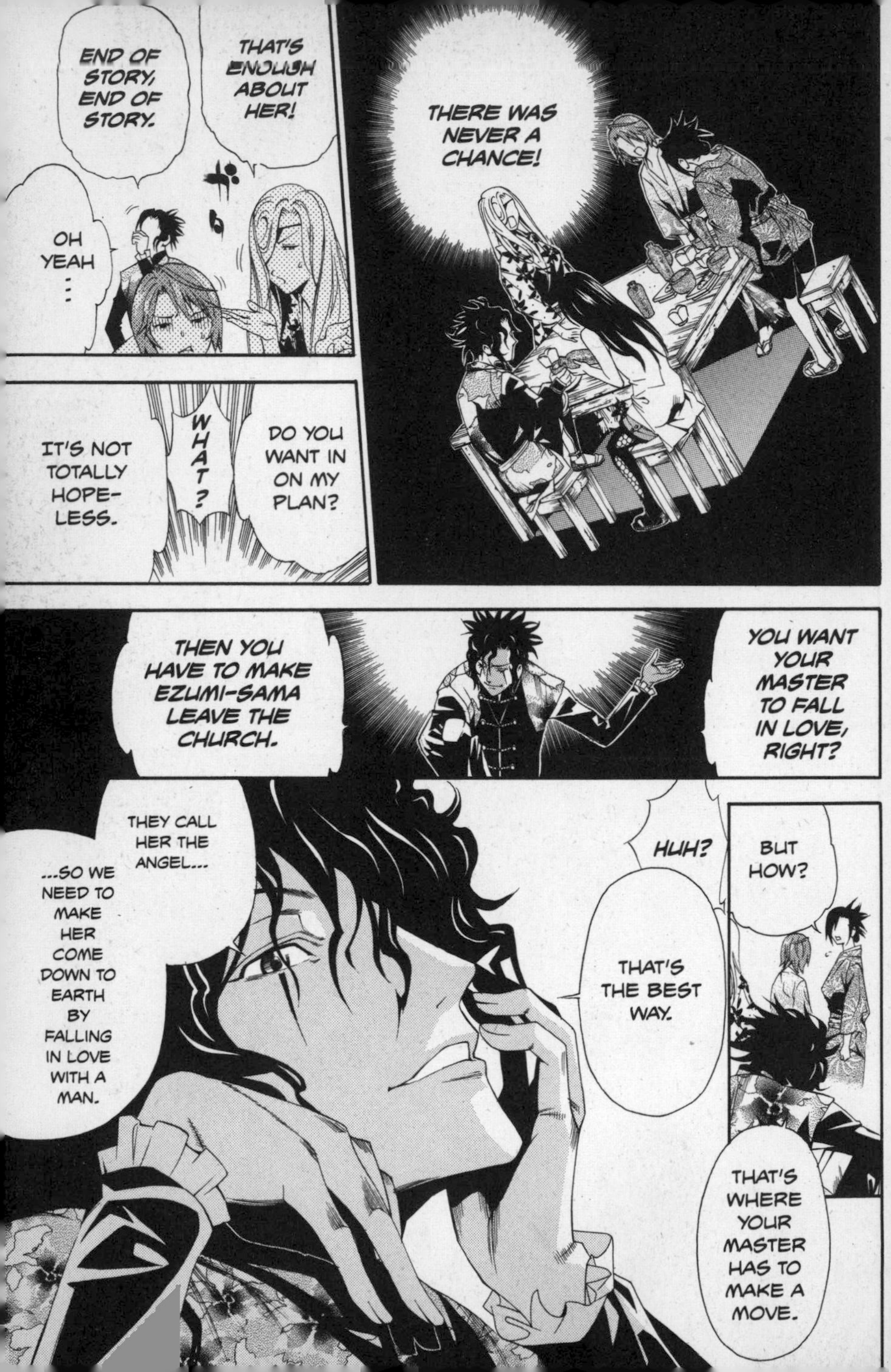
THERE WAS NEVER A CHANCE!
THAT'S ENOUGH ABOUT HER!
END OF STORY, END OF STORY.
OH YEAH...
DO YOU WANT IN ON MY PLAN?
WHAT?
IT'S NOT TOTALLY HOPE-LESS.
YOU WANT YOUR MASTER TO FALL IN LOVE, RIGHT?
THEN YOU HAVE TO MAKE EZUMI-SAMA LEAVE THE CHURCH.
BUT HOW?
THEY CALL HER THE ANGEL...
...SO WE NEED TO MAKE HER COME DOWN TO EARTH BY FALLING IN LOVE WITH A MAN.
HUH?
THAT'S THE BEST WAY.
THAT'S WHERE YOUR MASTER HAS TO MAKE A MOVE.

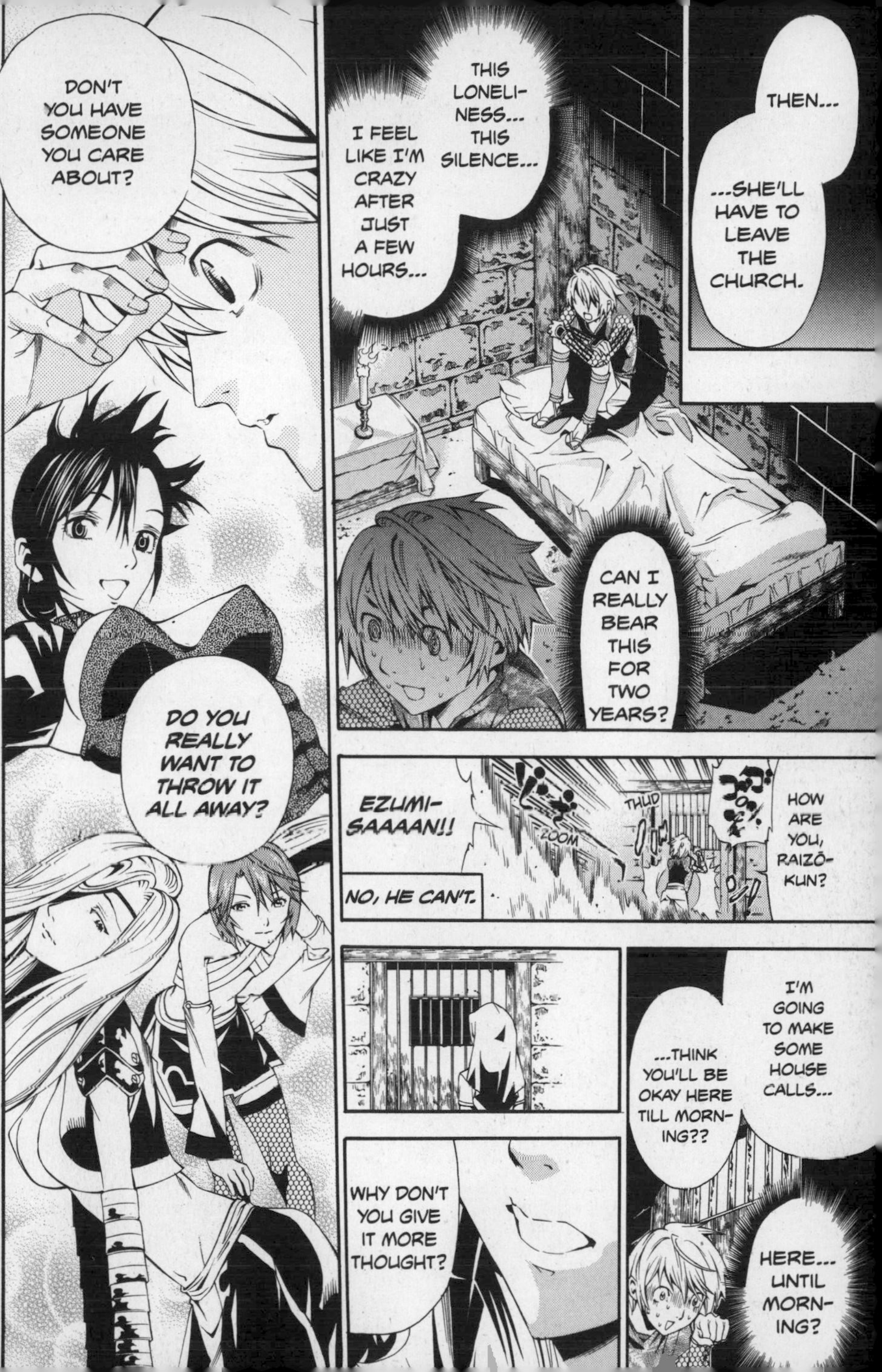

THEN...
...SHE'LL HAVE TO LEAVE THE CHURCH.
THIS LONELI-NESS... THIS SILENCE...
I FEEL LIKE I'M CRAZY AFTER JUST A FEW HOURS...
CAN I REALLY BEAR THIS FOR TWO YEARS?
HOW ARE YOU, RAIZŌ-KUN?
THUD
ZOOM
EZUMI-SAAAAN!!
NO, HE CAN'T.
I'M GOING TO MAKE SOME HOUSE CALLS...
...THINK YOU'LL BE OKAY HERE TILL MORN-ING??
HERE... UNTIL MORN-ING?
WHY DON'T YOU GIVE IT MORE THOUGHT?
DON'T YOU HAVE SOMEONE YOU CARE ABOUT?
DO YOU REALLY WANT TO THROW IT ALL AWAY?

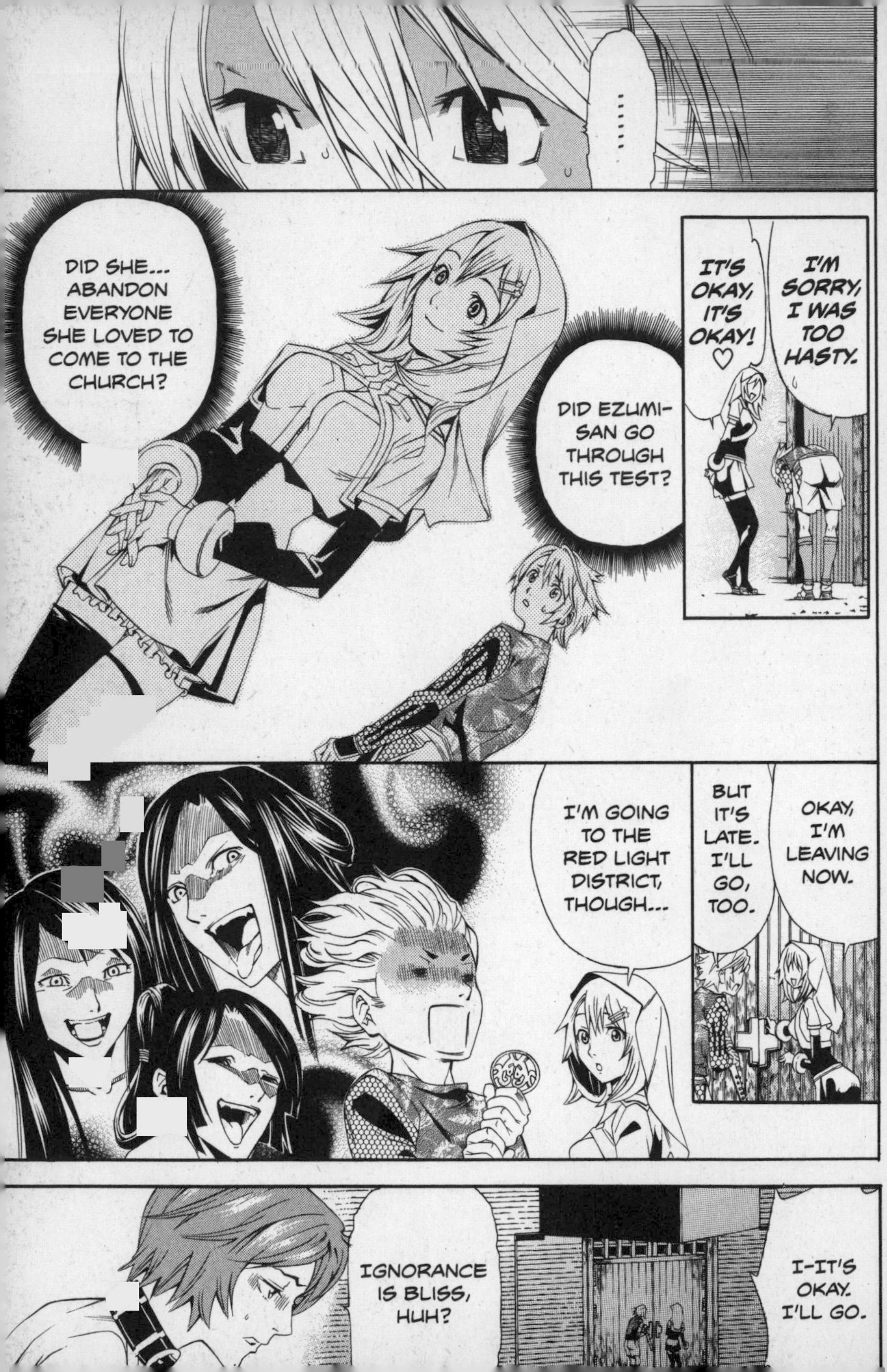
......
I'M SORRY, I WAS TOO HASTY.
IT'S OKAY, IT'S OKAY! ♡
DID EZUMI-SAN GO THROUGH THIS TEST?
DID SHE... ABANDON EVERYONE SHE LOVED TO COME TO THE CHURCH?
OKAY, I'M LEAVING NOW.
BUT IT'S LATE. I'LL GO, TOO.
I'M GOING TO THE RED LIGHT DISTRICT, THOUGH...
I-IT'S OKAY. I'LL GO.
IGNORANCE IS BLISS, HUH?

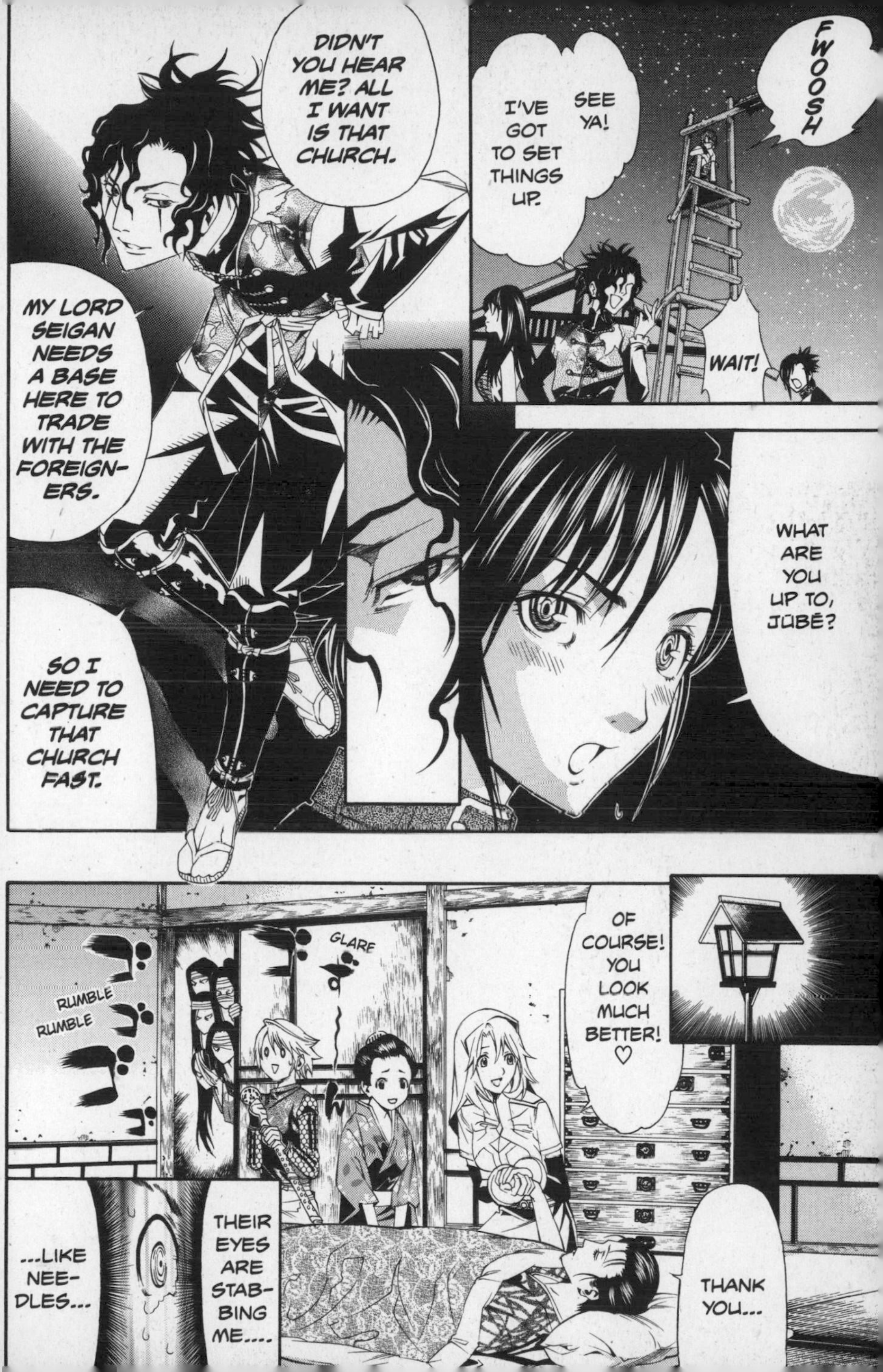
FWOOSH
SEE YA!
I'VE GOT TO SET THINGS UP.
WAIT!
WHAT ARE YOU UP TO, JŪBĒ?
DIDN'T YOU HEAR ME? ALL I WANT IS THAT CHURCH.
MY LORD SEIGAN NEEDS A BASE HERE TO TRADE WITH THE FOREIGN-ERS.
SO I NEED TO CAPTURE THAT CHURCH FAST.
OF COURSE! YOU LOOK MUCH BETTER! ♥
GLARE
RUMBLE RUMBLE
THANK YOU...
THEIR EYES ARE STAB-BING ME....
...LIKE NEE-DLES...

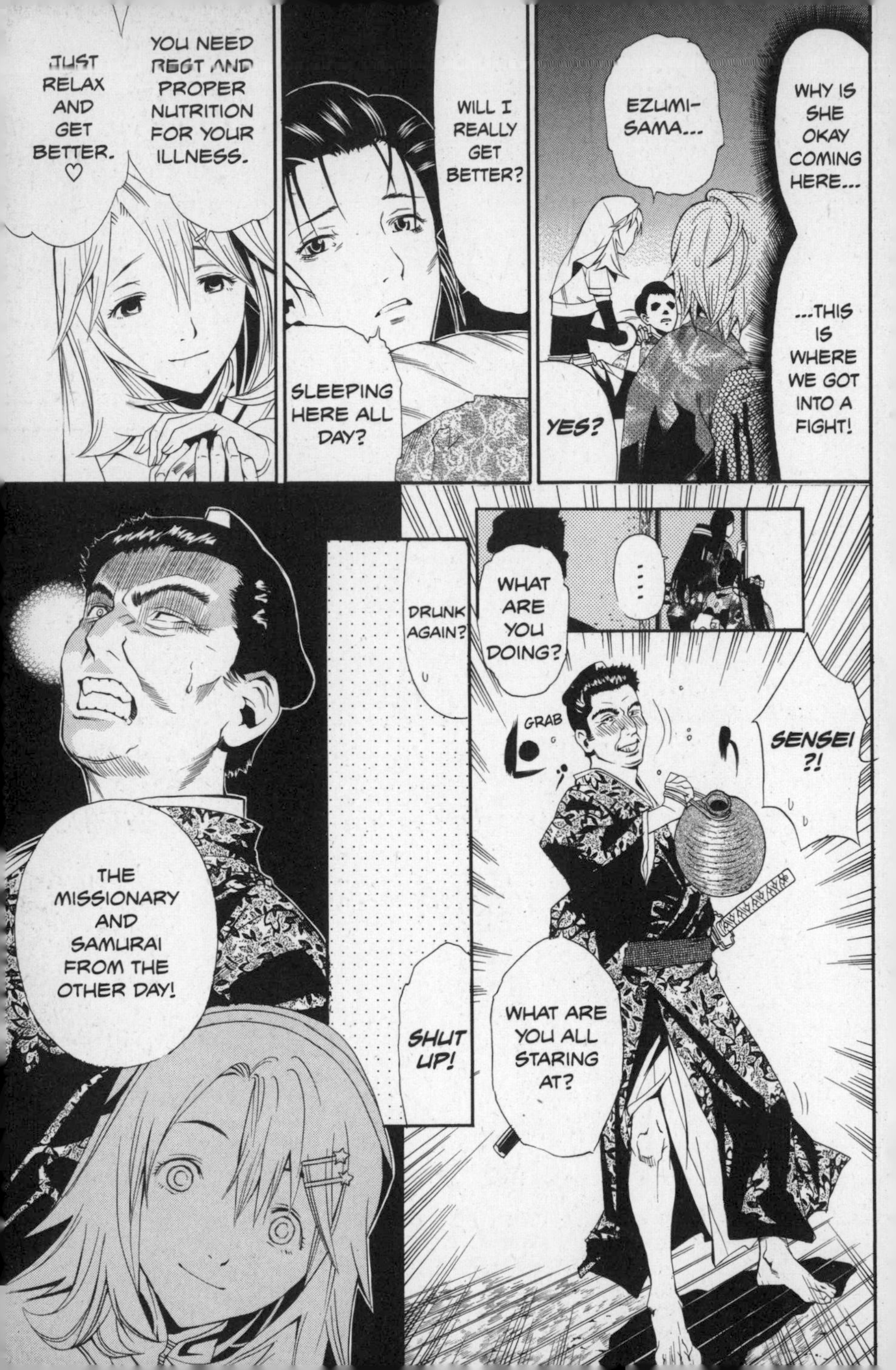
WHY IS SHE OKAY COMING HERE...
...THIS IS WHERE WE GOT INTO A FIGHT!
EZUMI-SAMA...
YES?
WILL I REALLY GET BETTER?
SLEEPING HERE ALL DAY?
YOU NEED REST AND PROPER NUTRITION FOR YOUR ILLNESS.
JUST RELAX AND GET BETTER. ♡
...
WHAT ARE YOU DOING?
SENSEI ?!
GRAB
DRUNK AGAIN?
WHAT ARE YOU ALL STARING AT?
SHUT UP!
THE MISSIONARY AND SAMURAI FROM THE OTHER DAY!

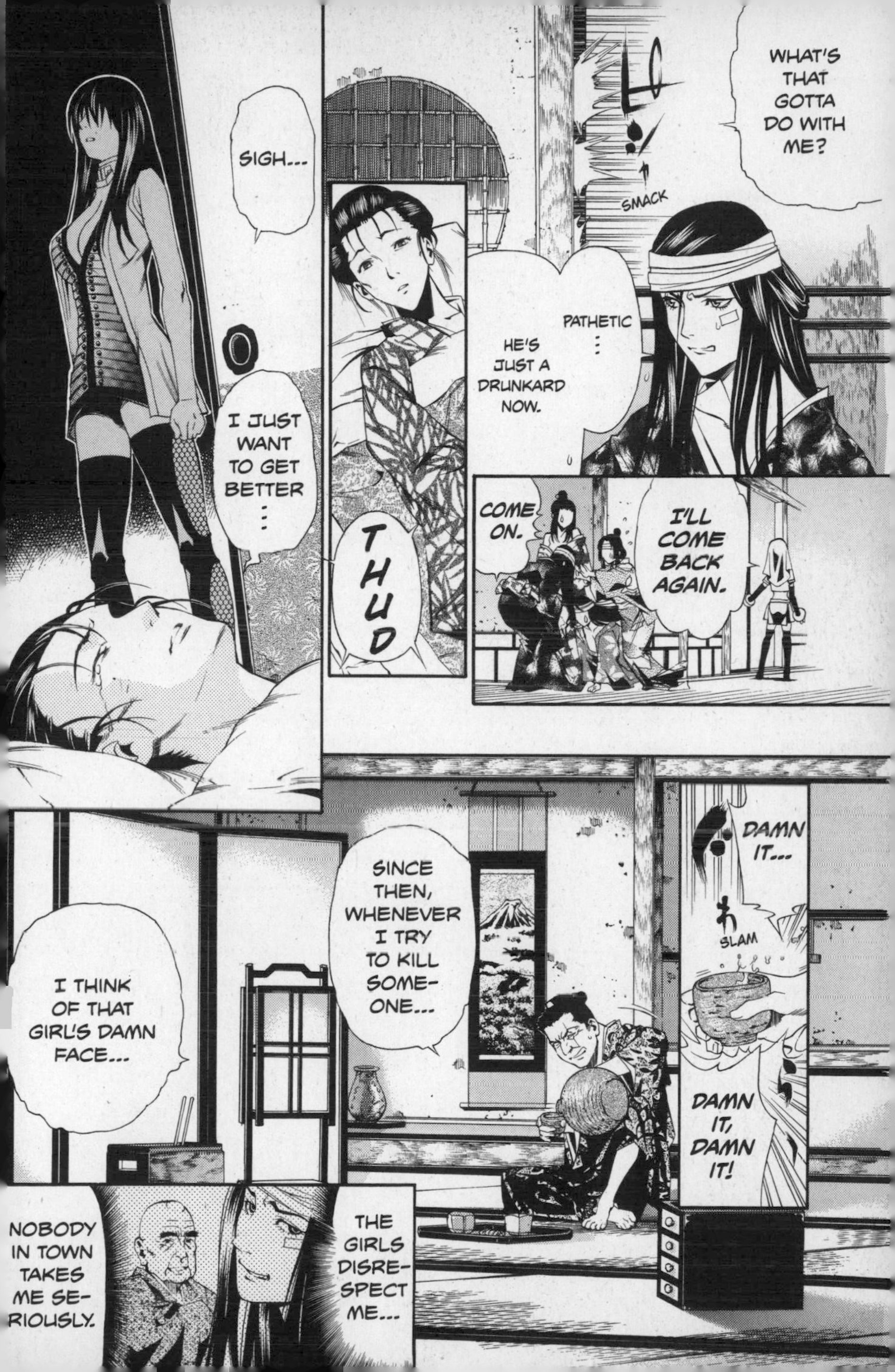
WHAT'S THAT GOTTA DO WITH ME?
SMACK
PATHETIC ...
HE'S JUST A DRUNKARD NOW.
I'LL COME BACK AGAIN.
COME ON.
THUD
SIGH...
I JUST WANT TO GET BETTER ...
DAMN IT...
SLAM
DAMN IT, DAMN IT!
SINCE THEN, WHENEVER I TRY TO KILL SOME-ONE...
I THINK OF THAT GIRL'S DAMN FACE...
THE GIRLS DISRE-SPECT ME...
NOBODY IN TOWN TAKES ME SE-RIOUSLY.

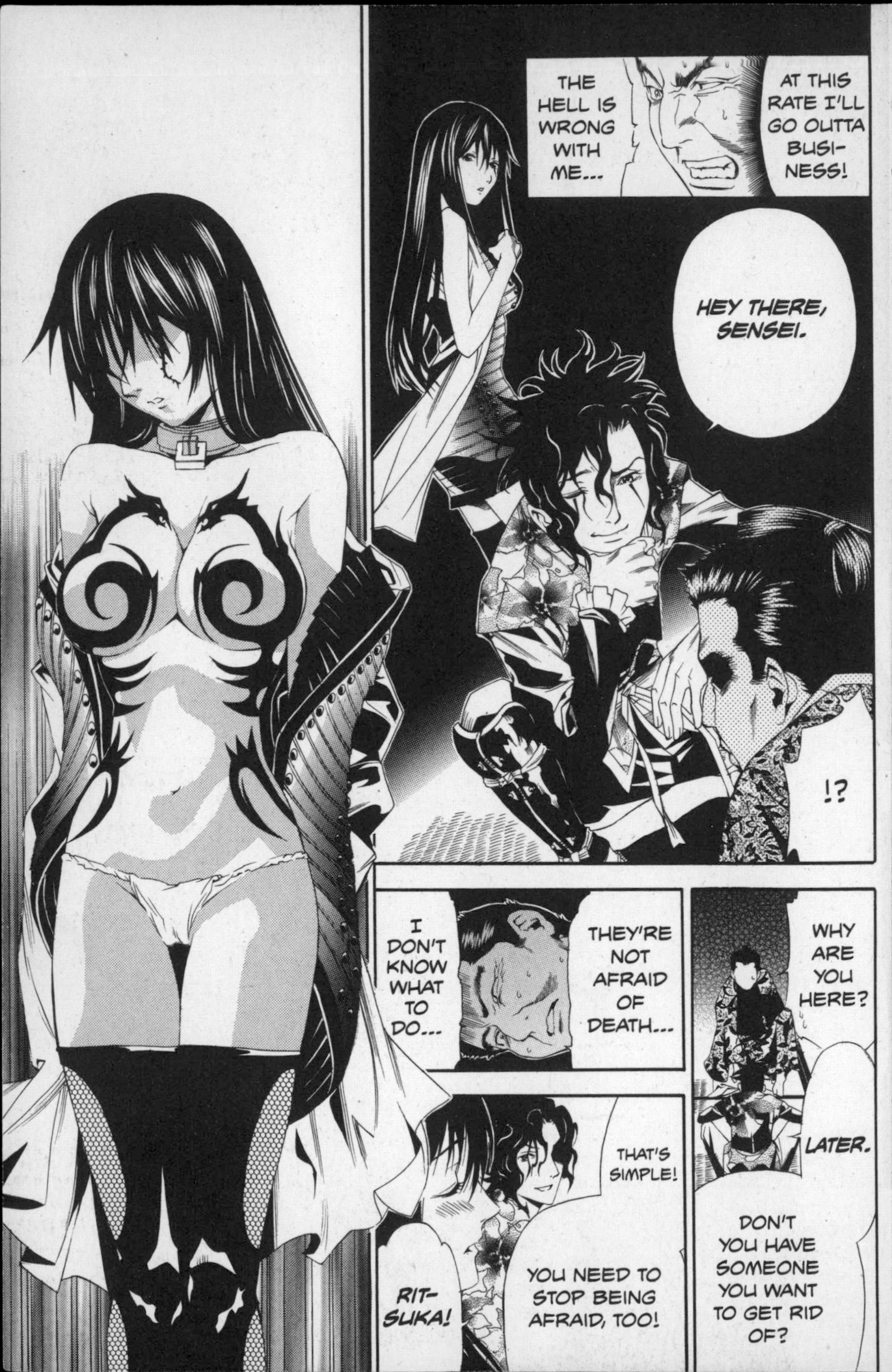
AT THIS RATE I'LL GO OUTTA BUSINESS!
THE HELL IS WRONG WITH ME...
HEY THERE, SENSEI.
!?
WHY ARE YOU HERE?
LATER.
DON'T YOU HAVE SOMEONE YOU WANT TO GET RID OF?
THEY'RE NOT AFRAID OF DEATH...
I DON'T KNOW WHAT TO DO...
THAT'S SIMPLE!
YOU NEED TO STOP BEING AFRAID, TOO!
RIT-SUKA!

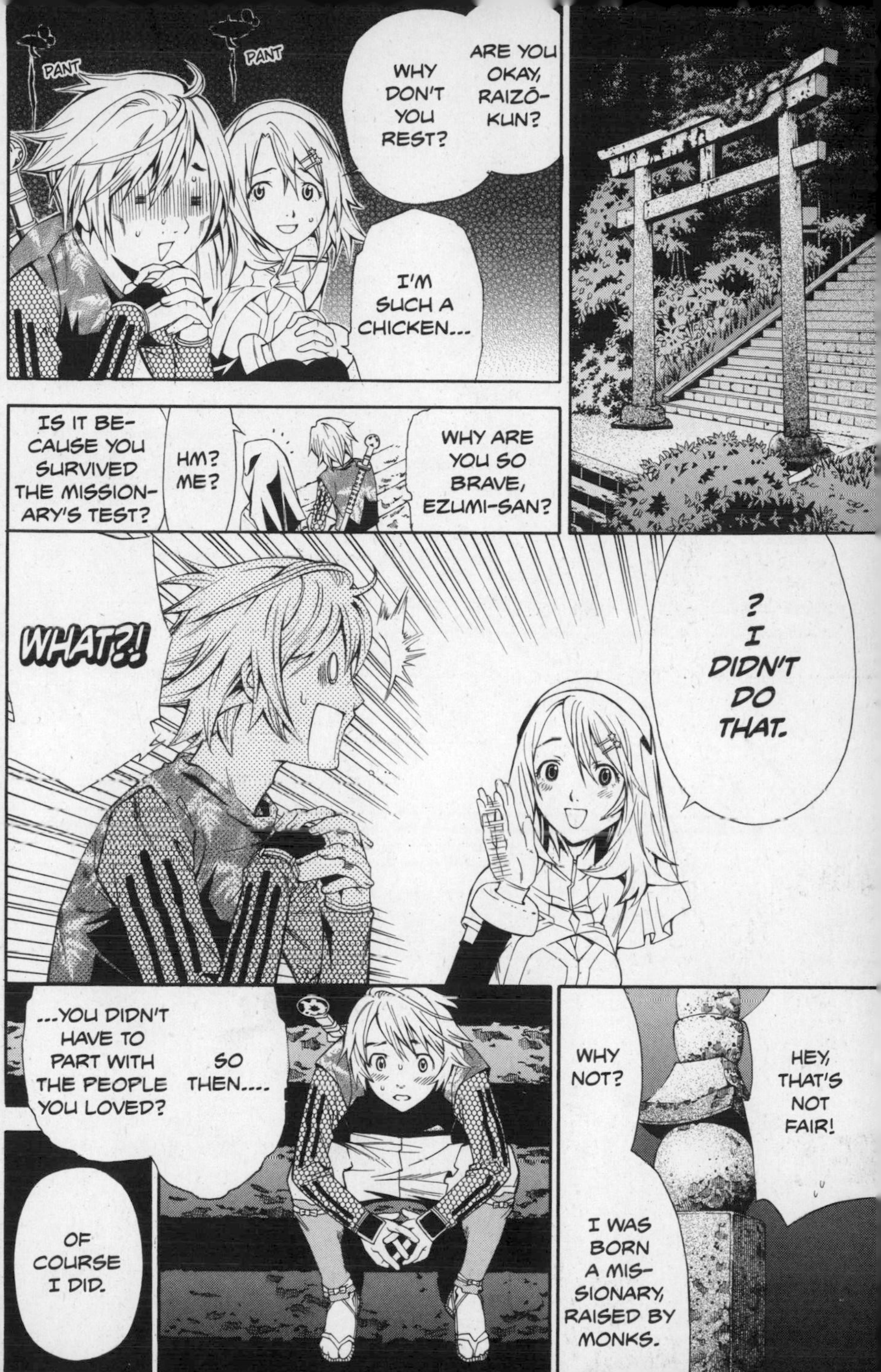
PANT
PANT
ARE YOU OKAY, RAIZŌ-KUN?
WHY DON'T YOU REST?
I'M SUCH A CHICKEN...
WHY ARE YOU SO BRAVE, EZUMI-SAN?
HM? ME?
IS IT BE-CAUSE YOU SURVIVED THE MISSION-ARY'S TEST?
? I DIDN'T DO THAT.
WHAT?!
HEY, THAT'S NOT FAIR!
WHY NOT?
I WAS BORN A MIS-SIONARY, RAISED BY MONKS.
SO THEN....
...YOU DIDN'T HAVE TO PART WITH THE PEOPLE YOU LOVED?
OF COURSE I DID.

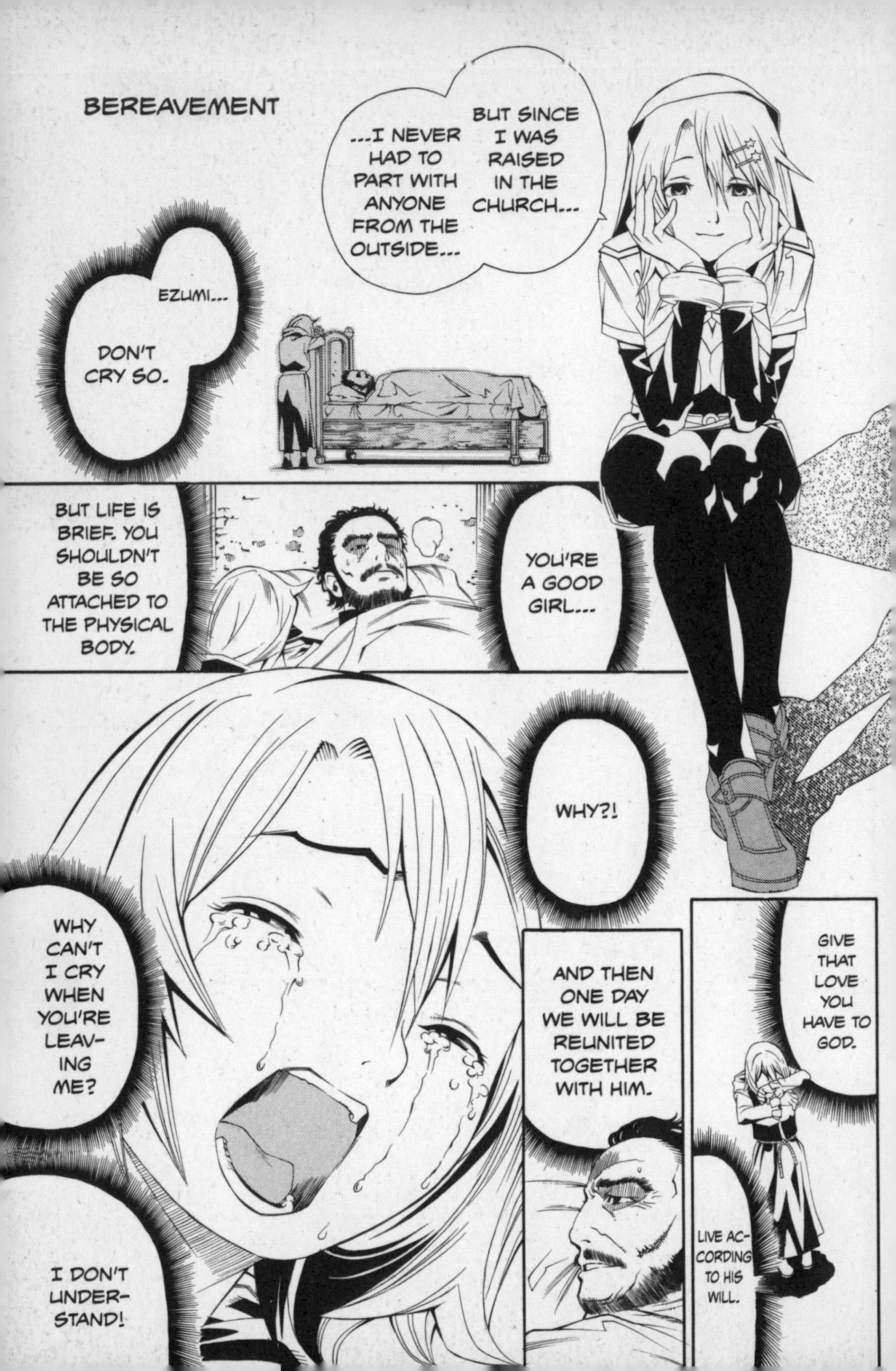
BEREAVEMENT
BUT SINCE I WAS RAISED IN THE CHURCH...
...I NEVER HAD TO PART WITH ANYONE FROM THE OUTSIDE...
EZUMI...
DON'T CRY SO.
YOU'RE A GOOD GIRL...
BUT LIFE IS BRIEF. YOU SHOULDN'T BE SO ATTACHED TO THE PHYSICAL BODY.
WHY?!
WHY CAN'T I CRY WHEN YOU'RE LEAV-ING ME?
I DON'T UNDER-STAND!
GIVE THAT LOVE YOU HAVE TO GOD.
LIVE AC-CORDING TO HIS WILL.
AND THEN ONE DAY WE WILL BE REUNITED TOGETHER WITH HIM.

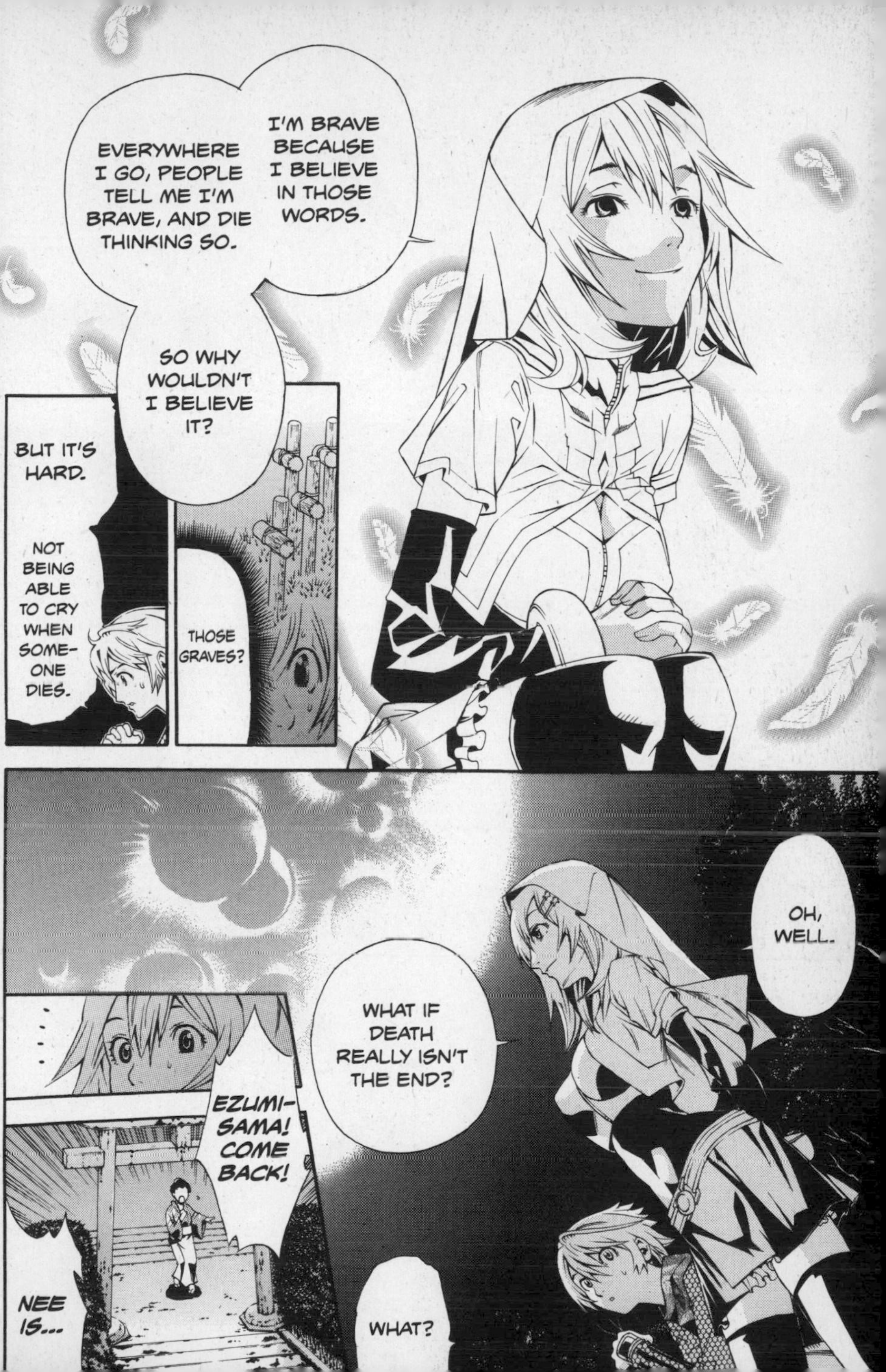

EVERYWHERE I GO, PEOPLE TELL ME I'M BRAVE, AND DIE THINKING SO.
I'M BRAVE BECAUSE I BELIEVE IN THOSE WORDS.
SO WHY WOULDN'T I BELIEVE IT?
THOSE GRAVES?
BUT IT'S HARD.
NOT BEING ABLE TO CRY WHEN SOME-ONE DIES.
OH, WELL.
WHAT IF DEATH REALLY ISN'T THE END?
WHAT?
...
EZUMI-SAMA! COME BACK!
NEE IS...

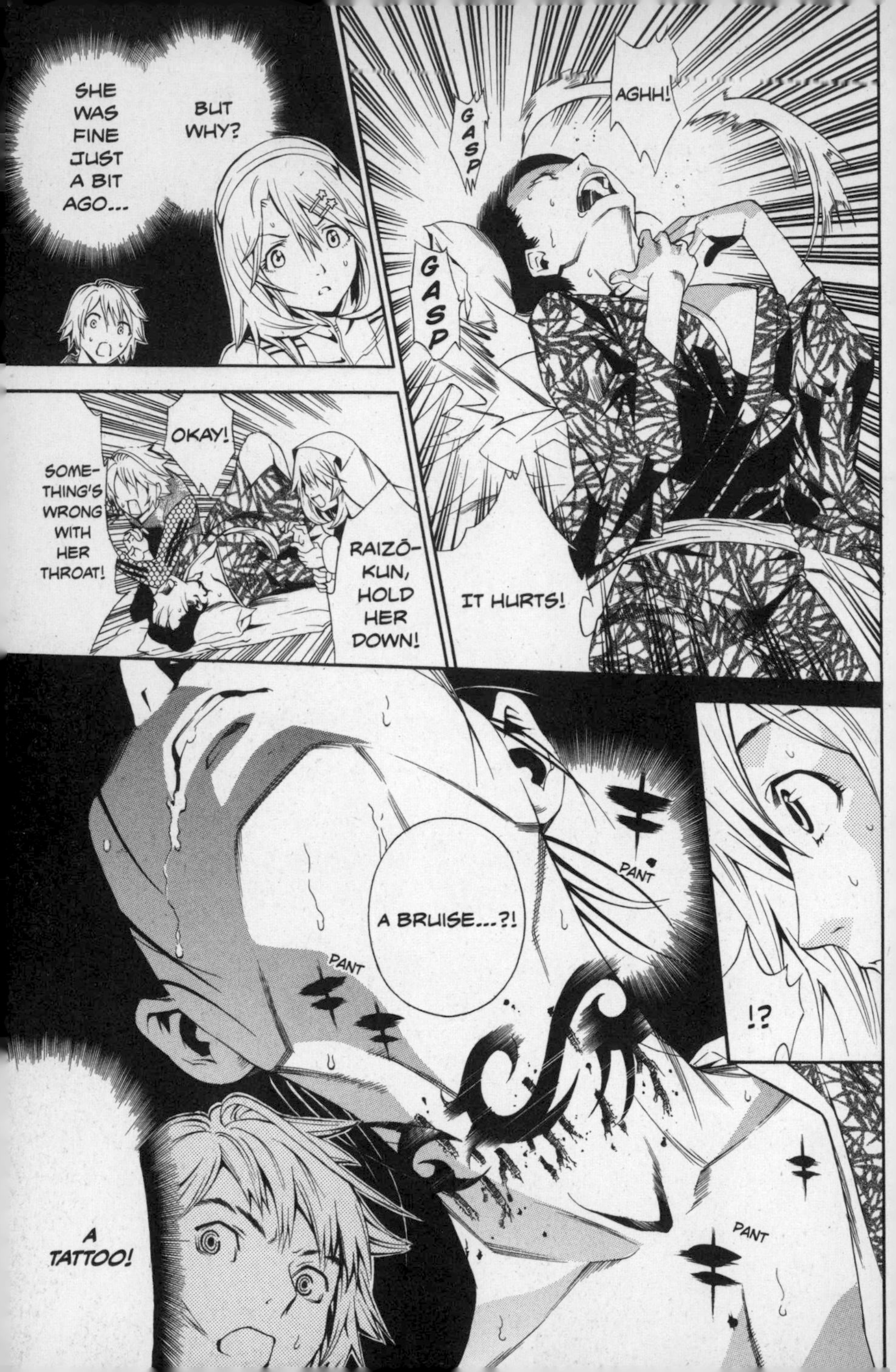
AGHH!
GASP
GASP
IT HURTS!
BUT WHY?
SHE WAS FINE JUST A BIT AGO...
RAIZŌ-KUN, HOLD HER DOWN!
OKAY!
SOMETHING'S WRONG WITH HER THROAT!
!?
PANT
A BRUISE...?!
PANT
PANT
A TATTOO!

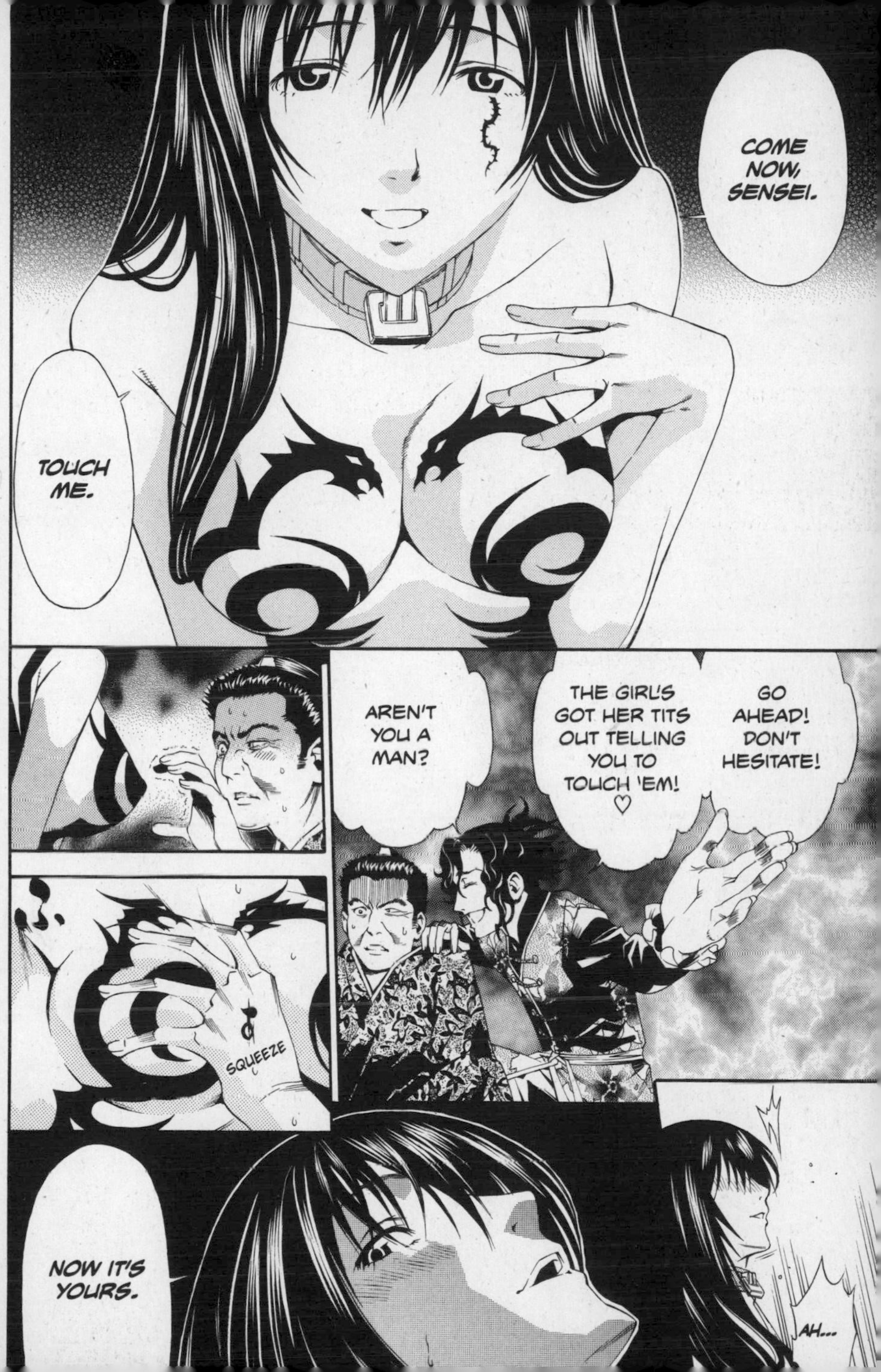
COME NOW, SENSEI.
TOUCH ME.
GO AHEAD! DON'T HESITATE!
THE GIRL'S GOT HER TITS OUT TELLING YOU TO TOUCH 'EM! ♡
AREN'T YOU A MAN?
SQUEEZE
AH...
NOW IT'S YOURS.

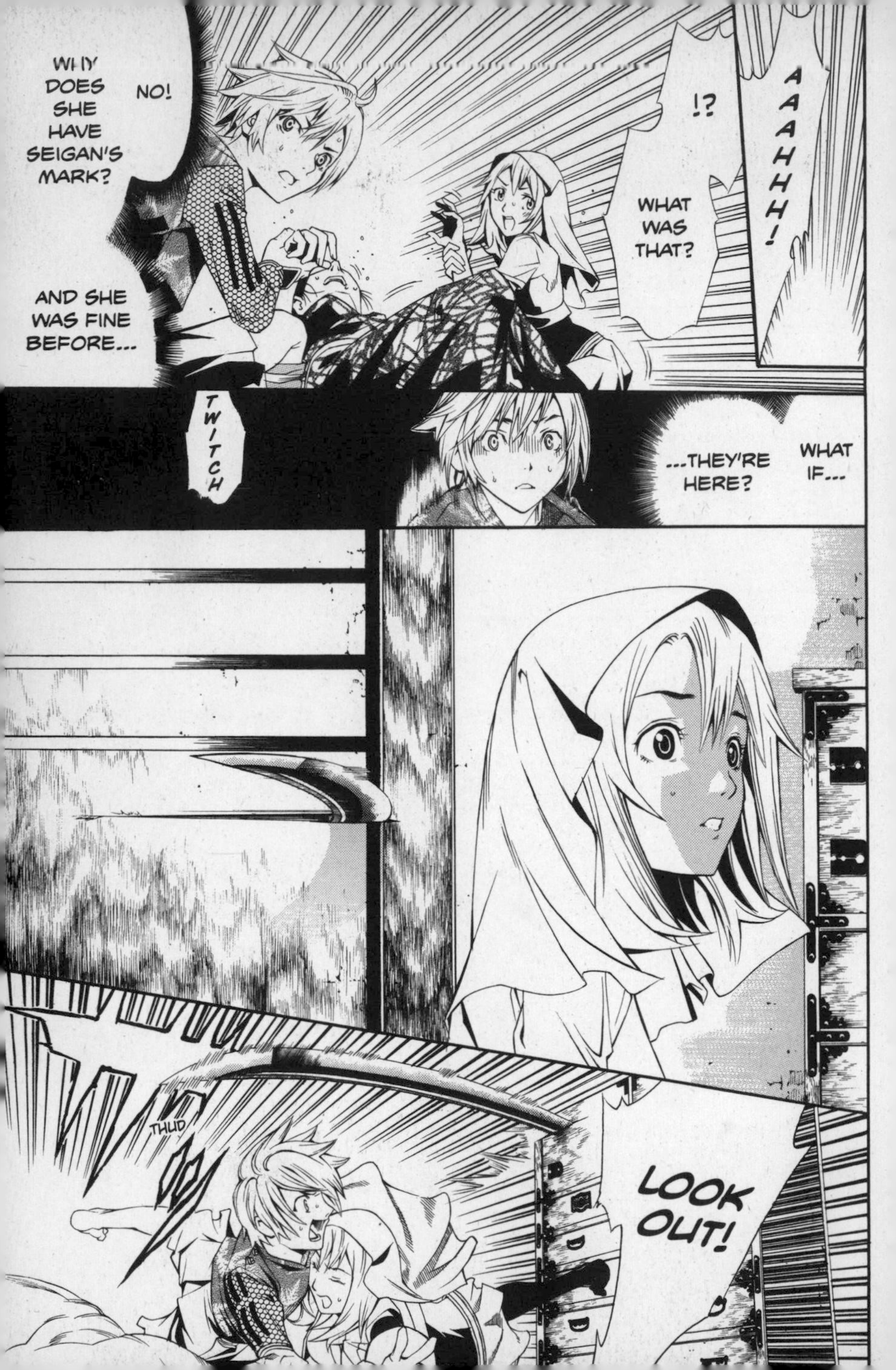
AAAAHHH!
!?
WHAT WAS THAT?
NO!
WHY DOES SHE HAVE SEIGAN'S MARK?
AND SHE WAS FINE BEFORE...
WHAT IF...
...THEY'RE HERE?
TWITCH
LOOK OUT!
THUD

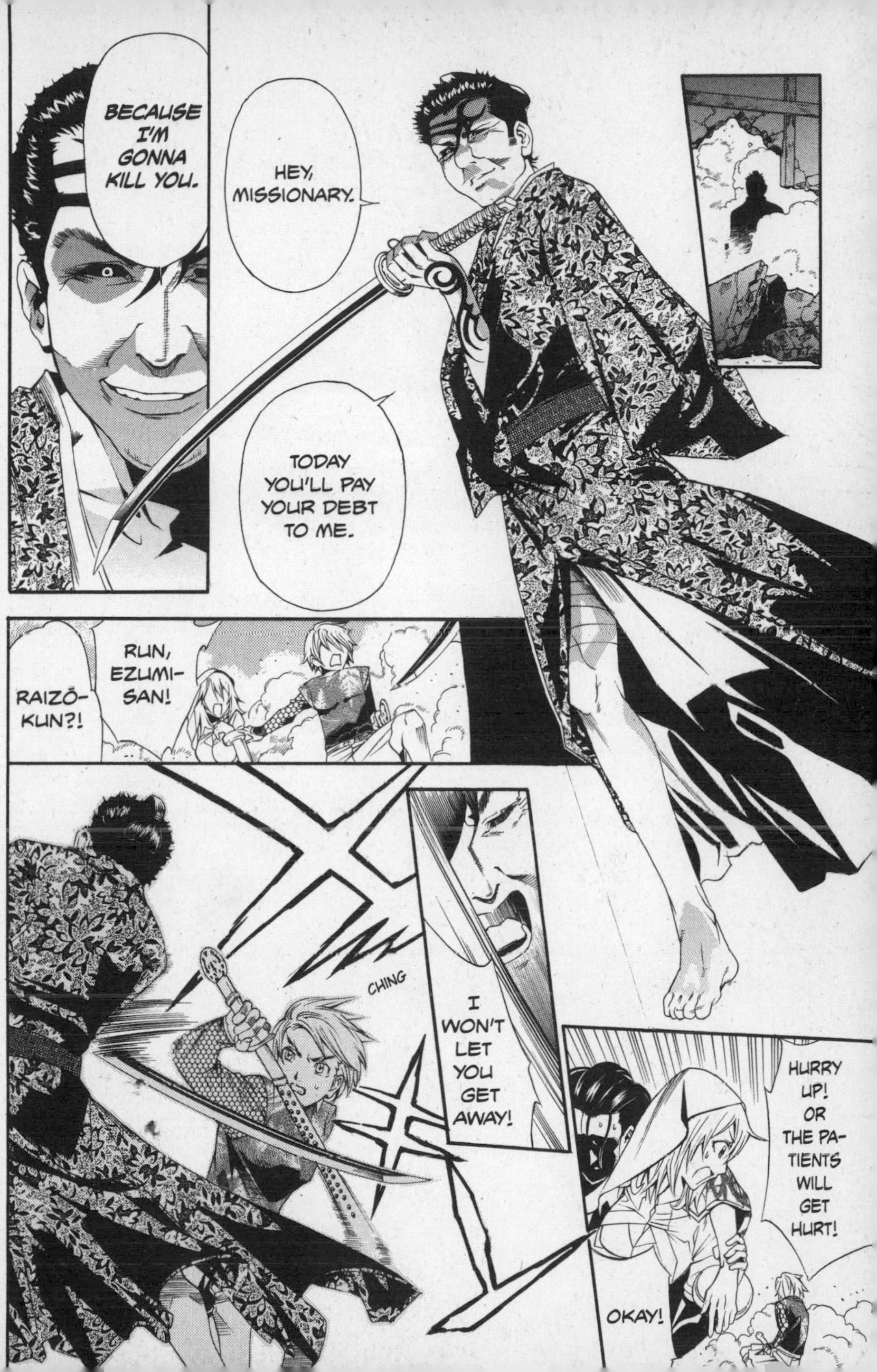
HEY, MISSIONARY.
TODAY YOU'LL PAY YOUR DEBT TO ME.
BECAUSE I'M GONNA KILL YOU.
RUN, EZUMI-SAN!
RAIZŌ-KUN?!
I WON'T LET YOU GET AWAY!
CHING
HURRY UP! OR THE PA-TIENTS WILL GET HURT!
OKAY!

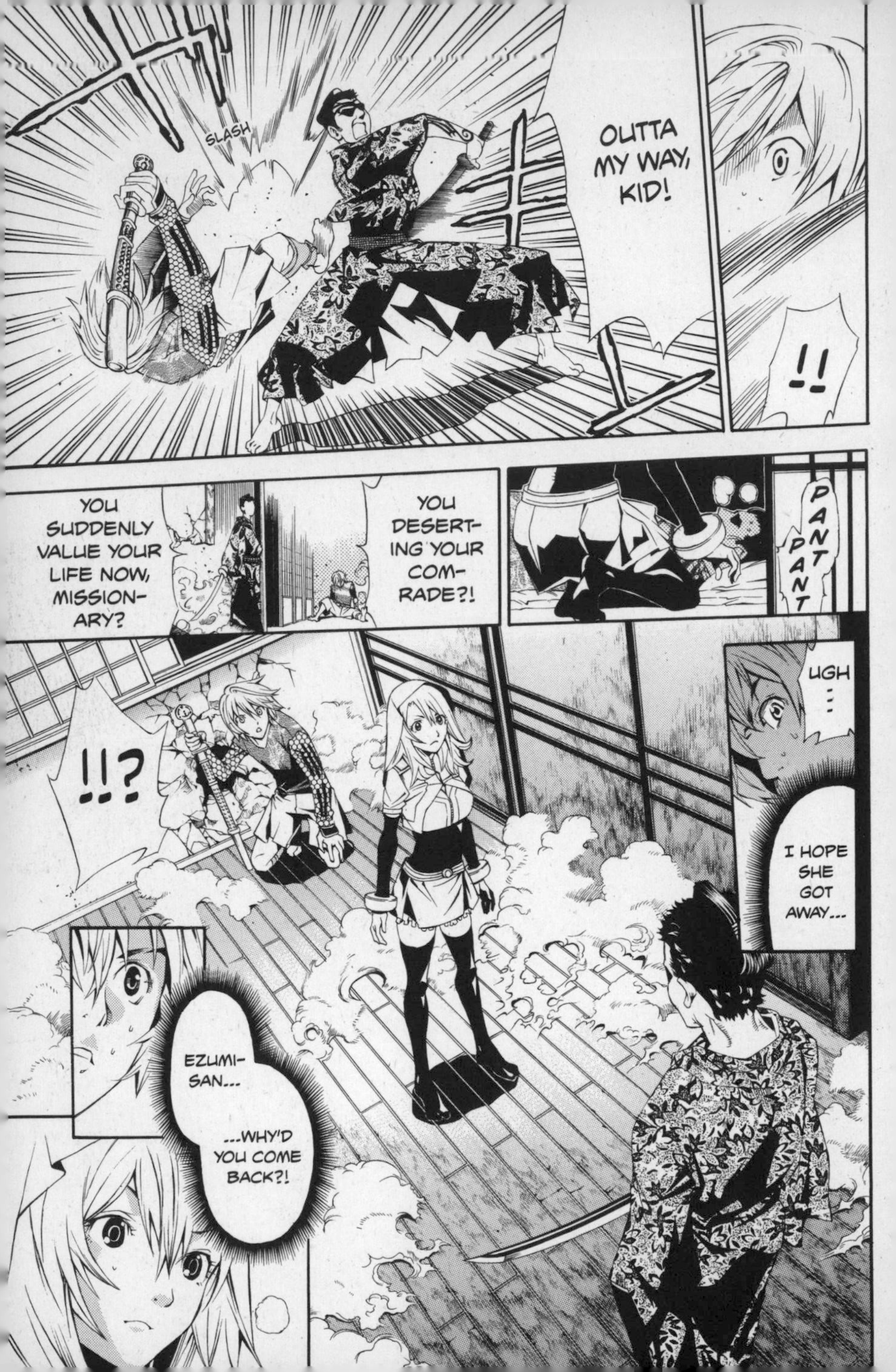
!!
OUTTA MY WAY, KID!
SLASH
PANT PANT
YOU DESERTING YOUR COMRADE?!
YOU SUDDENLY VALUE YOUR LIFE NOW, MISSIONARY?
UGH...
I HOPE SHE GOT AWAY...
!!?
EZUMI-SAN...
...WHY'D YOU COME BACK?!

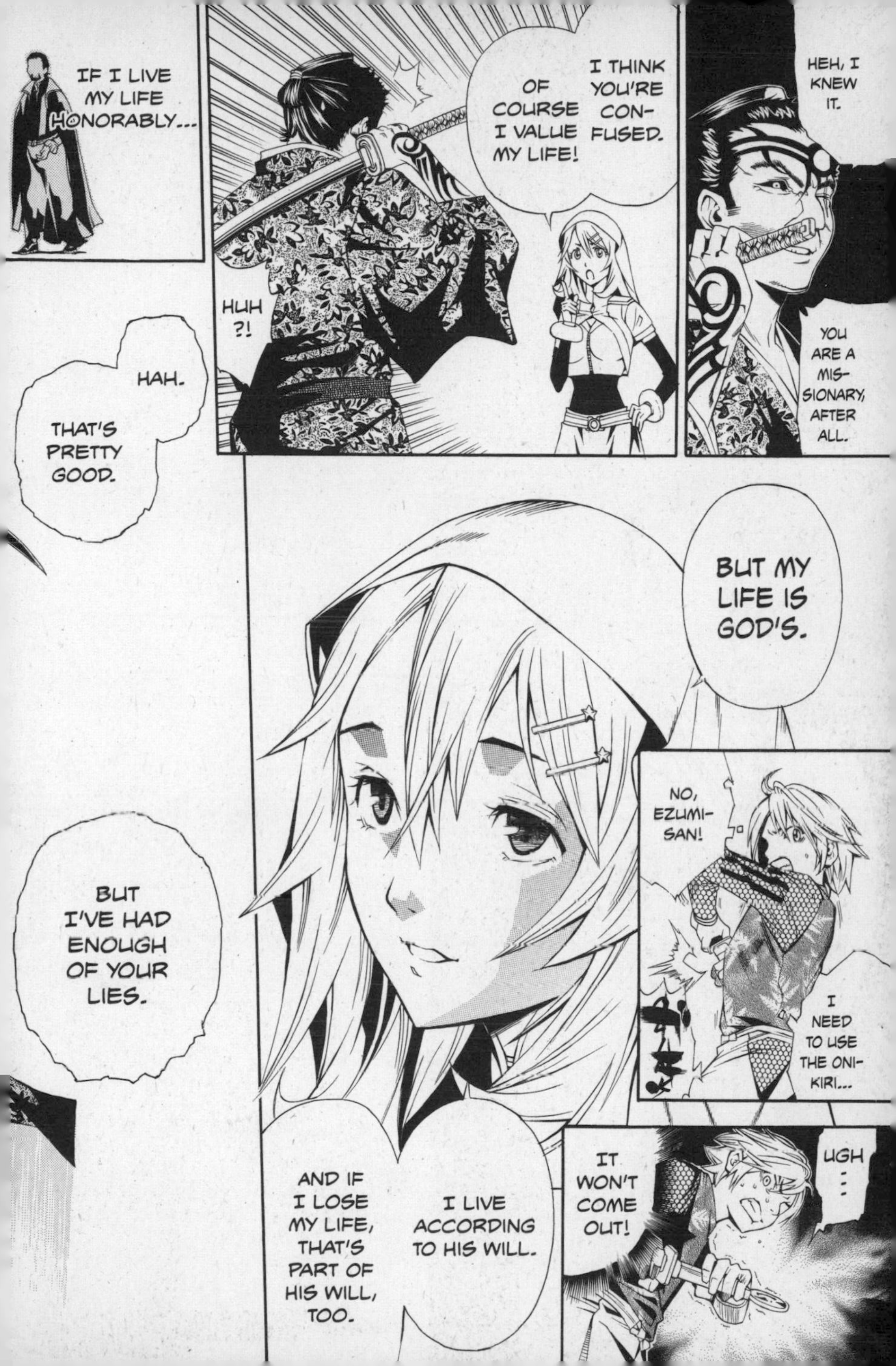

HEH, I KNEW IT.
YOU ARE A MISSIONARY, AFTER ALL.
I THINK YOU'RE CONFUSED.
OF COURSE I VALUE MY LIFE!
HUH ?!
IF I LIVE MY LIFE HONORABLY...
BUT MY LIFE IS GOD'S.
NO, EZUMI-SAN!
I NEED TO USE THE ONI-KIRI...
UGH ...
IT WON'T COME OUT!
I LIVE ACCORDING TO HIS WILL.
AND IF I LOSE MY LIFE, THAT'S PART OF HIS WILL, TOO.
HAH.
THAT'S PRETTY GOOD.
BUT I'VE HAD ENOUGH OF YOUR LIES.

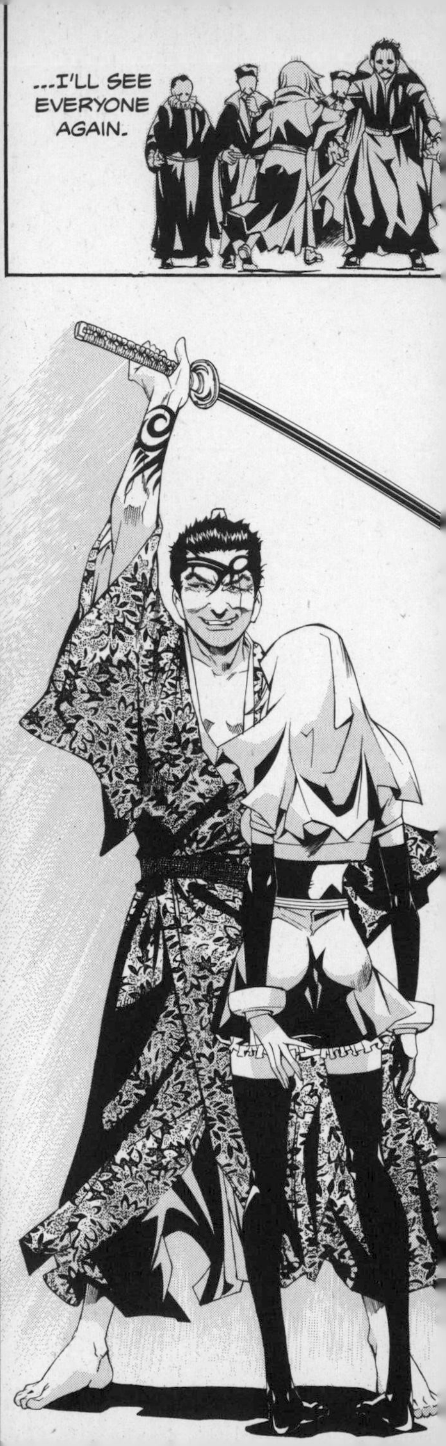
...I'LL SEE EVERYONE AGAIN.
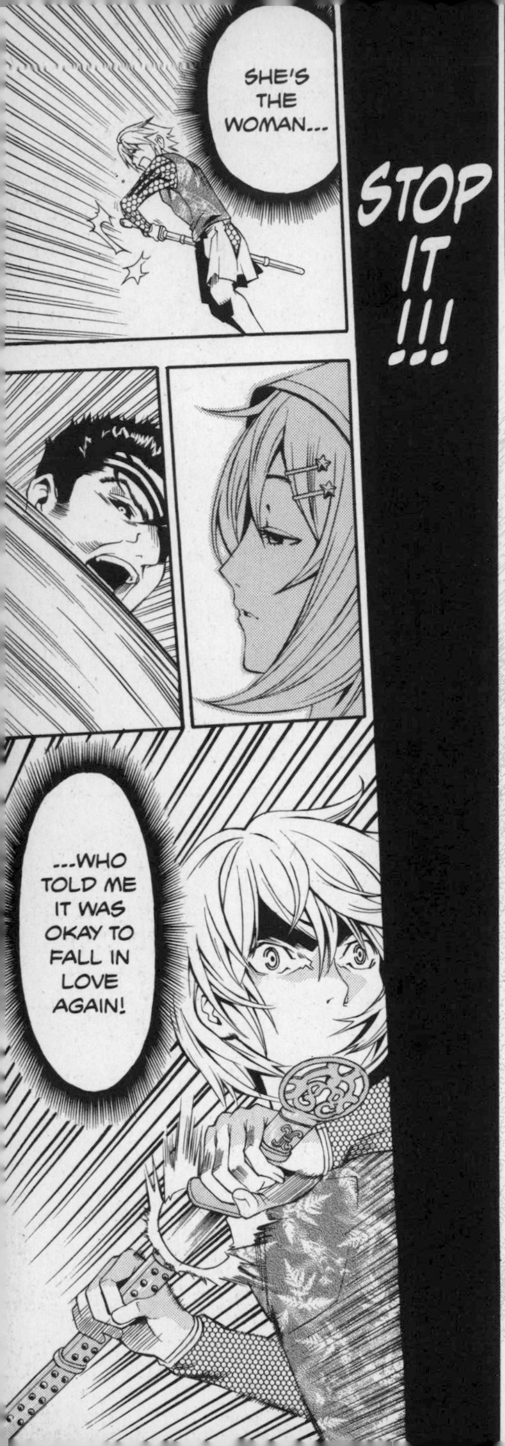
STOP IT!!!
SHE'S THE WOMAN...
...WHO TOLD ME IT WAS OKAY TO FALL IN LOVE AGAIN!

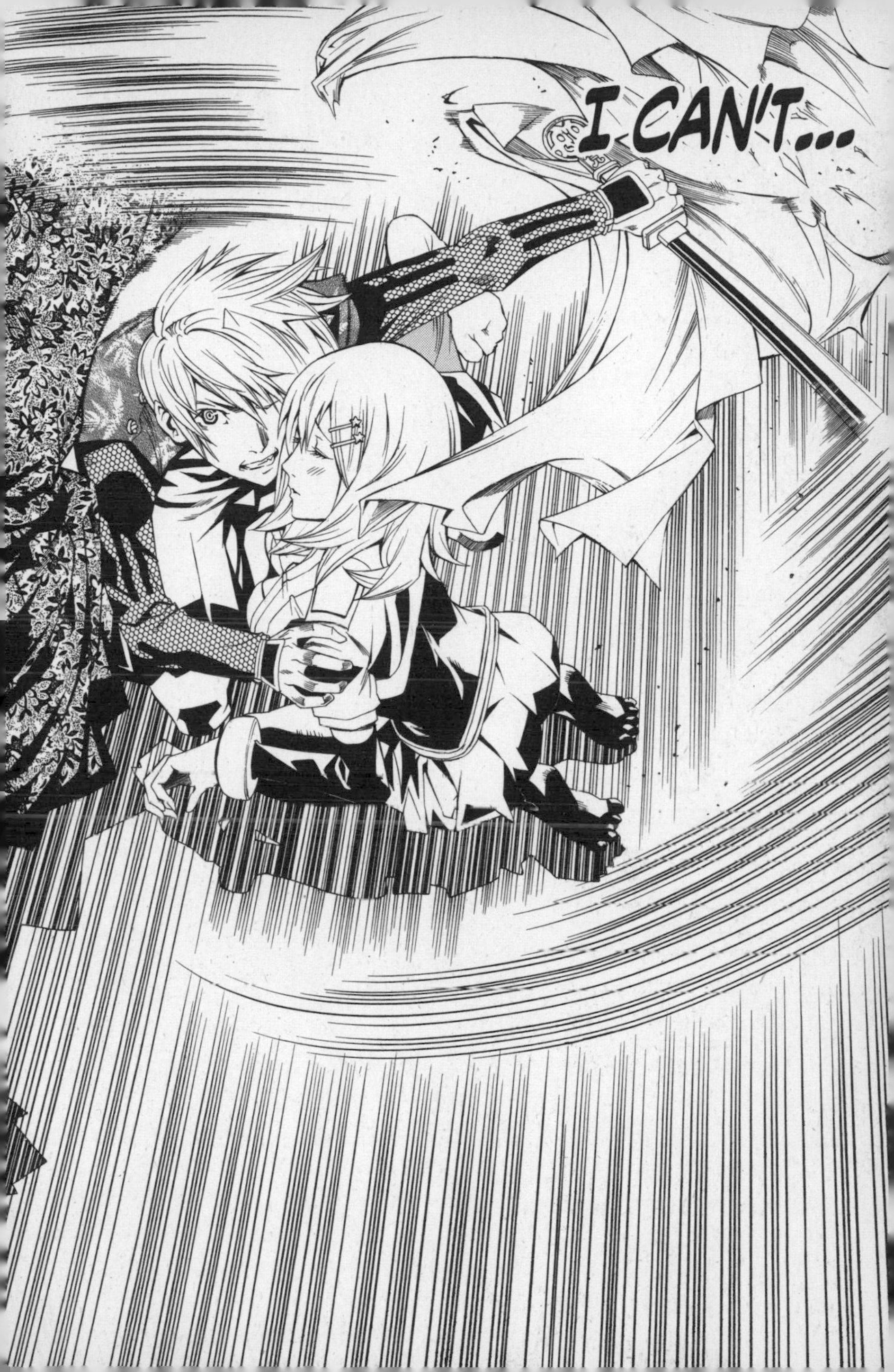
I CAN'T...

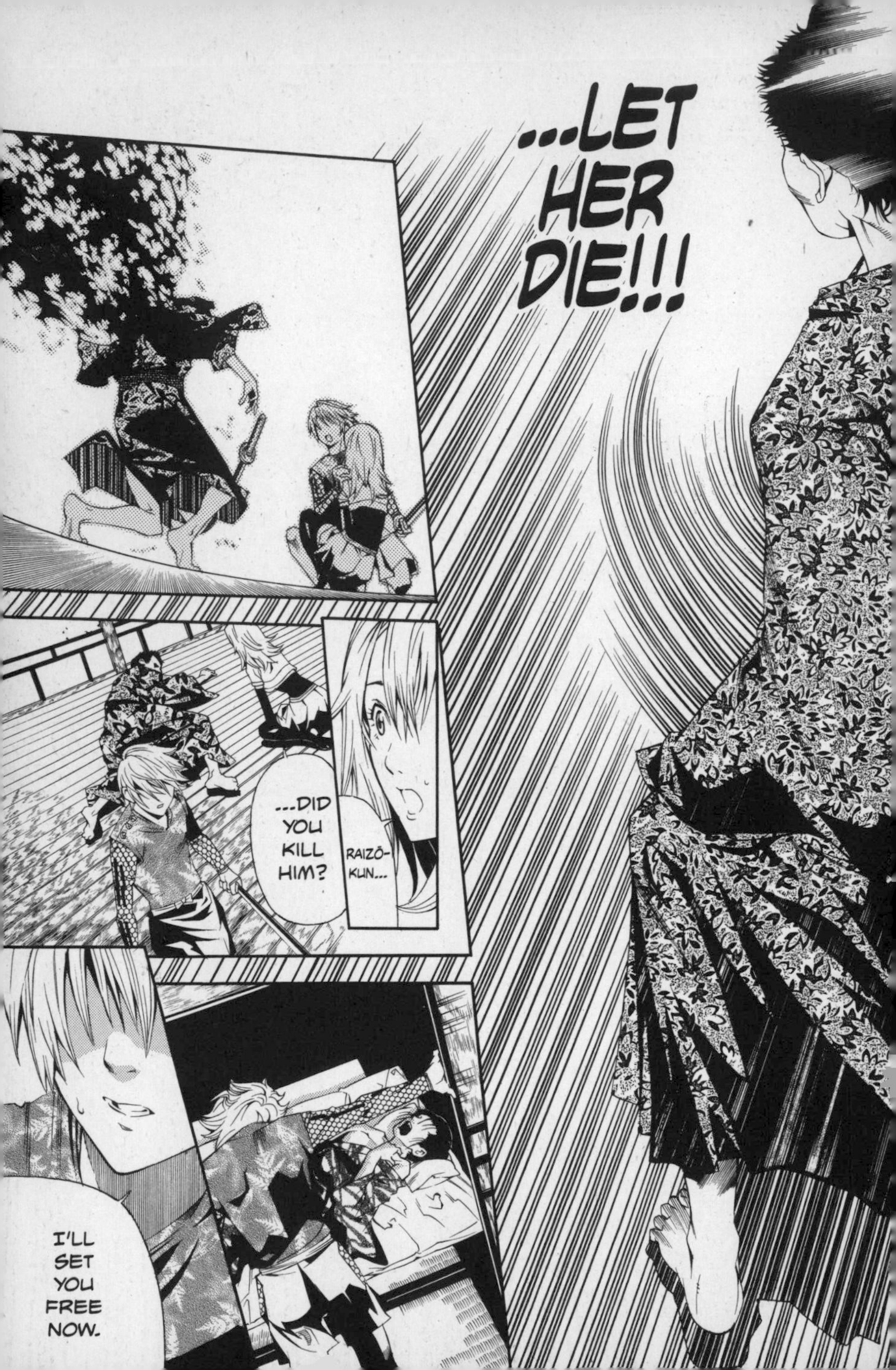
...LET HER DIE!!!
RAIZŌ-KUN...
...DID YOU KILL HIM?
I'LL SET YOU FREE NOW.

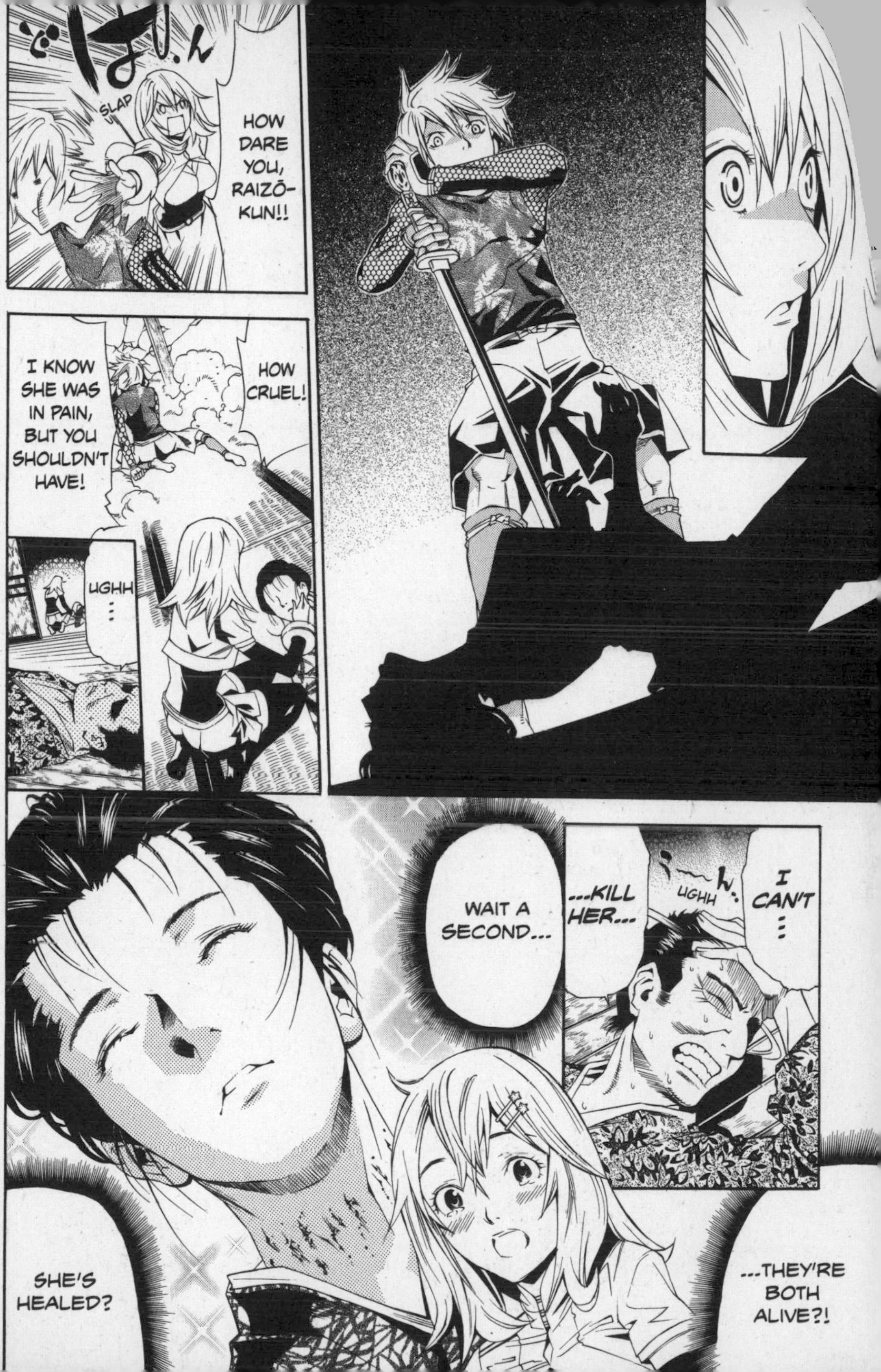
SLAP
HOW DARE YOU, RAIZŌ-KUN!!
HOW CRUEL!
I KNOW SHE WAS IN PAIN, BUT YOU SHOULDN'T HAVE!
UGHH ...
I CAN'T ...
UGHH
...KILL HER...
WAIT A SECOND...
...THEY'RE BOTH ALIVE?!
SHE'S HEALED?

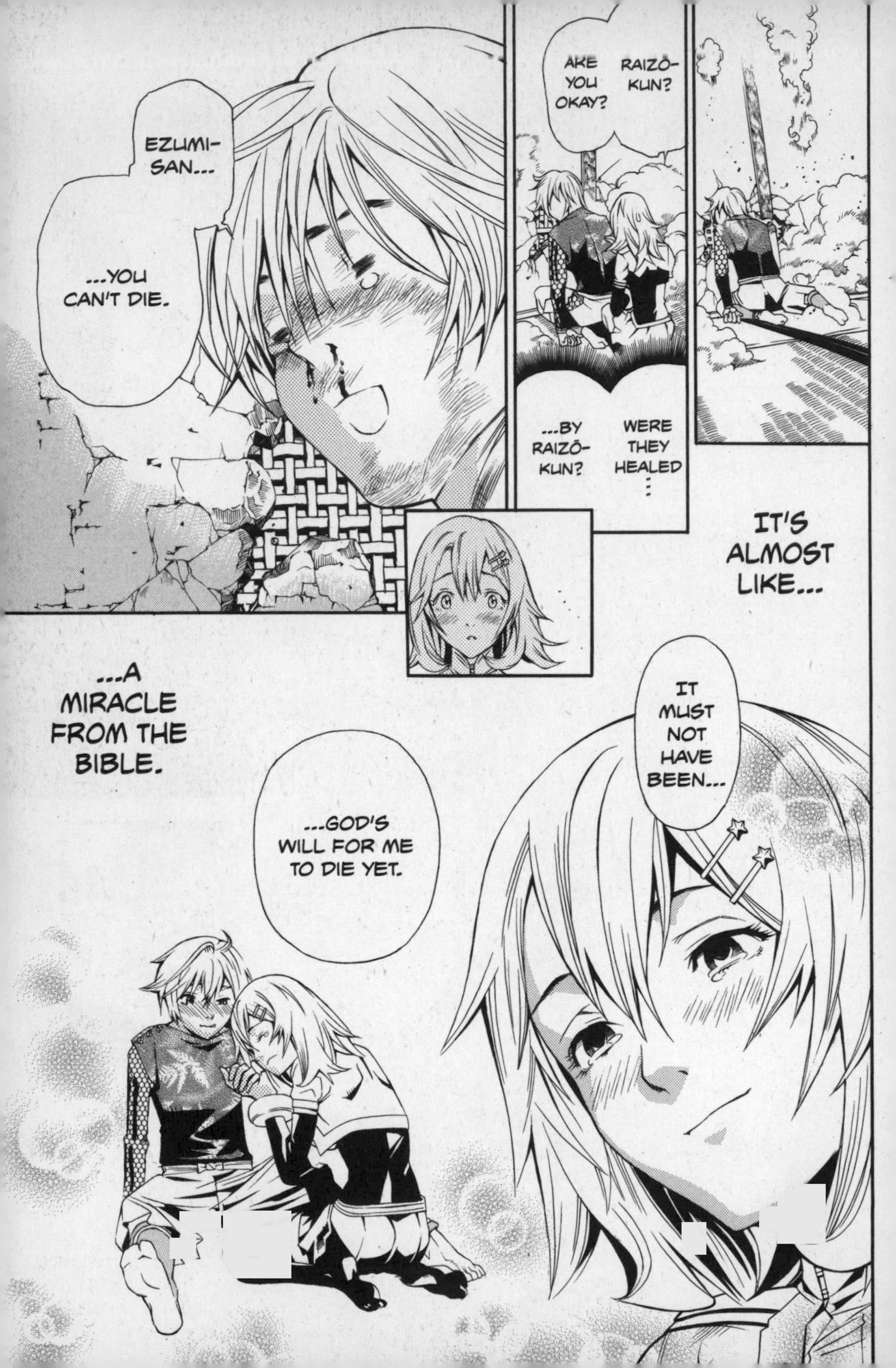
RAIZŌ-KUN?
ARE YOU OKAY?
WERE THEY HEALED...
...BY RAIZŌ-KUN?
EZUMI-SAN...
...YOU CAN'T DIE.
IT'S ALMOST LIKE...
...A MIRACLE FROM THE BIBLE.
IT MUST NOT HAVE BEEN...
...GOD'S WILL FOR ME TO DIE YET.

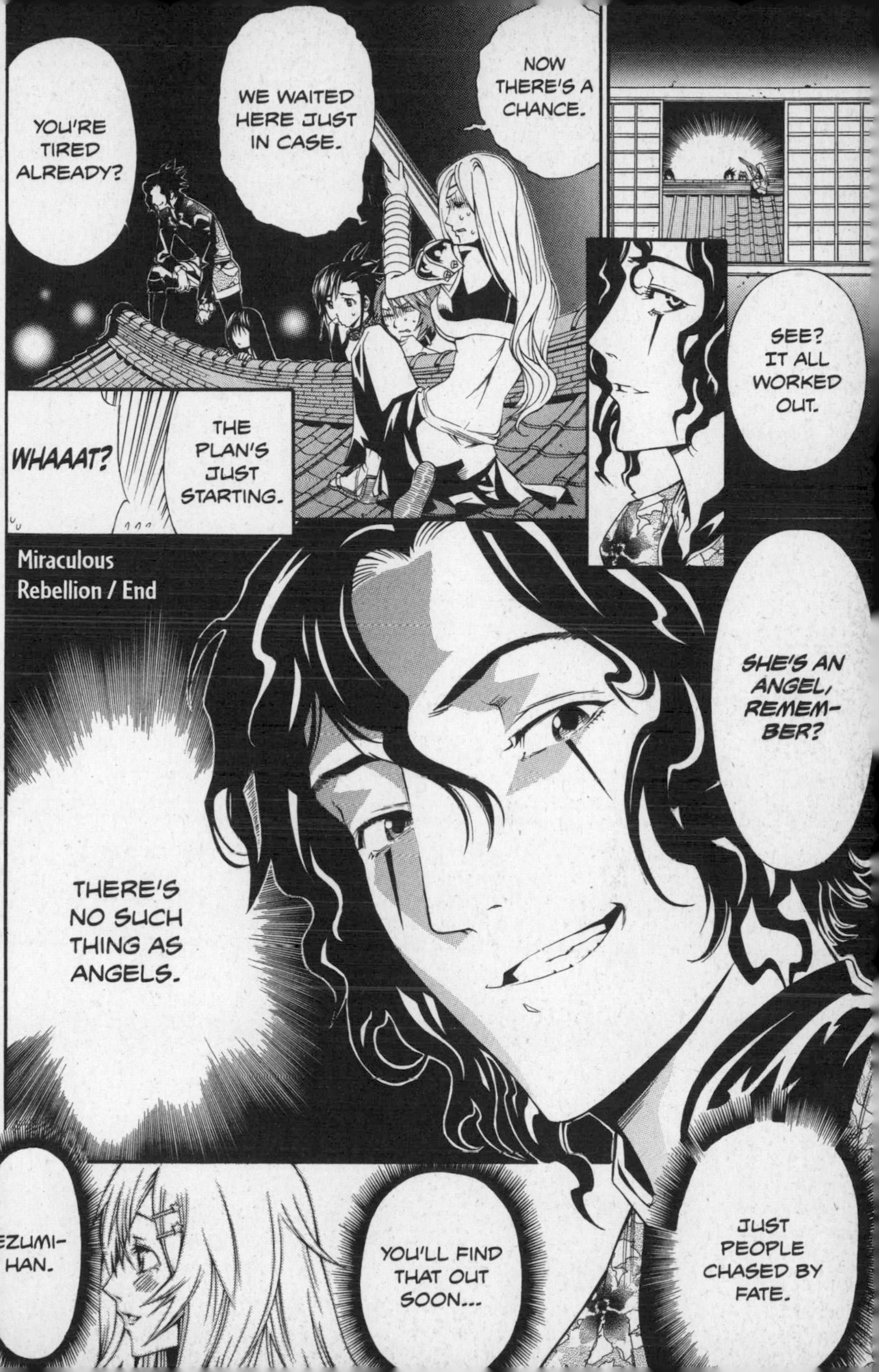
NOW THERE'S A CHANCE.
WE WAITED HERE JUST IN CASE.
YOU'RE TIRED ALREADY?
SEE? IT ALL WORKED OUT.
THE PLAN'S JUST STARTING.
WHAAAT?
SHE'S AN ANGEL, REMEMBER?
THERE'S NO SUCH THING AS ANGELS.
JUST PEOPLE CHASED BY FATE.
YOU'LL FIND THAT OUT SOON...
EZUMI-HAN.
Miraculous Rebellion / End

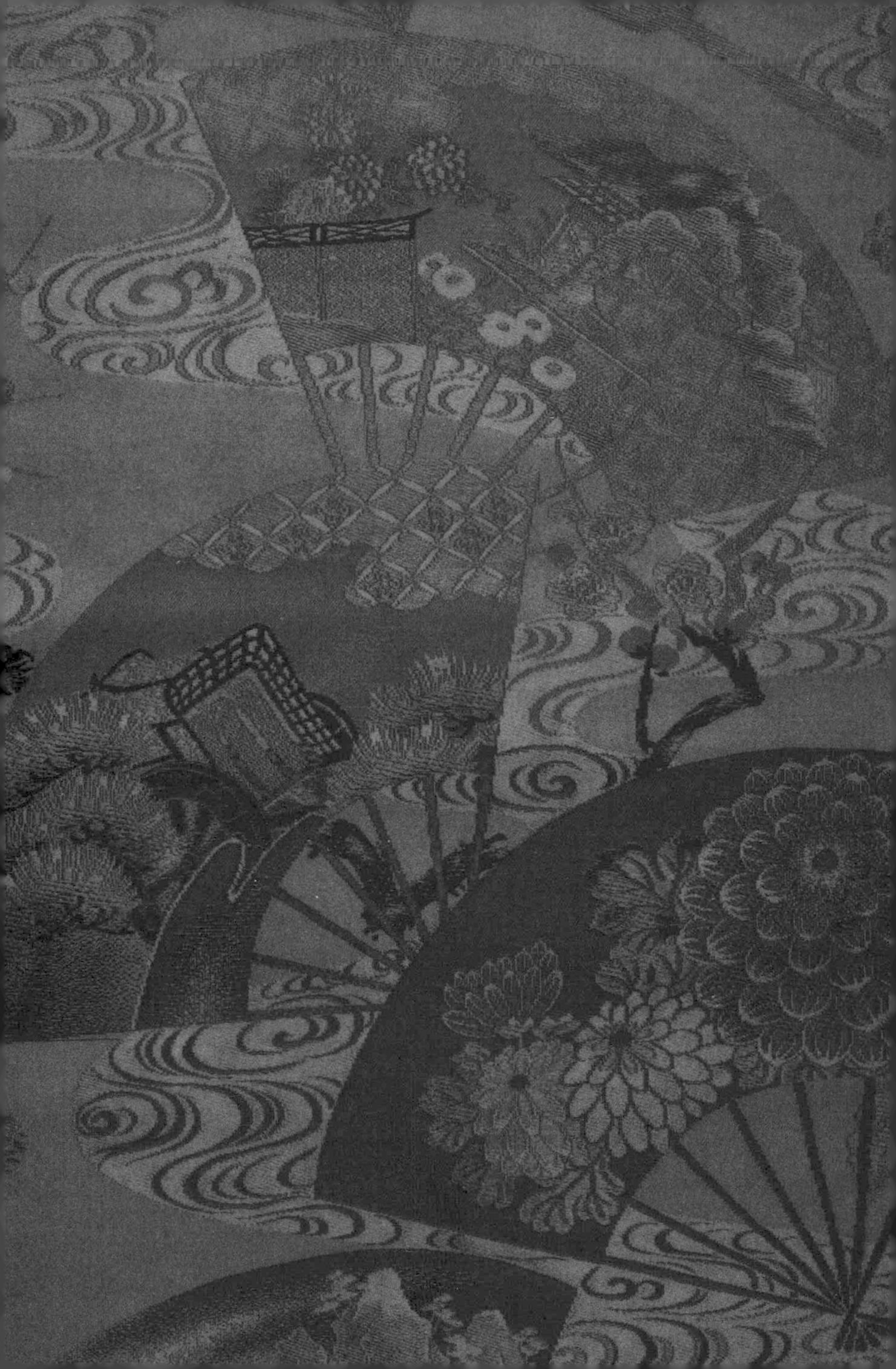

Ninja Girls

34 Fallen Angel Rebellion

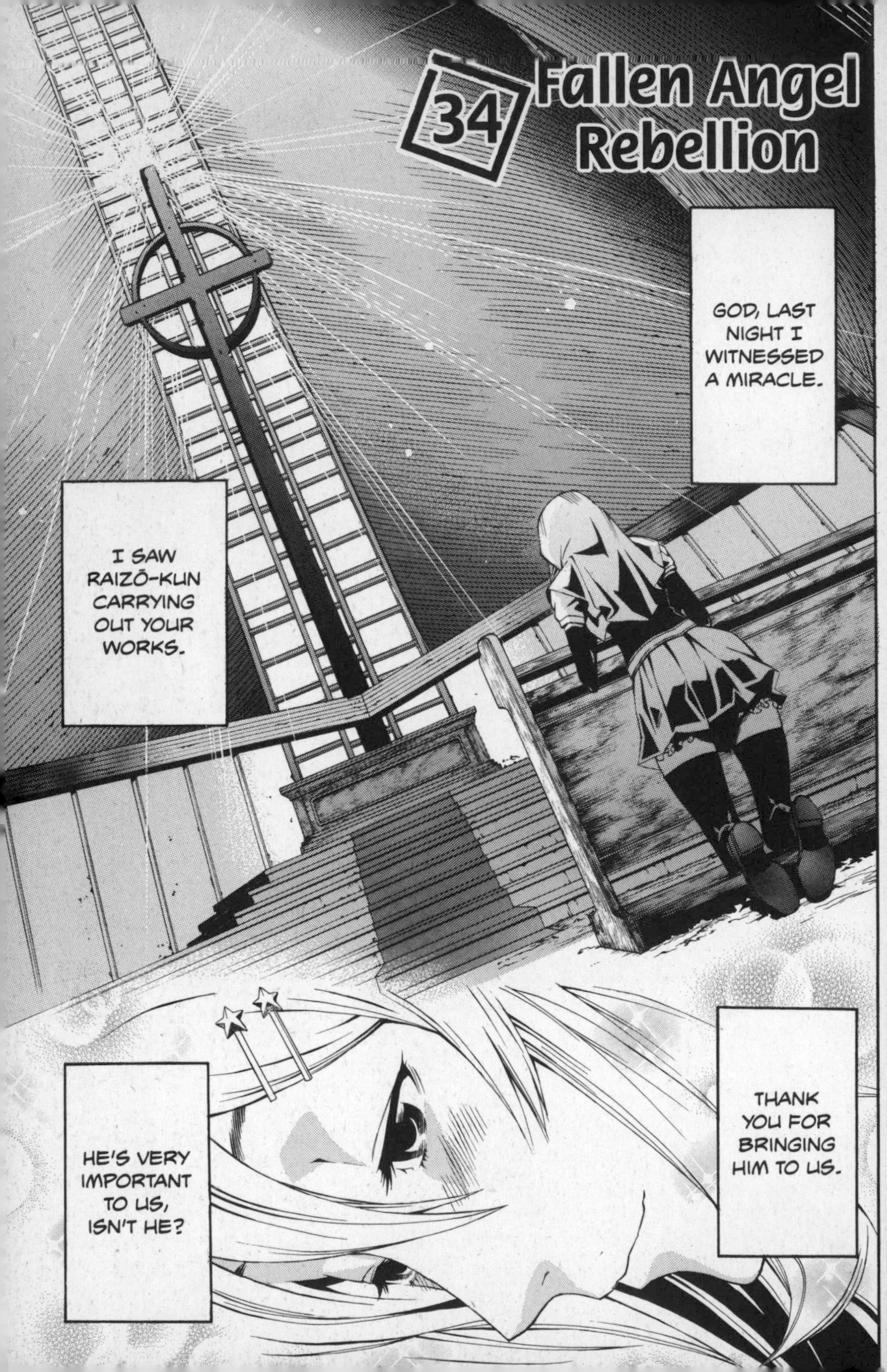
GOD, LAST NIGHT I WITNESSED A MIRACLE.
I SAW RAIZŌ-KUN CARRYING OUT YOUR WORKS.
THANK YOU FOR BRINGING HIM TO US.
HE'S VERY IMPORTANT TO US, ISN'T HE?

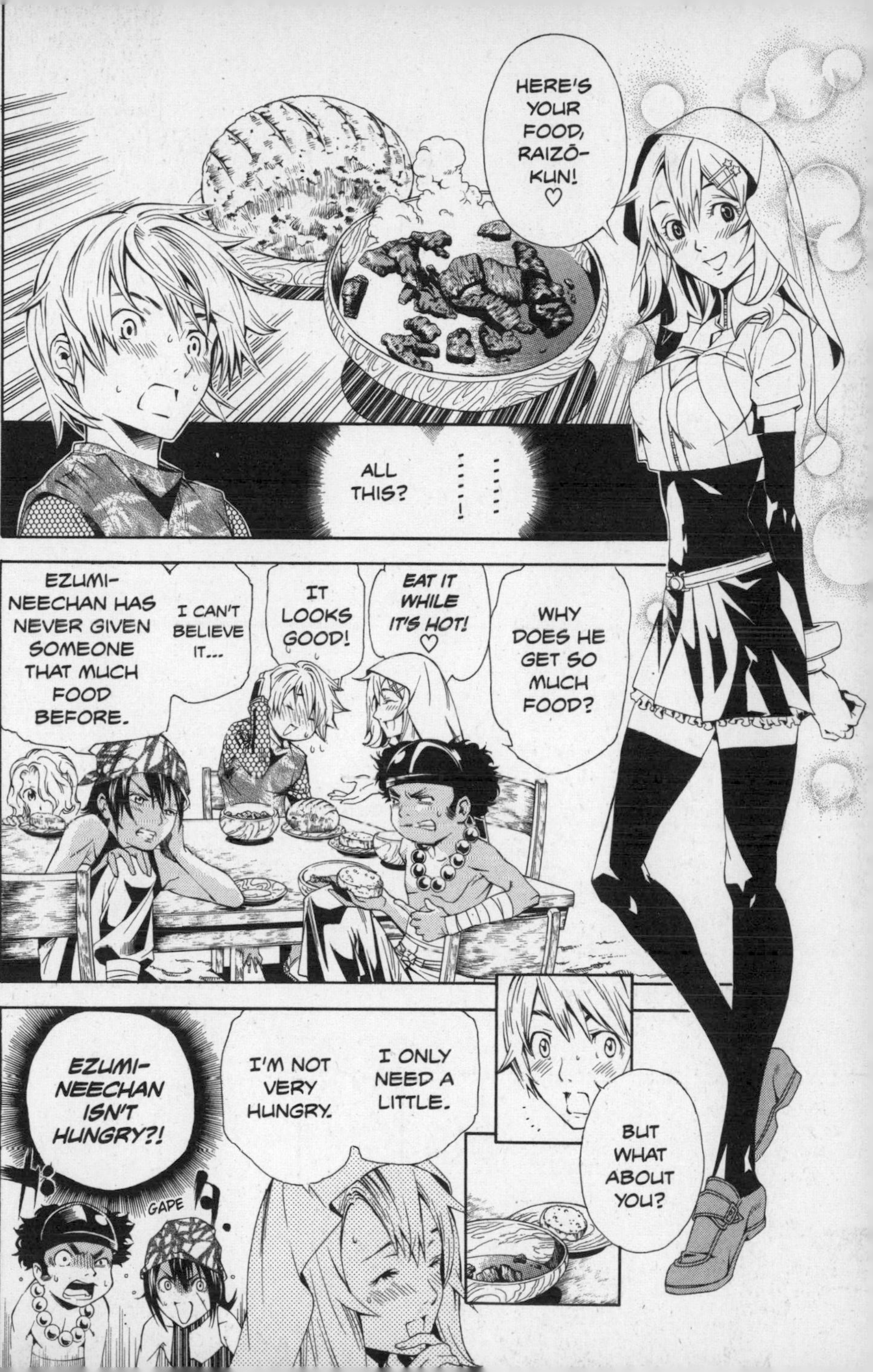
HERE'S YOUR FOOD, RAIZŌ-KUN! ♡
......
......!
ALL THIS?
WHY DOES HE GET SO MUCH FOOD?
EAT IT WHILE IT'S HOT! ♡
IT LOOKS GOOD!
I CAN'T BELIEVE IT...
EZUMI-NEECHAN HAS NEVER GIVEN SOMEONE THAT MUCH FOOD BEFORE.
...
BUT WHAT ABOUT YOU?
I ONLY NEED A LITTLE.
I'M NOT VERY HUNGRY.
EZUMI-NEECHAN ISN'T HUNGRY?!
GAPE

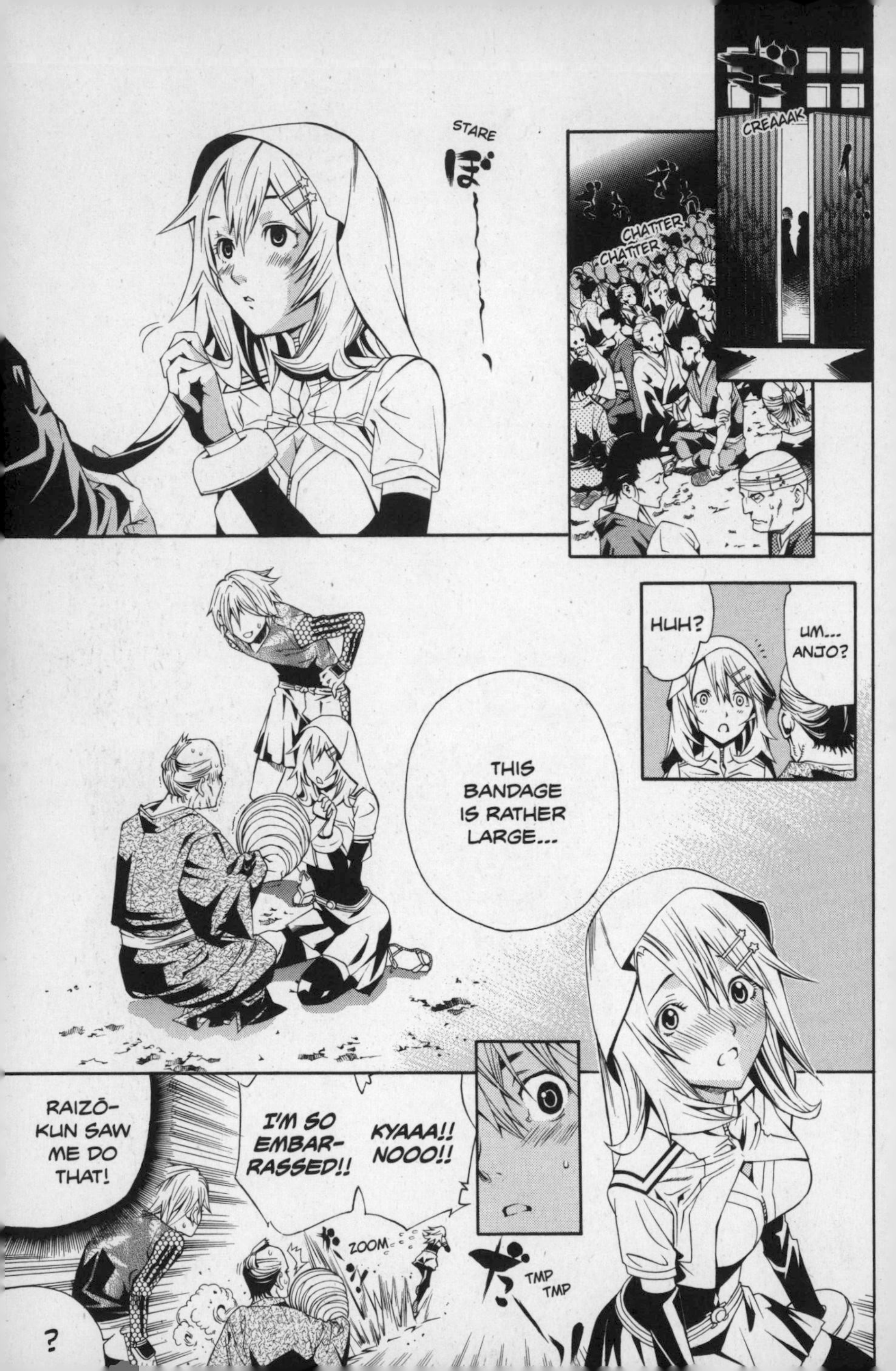
CREAAAK
CHATTER
CHATTER
STARE
ぼー
UM... ANJO?
HUH?
THIS BANDAGE IS RATHER LARGE...
KYAAA!! NOOO!!
I'M SO EMBARRASSED!!
RAIZŌ-KUN SAW ME DO THAT!
TMP TMP
ZOOM
?

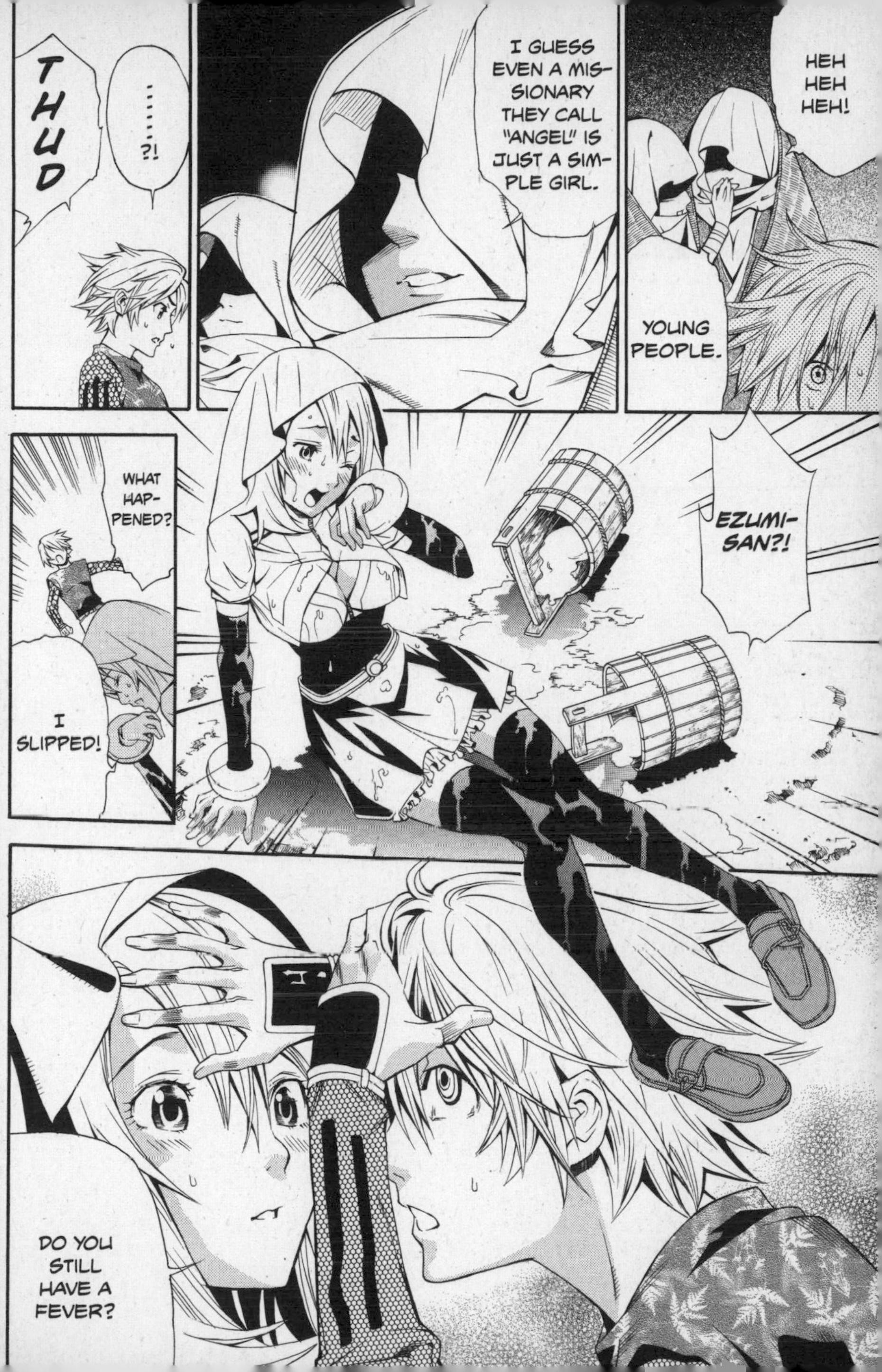
HEH HEH HEH!
YOUNG PEOPLE.
I GUESS EVEN A MISSIONARY THEY CALL "ANGEL" IS JUST A SIMPLE GIRL.
THUD
......?!
EZUMI-SAN?!
WHAT HAPPENED?
I SLIPPED!
DO YOU STILL HAVE A FEVER?

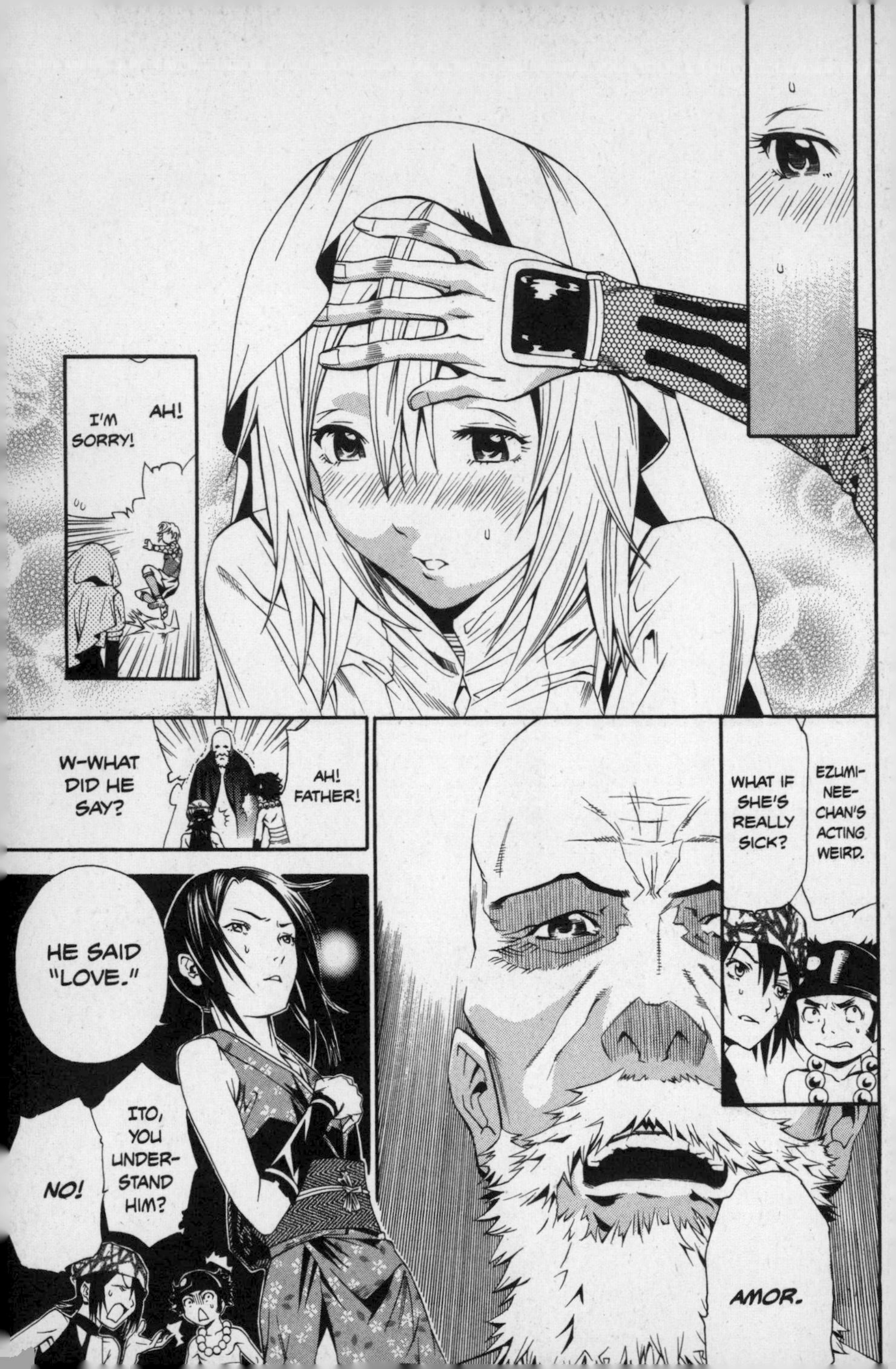
AH!
I'M SORRY!
EZUMI-NEE-CHAN'S ACTING WEIRD.
WHAT IF SHE'S REALLY SICK?
AMOR.
AH! FATHER!
W-WHAT DID HE SAY?
HE SAID "LOVE."
ITO, YOU UNDERSTAND HIM?
NO!

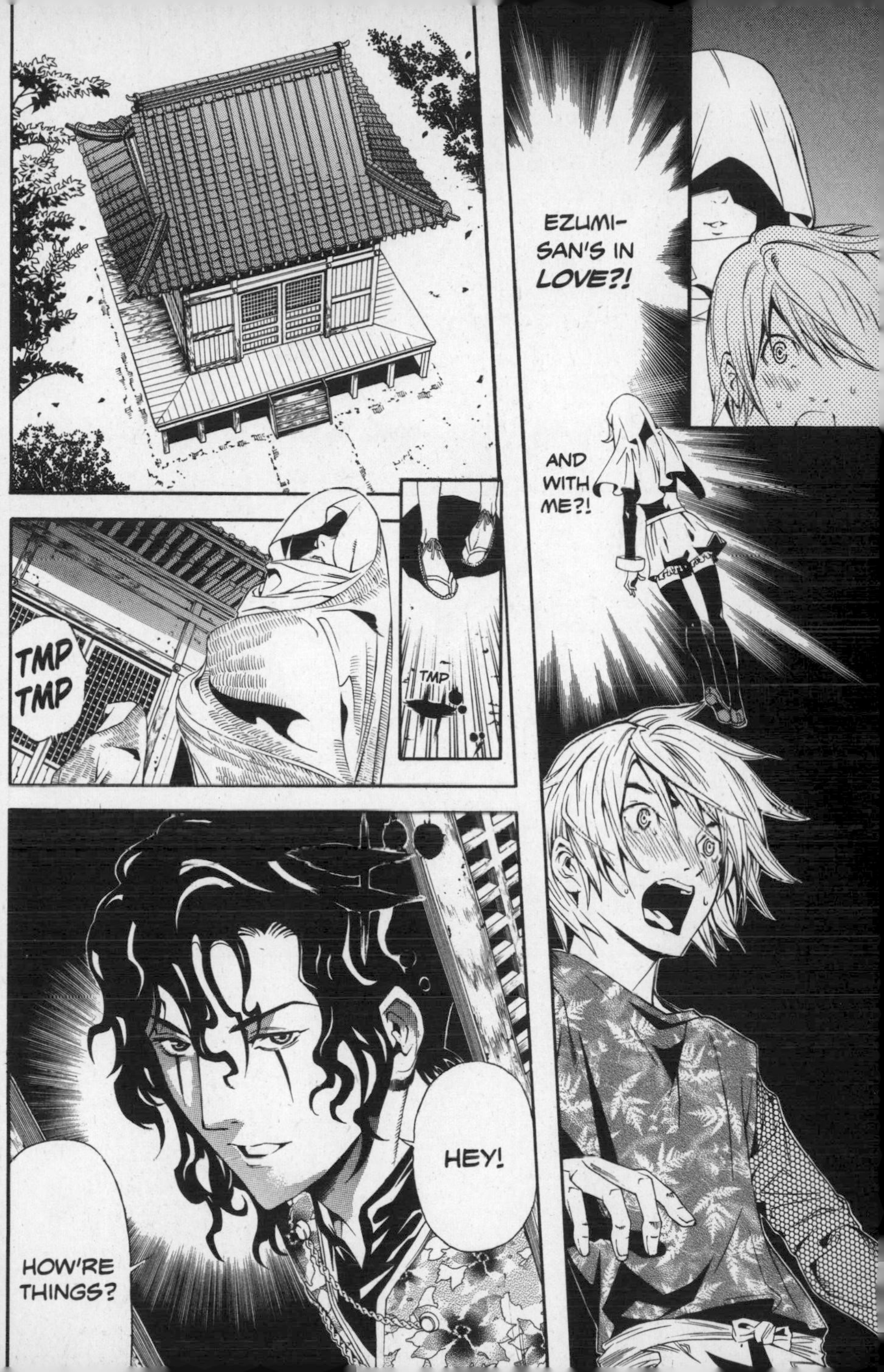
EZUMI-SAN'S IN LOVE?!
AND WITH ME?!
TMP
TMP TMP
HEY!
HOW'RE THINGS?

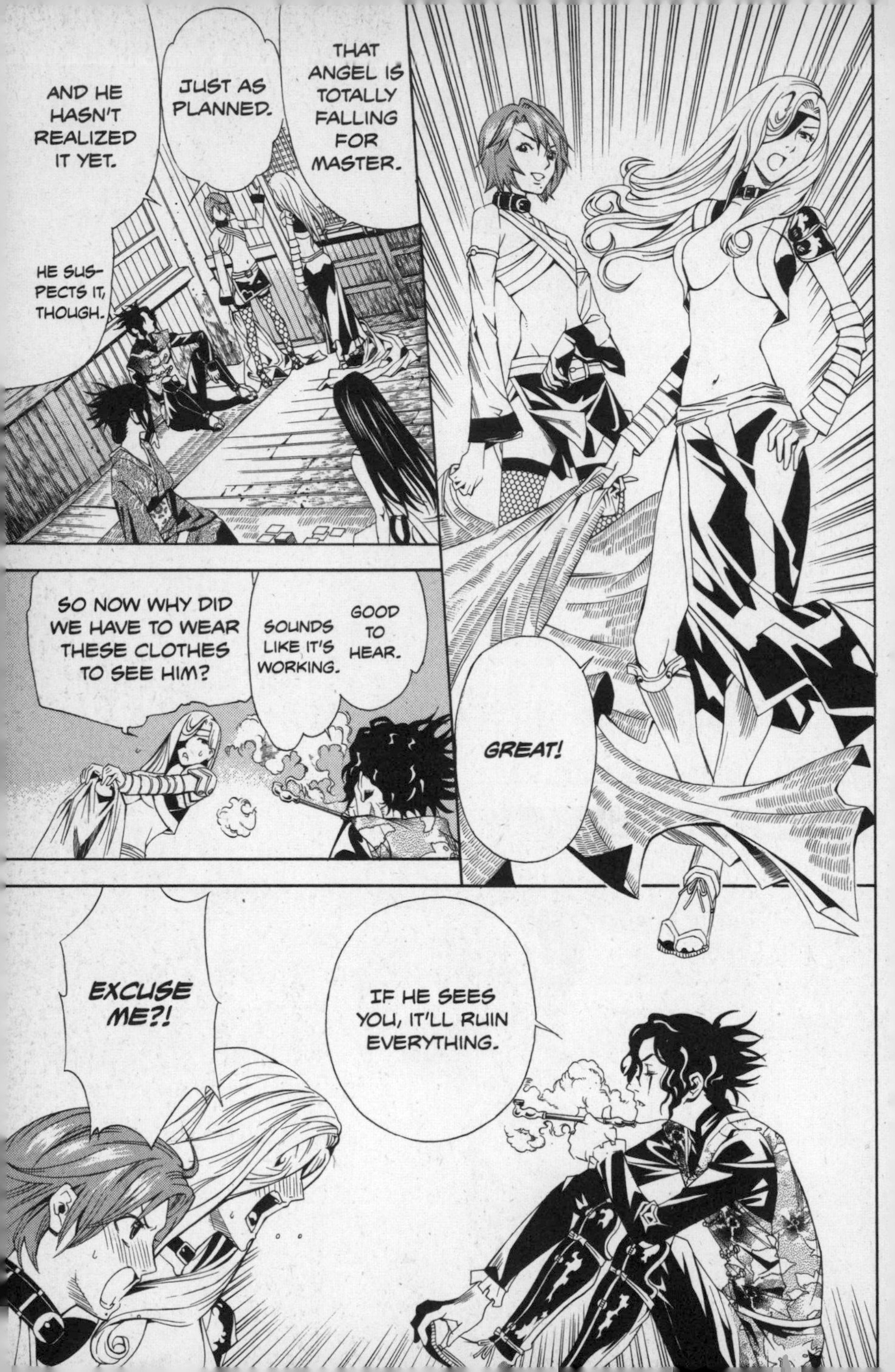
GREAT!
THAT ANGEL IS TOTALLY FALLING FOR MASTER.
JUST AS PLANNED.
AND HE HASN'T REALIZED IT YET.
HE SUSPECTS IT, THOUGH.
GOOD TO HEAR.
SOUNDS LIKE IT'S WORKING.
SO NOW WHY DID WE HAVE TO WEAR THESE CLOTHES TO SEE HIM?
IF HE SEES YOU, IT'LL RUIN EVERYTHING.
EXCUSE ME?!

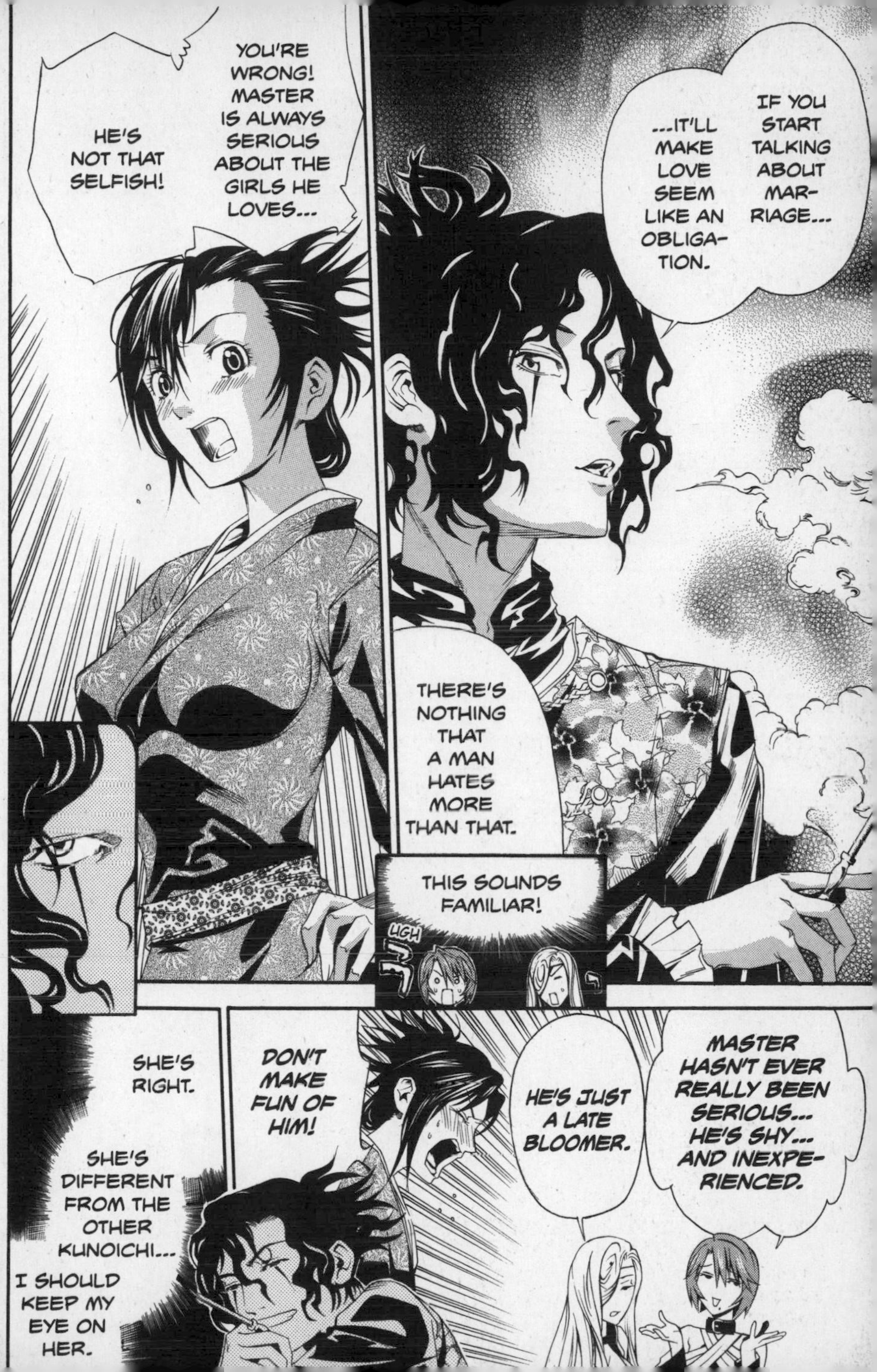
IF YOU START TALKING ABOUT MARRIAGE...
...IT'LL MAKE LOVE SEEM LIKE AN OBLIGATION.
THERE'S NOTHING THAT A MAN HATES MORE THAN THAT.
YOU'RE WRONG! MASTER IS ALWAYS SERIOUS ABOUT THE GIRLS HE LOVES...
HE'S NOT THAT SELFISH!
THIS SOUNDS FAMILIAR!
UGH
MASTER HASN'T EVER REALLY BEEN SERIOUS... HE'S SHY... AND INEXPERIENCED.
HE'S JUST A LATE BLOOMER.
DON'T MAKE FUN OF HIM!
SHE'S RIGHT.
SHE'S DIFFERENT FROM THE OTHER KUNOICHI...
I SHOULD KEEP MY EYE ON HER.

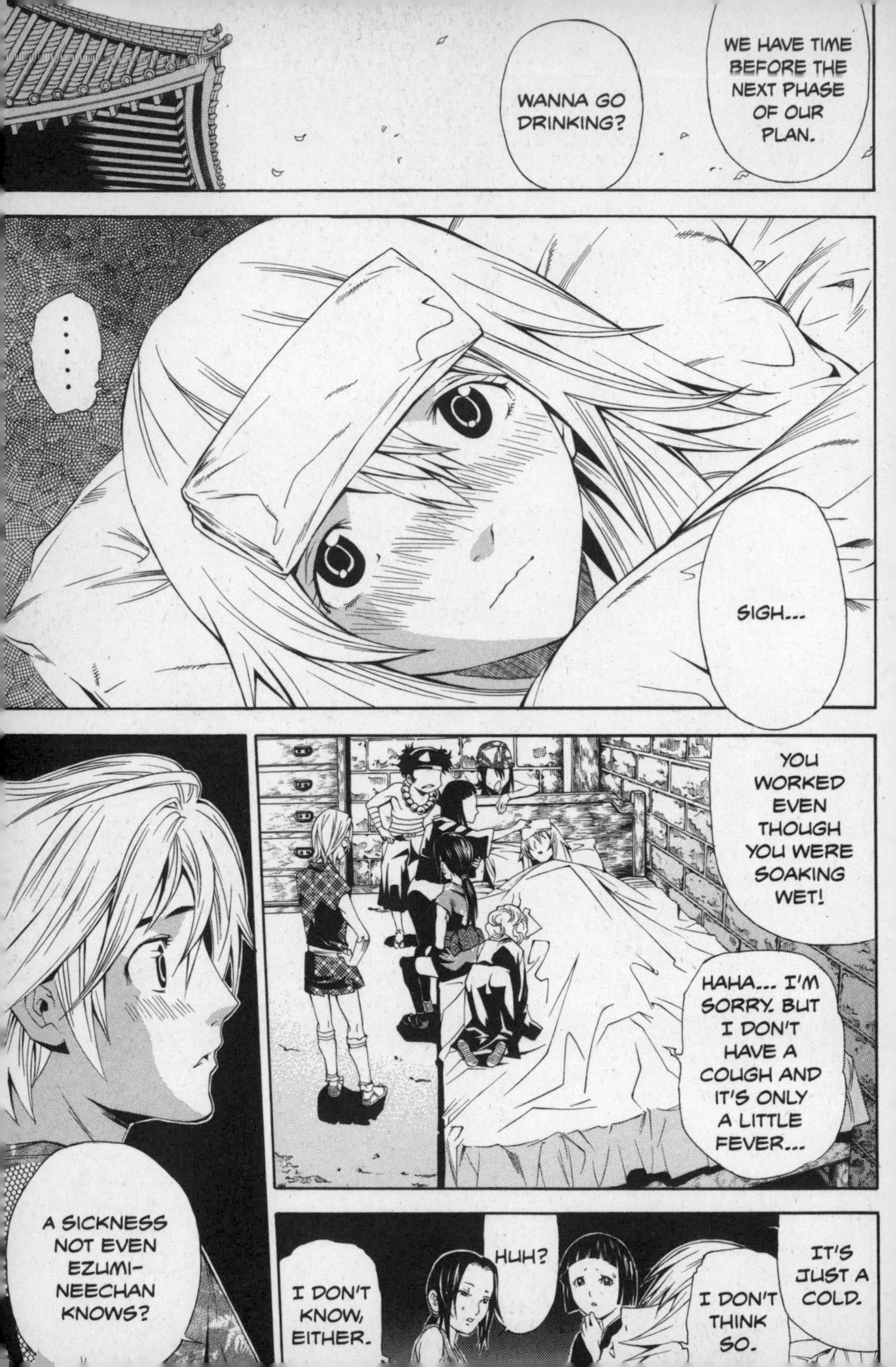
WE HAVE TIME BEFORE THE NEXT PHASE OF OUR PLAN.
WANNA GO DRINKING?
SIGH...
......
YOU WORKED EVEN THOUGH YOU WERE SOAKING WET!
HAHA... I'M SORRY. BUT I DON'T HAVE A COUGH AND IT'S ONLY A LITTLE FEVER...
IT'S JUST A COLD.
I DON'T THINK SO.
HUH?
I DON'T KNOW, EITHER.
A SICKNESS NOT EVEN EZUMI-NEECHAN KNOWS?

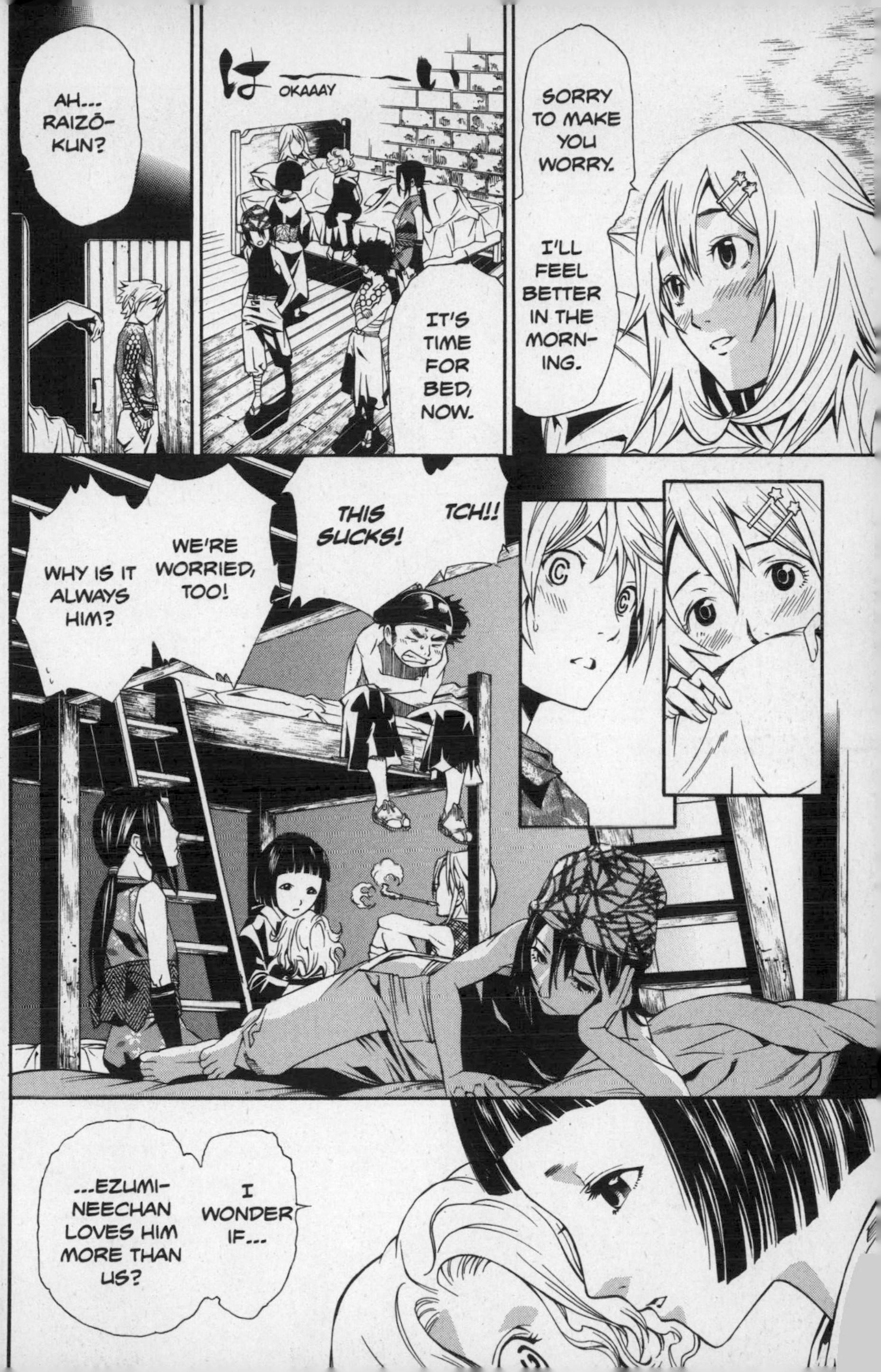

SORRY TO MAKE YOU WORRY.
I'LL FEEL BETTER IN THE MORNING.
IT'S TIME FOR BED, NOW.
は——い OKAAAY
AH... RAIZŌ-KUN?
TCH!!
THIS SUCKS!
WE'RE WORRIED, TOO!
WHY IS IT ALWAYS HIM?
I WONDER IF...
...EZUMI-NEECHAN LOVES HIM MORE THAN US?

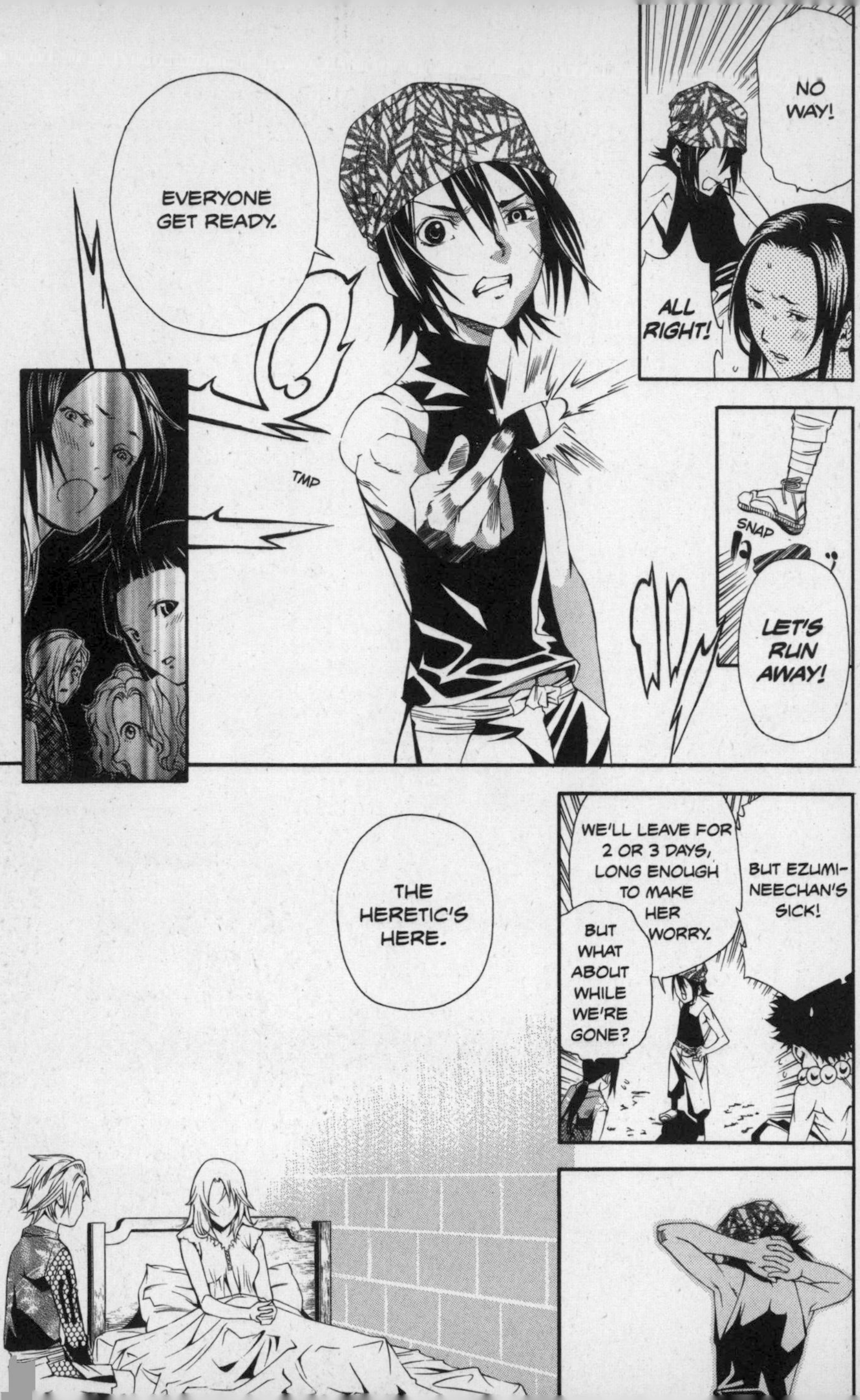
NO WAY!
ALL RIGHT!
SNAP
LET'S RUN AWAY!
EVERYONE GET READY.
TMP
BUT EZUMI-NEECHAN'S SICK!
WE'LL LEAVE FOR 2 OR 3 DAYS, LONG ENOUGH TO MAKE HER WORRY.
BUT WHAT ABOUT WHILE WE'RE GONE?
THE HERETIC'S HERE.

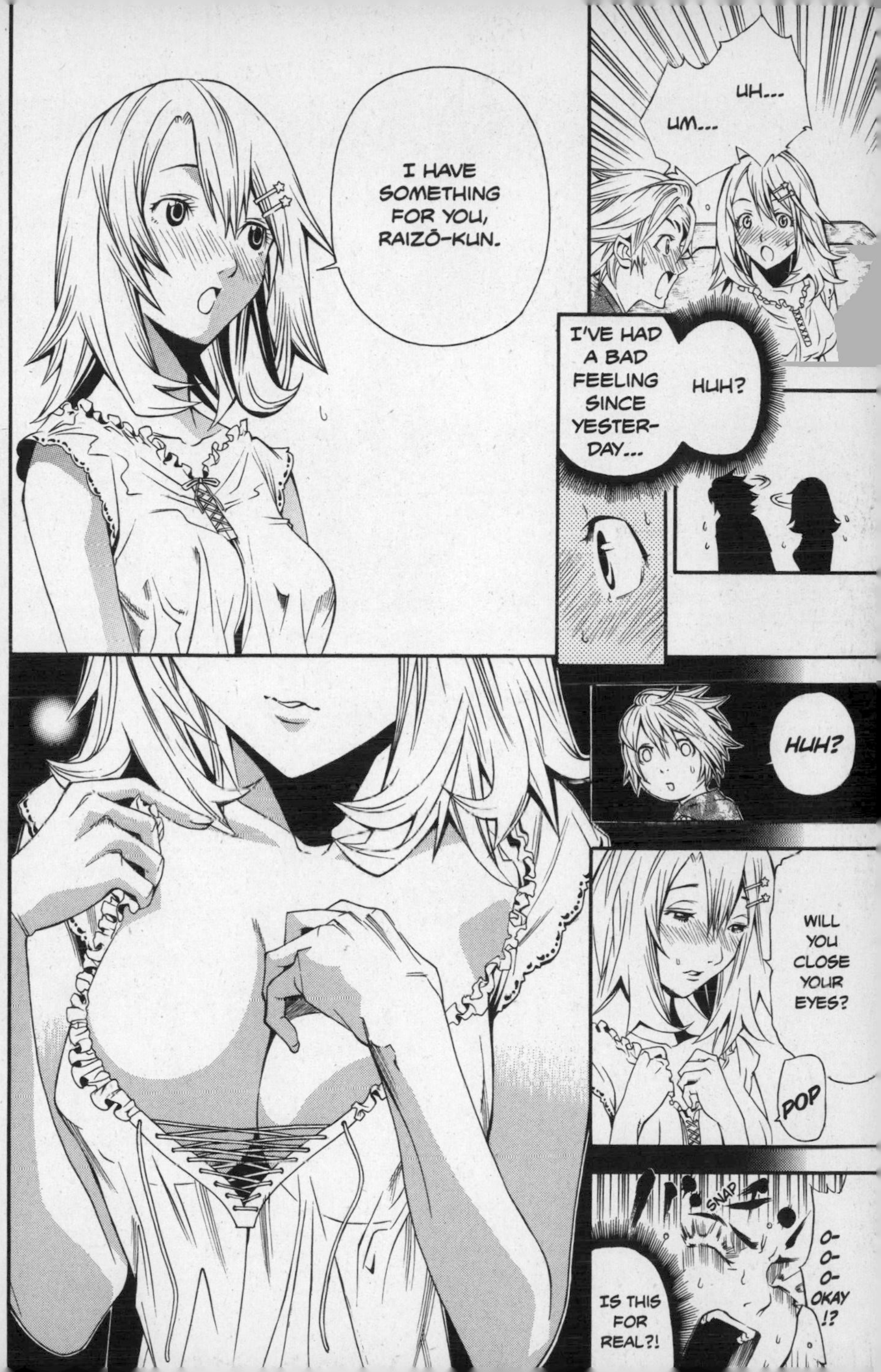
UH...
UM...
HUH?
I'VE HAD A BAD FEELING SINCE YESTER-DAY...
I HAVE SOMETHING FOR YOU, RAIZŌ-KUN.
HUH?
WILL YOU CLOSE YOUR EYES?
POP
SNAP
O-O-O-OKAY!?
IS THIS FOR REAL?!

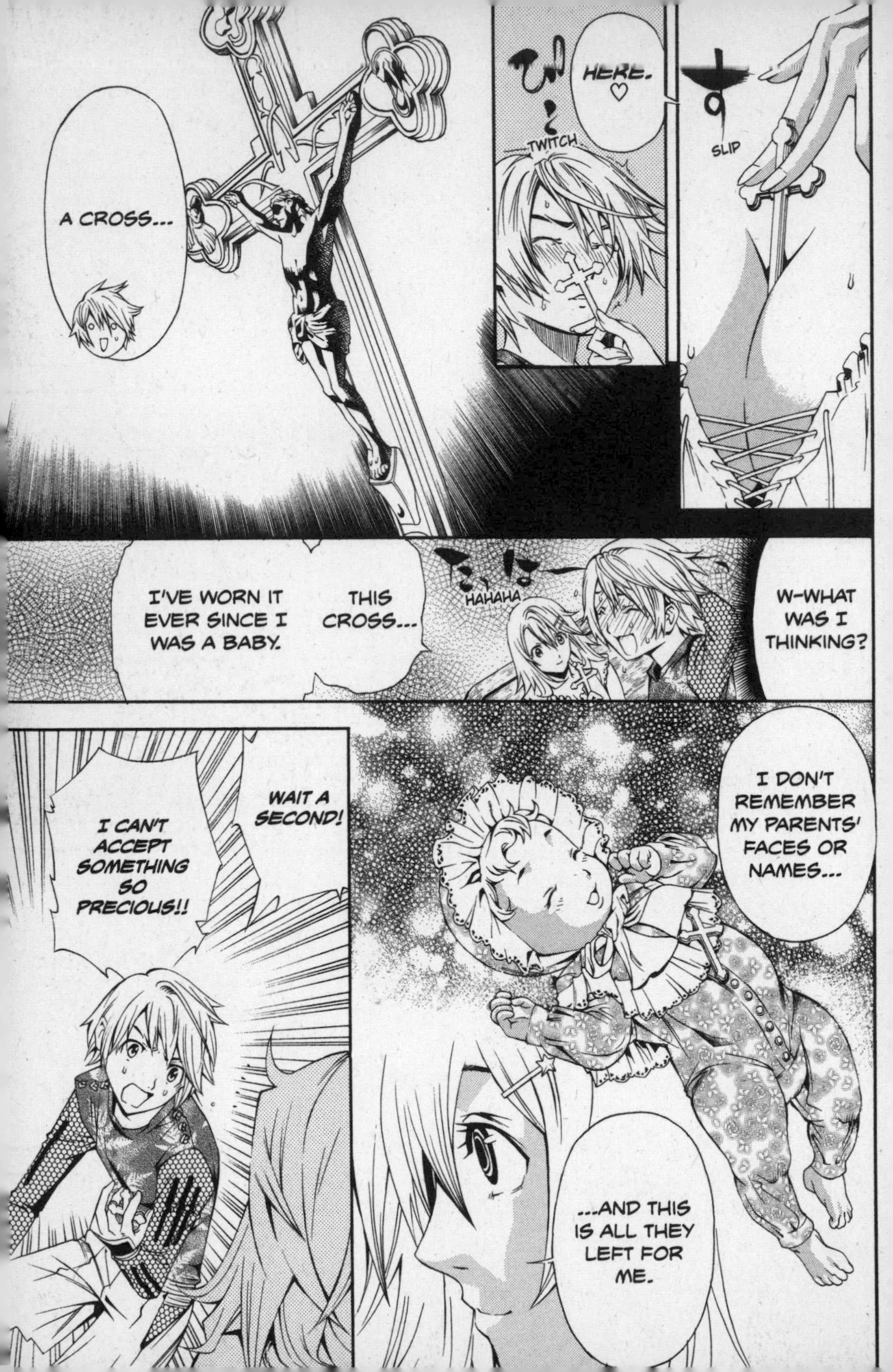
SLIP
HERE. ♡
TWITCH
A CROSS...
W-WHAT WAS I THINKING?
HAHAHA
THIS CROSS...
I'VE WORN IT EVER SINCE I WAS A BABY.
I DON'T REMEMBER MY PARENTS' FACES OR NAMES...
...AND THIS IS ALL THEY LEFT FOR ME.
WAIT A SECOND!
I CAN'T ACCEPT SOMETHING SO PRECIOUS!!

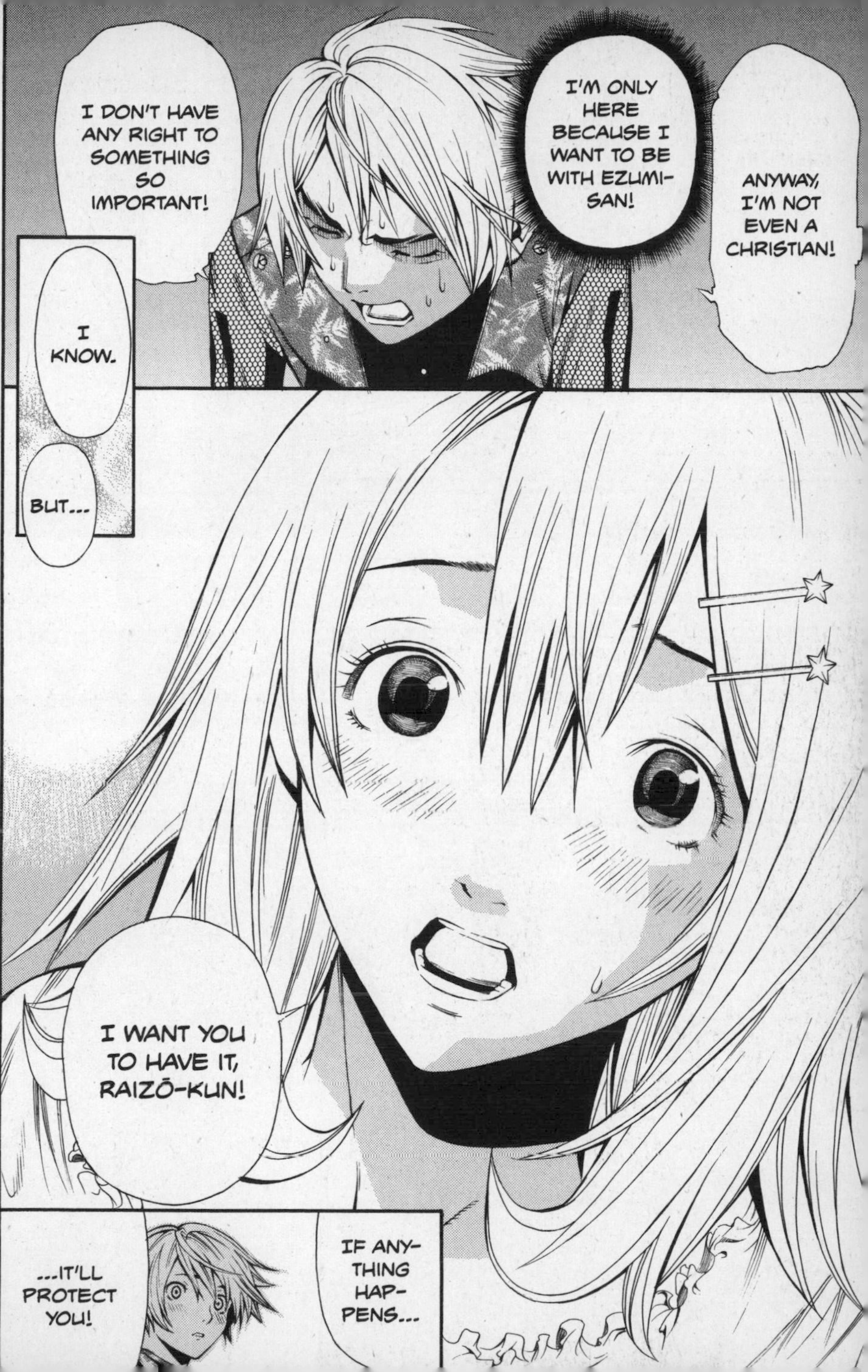
ANYWAY, I'M NOT EVEN A CHRISTIAN!
I'M ONLY HERE BECAUSE I WANT TO BE WITH EZUMI-SAN!
I DON'T HAVE ANY RIGHT TO SOMETHING SO IMPORTANT!
I KNOW.
BUT...
I WANT YOU TO HAVE IT, RAIZŌ-KUN!
IF ANYTHING HAPPENS...
...IT'LL PROTECT YOU!

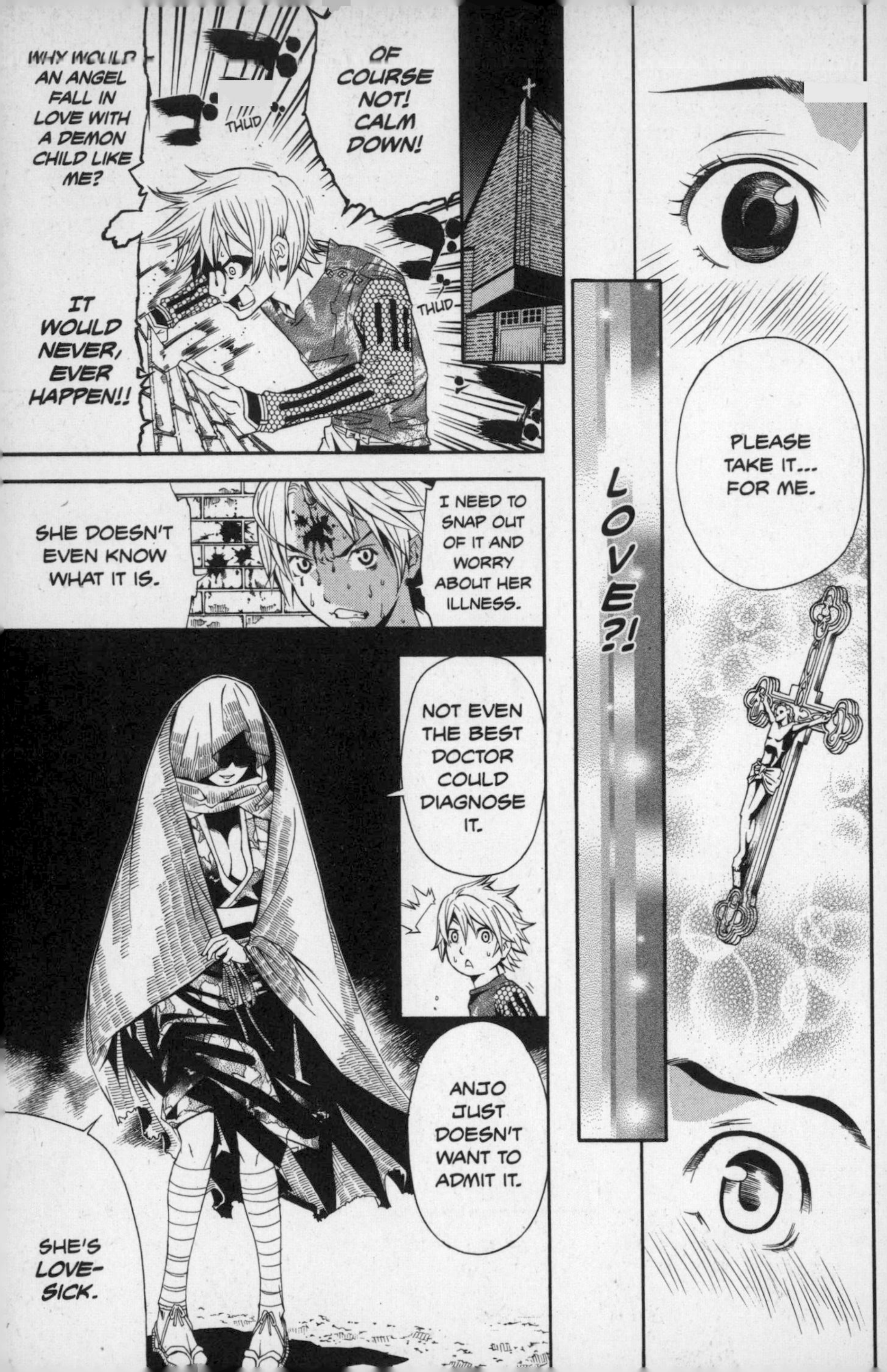
PLEASE TAKE IT... FOR ME.
LOVE?!
OF COURSE NOT! CALM DOWN!
WHY WOULD AN ANGEL FALL IN LOVE WITH A DEMON CHILD LIKE ME?
THUD
THUD
IT WOULD NEVER, EVER HAPPEN!!
I NEED TO SNAP OUT OF IT AND WORRY ABOUT HER ILLNESS.
SHE DOESN'T EVEN KNOW WHAT IT IS.
NOT EVEN THE BEST DOCTOR COULD DIAGNOSE IT.
ANJO JUST DOESN'T WANT TO ADMIT IT.
SHE'S LOVE-SICK.

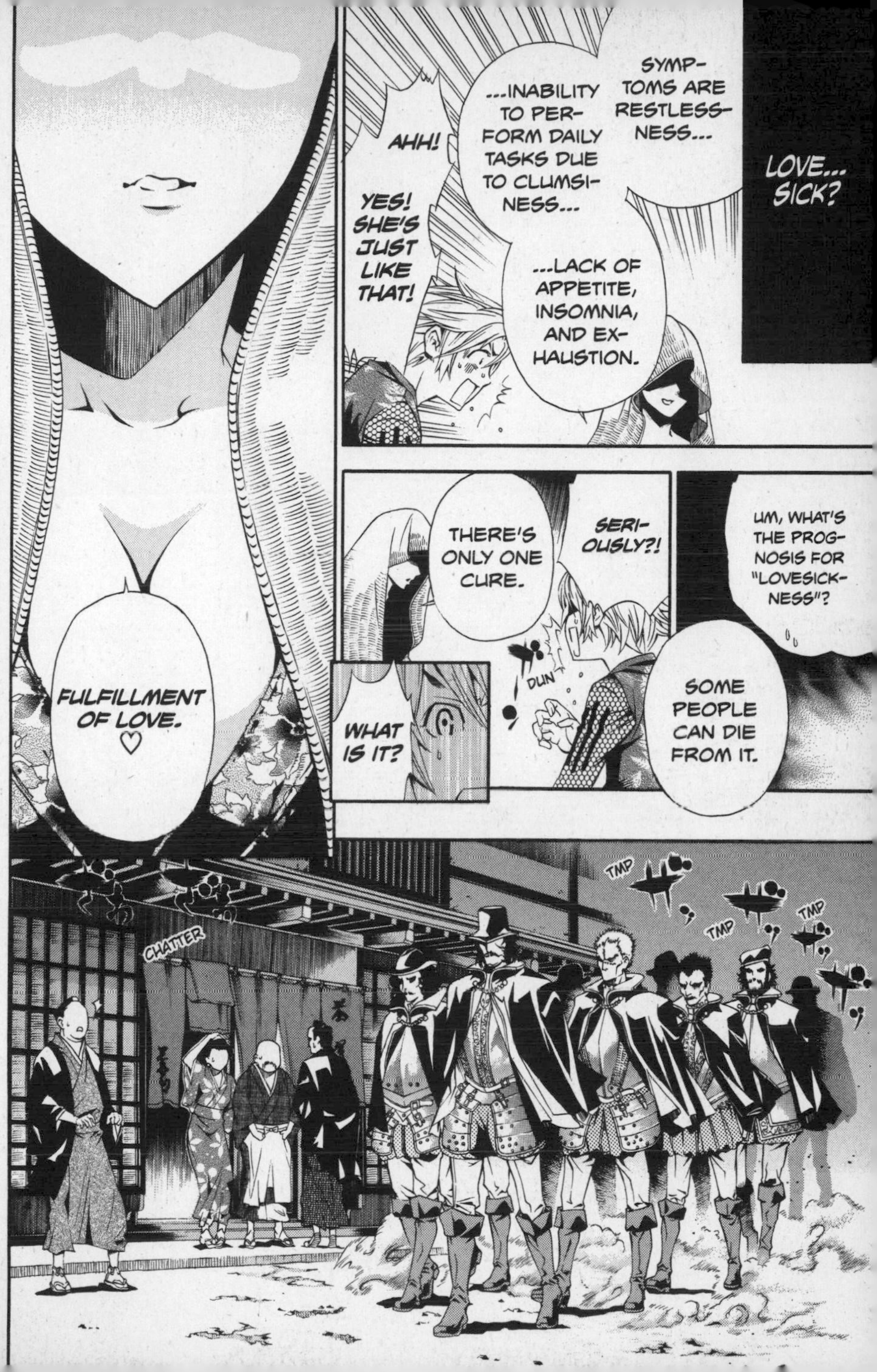
LOVE... SICK?
SYMPTOMS ARE RESTLESSNESS...
...INABILITY TO PERFORM DAILY TASKS DUE TO CLUMSINESS...
AHH!
YES! SHE'S JUST LIKE THAT!
...LACK OF APPETITE, INSOMNIA, AND EXHAUSTION.
UM, WHAT'S THE PROGNOSIS FOR "LOVESICKNESS"?
SOME PEOPLE CAN DIE FROM IT.
SERIOUSLY?!
THERE'S ONLY ONE CURE.
DUN
WHAT IS IT?
FULFILLMENT OF LOVE. ♡
TMP
TMP
TMP
CHATTER

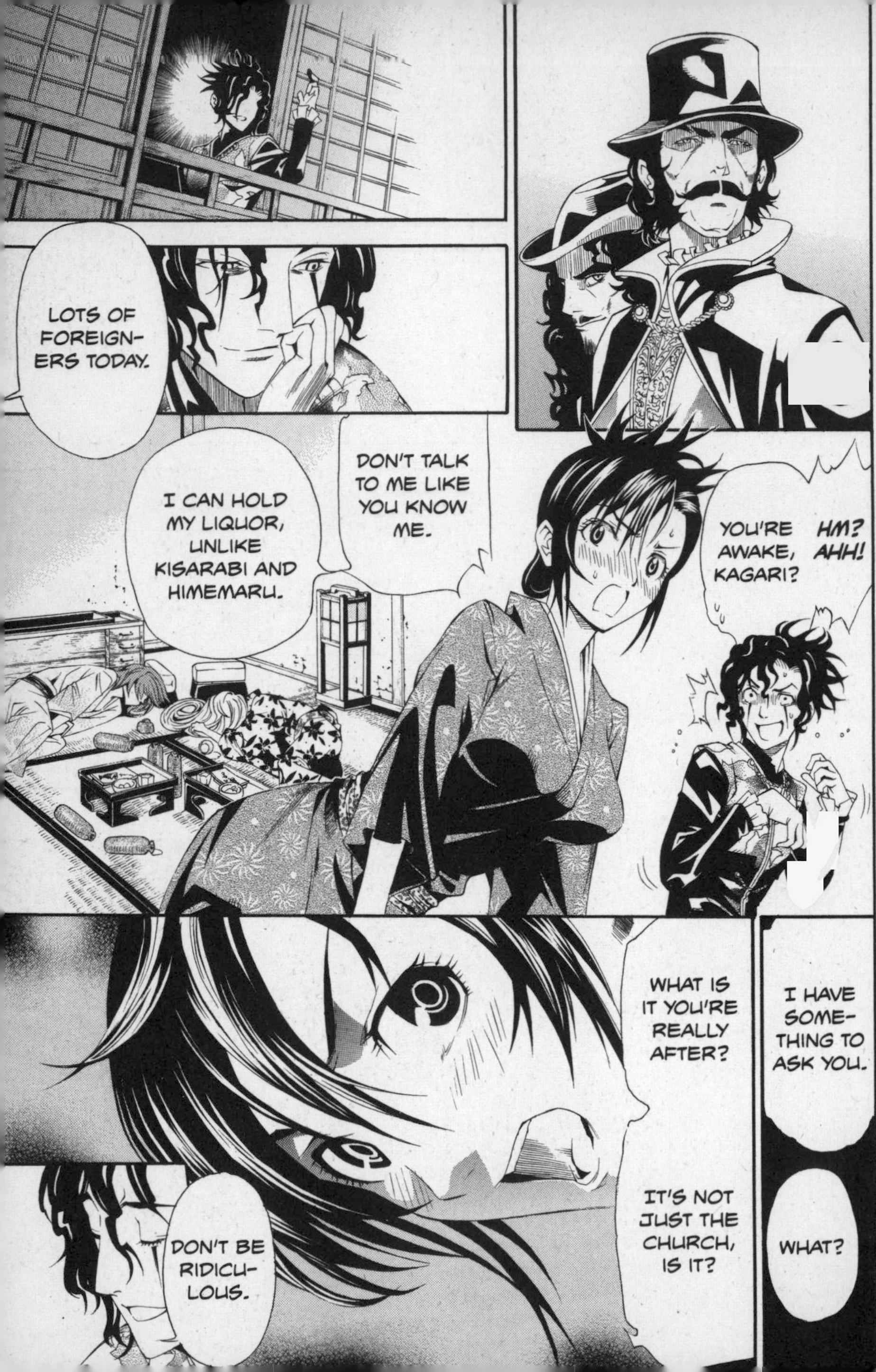
LOTS OF FOREIGNERS TODAY.
HM? AHH!
YOU'RE AWAKE, KAGARI?
DON'T TALK TO ME LIKE YOU KNOW ME.
I CAN HOLD MY LIQUOR, UNLIKE KISARABI AND HIMEMARU.
I HAVE SOMETHING TO ASK YOU.
WHAT?
WHAT IS IT YOU'RE REALLY AFTER?
IT'S NOT JUST THE CHURCH, IS IT?
DON'T BE RIDICULOUS.

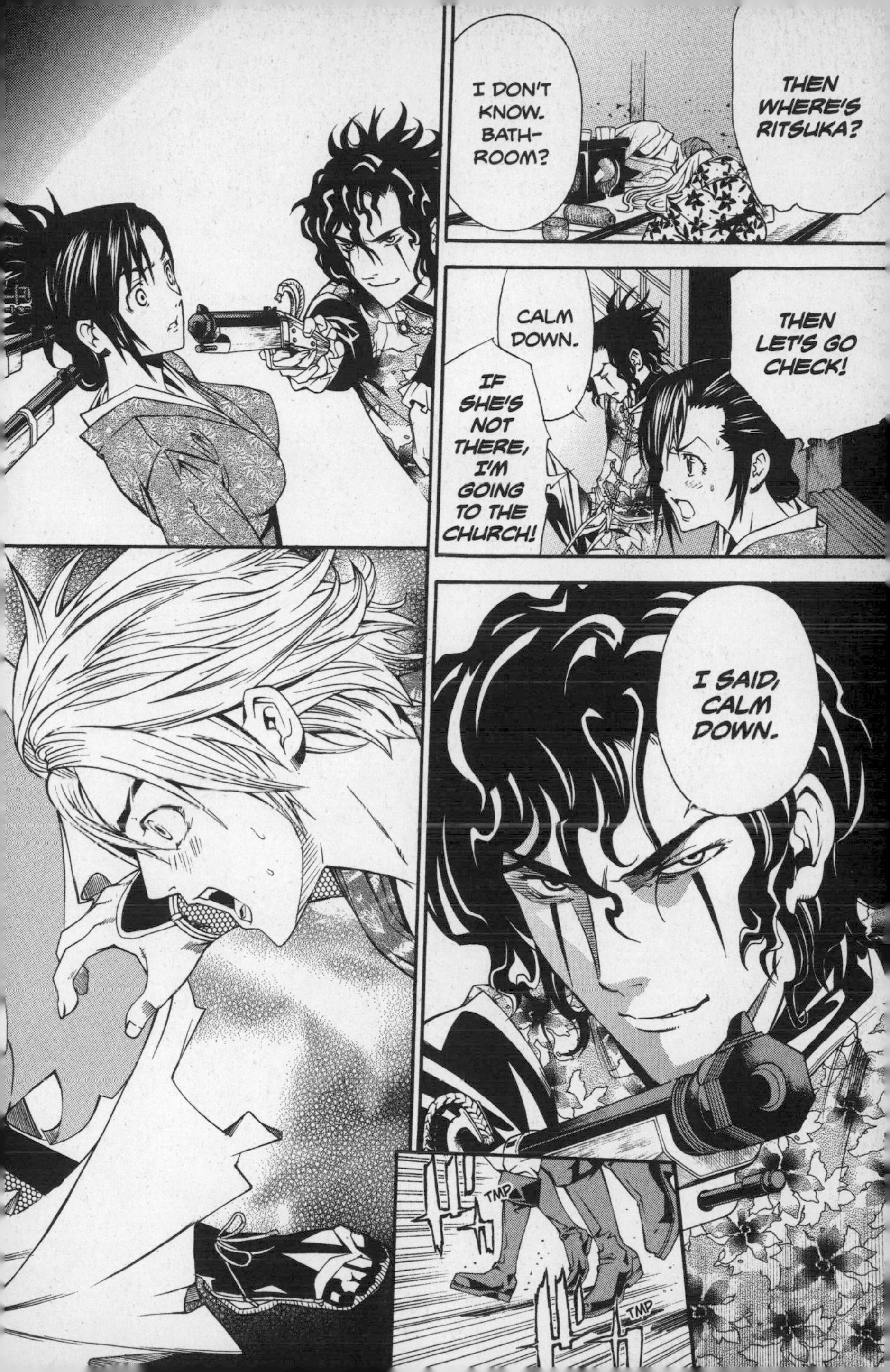
THEN WHERE'S RITSUKA?
I DON'T KNOW. BATH-ROOM?
THEN LET'S GO CHECK!
CALM DOWN.
IF SHE'S NOT THERE, I'M GOING TO THE CHURCH!
I SAID, CALM DOWN.
TMP
TMP

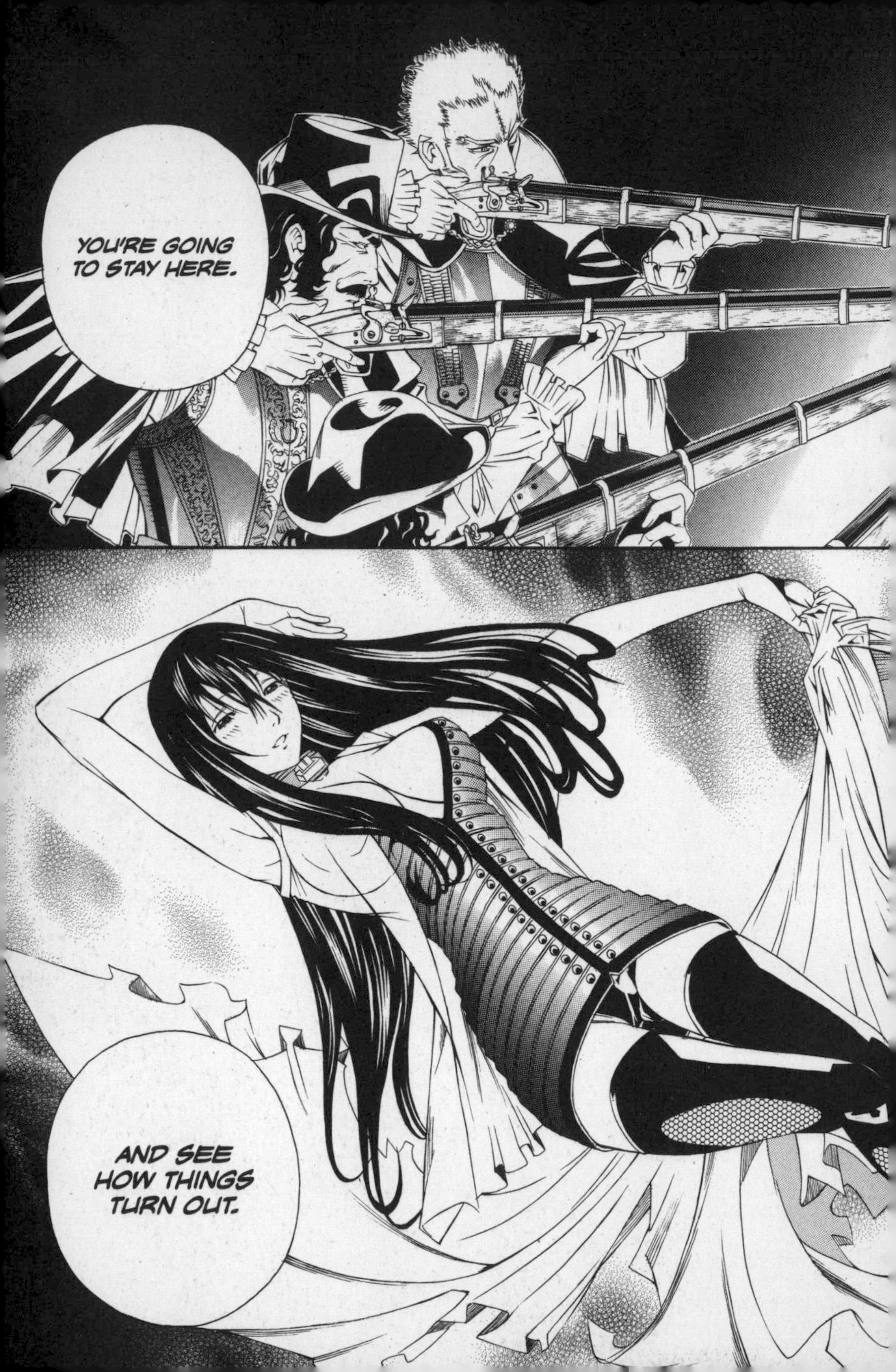
YOU'RE GOING TO STAY HERE.
AND SEE HOW THINGS TURN OUT.

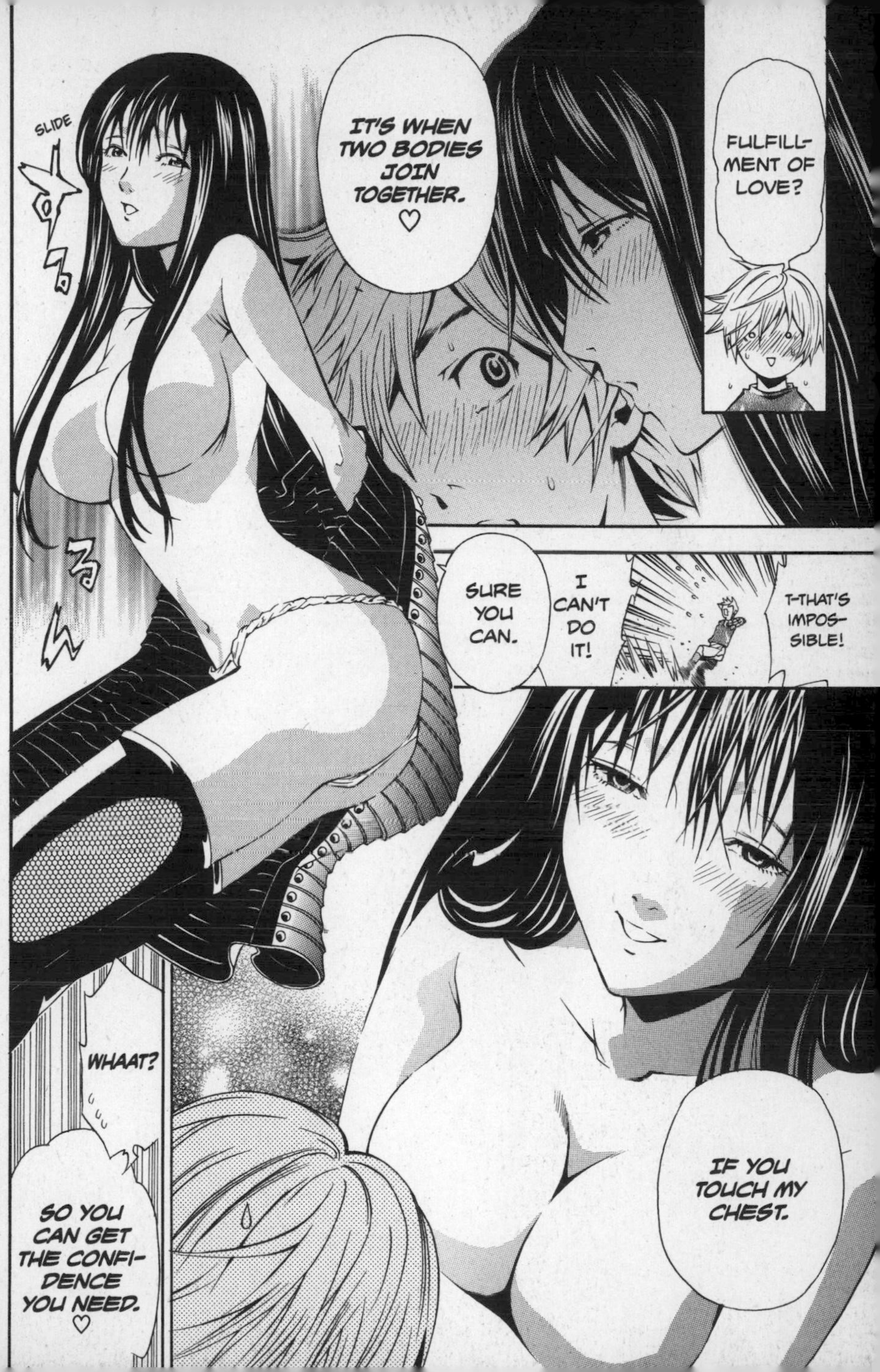
FULFILL-MENT OF LOVE?
IT'S WHEN TWO BODIES JOIN TOGETHER. ♡
T-THAT'S IMPOS-SIBLE!
I CAN'T DO IT!
SURE YOU CAN.
SLIDE
IF YOU TOUCH MY CHEST.
WHAAT?
SO YOU CAN GET THE CONFI-DENCE YOU NEED. ♡

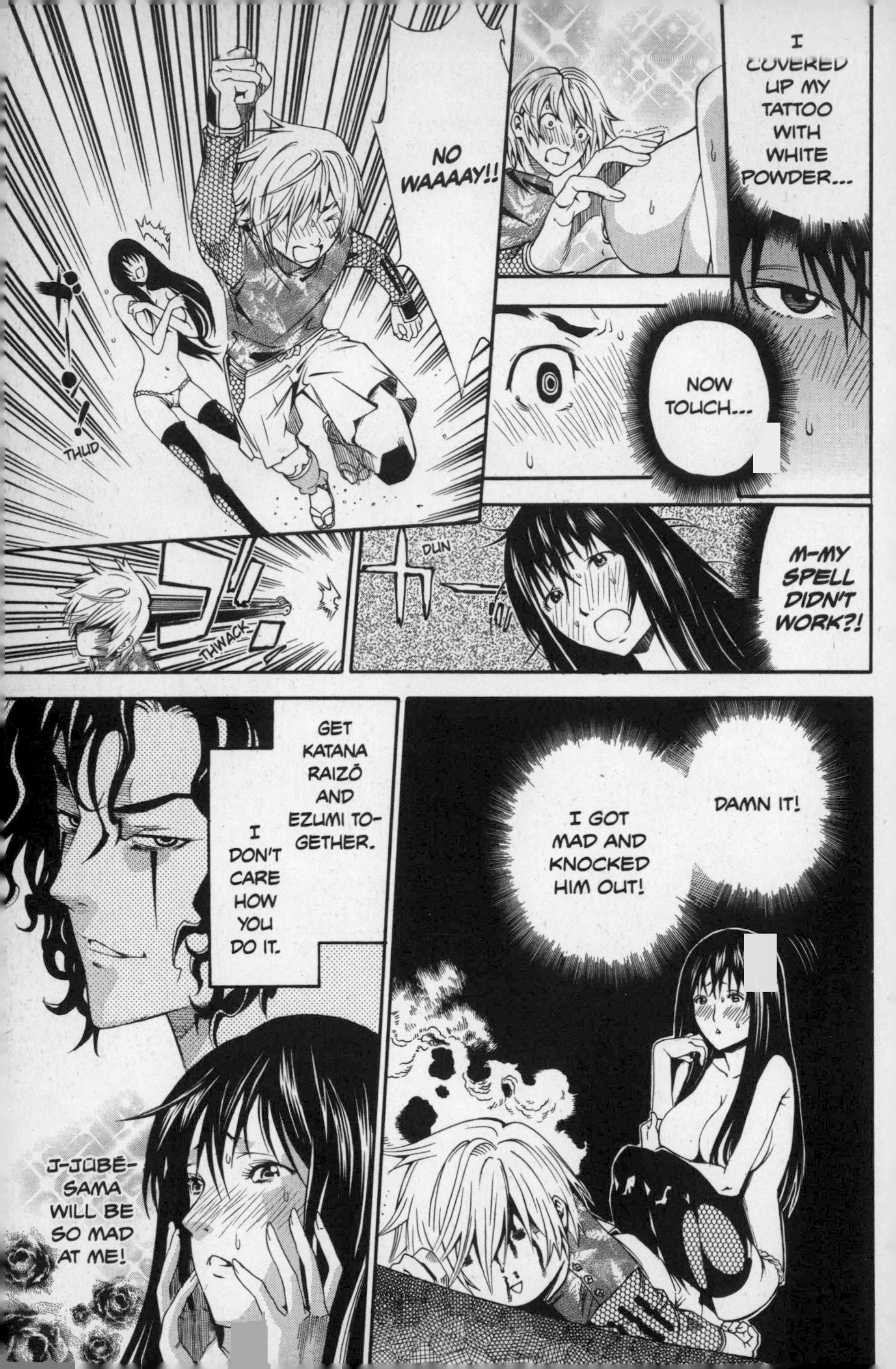
I COVERED UP MY TATTOO WITH WHITE POWDER...
NOW TOUCH...
NO WAAAAY!!
THUD
M-MY SPELL DIDN'T WORK?!
DUN
THWACK
DAMN IT!
I GOT MAD AND KNOCKED HIM OUT!
GET KATANA RAIZŌ AND EZUMI TO-GETHER.
I DON'T CARE HOW YOU DO IT.
J-JŪBĒ-SAMA WILL BE SO MAD AT ME!

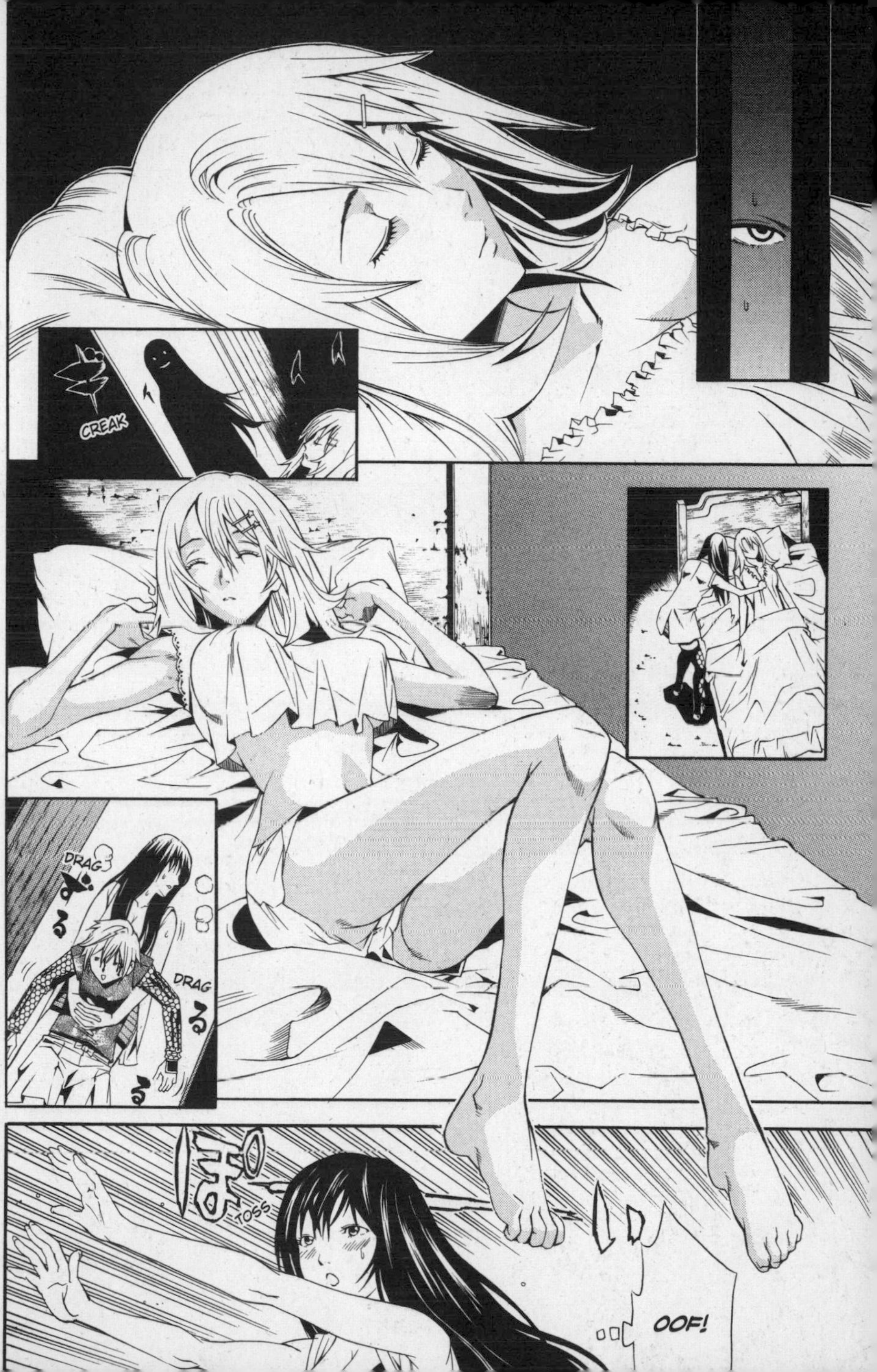
CREAK
DRAG
DRAG
TOSS
OOF!

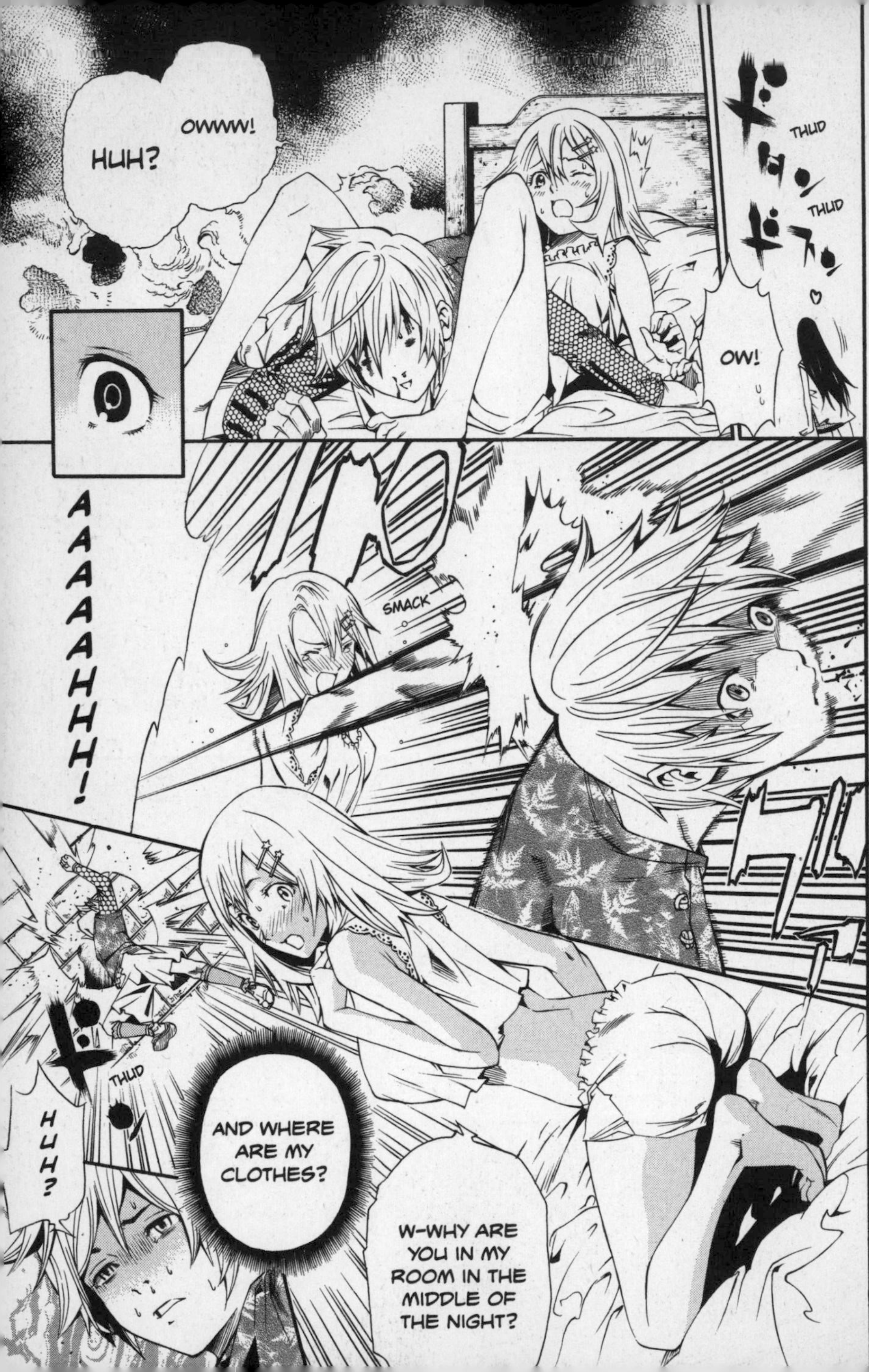
THUD
THUD
OW!
OWWW!
HUH?
AAAAAAHHH!
SMACK
W-WHY ARE YOU IN MY ROOM IN THE MIDDLE OF THE NIGHT?
AND WHERE ARE MY CLOTHES?
THUD
HUH?

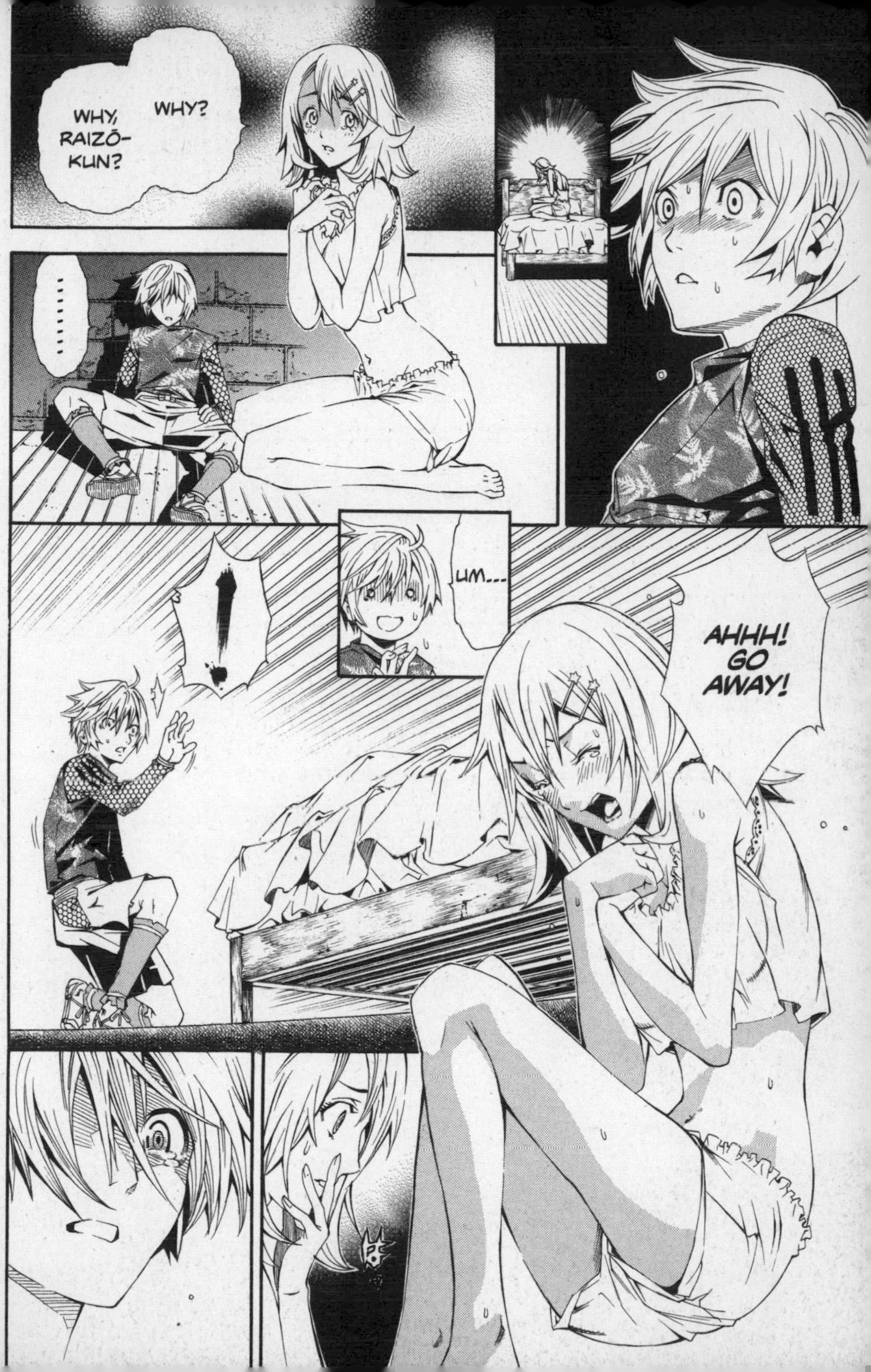
WHY?
WHY, RAIZŌ-KUN?
......
UM...
AHHH! GO AWAY!
!

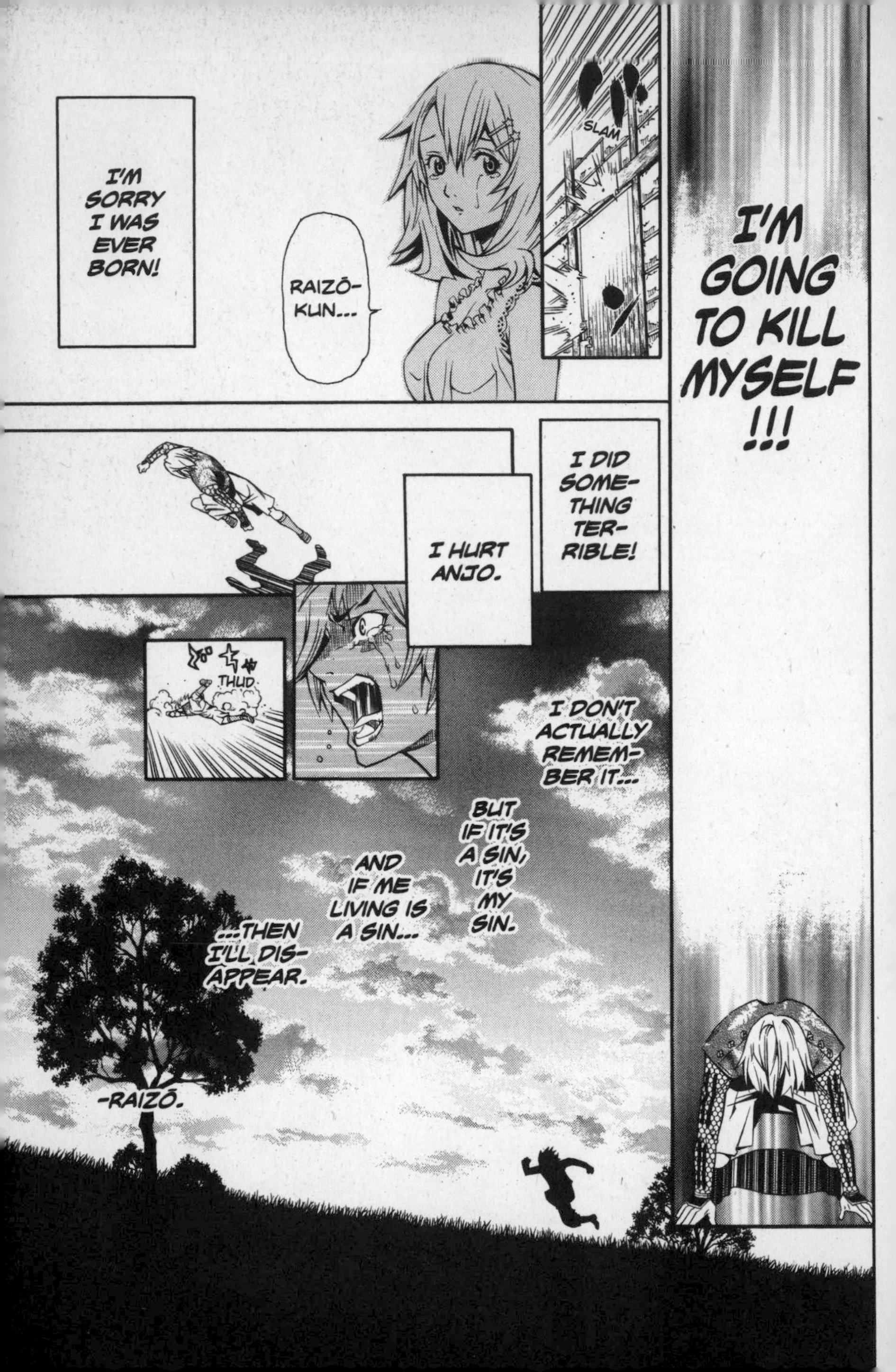
I'M GOING TO KILL MYSELF!!!
SLAM
RAIZŌ-KUN...
I'M SORRY I WAS EVER BORN!
I DID SOMETHING TERRIBLE!
I HURT ANJO.
THUD
I DON'T ACTUALLY REMEMBER IT...
BUT IF IT'S A SIN, IT'S MY SIN.
AND IF ME LIVING IS A SIN...
...THEN I'LL DISAPPEAR.
-RAIZŌ.

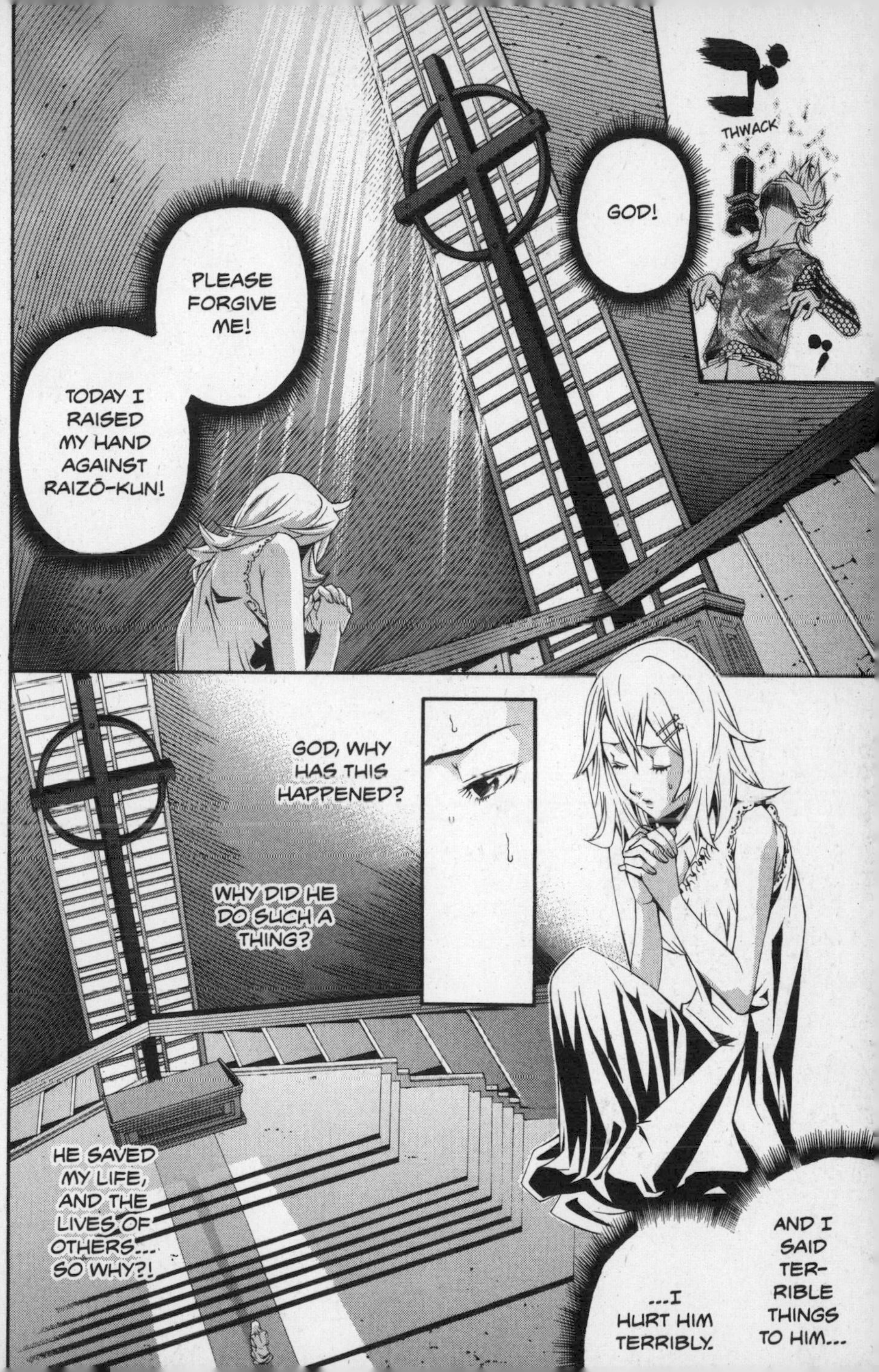
THWACK
GOD!
PLEASE FORGIVE ME!
TODAY I RAISED MY HAND AGAINST RAIZŌ-KUN!
GOD, WHY HAS THIS HAPPENED?
WHY DID HE DO SUCH A THING?
HE SAVED MY LIFE, AND THE LIVES OF OTHERS... SO WHY?!
AND I SAID TER-RIBLE THINGS TO HIM...
...I HURT HIM TERRIBLY.

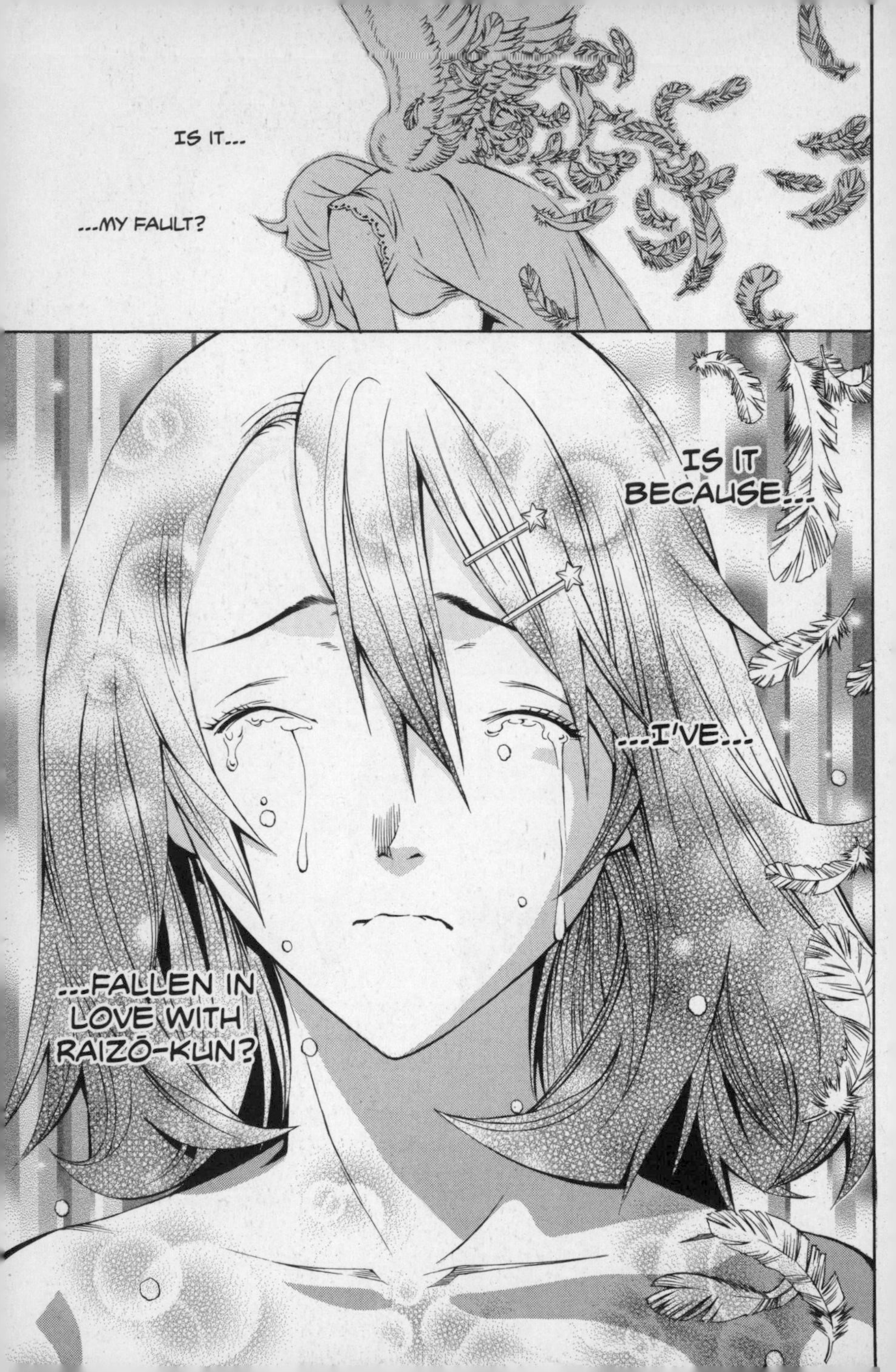
IS IT...
...MY FAULT?
IS IT BECAUSE...
...I'VE...
...FALLEN IN LOVE WITH RAIZŌ-KUN?

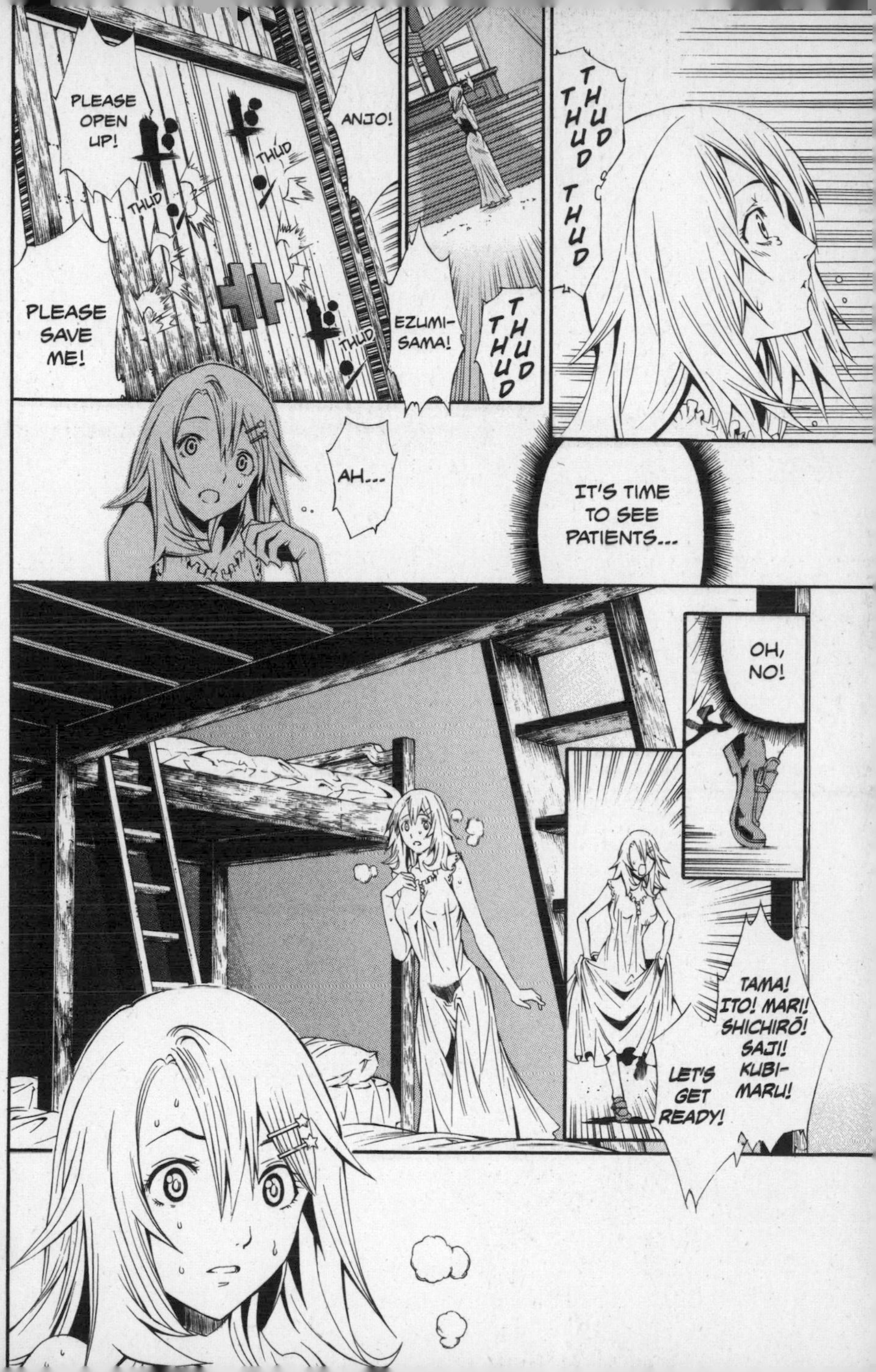

THUD THUD
THUD THUD
ANJO!
EZUMI-SAMA!
THUD THUD
PLEASE OPEN UP!
THUD
THUD
THUD
PLEASE SAVE ME!
IT'S TIME TO SEE PATIENTS...
AH...
OH, NO!
TAMA! ITO! MARI! SHICHIRŌ! SAJI! KUBI-MARU!
LET'S GET READY!

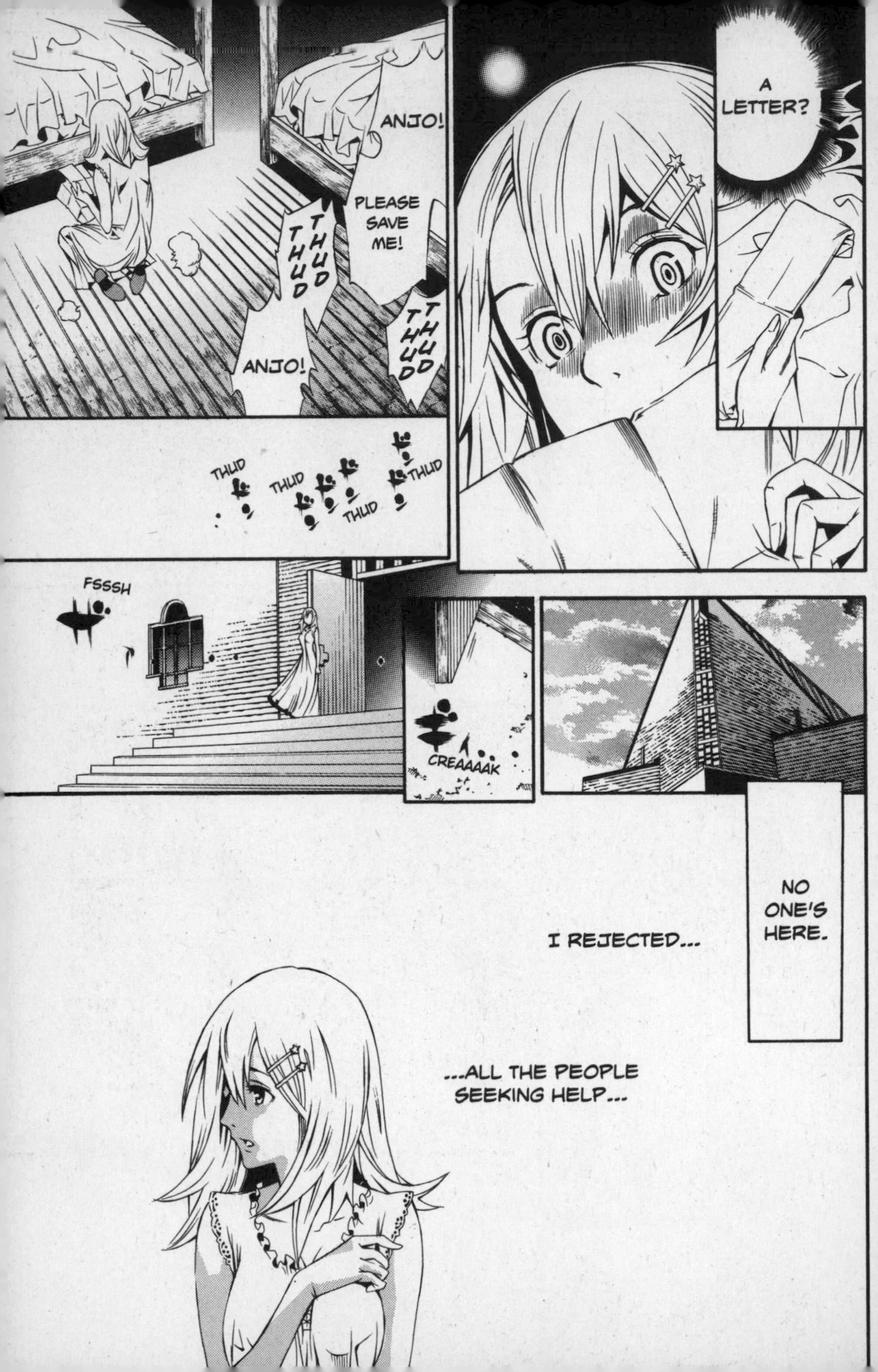
A LETTER?
ANJO!
PLEASE SAVE ME!
THUD THUD
THUD THUD
ANJO!
THUD
THUD
THUD
THUD
CREAAAAK
FSSSH
NO ONE'S HERE.
I REJECTED...
...ALL THE PEOPLE SEEKING HELP...

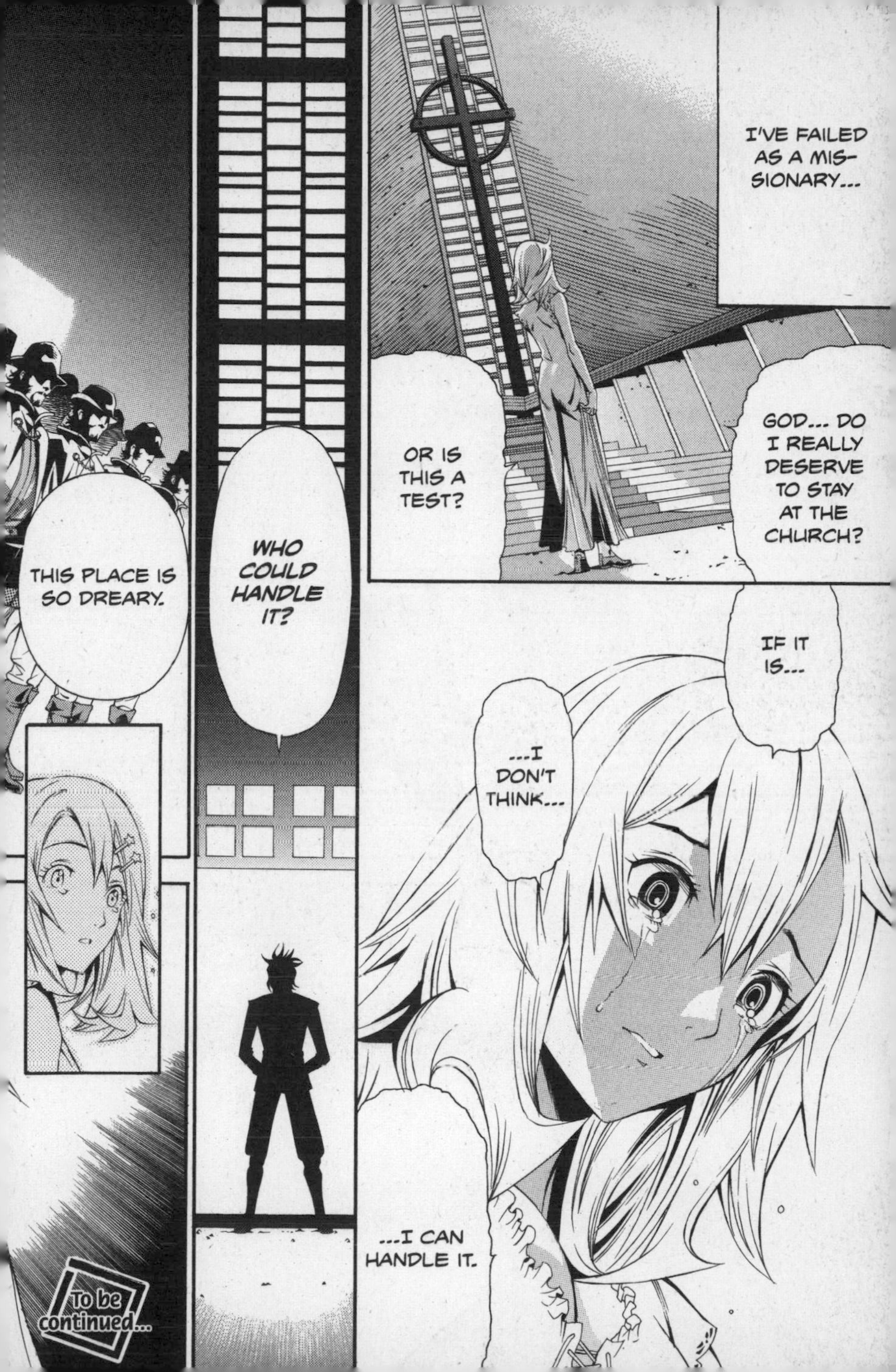
I'VE FAILED AS A MIS-SIONARY...
GOD... DO I REALLY DESERVE TO STAY AT THE CHURCH?
OR IS THIS A TEST?
IF IT IS...
...I DON'T THINK...
...I CAN HANDLE IT.
WHO COULD HANDLE IT?
THIS PLACE IS SO DREARY.
To be continued...

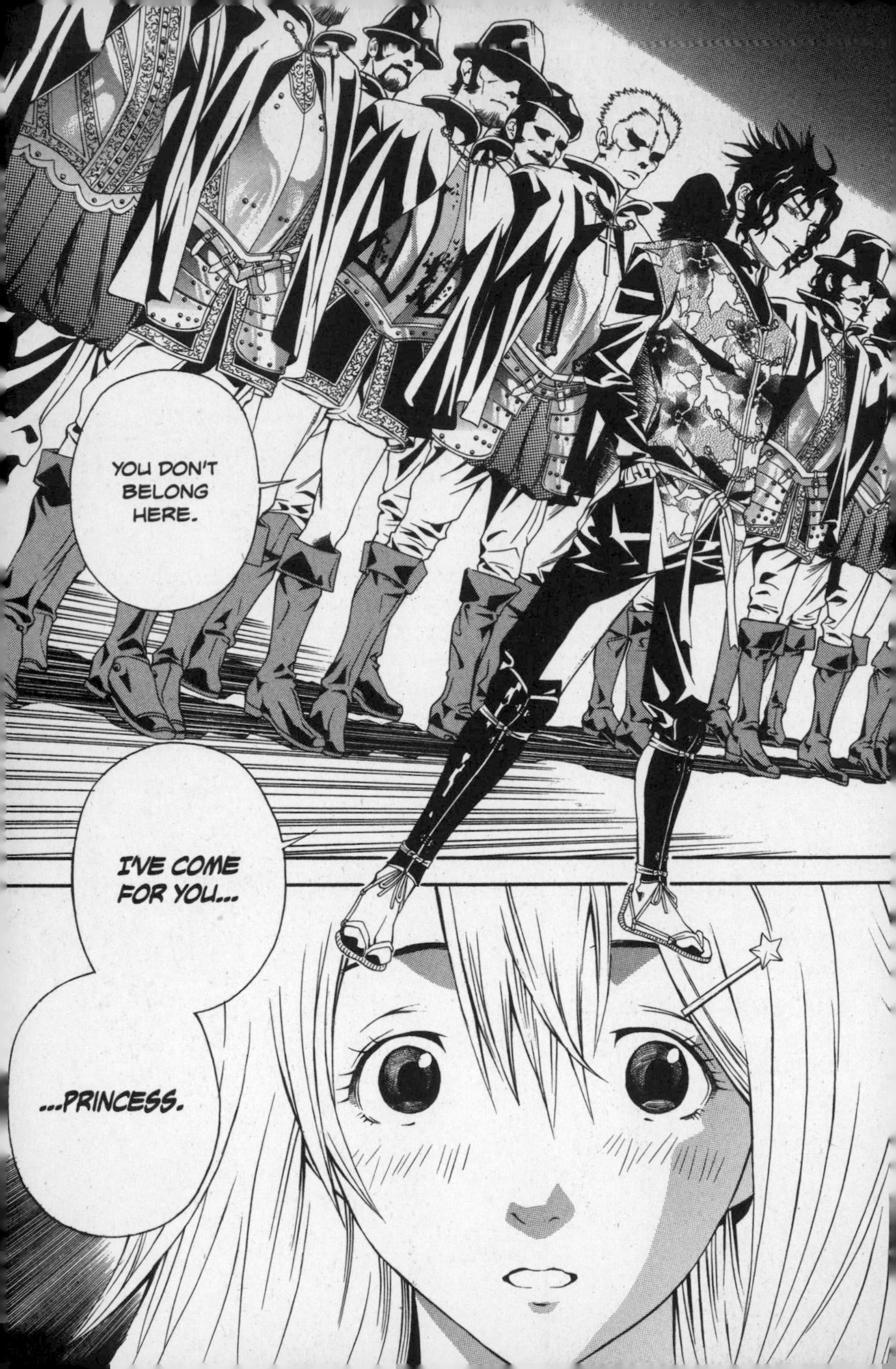
YOU DON'T BELONG HERE.
I'VE COME FOR YOU...
...PRINCESS.

TRANSLATION NOTES

Japanese is a tricky language for most Westerners, and translation is often more art than science. For your edification and reading pleasure, here are notes on some of the places where we could have gone in a different direction with our translation of the work, or where a Japanese cultural reference is used.

-dono
-dono is an archaic honorific roughly equivalent to –san or sometimes –sama.

Kunoichi
A *kunoichi* is a female ninja. It is written くノ一, which symbolizes the strokes necessary to write 女, "woman."

Sengoku era
Sengoku jidai (Warring States Era) lasted from the mid-15th century to the beginning of the 17th century. As its name suggests, it was a time of civil war in Japan, with regional lords (*daimyo*) taking control because of a weak central government. The most famous *daimyo* were Oda Nobunaga, known for his military prowess, and Tokugawa Ieyasu, who went on to become the first shogun of Japan's final shogunate.

Shinobi
Another word for ninja. *Shinobi* was the more commonly used term for ninja until its usage declined in popularity post-World War II.

Hime or himegimi
Hime means "princess." In this case it is also used towards any female of noble lineage, i.e. the daughter of a chief.

Ninpō
Ninpō literally means "ninja arts" or "ninja technique."

Shintaigō, page 17
Kagari's special ninpo attack. It's written with the characters "god," "body," and "conjuction."

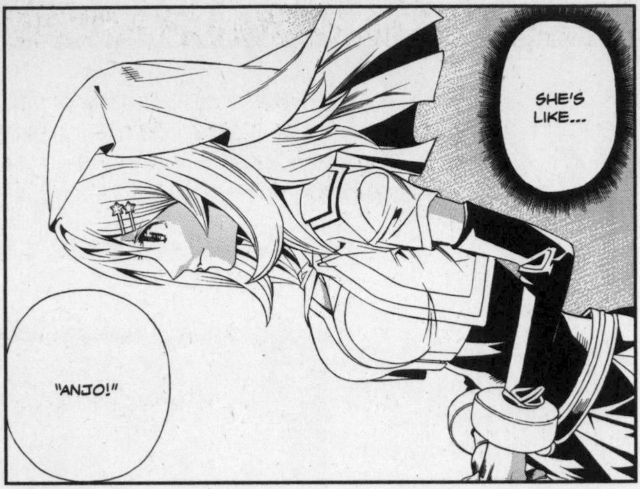
SHE'S LIKE...
"ANJO!"

***Anjo*, page 99**

Anjo means "angel" in Portuguese. There were many Portuguese missionaries in Japan at this time.

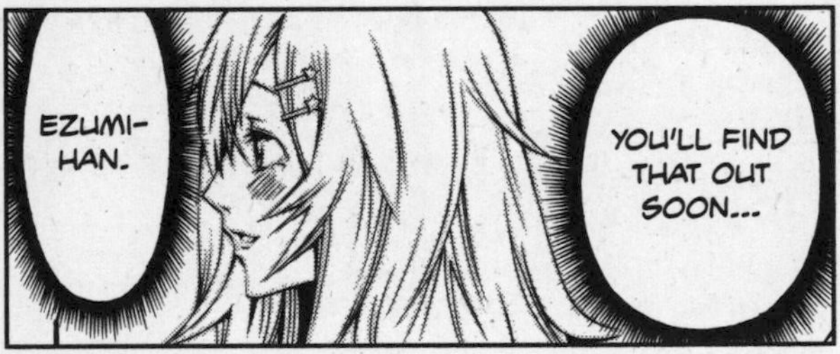
YOU'LL FIND THAT OUT SOON...
EZUMI-HAN.

***-han*, page 148**

-han is an honorific that means roughly the same thing as –san. It's largely outdated, but is still used today in some parts of Japan, particularly in Kyoto.

BY KEN AKAMATSU

Negi Springfield is a ten-year-old wizard teaching English at an all-girls Japanese school. He dreams of becoming a master wizard like his legendary father, the Thousand Master. At first his biggest concern was concealing his magic powers, because if he's ever caught using them publicly, he thinks he'll be turned into an ermlne! But in a world that gets stranger every day, it turns out that the strangest people of all are Negi's students! From a librarian with a magic book to a centuries-old vampire, from a robot to a ninja, Negi will risk his own life to protect the girls in his care!

Ages: 16+

Special extras in each volume! Read them all!

VISIT WWW.KODANSHACOMICS.COM TO:
• View release date calendars for upcoming volumes
• Find out the latest about new Kodansha Comics series

BY OH!GREAT

Itsuki Minami needs no introduction—everybody's heard of the "Babyface" of the Eastside. He's the strongest kid at Higashi Junior High School, easy on the eyes but dangerously tough when he needs to be. Plus, Itsuki lives with the mysterious and sexy Noyamano sisters. Life's never dull, but it becomes downright dangerous when Itsuki leads his school to victory over vindictive Westside punks with gangster connections. Now he stands to lose his school, his friends, and everything he cares about. But in his darkest hour, the Noyamano girls give him an amazing gift, one that just might help him save his school: a pair of Air Trecks. These high-tech skates are more than just supercool. They'll enable Itsuki to execute the wildest, most aggressive moves ever seen—and introduce him to a thrilling and terrifying new world.

Ages: 16 +

Special extras in each volume! Read them all!

VISIT WWW.KODANSHACOMICS.COM TO:
- View release date calendars for upcoming volumes
- Find out the latest about new Kodansha Comics series

TOMARE!

[STOP!]

You are going the wrong way!

Manga is a completely different type of reading experience.

To start at the *beginning*, go to the *end*!

That's right! Authentic manga is read the traditional Japanese way—from right to left, exactly the *opposite* of how American books are read. It's easy to follow: Just go to the other end of the book, and read each page—and each panel—from the right side to the left side, starting at the top right. Now you're experiencing manga as it was meant to be.